Dear Mike —

Thanks for introducing me to the Saxonusco and all your encouragement over the years.

Warm Regards,

Rob

THE BEGINNINGS OF MESOAMERICAN CIVILIZATION

Mesoamerica is one of several cradles of civilization in the world. In this book, Robert M. Rosenswig proposes that we understand Early Formative Mesoamerica as an archipelago of complex societies that interacted with one another over long distances and that were separated by less sedentary peoples. These early "islands" of culture shared an Olmec artistic aesthetic, beginning approximately 1250 BCE (uncalibrated), that first defined Mesoamerica as an area of culture. Rosenswig frames the Olmec world from the perspective of the Soconusco area of Pacific Chiapas and Guatemala. The disagreements about Early Formative society that have raged over the past thirty years focus on the nature of inter-regional interaction between San Lorenzo and other Early Formative regions. He evaluates these debates from a fresh theoretical perspective and integrates new data into an assessment of Soconusco society before, during and after the apogee of the San Lorenzo polity.

Robert M. Rosenswig is Assistant Professor of Anthropology at the University at Albany – SUNY. He has directed archaeological field work in Mexico, Belize and Costa Rica and has published numerous articles on the origins of agriculture and the development of sociopolitical complexity in Mesoamerica.

The Beginnings of Mesoamerican Civilization

INTER-REGIONAL INTERACTION AND THE OLMEC

Robert M. Rosenswig

University at Albany – SUNY

CAMBRIDGE
UNIVERSITY PRESS

CAMBRIDGE UNIVERSITY PRESS
Cambridge, New York, Melbourne, Madrid, Cape Town, Singapore,
São Paulo, Delhi, Dubai, Tokyo

Cambridge University Press
32 Avenue of the Americas, New York, NY 10013-2473, USA

www.cambridge.org
Information on this title: www.cambridge.org/9780521111027

First published 2010

Printed in the United States of America

A catalog record for this publication is available from the British Library.

Library of Congress Cataloging in Publication data

Rosenswig, Robert M.
The beginnings of Mesoamerican civilization : inter-regional interaction and the
Olmec / Robert M. Rosenswig.
    p.   cm.
Includes bibliographical references and index.
ISBN 978-0-521-11102-7 (hardback)
1. Olmecs – History.   2. Olmecs – Antiquities.   3. Soconusco Region (Mexico) –
Antiquities.   4. Mexico – Civilization – Indian influences.   I. Title.
F1219.8.056R67   2010
972.0009′ 01 – dc22   2009024177

ISBN 978-0-521-11102-7 Hardback

Dedicated to the loving memory of
Jeanne Newman
(1918–2002)

Contents

Figures

Tables

Acknowledgments

The research presented in this book was conducted under three permits issued by the Instituto Nacional de Antropología e Historia (INAH) Consejo de Arqueología from 2001 through 2003. I thank Ingeniero Joaquín García Barcena and Arqueóloga Leonor Merino for their assistance. The New World Archaeological Foundation (NWAF) provided logistical and curatorial support. Special thanks go to John Clark, NWAF director, for providing this support and to Ronald Lowe for his help in Chiapas – especially in the face of adversity.

The collection of data reported in this book was made possible by a National Science Foundation dissertation improvement grant; a Fulbright–Hays fellowship; a Foundation for the Advancement of Mesoamerican Studies, Inc., research grant; an NWAF research grant; two Yale Council of International and Area Studies grants and a series of grants from the Albers Travel Fund, Department of Anthropology, Yale University.

This project owes much to the pioneers of Soconusco archaeology: Michael Coe, Gareth Lowe and Carlos Navarrete. Their groundbreaking efforts in the region paved the way for all subsequent work. Michael Blake first introduced me to the Soconusco, and John Clark set me on the course to work at Cuauhtémoc. Together, Mike and John are responsible for this project's being undertaken, although not for the conclusions drawn.

Richard Burger steered me through many academic labyrinths, and I am grateful for his insights and for encouraging me to think of all Olmec issues in a comparative perspective. Richard Burger, Marcello Canuto and Thomas Tartaron provided much needed input and advice during the formulation and grant-writing stages of this research. Mary Miller has made my eyes a little less "wooden" when it comes to Mesoamerican art. For this and for her feedback on Chapter 6, I thank her. Takeshi Inomata and Louise Paradis generously gave assistance at key moments while I was at Yale.

Michael Love and Richard Lesure have provided their insights over the years, as have Philip Arnold, David Grove and Carl Wendt. I spent many days in San Cristobal with David Cheetham, who offered numerous helpful suggestions, not the least of which were related to Formative Period ceramics. Over the years, Marilyn Masson has given invaluable input that is much appreciated, as are her comments on Chapter 2. Christopher Pool and an anonymous Cambridge University Press reviewer made comments on a previous draft of this book, making the final product substantially stronger than I could have managed to make it on my own. In particular, Chris's detailed and thoughtful input is really appreciated. The interpretations in this book, however, do not reflect those of any of these individuals – credit can be laid at their doors, but fault should be delivered to mine alone.

Assistance in the field was provided by Cescilia Canal, Ruben Chuc, Travis Doering, Aaron Goldman, Jaime Holthuysen, Joe McGreevy, Yonny Mesh, Allison Perrett, Amanda Schrier, Samuel Sheehan and Joshua Silver. Artemio Villatoro diligently served as lab director during the 2002 and 2003 seasons, and his patience and hard work contributed tremendously to the data we collected. Barbara Arroyo, David Cheetham, John Clark, Janine Gasco, John Hodson, Andrew McDonald and Fred Nelson all visited the project while excavations were in progress.

Don Jorge Hernandez provided invaluable help in all aspects of the field work reported here. His sage advice and knowledge of the Soconusco were invaluable to the success of this project. I am grateful to the Comisario of Cuauhtémoc, Lucio López Gómez, who allowed us to turn the Cuauhtémoc Casa Ejidal into a home and laboratory during the 2001 season. I am indebted to the people of the Ejidos of Cuauhtémoc, La Libertad, Ignacio López Rayón and Emilio Zapata, who welcomed us into their towns with genuine hospitality and allowed us to work on their lands.

Roberto Hoover, Ronald Lowe, Carlos López and Artemio Villatoro helped me in different ways, and all provided welcome conversation during my stays in San Cristóbal. Doña Marie prepared delicious food for my crew and my family as the occasion required.

I am indebted to Wilberth Cruz Alvaro, Luis Flores Coba, Carlos Hoover, Willie Lowe, Joseph McGreevey, Ayax Moreno and Samuel Sheehan for all their wonderful illustrations. Thanks are due to Travis Doering for his obsidian analysis and to Ana Tejeda and Hector Neff for their ceramic sourcing analysis.

SECTION I

AN EARLY FORMATIVE MESOAMERICAN PROBLEM

1

Introduction

> Tell me, O Muse, of that ingenious hero who traveled far and
> wide after he had sacked the famous town of Troy. Many cities
> did he visit, and many were the nations with whose manners
> and customs he was acquainted; moreover he suffered much by
> sea while trying to save his own life and bring his men safely
> home . . .
>
> Homer, *The Odyssey*

Inter-regional exchange of goods and ideas is a distinctly human
practice that qualitatively separates us from other creatures on earth.
Why did people originally travel to faraway places and why did only
certain peoples reach out while others did not? Furthermore, after
inter-regional exchange networks were established, how did they
change the internal organization of interacting societies? The desire
for resources that are not locally available is the most obvious answer
to the first question. However, this explanation is not sufficient. To
understand the social processes that allowed people separated by
space, custom, language and religion to come together requires that
the political nature of exchange be addressed. Exploring the effects
of inter-regional interaction through the use of archaeological data is
the objective of this book.

Mesoamerica was one of a half-dozen original cradles of civilization in the world. The societies that occupied the Gulf Coast
of Mexico, particularly the early inhabitants that constituted the
San Lorenzo polity, were some of the first Mesoamerican peoples
to display clear evidence of social stratification. Despite (or more
likely because of) this, disagreements have raged for the past thirty
years over the nature of the San Lorenzo polity and its influence on

neighboring regions. These disputes currently provide one of the most challenging research topics for Mesoamerican archaeologists. The resolution of this disagreement is crucial to understanding the early prehistory of Mesoamerica as well as the comparative study of how complex societies developed worldwide.

Debate over the nature of Early Formative Gulf Coast civilization and its influence on other regions of Mesoamerica has been intense (e.g., Blomster et al., 2005; Clark, 1997, 2007; Diehl and Coe, 1995; Flannery and Marcus, 2000; Flannery et al., 2005; Grove, 1997; Neff et al., 2006a, 2006b; Sharer et al., 2006; Stoltman et al., 2005). Some authors adopt a "Sister Culture" perspective, which proposes that the inhabitants of many regions of Mesoamerica interacted on equal footing and together developed a distinctive inter-regional art style and new social institutions. There was therefore no center to the Early Formative Mesoamerican world. In contrast, others propose that the residents of San Lorenzo created a novel political and ideological system that was the "Mother Culture" of all subsequent Mesoamerican societies. In this second view, the elite at San Lorenzo disseminated innovations through ideological, political and economic exchanges. The inhabitants of San Lorenzo were thus qualitatively different from their neighbors whom they taught (and perhaps even conquered) to spread their ideas and institutions.

The essence of most disagreements about Gulf Coast Olmec civilization revolves around the nature of inter-regional interaction between San Lorenzo and other polities during the second part of the Early Formative period (ca.1250–900 BCE).[1] The Soconusco provides the single most sensitive region from which to explore competing ideas regarding the nature of Gulf Coast influence on other areas of Mesoamerica. This is the case because of prolonged and intensive contact between the two regions as well as a long history of investigation in the Soconusco (Blake et al., 1995; Ceja Tenorio, 1985; Clark, 1994; Clark and Pye, 2000; Coe, 1961; Coe and Flannery, 1967; Green and Lowe, 1967; Lesure, 1995; Love, 2002a; Lowe, 1975; Rosenswig, 2005). However, because the intensity of contact between the Gulf Coast and the Soconusco is exceptionally strong, it cannot be used to characterize the relationship between the Gulf Coast and other areas with weaker ties. In contrast, the intensity of Gulf Coast–Soconusco interaction provides one of the only plausible cases for evaluating whether the Gulf Coast polity of San Lorenzo was a colonizing empire (Clark, 1997).

This book addresses late Early Formative inter-regional interaction from the perspective of the Soconusco. Located primarily on Mexico's south Pacific coast, the Soconusco extends approximately 15 km into Guatemala on the hot, coastal plain between the Sierra Madre and the Pacific Ocean (Figure 1.1). This is the most fertile region of Mexico today and has been a center of innovation for the past 3,500 years. The Soconusco was the most distant province of the Aztec empire, and the tribute list of the Codex Mendoza evidences its richness in Prehispanic times (Gasco and Voorhies, 1989). Prior to the Aztec, the Quiché Maya had also invaded (Carmack, 1981; Navarrete, 1970). Cacao was always the most sought-after product from the Soconusco (Gasco, 2006), but other jungle products, such as jaguar pelts and tropical bird feathers, were also included on the Aztec tribute lists. Interestingly, the Soconusco was also required to provide jade and amber to the Aztec and, as these products were not locally available, fostered exchange with more peripheral areas (Blanton and Feinman, 1984). Just after the Spanish conquest, the population of the area was estimated at between sixty and one hundred thousand

Figure 1.1
Location of sites and areas of Mesoamerica mentioned in the text.

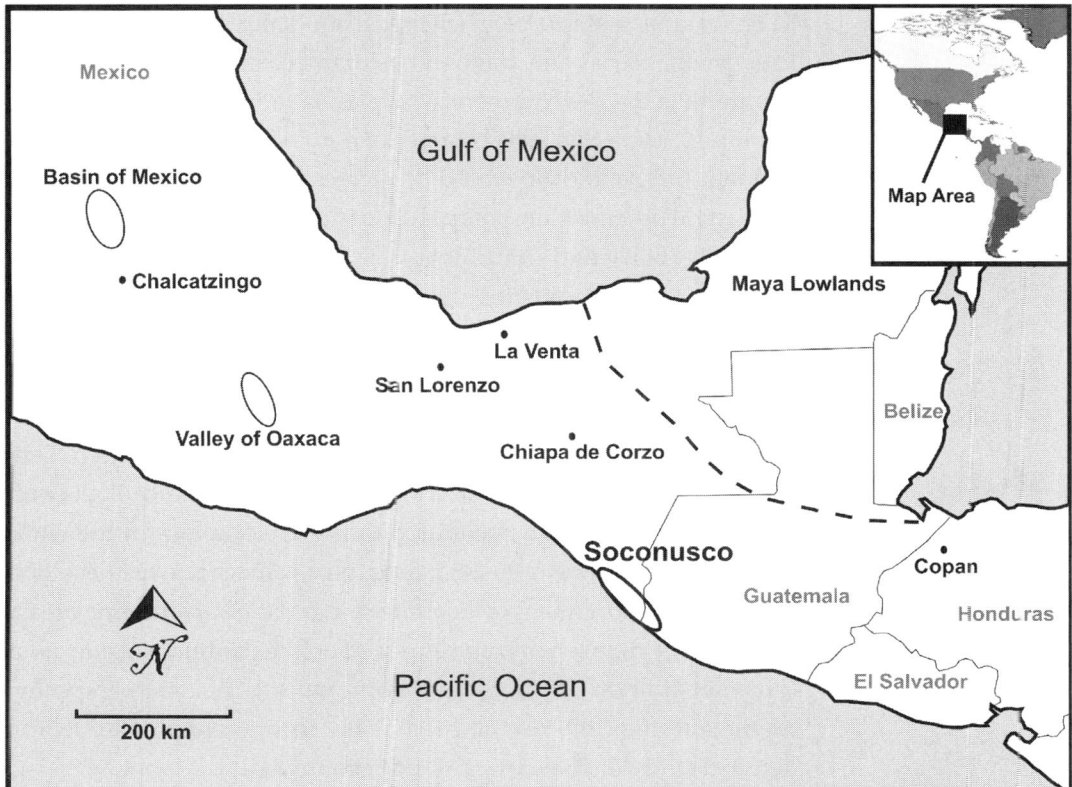

people (Orellana, 1995: 31), and the area was the center of a thriving trade network that connected the Mexican Gulf Coast and Central highlands with Guatemala and lower Central America. At the end of the Classic Period, the region was the source of Plumbate pottery that was traded across all of Mesoamerica (Neff, 2002). If we go back to the Late Formative period (300 BCE – CE 300), this region was a center of early carved stone stelae, depicting historical and mythological scenes, at the site of Izapa (Lowe et al., 1982). The subject of this book, however, is the centuries that precede the emergence of Izapa as a regional center.

The book explores the period between 1600 and 800 BCE that begins with the earliest settled villages and ceramic use in the Soconusco and extends through the rise and fall of San Lorenzo. The Soconusco has an exceptionally well-defined ceramic chronology that allows the fine-grained tracking of changes before, during and after the apogee of San Lorenzo (Blake et al., 1995; Clark and Cheetham, 2005). During the intervening 800 years, political rank (Blake and Clark, 1999; Clark and Blake, 1994) and stratification (Love, 1991, 2002a; Rosenswig, 2007) emerged in the Soconusco, maize began to be used as a staple crop (Blake, 2006; Blake et al., 1992a, 1992b; Rosenswig, 2006a) and trade in obsidian became organized at such a scale that the development of a prismatic blade technology was feasible (Clark, 1987; Jackson and Love, 1991). Population levels rose and fell, and people moved fluidly across the landscape while social interaction became more complex and integrated increasing numbers of people (Blake and Clark, 1999; Clark and Pye, 2000). The subject matter of this book begins when the inhabitants of the Soconusco had developed more sedentary societies and ends just as the first long-lasting hierarchically organized society emerged.

Data patterns from my investigations at the site of Cuauhtémoc serve as an index for regional developments in the Soconusco. They provide a unique opportunity to do this as Cuauhtémoc is the only documented site in the Soconusco that was occupied for the entire period in question (Rosenswig, 2005, 2009). The book further documents the abandonment of Cuauhtémoc and the surrounding area at precisely the time when Izapa emerged on the piedmont 20 km away (Lowe et al., 1982). This book thus provides a regional perspective on the effects of the rise and fall of the San Lorenzo polity from a detailed study of one corner of the Soconusco.

In Chapter 2, I explore ethnologically documented patterns of long-distance travel, exchange and distant cultural interaction. A core-periphery perspective for the study of long-distance interaction in Mesoamerica is discussed within the context of a reformulated World-systems theory. Such a perspective does not require a core-centered system that Wallerstein described for the fifteenth century. Instead, my approach here employs the macroregion as the unit for more fully understanding local processes.

I propose that the control of arcane knowledge can provide a powerful basis for maintaining an ideology of inequality. As the epigraph to this chapter emphasizes, the experiences that Ulysses gained in the course of his travels, including his knowledge of distant "manners and customs," are the stuff of legend. Such knowledge, shared through the telling, is what made Ulysses an exalted hero in Greek society. The elite control of ideas exchanged over long distances is described in this book as a knowledge kula that can operate in societies at various levels of complexity. I propose that such a knowledge kula emerged as the outgrowth of an archipelago of complexity in Early Formative Mesoamerica. This archipelago was formed by isolated pockets (or islands) of relatively more complexly organized peoples within a "sea" of less developed groups, some of whom maintained a mobile, foraging adaptation around the earliest sedentary food producers (see Rosenswig, n.d.). Within their respective islands of complexity, both Soconusco and Gulf Coast elites were able to maintain their elevated political position at home partly as a result of their *geographic distance* from each other and partly due to their *cultural distance* from their immediate neighbors. Chapter 2 concludes with examples of four other archipelagos of complexity: Trobriand Islanders in the Pacific, Eastern European Germanic tribes beyond the direct reach of the Roman Empire, Early Bronze Age Cycladic Islanders in the Mediterranean and Chavín Horizon communities in Peru.

In Chapter 3, Soconusco culture history is reviewed in relation to developments on Mexico's Gulf Coast with special attention to the San Lorenzo polity's rise and fall. I define an Initial Ceramic Period and three subsequent ceramic style horizons during the Early and Middle Formative periods. These four temporal epochs each encompass a number of ceramic phases. Although this is not the traditional manner into which time is divided in Mesoamerica, such a scheme facilitates inter-regional comparisons based on similar stylistic and technological changes through time.

In the second part of Chapter 3, I outline three hypotheses that have been used to account for the nature of Early Formative society in Mesoamerica. The first is what I term a "Peer Polity Model" (PPM) in which innovations are not centered on the Gulf Coast or anywhere else. Instead, a number of distinct yet equal polities across Mesoamerica inherited a shared iconographic system and developed sociopolitical complexity at roughly the same rate. Second is an "Elite Emulation Model" (EEM) that proposes that less politically developed areas borrowed ideas and material culture from the more advanced San Lorenzo polity. Third is an "Aztec Analogy Model" (AAM) that proposes a case of Early Formative Gulf Coast imperialism, which would have occurred in much the way that the Aztec later conquered their distant Soconusco province during the fifteenth century. For each of these three hypotheses, material expectations are outlined for the periods before, during and immediately after the apogee of San Lorenzo. These three models are formulated in this book to evaluate the nature of Gulf Coast–Soconusco relations. However, I hope that formally comparing these alternative hypotheses with be useful for researchers working in other areas of Mesoamerica.

Chapters 4 through 7 then present archaeological data from the Cuauhtémoc zone of the Soconusco as well as the arguments that attempt to link them to past human behavior. Each of these four chapters present a thread with which I will attempt to weave together 800 years of developments in the Cuauhtémoc region. In Chapter 4, settlement survey results are summarized and used to provide a basic demographic history of the area. The fluctuations in relative population levels within the Cuauhtémoc survey zone illuminate aspects of the overall political history of the Soconusco during the Early and Middle Formative periods. In the first part of Chapter 4, changing settlement patterns from the Cuauhtémoc and Mazatán zones of the Soconusco are compared to those at San Lorenzo. Results from each of these three survey areas document politically volatile landscapes during the Early and Middle Formative periods, where centers emerged for a few centuries and then collapsed. A network of polities with signs of incipient leadership emerged in the Mazatán zone during the Initial Ceramic Period. These were abandoned during the apogee of San Lorenzo, and the political center of the Soconusco shifted to the banks of the nearby Coatán River. Then, coeval with the collapse of the San Lorenzo polity, virtually all settlements in the Mazatán zone of the Soconusco were abandoned and population was drawn into a new, more hierarchical polity around La Blanca to the south. For the first time in the Soconusco, four tiers of settlement are documented based on the extent of sites and the size of their central mounds.

The history of architectural construction at Cuauhtémoc is presented in the second part of Chapter 4. During the Initial Ceramic Period, two structures at Cuauhtémoc were oriented northwest–southeast, which is parallel to the coastal plain. Then, during Horizon I, a low platform mound was oriented east–west with no obvious referent on the local landscape but consistent with the arch of the sun. The first conical pyramid mounds were then built at the center of Cuauhtémoc during the Conchas phase. The significance of building conical mounds for the first time is explored. These construction projects are discussed both in terms of labor organization as well as the transformation of the built landscape. The emergence of social stratification and the building of large mounds in Hawaii (Kolb, 1994, 2006) are discussed, and parallels are drawn to the organization of labor in the Soconusco.

Chapter 5 explores the changing domestic economy of Cuauhtémoc society. Faunal analysis and isotope data are presented to explore past diet and illuminate the manner in which the inhabitants of the Soconusco fed themselves. Food-processing practices are subsequently presented as the proportion of the ceramic assemblage made up by utilitarian tecomates (i.e., neckless jars) as well as changes in the size of these vessels. Changing quantities of fire-cracked rock, ground stone and obsidian from Cuauhtémoc are presented as are changing proportions of manos and metates versus mortars and pestles. These classes of data each indicate continuity in domestic patterns throughout the Early Formative period, followed by a marked reorganization of the domestic economy during the Conchas phase (see Rosenswig, 2006a). The most dramatic changes in the Soconusco domestic economy were therefore not the result of contact with San Lorenzo but instead occurred after its fall during the early Middle Formative period.

Feasting behavior is then explored using ceramic data. The proportion of serving-to-cooking vessels is tracked through time as is the size of slipped tecomates. Changing overall proportions of decorated serving dishes is quantified as is the distribution of their sizes. These data indicate that there were significant changes in the Soconusco with the political reorganization that corresponded to the rise of San Lorenzo. In contrast to dramatic changes in the domestic economy, Conchas-phase patterns show an overall continuity in food presentation practices. Thus, the political superstructure was transformed first and then the economic base followed. This view is contrary to traditional materialist assumptions and highlights the importance of relying on empirical evidence to document political evolution.

Changes to the Soconusco representational systems are presented with specific examples from Cuauhtémoc in Chapter 6. Ceramic vessels and figurines are the most important classes of data employed for this task. A dramatic change in the overall appearance of ceramic assemblages from small red tecomates to an assemblage dominated by larger black and white dishes is quantified and its meaning explored. Parallels are drawn between the use of late Early Formative white-rimmed blackwares and the equally distinct Ramey Incised pottery that was widely distributed in the American Southeast during the eleventh through the fourteenth centuries (Pauketat, 2004). In this example from the southeastern United States, a black and red color scheme contrasted the rest of the ceramic assemblage and encoded a political message in the vessels. Another Soconusco novelty documented during Horizon I, along with the change in color aesthetic, was the introduction of abstract iconography for the first time. This iconography depicted mythical creatures such as the Olmec dragon – part caiman, part harpy eagle. The function of abstract iconography is explored as is its introduction into a society for the first time.

The evolution of three successive figurine complexes during the course of Cuauhtémoc's occupation reveals a changing worldview expressed symbolically in the representation of the human form. First, human representation was naturalistic during the Initial Ceramic Period with two figurine types: young, naked females and fat, clothed elders who were generally seated. Then, as part of a new aesthetic during Horizon I, figurines depict androgynous, infantile individuals whose age and sex are ambiguous. During Horizon II, a wider range of individuals are depicted but age and sex continue to be unclear. These patterns indicate that the most significant changes in Soconusco representation conventions of the human form coincided temporally with the florescence of San Lorenzo. Therefore, whereas the most dramatic economic change occurred at Cuauhtémoc after the fall of San Lorenzo, the local political and aesthetic superstructure was transformed during the rise of this distant Gulf Coast polity.

A review of Spanish ethnohistorical sources on trade between the Soconusco and Gulf Coast is presented in the first part of Chapter 7. Travel times and trade routes to and from the ancient Soconusco can be more accurately reconstructed with the aid of these documents. Such accounts provide estimates of the time required to move from one area of Mesoamerica to another using preindustrial technology.

Exchange patterns from Cuauhtémoc are evaluated in the second part of Chapter 7 based on the results of obsidian and ceramic sourcing studies. These analyses link changes in the Soconusco to materials brought in from other parts of Mesoamerica. I argue that obsidian was deposited at Cuauhtémoc at the beginning of Horizon I as the exchange of this material from the Guatemalan highland sources brought this material through the Soconusco, on its way to the Gulf Coast. In the opposite direction, ceramics vessels decorated with a novel black and white aesthetic (some of which were the distinctive white-rimmed black wares) were being transported to many parts of the Soconusco, including Cuauhtémoc.

In Chapter 8, the patterns presented in the preceding four chapters are evaluated in relation to the expectations outlined in Chapter 3. A pragmatic positivism (Kelly and Hanen, 1988) is employed as the most productive way in which to evaluate data and enhance our knowledge of the past. Evidence is synthesized for this assessment, which describes changes in the Soconusco through Cuauhtémoc's rise and fall. I conclude that the EEM more fully and parsimoniously accounts for the available data than does either the PPM or the AAM.

In Chapter 9, I review the empirical contributions of this book and summarize the Cuauhtémoc data. The review and summary are followed by assessing whether it is productive to use the Mother Culture and Sister Culture concepts to achieve an anthropological understanding of Cuauhtémoc society. I argue that such concepts (along with the typology of chiefdom and state) have obscured our understanding of how Early Formative polities in Mesoamerica actually operated. Instead, I propose that Horizon I society in the Soconusco is best understood diachronically in terms of how things changed from the previous Initial Ceramic Period and were, in turn, transformed again during Horizon II. Chapter 9 concludes with a historical materialist interpretation of the data that focuses on evidence for the exploitation of labor in the Soconusco. Contrary to conventional materialist wisdom, these data suggest that political and ideational aspects of the superstructure were transformed in the Soconusco prior to the economic base and that changes to the former likely spurred a reorganization of the latter.

NOTE

1. Uncalibrated dates are used throughout this book as has traditionally been the standard among scholars studying Formative Period Mesoamerica. Please see Pool's (2007: Figure 4.1; 303 note 1) discussion of using calibrated dates for making comparisons across Mesoamerica at this time and Clark's (2007: Figure 2.3) most recent assessment of the calibrated phase limits for the period dealt with in this book.

2

Knowledge in an Archipelago of Complexity

> On the pretext of saving the producers the trouble and risk of exchange, of finding distant markets for their products, [traders] thus become the most useful class in society . . . amass enormous wealth and corresponding social influence, and for this reason are destined to reap ever new honors.
>
> Engels 1972[1891]: 210

In this chapter, I explore the political behavior entailed by long-distance ties between early complex societies. I propose that it is productive to explore the evolution of early Mesoamerican societies from a core/periphery perspective, distinct from the World-systems approach (Wallerstein, 1974) from which it is derived. I then present a discussion of inter-regional interaction inspired by Mauss's (1990) original formulation of the long-term meaning of gift giving and Malinowski's (1922, 1935) classic Trobriand ethnography that defined kula exchange. My goal is to explore the behaviors that are implied when archaeologists document the trade of objects and sharing of ideas over long distances. Mary Helms's (1979, 1993a) model for the local political salience of knowledge acquired from distant sources is reviewed, and the commonly documented quest for arcane knowledge is discussed. I argue that any study of exchange should give weight both to the movement of material goods and the ideas that accompany them. The movement of potentially prestigious ideas and concepts (or those that are desirable in some way) over long distances I call a "knowledge kula." As such, ideas/concepts can move across long distances and be exchanged between elites, and they can remain tied to specific individuals or particular places. In Melanesian, kula exchange is circular with objects traveling in opposite directions.

My use of the term kula here presupposes no necessary patterns or direction of exchange. Instead, it is the integration of local and long-distance exchange relationships on which I focus. Ideas or concepts (and objects) from afar link local exchange with long-distance exchange, as Helms discusses at length. This can be true after foreign objects arrive into a local system, but, as I review below, equally important is how labor is mobilized and rituals are enacted to "gear up" for launching exchange trips.

Drawing on Braudel's (1992) conception of medieval European towns forming an archipelago of cultural islands, I end this chapter by defining an "archipelago of complexity." This concept both describes the geographic separation of interacting exchange partners and provides a model to interpret the manner in which foreign objects and knowledge functioned locally. I argue that exotic objects and ideas can be effectively employed by an elite for political ends only when their distribution and use can be controlled. Examples are provided from the Trobriand Islands, Roman Europe, the Bronze Age Cyclades and Peru's Early Horizon. These examples, widely separated in space and time, suggest that common processes may be at work in how local prestige is constructed from exotic goods and ideas. Material objects that are imbued with knowledge (through the use of iconography or other symbolism) provide archaeological evidence through which to explore these processes in prehistoric contexts.

A CORE/PERIPHERY PERSPECTIVE

A reformulated World-systems approach is relevant in modeling Early and Middle Formative long-distance interaction in Mesoamerica. An advantage of this perspective is that it necessarily situates the Cuauhtémoc research area, and the Soconusco in general, within a broader geographic and diachronic context. Changing sociopolitical structure is explored as the dynamic interplay between developments at both a regional and an inter-regional scale (Frank, 1990; Frank and Gills, 1993). Therefore, the unit of analysis is central to understanding the manner in which societies change (McC. Adams, 2001: 349–350). So, although large spatial scales are generally required to understand local phenomena, it is equally important to account for how the geographic extents of interaction changed through time (Wallerstein, 1991).

World-systems analysis was first proposed by Immanuel Wallerstein (1974) to explain European colonial expansion but has been modified over the past two decades to be more applicable to prehistoric contexts (e.g., Blanton and Feinman, 1984; Burger and Matos, 2002; Chase-Dunn, 1992; Chase-Dunn and Hall, 1993, 1995; Ekholm and Freidman, 1985; Frank, 1990, 1993, 1995; Frankenstein and Rowlands, 1978; Freidman and Rowlands, 1978; Kohl, 1987; McGuire, 1987; Peregrine and Feinman, 1996; Rowlands et al., 1987; Schneider, 1977; Schortman and Urban, 1987, 1992a). There are, however, a number of critics of this reformulation (e.g., McGuire, 1996; Renfrew, 1986a; Stein, 1999; Wallerstein, 1991: 242), and there is little consensus regarding the societies to which it can be applied (Abu-Lughod, 1989; Braudel, 1992: 57; Frank, 1990, 1993; Frank and Gills, 1993). To escape a semantic cul-de-sac, World-systems theory is employed here in its reformulated guise and referred to in this book as a core/periphery perspective that is relevant to precapitalist societies (Santley and Alexander, 1992: 24; Schneider, 1977). This reformulation requires: 1) exploring the potential of luxury goods to transform society; 2) imbuing archaeologically recognizable style horizons with processual explanations; and 3) recognizing that a core area can become peripheral and that more than one core can exist at a time within a given macroregion.

The first basic premise required to make the core/periphery perspective relevant to precapitalist societies is to discard the dichotomy Wallerstein creates between luxury and bulk goods (Schneider, 1977). Wallerstein (1974: 41–42) claims that staple foods and raw materials provide the impetus for the expansion of the world system. However, in Europe the trade of luxuries such as pepper, sugar and furs sparked the intensification of inter-regional integration (e.g., Braudel, 1992: 183–265; Mintz, 1985; Wolf, 1982). Therefore, Wallerstein does not in fact accurately account for the factors that were responsible for the development of the capitalist World-system. The trade in luxury goods plays an even more central role in precapitalist societies. Long-distance exchange in goods and ideas further provides opportunities for individuals to organize the production, procurement and distribution of such goods (Hodder, 1982a: 209). Leadership can be maintained through control of resources or knowledge of trade routes, and an elite segment of society can be perpetuated through the social relationships that develop through long-distance trade (e.g., Helms, 1979, 1992). Therefore, emergent elites can employ inter-regional exchange for social and political advantage at a local scale (Frankenstein and Rowlands, 1985). After an elite segment of society has grown to depend on long-distance trade to maintain their elevated position, one can imagine that there would have been a self-interested motivation to expand it in response to local challenges (Champion, 1989: 14). Luxury goods are then not that "luxurious" but instead crucial to the operation of society. This perspective is dynamic as sociopolitical change is proposed to occur due to competition between elites in distant areas, as well as among those in any given local area. In the next sections of this chapter, I return to this point and explore the behavior entailed by elite inter-regional interaction.

A second requirement of the core/periphery perspective is that regional similarities in material culture be interpreted in terms of the social processes responsible for generating the spread and maintenance of recognizable artifact styles. As Kristiansen and Larsson (2005: 37) observe: "Exchange and interaction cannot be understood as a neutral flow of material goods. They were embedded in a complicated system of social and political exchange rituals that had to do with the ways in which value, status and power were produced and reproduced." Areas of interaction that result in archaeologically recognizable "style horizons" have long been recognized in the New World (Willey, 1945, 1948, 1962, 1991 and see Rice, 1993). The definition of such stylistic "horizons" (i.e., geographically extensive use of objects containing similar symbolic information) can be useful for cross-dating sites and establishing the contemporaneity of groups of people from disparate locations. Horizon styles and style markers were basic tools of culture-historical reconstruction that allow temporal ordering of cultures within a defined region (Phillips and Willey, 1953). The processual backlash against such explanations encouraged the scale of interpretation to contract and explore local processes by underestimating macroregional processes (McGuire, 1996: 51; Schortman and Urban, 1987). The perspective advocated here focuses on the interplay of local and inter-regional processes, embraces the empirical reality of horizon styles and proposes that their meaning be explained in behavioral terms. In Chapter 3, an Initial Ceramic Period and three style horizons are defined for Early and Middle Formative period Mesoamerica to help understand the changing macroregional system of interaction. These four temporal epochs are thus understood in terms of the inter-regional behavior that resulted in the production of similar material culture.

A third requirement for a core/periphery perspective to make it relevant to ancient times is to define an inter-regional system without a permanent or solitary core area (see Chase-Dunn and Hall, 1991; Ekholm and Freidman, 1985; Hudson, 2004; Kristiansen, 1987). Furthermore, core areas should not be seen as the sole location of innovations that were then spread to peripheries (Hall, 1986; Stein, 2002: 905). People in all regions act in their self-interest and are equally capable of all sorts of innovation. For example, Kohl (1987: 20–21) discusses Bronze Age Omani society, where elite exchange relationships with both Harappa and Sumer allowed for a more complex level of local organization without being dependent on either system (also see Blackman et al., 1989). In this Omani case, two distant core areas coexisted, which allowed for local developments to follow an independent course. Without technological advantages in communication, transportation and military power, ancient elites in core areas did not occupy a comparably dominant position as in modern core states (contra Wallerstein, 1974: 349). Abu-Lughod (1989: 38) observed that: "The term 'world system' as it is currently used, has unfortunately been conflated with the *particular hierarchical structural organization* that developed from the sixteenth century onward" (emphasis in original). She further argues that:

The world economy of the thirteenth century is not only fascinating in itself but, because it contained no single hegemonic power, provides an important contrast to the world system that grew out of it: the one Europe reshaped to its own ends and dominated for so long. This contrast suggests that the characteristics of world systems are not invariant. There is no unique way for the parts to be organized.

Abu-Lughod, 1989: 4, 6

As documented in the ancient world, polities in core areas tended not to be stable, and those in peripheral areas could surpass them in terms of organizational complexity (Champion, 1989: 17–18). If core and peripheral areas can change through time, then inter-regional domination is not essential to provide insight into pre-capitalist societies. Instead, unequal levels of complexity can result when one region differentially influences another (Schortman and Urban, 1994). A core/periphery perspective defined in this way also addresses critiques that World-systems analysis treats people in the periphery as passive victims (Sahlins, 1994: 412; Wolf, 1982: 23). In this book I argue that the most organizationally complex polity in Mesoamerica at the end of the Early Formative period emerged on Mexico's Gulf Coast at San Lorenzo. However, this was relatively short-lived. San Lorenzo had collapsed by the beginning of the Middle Formative period, and numerous other polities then emerged after its demise. The political landscape of the Soconusco was similarly dynamic during the Early and Middle Formative periods, and political centers did not last for longer than a few centuries.

Core/periphery perspectives in Mesoamerica

Blanton and Feinman (1984) were among the first to explicitly address the applicability of a World-systems approach to Mesoamerican archaeology. They posited that macroregional interaction was maintained by the desire of core area elites to acquire luxury goods but also had the effect of stimulating economic activities in both core and peripheral zones. Peripheral areas were not only drawn in directly by tribute obligations; the exchange of goods transformed societies in such zones as a result of new social and political dynamics linked to labor reorganization. A recent model proposed by these authors attempts to characterize Mesoamerica in terms of general organizational principles that oscillate between local and inter-regional strategies (Blanton et al., 1996; and see Pool, 2007: 29–31; Rosenswig, 2000). Such coordinated pan-regional cycles are reminiscent of those proposed by Frank (1993) to characterize the past 5,000 years of Eurasian history, as both identify simultaneous, pan-regional changes in organizational strategies over great distances.

Mesoamerican scholars modeled inter-regional interaction in various ways that anticipated Wallerstein's (1974) seminal publication. In fact, the basic idea of Mesoamerica as a culture area implies regular long-distance interaction (Kirchoff, 1952) as does the concept of style horizons (discussed at more length in Chapter 3). Whereas the idea of culture areas attributes empirically observed cultural traits and artistic styles to diffusion, other early models proposed explanations that link inter-regional interaction to the emergence of inequality in the Early and Middle Formative periods (e.g., Flannery, 1968; Rathje, 1971, 1972).

In the years prior to the publication of Wallerstein's seminal book, William Rathje (1971, 1972) proposed a "core/buffer" model of inter-regional economic interaction to explain the emergence of complexity among the Gulf Coast Olmec and lowland Maya. He argued that the lack of salt, ground stone and obsidian in the lowlands required suprahousehold organization to obtain them (Rathje, 1971: 276–277). Because these three products were available only in the highlands and yet were essential to an agricultural adaptation, "The need within every household for basic resources therefore created a bridge between ecology and sociopolitical organization" (Rathje 1972: 371). In their trade with "buffer polities," lowland core polities exchanged arcane knowledge and associated ritual objects for highland resources and quickly rose to power as this set up an unequal flow of wealth. However, as a monopoly over arcane knowledge was difficult to maintain, the core polities collapsed as those in the highlands rose to prominence by usurping and redefining the ideology of power. Rathje's core, highland and buffer zone distinctions parallel quite closely Wallerstein's definition of core, periphery and semiperiphery. Over the past thirty years, the variables that Rathje discussed have been reevaluated. The impetus for exchange may not be that the lowlands lack salt and ground stone for a successful agricultural adaptation (see Arnold, 2000: 121–122; Stark, 2000: note 7). Furthermore, that agricultural dependence had not fully developed during the Early Formative period (Blake, 2006, Blake et al., 1992b; Rosenswig, 2006a). In addition, Rathje's model cannot explain why some of the most intensive Early Formative period interaction was between the Gulf Coast and the Soconusco as both regions contain roughly the same environments and resources.

Even prior to the publication of Rathje's papers, Flannery (1968) modeled long-distance interaction with Gulf Coast societies from the perspective of an emergent Oaxaca elite (but see Flannery and Marcus, 1994: 389). He proposed that external relations were used to bolster internal, elite status differentiation in both regions. The Gulf Coast elite received a supply of exotic goods that could be used to "reinforce commitments to the Olmec social and religious systems" (Flannery, 1968: 81). For their part, the Oaxaca elite "emulate the religion, symbolism, dress and behavior of the Olmec elite insofar as it would enhance their own status among their own people" (Flannery, 1968: 79–80). Flannery's model emphasizes that the inter-regional exchange of preciosities can be fundamental to political systems within two regions at different levels of organizational complexity. The self-interest of leaders in both regions therefore provides the impetus for long-distance trade of material goods as well as the potential for exchange of technological knowledge, innovative methods of social organization and religious practices. In terms consistent with a core/periphery perspective, he posits that "... the overall function of the whole system may have been to create one big economic sphere where previously many small ones had existed ... " (Flannery, 1968: 108). In other words, as I argue in this book, the creation of "one big economic sphere" at the end of the Early Formative period established Mesoamerica's first World-system.

Rather than simply describe Gulf Coast–Soconusco interaction at the end of the Early Formative period, my goal is to evaluate the relationship between inhabitants of the two regions from the perspective of the Soconusco cultural system: before, during and after the apogee of the San Lorenzo polity. This book is thus an attempt to understand the first 800 years of settled life in one corner of the Soconusco from a diachronic perspective. However, although helpful at conceptualizing the "big picture," a core/periphery perspective does not work as well for explaining specific material patterns. To explore such patterns, in the remainder of this chapter I articulate a more detailed model from which to interpret inter-regional interaction among early complex societies.

GIFT EXCHANGE AND SOCIAL DEBT

Mauss's (1990) definition of a gift exchange economy was seminal in laying out the underlying political and economic mechanisms established through the competitive exchange of material goods. His thesis provides insight into the process of economic interaction between people who had no money or other form of absolute value for exchange items. Explicitly framed within Durkheim's proposal of the division of labor, the main question addressed in *The Gift* was to:

... indicate in detail the various principles that have imposed this appearance on a necessary form of exchange, namely, the division of labour in society itself – among all these principles we shall nevertheless study only one in depth. *What rule of legality and self-interest, in societies of a backward or archaic type, compels the gift that has been received to be obligatorily reciprocated? What power resides in the object that causes its recipient to pay it back?*

Mauss, 1990: 3, emphasis in original

Written in 1925 and drawing primarily on the then recently acquired, ethnographic data of the Northwest Coast Potlatch and the
Polynesian Kula, Mauss defines the fundamental social obligations of
gift exchange. These obligations – to give, to accept and to reciprocate
– create a web of social relations that can be broken only with the loss
of political authority or under threat of war (Mauss, 1990: 39–42). For
example, a chief on the Northwest Coast could preserve his authority
only by giving as much as he could at a potlatch. In addition to
the economic transaction, the act of giving provided evidence of his
power, as it was a material and visible representation of his political
power and (by implication) his spiritual power. Among the Trobriand
Islanders, the extent of a chief's gift-giving ability and his ability to
redistribute the gifts he receives, is a material manifestation of his
mana (Mauss, 1990: 75). As Mauss (1990: 39) says:

A chief must give potlatches . . . He can only preserve his authority over his
tribe and village . . . he can only maintain his rank among the chiefs – both
nationally and internationally – if he can prove he is haunted and favoured
both by the spirit and by good fortune . . . he can only prove this good fortune
by spending it and sharing it out . . .

The obligation to accept a gift is as stringent as to give in the first
place. Mauss (1990: 41) observes: "One has no right to refuse a gift,
or to refuse to attend the potlatch. To act in this way is to show that
one is afraid of having to reciprocate . . . It is either to admit oneself
beaten in advance or, in certain cases, to proclaim oneself the victor
and invincible." The obligation to reciprocate is the essence of the
gift exchange and the factor that makes it a self-perpetuating system
of social relations. The obligation to reciprocate means that the social
obligation is not terminated and that there is always a ceremony of
gift exchange pending that maintains social bonds between groups
of people and between their chiefs.

When given a gift, a Northwest Coast chief could reciprocate, fail
to do so and lose face, or go to war. If one loses face, one drops out of
the running and is no longer a chief. Reciprocating and going to war
are both antagonistic actions, representing either political/economic
competition or military confrontation. With war, the exchange system
breaks down between the particular groups of people. However, by
far the most common result is to reciprocate in the exchange of gifts,
and so, put the other group into a position where they are socially

indebted – and the cycle continues (see also Drucker and Heizer, 1967; Jonaitis 1991).

Sahlins (1972: 171) notes that, as a political philosopher, Mauss adopts a rather Hobbesian position as the two share "... a basic agreement on the natural political state as a generalized distribution of force, on the possibility of escaping from this condition by the aid of reason, and on the advantages realized thereby in cultural progress" and, further, that: "The gift is alliance, solidarity, communion – in brief, peace, the great virtue that earlier philosophers, Hobbes notably, had discovered in the State.... The primitive analogue of social contract is not the State, but the gift" (Sahlins, 1972: 169; and see Komter, 2005). However, rather than being a static form of political organization, gift giving is a strategy of political interaction. It thus provides a more dynamic forum for analysis by focusing on a reciprocal process of interaction. Mauss's thesis in *The Gift* therefore presents a nuanced, historical assessment as: "... it corrects just this simplified progression from chaos to commonwealth, savagery to civilization, that had been the work of classical contract theory. Here in the primitive world Mauss displayed a whole array of intermediate forms, not only of a certain stability, but that did not make coercion the price of order" (Sahlins, 1972: 179–180). Gift giving, as a basic social mechanism, provides a starting point from which to understand inter-regional interaction.

CONSPICUOUS CONSUMPTION AND SOCIAL CAPITAL

Competitive gift giving is a form of social interaction governed by the logic (or illogic) of conspicuous consumption. Measuring the value of goods, in societies that do not use abstract forms of value such as money, is most simply accomplished through the labor theory of value (Marx, 1978: 254–261).[1] That is, at a fundamental level, an item's value can be measured as the quantity of labor invested in its production and acquisition (see Graeber, 2002: 54–56, 66–67). Therefore, the value of goods given and consumed can be translated, on some level, to a measure of labor expenditure. The consumption of resources therefore results in the creation of social currency that is maintained by the giver until the gift is reciprocated. Labor is transformed into goods through their production, and goods are, in turn, transformed into social capital through their distribution to others. But why is the process of gift exchange consistently able to create social capital that circulates within society? Furthermore, why is it that the social capital of the gifts exchanged is so obvious to archaeologists and often appears to have cross-cultural salience?

To answer these questions, I follow an argument presented by Bruce Trigger (1990, 2004) that accounts for the common use of monumental architecture and elaborate burial practices in early complex societies. This argument was designed to explain the inherent value of expending labor to create monuments. However, the logic of using labor to create symbols of power functions equally well when applied to the exchange of gifts; both rely on the labor theory of value to create cross-culturally recognizable prestige. In fact, without assuming a cross-cultural theory of value it would be difficult for archaeologists to understand the valuables circulating in societies with which they share no historical connection.

The defining feature of a monumental construction project "... is that its scale and elaboration exceed the requirements of any practical functions that a building is intended to perform" (Trigger, 1990: 119). Trigger begins with Zipf's theory of least effort, which posits that "... a person in solving his immediate problems will view those against the background of his probable future problems *as estimated by himself* [and] he will strive to solve his problems in such a way as to minimize the *total work* that he must expend in solving *both* his immediate problems and his probable future problems" (Zipf, 1949: 1). Citing examples from a wide array of prehistoric cultures and early civilizations that support the basic cross-cultural reality of the principle of least effort, Trigger (1990: 122) rejects "efforts to discredit it as Western ethnocentrism" due to the empirically documented ubiquity of such behavior. Establishing the principle of least effort as guiding behavior among prehistoric hunter-gatherers, tribal agriculturalists, preindustrial states and modern economic planners, Trigger (1990: 124) concludes that "The main difference between them is that the modern planners seek to conserve the expenditure of energy in order to maximize profits, while people living in egalitarian societies generally used it to satisfy their wants with minimal personal effort..."

It is the pervasiveness of the principle of least effort which provides social salience when violated. More than a century ago, Veblen (1994 [1899]) systematically described the common elite practice of wasting, or conspicuously consuming, large amounts of resources. Originally intended as an ironic critique of nineteenth-century capitalism in the United States, Veblen identified a fundamental manner through which the elite expressed their "eliteness." That is, being part of the elite is put into evidence only by acting in an elite manner, and having wealth is only evidenced by displaying it.

The translation of nonsubsistence labor into material objects that serve no "practical" purpose imbues them with socially recognizable power. As Trigger (1990: 122) puts it, " . . . monumental architecture makes power visible and hence becomes power rather than merely a symbol of it." The relevance of such a proposal to archaeology is clear as it is from the material remains of the past that behavior must be inferred. Therefore, the valuable prestige goods and monumental architecture documented by archaeologists can be employed as proxy measures of power (DeMarrais et al., 1996), and their spatial distribution reflects such power in action (see Smith, 2003). At some basic level, the labor value of these undertakings provides the "common currency" for the expression of power in many types of material culture.

PERSUASIVE DISPLAY AND SOCIAL POWER

One is powerful if one can exercise power. Rather than being self-evident, this is fundamental to understanding how the symbols of power relations function within society. As Veblen (1994 [1899]: 36) noted in regard to esteem, "In order to gain and hold the esteem of men it is not sufficient merely to possess wealth or power. The wealth or power must be put in evidence, for esteem is awarded only on evidence." The same logic holds for political authority. Public claims of power are salient only if the control over the labor of others is displayed. For example, monumental constructions and valuable artifacts are symbols of power only because the control of human labor was required to create them.

As defined above, power is generally expressed in two time frames. The first is during the construction, or acquisition, of valuable objects. At such times, labor is controlled directly and mobilized for a specific purpose. Therefore, the act of creating valuable objects is a concrete method of exercising power as it affirms that a leader has the power to bring valuable objects into existence. If a ruler has 1,000 people toil for two years to build his palace, then they are all aware of the power he exercises over them. The exercise of power is most blatant when work is undertaken by slaves who may refuse only on penalty of death. However, if people provide their labor through some sort of corvée system, which is legitimized through a religious ideology of divine kingship, the use of their labor is no less evident. Equally evident is the power required to, for example, import gold from a distant land and to have it fashioned into fine ritual paraphernalia by local smiths. The traders and specialized workers will undoubtedly be better treated than the slave, but there is no doubt as to who has the power or whose political interests drive these economic activities. Even in situations where labor is considered to be cooperative, there are nonetheless individuals who organize work parties. In such cases, it may be an age and/or sex (e.g., senior men) who are in charge and the "cooperative" undertaking still reaffirms established social norms.

During the initial acquisition and creation of valuable objects, the expenditure of labor is most evident. However, a second time frame for the expression of power is the persistent use of valuable objects as well as the transformation of landscapes by monumental architecture. The memory of this control of labor imbues the objects with a value related to the level of effort that was required to create them. Such historical "bookkeeping" would not be as precise as, for example, this monument required one million person-hours to construct whereas that gold scepter required two thousand person-hours to acquire the gold and jewels and have a master artisan make it. Although, in a modern example of such labor bookkeeping, Grahame Clark (1986: 109) notes that the robes worn by Prince Philip as Chancellor of the University of Cambridge took more than 440 person-hours to make – not including the cost of the cloth or the gold used for elaborate ornamentation. My point here is simply that the value of objects and monuments are maintained in approximate accordance with the labor required for their creation and the resulting culturally defined power of their use. As monuments are on permanent display and badges of authority, such as crowns and scepters are employed at specific times for public ritual, individuals who control their use remind others of the social power that such objects have symbolically embedded in them. In the case of earthen mounds, their periodic maintenance would function in a similar manner by reminding people of their initial construction and continued use by a restricted segment of society.

In an insightful analysis of money and the Madagascar slave trade, David Graeber (1996) carries this line of reasoning one step further in his exploration of the politically negotiated nature of elite power. He states that:

> ... in the final analysis a king's status is based on his ability to persuade others to recognize him as such, and to pay him tribute for that reason. By making a show of magnificence, a king is able to define himself in such a way that others are moved to transfer some of their wealth to him ... By covering themselves with gold, then, kings persuade others to cover them in gold as well ... By engaging in persuasive display, then, all one is really doing is calling on others to imitate actions that are implicitly being said to have already been carried out in the past.
>
> Graeber, 1996: 9

Graeber stresses the importance of historical referents used to convince people of a king's social power and thus his right to rule. Not only does the creation of impressive monuments and opulent objects represent the power of a ruler, but the process of displaying and using such material symbols of power is fundamental to legitimizing power through a socially salient public discourse. Yet such discourse is not static, and authority must be constantly invigorated through persuasive display. New and innovative sources of social capital need to be acquired and infused into the system as:

> Few objects are simply one thing or another ... in any system of value there are, at the very least, constant diversions and slippages back and forth, continual struggles over definition. Often – as in the case of the Greek polis – these struggles are quite openly political ones. And insofar as they involve attempts to reconcile such contrasting values as artistic beauty, wealth, and civic authority, one might say that, in essence, they are *always* political.
>
> Graeber, 1996: 12

Therefore, if the possession of wealth is a manifestation of power, then its display is a necessarily political endeavor. In addition, regularly displaying the evidence of such wealth represents the process necessary for maintaining power. Based on the argument that conspicuous consumption creates social capital, the archaeologist can identify persuasive display behavior through such wealth items that far surpass any functional requirements.

Mesoamerican leaders were not covering themselves in gold during the second part of the Early Formative period (or what I define as Horizon I in Chapter 3). What they were doing was infusing exotic, supernaturally charged customs into the societies that they were directing. Flannery (1968: 105) states that " ... there may have been an attempt on the part of the elite of the less sophisticated society to adopt the behavior, status trappings, religion, symbolism, or even language of the more sophisticated group . . . in short, to absorb some of their charisma." Therefore, rather than being covered in gold, the Soconusco leaders I discuss in this book wrapped themselves in exotic charisma and by doing so they encouraged others to regard them accordingly.

LOCAL COHESION CREATED THROUGH THE PRODUCTION OF GIFTS

The majority of this chapter has thus far addressed the competitive and political nature of gift exchange and wealth display from a top-down perspective. However, the social organization required to produce gifts, and acquire goods for display, can also provide a unifying force within society as a leader coordinates local groups for a single purpose. The numerous social processes required to acquire and/or produce prestige items may thus be equally important as what was done with them. Elites would have provided gifts to other local (or nearby) elites as well as their followers to make long-distance exchange trips possible.

Malinowski's (1922) description of the kula exchange was seminal in the creation of Mauss's thesis on the gift and the nature of competitive exchange. However, significant parts of kula voyages were the collective purpose and the social cohesion created by the preparation for such trips. Therefore, although long-distance exchange may result in differentiation, the production and acquisition of goods to be exchanged can also generate solidarity within society. As Uberoi (1962: 108) notes, " . . . *kula* expeditions act as a channel whereby the quarrels which arise within one district . . . are turned outward, and made to emphasize and renew the district's foreign relations."

Most discussions of kula exchange focus on the long-distance exchange of white shell bracelets (*mwali*) and red shell necklaces (*soulava*), together called valuables (*vaygu'a*). However, the large scale, intertribal kula trade is just one level of exchange operating within Trobriand society. Malinowski (1922: 167) tells us that "every legal and customary act is done to the accompaniment of material gift and counter gift; that wealth given and taken, is one of the main instruments of social organization, of the power of the chief, of the bonds of kinship, and of the relationship of law."

In preparation for the kula expedition, many activities were undertaken such as "the building of canoes, preparation of the outfit, the provisioning of the expedition, the fixing of dates and social organization of the enterprise" (Malinowski, 1922: 99). As well as the trade of *vaygu'a*, an important secondary trade of more mundane goods, such as food and ceramic vessels, was carried out during the kula exchange (Uberoi, 1962: 156–157). Although these activities are subsidiary to the kula, they (along with the actual voyage) require the majority of the time of those involved. As Malinowski (1922: 100) states, "... if we look at the acts from the outside, as comparative sociologists, and gauge their real utility, trade and canoe-building will appear to us as the really important achievements, whereas we shall regard the Kula only as an indirect stimulus ... " In other words, although the motivation for long-distance trade is the political aspirations of individuals who organize these voyages, they result in important economic exchange occurring as well.

The inland kula exchange of *vayagu'a* (occurring after the long-distance trips were completed) is equally significant as the long-distance trips and acquisition of goods. No magic was performed and no large public gatherings were convened, but the goods acquired from overseas kula were distributed by the chief in exchange for goods from local communities (Malinowski, 1922: 464–477). Therefore, to view gift giving solely in terms of an exchange between communities reduces it to an economic activity with very short duration when, in fact, it is an elaborate intracommunity process that begins before the kula party sets out and continues long after they have returned. This, of course, is the essence of Mauss's (1990: 5) concept of exchange as the "system of total service." It is also significant that, through all of these activities, it is the chiefs who orchestrate and direct tasks. Therefore, in addition to any material gains achieved during the course of inter-regional exchange trips, they also reaffirm their political dominance by directing the labor of others (Goldman, 1970: 498). Mauss (1990: 27) observes, " ... in the end, only the chiefs, and even solely those drawn from the coastal tribes – and then only a few – do in fact take part in it. The *kula* merely gives concrete expression to many other institutions, bringing them together." Given this quote, Adams's (1975) and Weiner's (1976: 220) critique, that Mauss does not address the reinforcement of dominant power relations embedded in gift exchange, seems unfounded. Mauss appears only too aware of the political implications of the gift exchange and its ability to generate social capital (Godelier, 2004: 11).

In terms of time expenditure, the giving and receiving of gifts (both locally and in distant lands) are a relatively small part of the overall function of these gifts. Scholars are often focused too narrowly on the exchange of gifts or on how leaders bribe their followers through the redistribution of gifts. As a result, less attention is paid to the integrative effect of producing the objects that act as gifts or to gearing up for feasts and other processes of exchange (e.g., Scheffler, 1965: 216). Such integrative mechanisms have the potential to establish, and naturalize, the power of a leader as much as the "payoff" of formal exchanges between chiefs or the later redistribution to followers. The essence of kula is the use of exotic objects (and the histories they possess) in local practices. Such a melding of the local with the distant is cross-culturally salient.

KNOWLEDGE KULA AND SOCIAL INEQUALITY

Gift exchange forms the basis of the nonmonetary political economy and helps explain the process of establishing the value of luxury goods. As Sahlins (1972: 133) observes, "The economic relation of giver-receiver is the political relation of leader-follower." To maintain political inequality, a leader must restrict the ability of potential political competitors within his polity to acquire wealth and power. Once in a dominant position, a ruler can maintain political power (and social capital) only as long as he can continue to give away gifts and potential rivals cannot.

Gosden (1989) proposes two potential ways in which access to prestige items can be restricted: through long-distance trade and through craft production. The former refers to a situation in which the elite segment of a population trades with distant groups for valuable goods not available locally. In this case, Gosden (1989: 361–363) uses the kula as an example and points out that all members of society have access to identical local products. The latter (i.e., use of craft production) refers to the situation in which a local elite derives power through the control of craft specialists who can produce prestige goods that cannot be made without restricted skills that are known only to them. As examples, he describes the Central and West African manufacture of fine metal and cloth objects by elite specialists. Gosden (1989: 367) posits that it is difficult to maintain a monopoly over trade, and sees the creation of craft products as a more stable system with which to maintain permanent differentiation in the flow of unreciprocated gifts.

Gosden's (1989) scenario assumes that long-distance trade does not result in restricted skills or learned knowledge in the way that craft production does. However, Gosden (1985: 476–478) himself provides a counterexample with his intriguing discussion of how the king of the Kongo significantly decreased local production of iron, copper, cloth and salt because it was simpler to control the import of prestigious Portuguese trade gifts. Mary Helms (1979) provides a further example from the sixteenth-century Cuna of Panama where long-distance exchange forms the basis of unequal power relations. Unequal relations among the Cuna were not based solely on the procurement of material goods from afar, but were also dependent on the acquisition of esoteric knowledge. Malinowski (1922: 181) tells us that, among the Trobriand Islanders, payment is made to those who possess magic and can affect, among other things, the weather, the state of crops or the health of sick persons. Knowledge of magic is thus a valued commodity that is paid for. In addition, among the Trobriand people, "The power of magic is exploited at the highest political level . . . magic becomes the most creative and powerful tool that anyone can wield . . . magic is accompanied by great ritual and political display" (Weiner, 1976: 216). In her diachronic study of the Enga, Polly Wiessner (2002: 247–248) also documents that control of knowledge increased precisely as the level of inequality within society increased. If a distant source of esoteric knowledge exists and control of its dissemination can be controlled, then the exchange of such knowledge (regardless of the particular objects traded) provides social power to persons who trafficked in it. Thus, contrary to Gosden's (1989) claim, both trade and craft specialization each have the potential to provide controllable sources of prestige. Such prestige is most relevant to archaeological inquiry when materialized as wealth items that are gifted and displayed. In the case of Early Formative period societies, iron ore, obsidian, greenstone and ceramic vessels are the only traceable goods that were exchanged. However, as I argue in this book, knowledge of different places, distant customs and the routes one follows to get there are all associated forms of knowledge that leave no material residue.

Helms's (1979) main thesis is that contact among Panamanian elites and long-distance interaction with Columbian rulers served primarily political purposes. Such contact was, for the most part, " . . . a search for politically useful knowledge, that is, as intellectual quests that then paid political dividends" (Helms, 1979: xiii). Based

on early Spanish accounts, Helms defines seven paramount chiefdoms operating in Panama prior to Spanish contact. Each chief lived
in his principle city (*bohio*), and his territory was located on a major
transportation artery – both river and land trails. These chiefdoms
were often surrounded by minor dependent chiefs who all traded,
and went to war, with each other (Helms, 1979: 39).

It is reported that much trading was carried out among the Cuna
chiefdoms and that this was often prefaced with hostility (see Helms,
1979: 61). In addition, the sixteenth-century accounts make it clear
that a chief evidenced his ability and right to rule through the display of material goods and the quantity of such goods that he could
distribute to his followers (see Helms, 1979: 32). Helms's account of
Panamanian chiefdoms thus closely resembles those that Mauss used
in his initial formulation of the gift exchange economy.

Cuna trade was predominantly in shells from the Atlantic coast,
pearls from the Pacific coast, gold from the highlands, woven cotton
cloth, pottery, agricultural products and slaves. Gold was the most
important trade item, and all members of the elite wore gold ear
and nose rings. Considerable skill was required to procure these
valuable goods as, for example, oyster divers were trained from birth
(Helms, 1979: 49). Spinning and weaving cotton, goldsmithing and
pottery production were all craft specialties that also required lengthy
training. However, contra Gosden (1989), the trade and manufacture
of goods was a fluid relationship, and groups that procured raw
materials were not always those that fashioned them into sought-
after prestige items. The point here is that, among the Cuna, it was not
solely trade nor purely manufacturing that rulers used to monopolize
political power.

The most fundamental form of political power was instead
established and maintained among the Cuna by traveling to distant Colombia to acquire arcane knowledge. Helms (1979: 107–108)
explains that "the geographically distant and the supernaturally distant were closely related, and that this association was succinctly
stated by the acquisition from distant geographical regions of elite
prestige items with sacred significance." Knowledge can itself be
viewed as a commodity that is traded, hoarded and exploited for
political ends (e.g., Braudel, 1972: 365–368; Broodbank, 2000: 249–262;
Helms, 1988: 118–119; Kristiansen and Larsson, 2005: 49; Renfrew,
1993). Different societies may favor traded objects, crafted objects
and exotic knowledge in various degrees, but it is likely through the

self-reinforcing use of all three that the elite of a given society will maintain their dominant position.

In early twentieth-century Cuna society, there was a hierarchy of knowledge. Women and young people possessed basic knowledge of their society's World view and ceremonial behavior; older men acquired knowledge of other myths, chants and medical lore. Village chiefs knew more lore and learned a distinctive chief's language (Helms, 1979: 122). Chiefs with regional influence were even better versed in matters of lore and ritual. Such knowledge was compared at political occasions and functions in the same manner as were any other scarce goods (Helms, 1979: 128). Up until the late nineteenth and early twentieth centuries, Cuna elite traveled to northern Colombia to be schooled in religion, medicine, history and leadership skills. Therefore, traveling to distant lands to acquire arcane knowledge and returning with exotic prestige goods appears to have been a significant source of social capital among the Cuna. In Mesoamerica, a similar role for objects executed in the Olmec style has long been proposed by Drennan (1976a: 357–358), Earle (1990: 75) and others (Coe, 1965a; Flannery, 1968: 106; Grove, 1970: 32, 2000). Similar models also have been advanced lately for the Philippines (Junker, 1999), the southeastern United States (Pauketat et al., 2002; Turbitt, 2000) and Bronze Age Europe (Kristiansen and Larsson, 2005). Barbara Stark (2000) has used Helms's 1993 book *Craft and the Kingly Idea* when addressing the Olmec (and see Clark, 2007).

In that work, Helms (1993a: 6) attempts to meld "... aesthetics and symbolism on the one hand and economics on the other..." She provides ethnographic examples of the manner in which persons who engage in long-distance exchange employ the prestige and goods thus acquired to bolster their social position at home. Helms proposes that there is a cross-culturally consistent division between what exists "inside" society and what exists "outside" society. The outside realm is conceived of both horizontally (in terms of geographically distant places) as well as vertically (in terms of different planes of existence). Through the association of physically and spiritually distant places, the former takes on a sacred character (also see Helms, 1988). In terms reminiscent of Graeber's (1996) idea of persuasive display, Helms (1993a: 9) states:

... not only do crafted goods and foreign-derived goods encapsulate power from that portion of the universe lying outside society, but the very acts of skilled crafting and of long-distance acquisition are important precisely because they channel and concentrate such energy. Consequently, individuals who do this crafting or who acquire such goods become associated with, perhaps filled with, this same power, as do those who come to possess such goods and surround themselves with such extraordinary objects.

The consistent association of foreigners, or least foreignness, with high status is documented in most early civilizations. As Trigger (1993: 86) notes, "Kings and nobles frequently trace their origins to strangers in order to minimize their kinship and ethnic obligations to the people they dominate." There are numerous examples of rulers being associated with foreignness and here I mention just two from Mesoamerica. First, the Classic period Maya rulers of Tikal and Copán asserted ties between their founding ancestors and the ancient center of Teotihuacan as part of the political discourse that justified their right to rule (Stuart, 2000). Second, the Aztec also traced their ancestry to northern peoples who migrated and subsequently dominated the Valley of Mexico (Gillespie, 1989). These examples may or may not be demonstrable with archaeological data, but both established foreign ethnicity as emic characteristic of elite status. In prestate societies, creation myths might not have established such a wide divide between elite and commoner as the Maya and Aztec cases, but the exotic was nonetheless associated with the powerful.

The powerful effect of foreignness and of accruing local prestige and political authority from the association with the "distant" is significant for understanding the Olmec iconography recovered at Cuauhtémoc that I present in Chapter 6. As we see in Chapter 3, there is little consensus on the meaning and political role of such iconography. In the following section of this chapter, I propose that the regions of Mesoamerica inhabited by people employing Olmec iconography can be conceived of as forming an archipelago of complex societies separated by large areas where such imagery (and the ideas it materializes) had little salience.

Kristiansen and Larsson (2005) have presented an interpretation of European Bronze Age society in terms similar to those proposed here for Early Formative Mesoamerica. They also rely on Helms's work, discuss long-distance travel and local use of esoteric knowledge and explain the diffusion of ideas in behavioral terms. Their treatment of past societies is, however, quite different from mine as they interpret the cognitive meaning of the iconography they examine based on the traditional structuralist assumption of binary opposition. For example, "The idea of boundaries between inner and outer space, nature and culture, civilized and barbarian, them and us, is rooted in every society" (Kristiansen and Larsson, 2005: 43). Hodder (1990) presents an equally structuralist interpretation of the Neolithic through the concepts of domus and agrios forming a fundamental cognitive opposition that permeates all aspects of life. Such dichotomous assumptions seem unfounded in the details of Formative Mesoamerica even if they might be accurate for the European psyche as Hodder (1990: 275, 283) proposes. In this book, I make no claim to understand the specific meaning of Olmec iconography or the particular cognitive structure of Mesoamerican peoples.

AN ARCHIPELAGO OF COMPLEXITY

Braudel (1992) employs the term "Archipelago of Towns," (originally coined by Richard Hapke) to describe the spottiness of innovation in Medieval Europe against a "sea of backwardness." The analogy is to a network of "cultural islands," forming an archipelago of interaction across the continent. These cultural islands are described as "Exceptional and enigmatic, this handful of extraordinary cities dazzled observers" (Braudel, 1992: 30). Despite the dazzle, in nearby areas, people lived a traditional, subsistence-level existence. Even in eighteenth-century England and Holland, there were extensive regions of the countryside surrounding London and Amsterdam where people lived by hunting and fishing as they had for millennia (Braudel, 1992: 42–43). Abu-Lughod (1989: 13) succinctly reiterates this idea: "once one moved away from the city centers that maintained links to the outside, one was clearly in the shadowy world of subsistence." She describes the internal undeveloped realm of peasants that (like the distant world of barbarians) was not as culturally integrated into the other urban centers that defined Medieval Europe.

Recently, Upham (1992, 2000) has focused attention on the archaeologically "empty" spaces in a Desert West macroregional system of the Southwestern United States. He points out that, rather than really being empty, those areas were actually occupied by hunter-gatherers or others not tied into regional systems, and whose remains have low archaeological visibility. I posit that in Mesoamerica during the Early Formative period along with early villagers, less sedentary peoples were present, and probably quite common (see also Arnold, 1999;

Kennett et al., 2006: 104–105; Neff et al., 2006b: 308; Rosenswig, 2006a, 2006b). During the course of the second millennium BCE, sedentary, food-producing villagers went from an anomaly to the most pervasive settlement/subsistence strategy across Mesoamerica. The implication of this proposal is that, when studying sedentary Mesoamerican peoples during the Early Formative period, it is worth exploring the distinct possibility that they were surrounded by groups of people who maintained an adaptation characterized by residential mobility, minimal ceramic use and subsisting by hunting, fishing and gathering wild resources.

One of the ways in which mobile peoples can be understood is in terms of their effect on inter-regional interaction. From the perspective of sedentary villagers, the importance of "empty" areas, and the nonsedentary peoples that occupy them, " . . . often pose significant logistical obstacles to travel, trade, and communication" (Upham, 1992: 149). Knowledge of such peoples, as well as their customs and languages, would have been as important to persons engaged in inter-regional trade as would have the knowledge of the actual routes to get from one place to another. The ability to travel between distant islands of complexity was likely one reason why persons with the skills to do so gained prestige when they returned home bearing exotic goods, familiarity with foreign customs and desirable esoteric knowledge (Helms, 1979, 1988).

Foraging peoples also possess, or can procure, things that sedentary villagers desire. Laura Junker (2003: 204) reviews an "ethnohistorically well-documented system of exchange and social interaction between interior tropical forest hunter-gathers and lowland intensive rice farmers in the Tanjay Region of Negros Island in the central Philippines." These Filipino foragers have a high rate of residential mobility, moving as many as twenty times per year. They trade gold and iron ore as well as meat, animal pelts, hard woods and other forest products for rice, iron tools, ceramics, textiles, salt and other lowland products, and some groups provide seasonal agricultural labor for lowland farmers (Junker, 2003: 212). In addition to these hunter-gatherers (known historically as the Agta, Ata and Batak), there were also tribally organized swidden farmers who occupied areas of the highlands. Thus, the coexistence of three separate subsistence/settlement systems provides an even more complex example of intermixed groups than I propose for Early Formative Mesoamerica.

The hunter-gatherer inhabitants of the tropical highland Tanjay region provide a good analogy for the nonsedentary peoples I suggest existed in Mesoamerica during the Early Formative period. Junker (2003: 208) argues that the "archaeological evidence, though meager, points to the early co-existence of food producers and hunter-gathers in the heavily forested interior of the Philippines, a co-existence that may have been maintained through ecological specialization and economic symbiosis." These foraging groups exchanged goods with "maritime trade-oriented coastal chiefdoms engaged in foreign luxury good trade with the Chinese" (Junker, 2003: 205). The Philippine example is thus of a relatively stable, tropical adaptation of foragers and farmers, and the latter were engaged in long-distance trade across a maritime archipelago. However, Philippine foragers lived in areas that agriculturalists do not want, and the former are surrounded by the latter – instead of the other way around. Despite this difference between the Filipino case and the situation in Mesoamerica, two basic points are clear. First, foraging is a stable adaptation that can exist alongside more sedentary food producers. Second, neighboring farmers and foragers will interact with each other in numerous ways.

Pastoralists also can occupy areas between sedentary states, creating apparently "empty" areas. In the context of assessing the degree of inequality among ethnographically documented pastoralists, Salzman (1999: 36) notes:

Not unusually, the effective reach of one state fell far short of neighboring states, sometimes for long periods and large areas. Thus there were often large stateless areas in which other kinds of social groupings could and did flourish and hold sway. Often these stateless polities engaged in predation against populations and resources claimed by neighboring states, and sometimes they entered into direct conflict with the forces of these states.

Pastoralism provides another example of peoples with different subsistence strategies living between sedentary centers that produce much greater quantities of material culture. Although unlikely to attack sedentary centers, travelers laden with desirable goods could have been vulnerable to nonsedentary peoples they encountered (and whose territories they passed through) on exchange voyages. Knowledge of where these peoples were located (and how to avoid them) as well as personal alliances and/or trade relationships with their leaders all would have been valuable information that could be restricted and passed on to one's descendants. The idea of a cultural archipelago has an empirical reality in Early Formative Mesoamerica, where a number of concentrations of villages are known, whereas in intervening areas, hunter-gatherers and semisedentary peoples persisted for centuries (see Pool, 2007: 144). The best known pre-ceramic groups that persisted through the entire Early Formative period are found in northern Belize (Lohse et al., 2006; Rosenswig, 2004; Rosenswig and Masson, 2001). Philip Arnold (1999, 2005) also describes the variability of Early Formative adaptation on the Gulf Coast and argues that semisedentary peoples lived at La Joya, which was only a two-day walk from San Lorenzo. Other second millennium BCE non–ceramic-using peoples – especially those who relied on more perishable forms of material culture – likely have gone undocumented in much of Mesoamerica.

The date of the first sedentary villagers has long been recognized to be variable across Mesoamerica (Sanders and Price, 1968: 25–26, 111; Willey and Phillips, 1958: 150; and see Clark and Cheetham, 2002). Barbara Stark (1997: 288) notes that "It is possible that some sedentarization of mobile groups and shifts in the degree of seden-tarism continued through the Early and perhaps the Middle Pre-classic periods, despite the fact that scholarship has emphasized a transition to sedentary life during the Archaic period, rather than the Preclassic period." Sedentary, Early Formative period villagers pro-duced larger sites and more material that accumulated in deeper mid-dens that have resulted in a much higher level of visibility compared to nonsedentary and non–ceramic-using peoples. As Niederberger, (2000: 169) observes:

At the end of the second millennium B.C., large regional centers, constituting the expression of a new type of territorial organization, appeared in various zones of Middle America, from Guerrero to the Gulf Coast. Emerging from a rather homogeneous social landscape of independent farming villages, these new regional centers were greater in size, and with higher population densities and more varied functions, than earlier villages and were able politically and economically to control their surrounding territories.

In the Soconusco, John Clark and Michael Blake (1994: 23) ob-served that "Although settlement survey coverage of adjacent areas is not complete, available data suggest that during the Early Forma-tive period the Mazatán area was ringed by uninhabited or sparsely occupied land . . . " With the increase in our knowledge during the subsequent fifteen years, we can define the entire southeastern part of the Soconusco, and not just the Mazatán zone, as being ringed by sparser occupation and people who apparently followed different subsistence strategies. Elsewhere, I present a more complete case for the Soconusco being a cultural island of complexity (Rosenswig, n.d.). In that article, relying on differences in settlement patterns and depictions of the human form, I show how the southeastern section of the Soconusco between the Cantileña and Guamuchal/Manchón swamps formed a cultural and demographic island (Figure 2.1). This was true during the entire Early Formative period, and the Soconusco cultural island became even more circumscribed during the early Middle Formative Conchas phase, as I describe in more detail in Chapter 3.

My intention in this book is not to redress the imbalance of the less studied "homogeneous social landscape" but to explore how the long-distance interaction between elites in the centers of complexity used their isolated position to their political advantage (see Schortman and Urban, 1992b: 240–242). In the remainder of this chapter, I review four examples drawn from distant reaches of time and

Figure 2.1
Map of the land between two large swamps in the southeastern Soconusco.

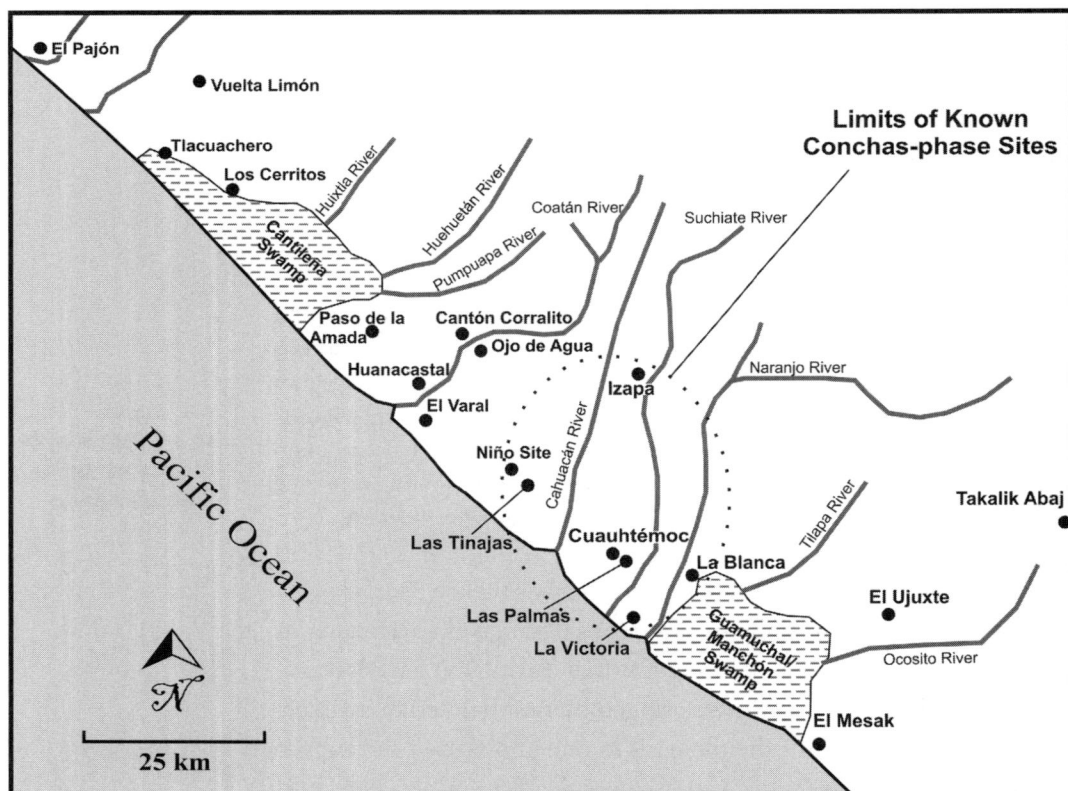

geography to explore how elites in other regions of the world employ the exchange of goods and knowledge to maintain their elevated position.

Trobriand Islanders

I discussed the Trobriand Islands and the kula exchange earlier in this chapter. Here, I briefly revisit this canonical ethnographic case to highlight an argument presented by Ron Brunton more than a quarter century ago. Brunton (1975) argued that geographic isolation is why chiefdoms emerged in the Trobriand archipelago and not in more centrally located areas of Melanesia. The Trobriand Islands are recognized as anomalous in the area as subclans each have a single recognized leader rather than a number of competing Big-men (Powell, 1960). Brunton (1975: 547–550) convincingly shows that the area was in a precarious position and had difficulty acquiring kula valuables. Rather than being central in the kula ring as Malinowski originally proposed, these islands were remote and no kula items were locally produced. The Kiriwina elite " . . . was thus in the unique position of being able to close off the exchange system and erect barriers to the convertibility of kula items" (Brunton, 1975: 553). Prestige items were controlled and Kiriwina also had some of the most productive soils in the Trobriands, which meant that a relatively large local population could be supported (Irwin, 1983: 31). Therefore, local environmental richness and control of external exchange appear to have been jointly responsible for the emergence of hereditary ranking. In contrast, the nearby island of Vakuta was in the most central kula position but was " . . . the one place in the Trobriands where rank is hardly operative" (Brunton, 1975: 551).

This example highlights the local political ramifications of controlling trade and interaction with other regions. As reviewed earlier in this chapter, Gosden (1989) discounted trade as an important factor in the emergence of inequality because he claims it cannot be monopolized. However, Brunton's (1975) interpretation of the kula ring provides an example of how the importation of foreign prestige goods can be controlled by the elite in a geographically isolated location. Schortman and Urban (1992b: 240–241) observe that a low level of inter-regional interaction, accompanied by a steady flow of trade goods, appears to be a cross-cultural characteristic of emergent stratified societies. They further note that a large influx of exotic goods (often documented ethnographically as the result of colonial period European intervention) actually resulted in political decentralization and loss of local authority. It is not trade per se, nor is it the existence of distant trading partners, but instead the control of inter-regional interaction is the crux of creating and maintaining inequality. Similarly, in the model presented in this chapter, it is not the existence of exotic or esoteric knowledge that is significant but the control of its circulation between isolated islands of more complex societies. Therefore, I am making for the circulation of knowledge the same argument that Brunton made for kula goods – their control can be used for political ends.

Germanic Barbarians

The Germanic tribes north of the limit of the Roman Empire (during the period from 100 BCE through CE 300) provide another example of the importance of isolation from larger systems in the establishment of local rank distinction (Wells, 1992, 1999). Communities that traded directly with the Romans on a regular basis (such as Westick just north of the Rhine River and Feddeersen Wierde on the North Sea coast) employed a large number of Roman everyday objects and coins in burials and other ways that altered their original social and economic function. However, these exotic Roman goods were not employed as status markers (e.g., they were not included in high-status burials but more widely distributed and found in burials of all statuses). In contrast, in northeastern Europe (which was beyond direct contact with the Roman world) the situation was very different. In this region, a series of twenty-five cemeteries (referred to collectively as the Lübsow Graves) contain individuals buried with Roman metal and glass serving vessels as well as Roman metal jewelry. However, absent from these graves and adjacent northeastern European communities were Roman coins or other utilitarian objects. In fact, at the site of Gudme, in Southern Denmark, burials with Roman grave goods were found associated with the emergence of local kings.

Isolated from Imperial culture, the northern Germanic peoples employed exotic Roman jewelry and serving vessels to express differences in social status through mortuary ritual. Wells (1992: 179) notes that "The great numbers of bronze containers, and smaller numbers of glass vessels, of Roman manufacture . . . can be attributed principally to the fascination that Mediterranean rituals of wine-drinking and banqueting, and the material paraphernalia that went with them, held for the northern Europeans." Therefore, the feasting rituals of the distant Roman society were emulated and their distinct serving vessels were employed by isolated Germanic leaders for local political ends in much the same way as the Kiriwina elite controlled the use of kula goods. In contrast, such control was not possible on the island of Vakuta and in communities that traded directly with Romans, so neither could limit the access of foreign goods and employ them for political ends. Both the Trobriand and Germanic examples highlight the importance of isolation from a regional exchange system to an elite ability to control the political use of the objects (or ideas) that were circulating. This is why the existence of an archipelago of complexity, where travel between islands requires skill and knowledge, is an important element in the political use to which circulating objects can be put.

Early Bronze Age Cyclades

The transition from Early Bronze I to Early Bronze II (2800–2200 BCE) in the Cycladic islands of Greece provides another archaeological example of the emergence of a complex society in the context of travel between isolated islands (Broodbank, 2000). In the Early Bronze II period, four village-sized centers emerged together each with elaborate burials that contained hordes of traded prestige goods, such as silver jewelry, elaborate ceramics, marble bowls and the well-known marble figurines. Although proximity to arable land was found near two of these sites, the primary determining factor for site location appears to be centrality in terms of trade networks (Broodbank, 2000: 237–244). Therefore, both subsistence and commercial factors appear to have determined Early Bronze II settlement choice. However, these factors explain neither the processes responsible for community cohesion nor the manner in which the emerging elite legitimized their newly acquired power. Broodbank outlines the social dynamic of long-boat activity as the emergence of:

...an ideology of seafaring and an associated one of armed male power, we can explore the likely roles of prestigious seafarers in assuring community safety and advancing community power through organizing people to build and crew canoes . . . [and] . . . a demographic pool of roughly a hundred people would be needed to produce a suitable crew for one of the latter craft. But numbers alone would not suffice without the presence of someone with the authority to attract and mobilize people, either inside or outside of kin group relations.

Broodbank, 2000: 256

Although not a demographic cause per se, population concentration did have to reach a critical level before hierarchy began to emerge. As Clark and Blake (1994) outline in their model for the emergence of rank, it is the acquisition of status (rather than resources themselves) that provides the motivation for setting off on trading voyages to distant lands. Also in keeping with Clark and Blake (1994), Broodbank proposes that the quest for status resulted in leaders trying to attract more followers – rather than population pressure necessitating their emergence. Dramatic population growth and, perhaps most importantly, centralization were therefore the results, not the causes, of emerging hierarchies.

Broodbank goes one step further (in a direction that parallels my idea of a knowledge kula engaged in by an elite, status-seeking segment of society) when he states:

Conceptions and experience of distance under such circumstances would become increasingly diverse, and knowledge of the world beyond a scrap of lived-in islandscape increasingly filtered by people and places that did maintain seafaring traditions . . . The scope for people living in places that still practiced seafaring to a serious degree to manipulate flows to their advantage, in the pursuit of strategies of social power and enhancement of values is apparent.

Broodbank, 2000: 258–259

Status and wealth were therefore acquired by long-distance exchange and the knowledge of distant places. Although this occurred within a local context, it was also during Early Bronze II that the scale of trade in the Aegean expanded so that the Cycladic islanders began to participate in interaction networks that stretched over larger geographic areas.

Very much like the ethnographically documented Trobriand and Panamanian examples outlined in this chapter, the Early Bronze II seafarers derived prestige through boat travel to distant lands with the goal of acquiring exotic goods and knowledge. The Early Cycladic societies (as the Melanesian societies engaged in kula exchange) were limited in the degree of political complexity they could achieve due to the physical limits of the environments of these islands. In the Cycladic and Melanesian examples, groups of people were physically separated from each other by large expanses of water. Similarly, my idea of an archipelago of complexity for Early and Middle Formative Mesoamerica is that an analogous relationship occurred on land across a cultural sea of less politically complex peoples (who were not directly connected to inter-regional exchange networks) who separated islands of cultural complexity.

Chavín Horizon Peru

The Chavín Horizon of Formative South America provides an example of a land-based cultural archipelago. Richard Burger (1992, 1993) presents a model of the Chavín cult forming a series of shrine centers in Early Horizon Peru. According to this model, the site of Chavín de Huántar, which measured 6 ha when founded during the late Initial Period Urabarriu phase (1000–500 BCE), became the center of a regional cult. The site was located in the Mosna river valley at a natural gateway between the Pacific coast and the Amazon jungle (Burger, 1992: 129). There were a few imported items documented in late Initial Period contexts at Chavín de Huántar such as ceramic vessels and obsidian (Burger, 1992: 162), but the inhabitants of the site were largely self-sufficient as was typical of small highland centers at that time. However, labor and/or tribute were extracted by the leaders of Chavín de Huántar to build the Old Temple – a 125 m by 75 m U-shaped monumental platform that reached 16 m in height. The power from which to build the Old Temple seems to have come from controlling inter-regional trade as indicated by the construction of a megalithic stone wall that blocked movement on the Mosna Valley floor and stone monuments located in surrounding small communities, carved in Chavín style, depicting priests wielding a variety of weapons as well as bloody trophy heads (Burger, 1992: 163–164).

During the late Initial Period Urabarriu phase, a distinctive art style was used for the first time at the site of Chavín de Huántar. Chavín art consisted of stylized conventions and a set of visual metaphors that create visual confusion for the uninitiated (Burger, 1992: 146–149). Another striking feature is that all of the predatory animals depicted by Chavín art inhabit lowland environments. Burger (1992: 155) proposes that "... Chavín's religious leaders justified the promotion of alien symbols by claiming that the exotic lowland groups had esoteric knowledge unusually effective in controlling supernatural forces." As well as Amazonian animals, images of the "Great Cayman" are depicted carrying lowland crops such as manioc and hot peppers. Therefore, iconographic subjects were drawn from the Amazon and architectural styles were adopted from the Pacific coast to create a new highland religious complex. Although this style was first invented at Chavín de Huántar at the end of the Initial Period, it was during the following Early Horizon that it was spread across the Andes.

At Chavín de Huántar, the Early Horizon is defined as the Chakinani (500–400 BCE) and the Janabarriu (400–200 BCE) phases. At the end of the Initial Period, many of the monumental centers on the coast collapsed, yet Chavín de Huántar expanded by nearly threefold to cover 15 hectares. During the Chakinani phase, exceptionally fine ceramics were much more commonly found in domestic refuse and " . . . the *pervasiveness of religious symbols on everyday pottery* manifests the profound connection between the settlement and the temple, and also suggests the degree to which the religious ideology of the center structured daily life . . . " (Burger, 1992: 166, italics mine). During the following Janabarriu phase, Chavín de Huántar expanded again to cover 42 hectares and was 20 times larger than any of the villages that supported it. Llama continued to dominate the faunal assemblages and most domestic artifacts, including pottery, and show considerable continuity from the preceding phase. The import of obsidian increased dramatically, craft activities were restricted to certain areas of the site and social stratification is suggested for the first time (Burger, 1992: 171–172).

To understand the Chavín cult, and its spread beyond Chavín de Huántar, it is necessary to expand the geographic scale considered. By the end of the Initial Period, on the lower river valleys of the coast of Peru, the early U-shaped monumental constructions for which the area is famous were abandoned and regional population levels fell. This occurred across the central coast from the Lurín to the Casma Valley, where monumental construction projects appear to have been abandoned rapidly (Burger, 1992: 185). The Casma Valley was reoccupied during the late Early Horizon period (i.e., contemporary with the Janabarriu phase at Chavín de Huántar) with large centers that lack monumental constructions. Furthermore, a series of hilltop forts were built during the Early Horizon, suggesting increased violence during the disintegration of Initial Period society (Burger, 1992: 188).

Along with the spread of stylistic elements and images, the Early Horizon also witnessed a diffusion of technological developments in textiles and metallurgy (Burger, 1992: 201). Textile technology changed and included the integration of camelid hair into cotton textiles and various forms of textile painting. The former demonstrated the inter-regional integration of highland camelid hair with lowland cotton cloth – the latter greatly expanded the range of symbolic expression possible on this medium. In addition, it was during Early Horizon that domestic camelid remains became commonplace on the coast and a system of intervalley roads were built (Burger, 1992: 210). Along with new iconography, the Chavín cult appears to have facilitated the diffusion of new technologies used to spread the accompanying ideology (Burger, 1992: 202). In this way, Gosden's (1989) division between long-distance imports and craft products is melded in such objects, as Helms (1993a) discusses at length.

The adoption of foreign status symbols occurred at Early Horizon Andean sites where local leaders sought such connections for their own political purposes and used locally available goods desired by the rulers of Chavín the Huántar to do so. Located close to one of the world's largest sources of cinnabar, Atalla provides an example of a site that owed its status as a local center to the wants of the Early Horizon elites at Chavín de Huántar and elsewhere. This site was located quite far south of any other Early Horizon center. Cinnabar has been documented covering the faces of rich Cupisnique burials on the coast and at the highland center of Kuntur Wasi, and so was generally in high demand during the Early Horizon (Burger and Matos, 2002: 166). The source of this scarce mineral was spread over 30 sq km in a harsh, high-altitude environment making direct control of this resource untenable. Instead, Atalla is located in an ideal location to control the transport of cinnabar to Chavín de Huántar. Finally, not only does Atalla's occupation begin when Chavín de Huántar emerged as a regionally important polity, but its abandonment also corresponds to the later collapse (Burger and Matos, 2002: 173). As I argue in the pages that follow, the collapse of a number of sites together can be as informative as their contemporaneous rise.

SUMMARY

In this chapter, I have outlined a model of inter-regional relations between early complex societies. I propose that long-distance exchange, fueled by competition at home, can provide a potent method of accruing social prestige and political power through the acquisition of goods and knowledge from distant lands. The political use of such goods and knowledge is effective only when local elites can control their access. I argue that islands of cultural complexity separated by areas inhabited by less politically complex groups not participating equally in inter-regional exchange networks provide an ideal situation for such elite control. I further propose that, in Mesoamerica, Early Formative hunter-gatherers (or other semisedentary peoples) inhabited the areas between the better studied villages with incipient elites. Furthermore, nonsedentary peoples create the illusion of empty space to the modern day investigator due to their low archaeological visibility. The areas occupied by such peoples were the "seas" that elites from one "island" of complexity had to travel through to reach another center of cultural complexity. In the following chapters, I employ this model of inter-regional interaction to help understand the Early Formative world of Mesoamerica. I argue that the land between two large swamp systems in the Soconusco defined one such cultural island. I further propose that members of the emerging elite from within this cultural island traveled to, and interacted with, elites in another cultural island on Mexico's Gulf Coast as well as with those in more distant islands of complexity in the Mexican highlands, and elsewhere.

NOTE

1. Marx did not invent the labor theory of value. Smith and Ricardo had each previously articulated the idea that commodities in the marketplace are set by the direct and indirect labor required for their production (see Heilbroner, 1980: 153–155). However, it was Marx who first addressed the political role of labor as being more than simply a price-setting index.

3

Mesoamerica's First Style Horizons and the "Olmec Problem"

> We seem to have reached a watershed in Olmec studies – the disintegration of a traditional perspective and a realignment into a series of alternative interpretations.
>
> Demarest 1989: 303

This chapter provides the regional culture history for the Gulf Coast and Soconusco as well as expectations for the inter-regional relationship between the elites in the two regions. I begin by defining four epochs (i.e., temporal periods that can contain more than one ceramic phase) that make up Mesoamerica's Early and Middle Formative periods: an Initial Ceramic Period and three subsequent style horizons. Sketches of Soconusco and the Gulf Coast culture history are provided for each of these periods. I then review the "Olmec Problem" in Formative Mesoamerican studies (Pool 2007: 15–17, 197). That is, how do we understand the occupants of Mexico's Gulf Coast, particularly those inhabiting San Lorenzo during the second part of the Early Formative period? Furthermore, what is their relationship with the inhabitants of other regions? In the context of this book, I limit discussion as much as possible to the impact of changes occurring on the Gulf Coast to developments of the inhabitants across the Soconusco. My focus on these two regions is admittedly a bit myopic but necessary to provide a sufficiently detailed treatment of the data used to evaluate the competing hypotheses I present in this book. I then outline three competing models that describe Soconusco–Gulf Coast interaction. These models are presented as competing hypotheses that may be of use to evaluate date from other areas of Mesoamerica but are formulated here specifically for the Soconusco. This chapter ends with an elaboration of the expected material patterns for each model, and so, provides expectations for the data from the Cuauhtémoc zone of the Soconusco that I present in the following four chapters of this book.

EARLY AND MIDDLE FORMATIVE MESOAMERICAN STYLE HORIZONS AND CULTURE HISTORY OF THE SOCONUSCO AND THE GULF COAST

Horizon styles are chronological cross-dating tools and, as discussed in relation to core-periphery theory in Chapter 2, help to frame the spatial extents of inter-regional interaction systems. The idea of Mesoamerican Early and Middle Formative style horizons has been explored at length, and defined in a variety of ways, by Coe (1965a, 1977), Lowe (1971, 1977, 1978, 1981, 1998) and others (e.g., Agrinier 1984; Henderson 1979; Tolstoy 1989a, 1989b; Tolstoy et al. 1977). Grove (1993: 88) reviews the use of Olmec style horizons and worries that:

... because horizons and their attributes are given Olmec-associated names, the discovery of such attributes at any site frequently leads otherwise cautious scholars to assume incautiously that the horizon attributes are indicative of "Olmec" influence or "interaction." Although most Formative period researchers do not write explicitly of Olmec horizons in their publications, I believe that a great many do implicitly accept the "Olmecness" of the horizons.

It is my intention to *explicitly* address the horizon styles that are so evident in the archaeological record of Formative Mesoamerica. I follow the original formulation of a horizon as a "spatial continuum represented by the wide distribution of a recognizable art style" (Phillips and Willey 1953: 625). Noncontiguous distributions of such styles and changes in the extents of their distribution over time provide a point of embarkation to explore what local and long-distance processes may be responsible for such macroscale patterns. As Lesure (2004: 74) observes:

... Olmec iconography was widely but unevenly distributed across Mesoamerica. In some periods and places it seems very pure; in others, it is mixed with more localized themes and styles. The artistic media used are also diverse. They include monumental stone sculptures, portable stone objects, modeled ceramic artifacts, and pottery vessels.

In addition to employing horizon styles as a tool for cross-dating, my aim is to begin with a set of material culture artistic styles employed in many parts of Mesoamerica from which to explore the process of changes occurring in the Soconusco (see Lesure 2004: 88–92).

I use the term "Olmec" in this book to refer to an art style and the Early and Middle Formative people of various regions of Meso-america are referred to geographically by the area or the site that they inhabited (following Lesure 2004). This is in contrast to the term being used to denote the inhabitants of the Gulf Coast as a number of recent scholars have (Diehl 2004; Pool 2005: 22; 2007: 15). Instead, Olmec is used like Victorian, Roman or Byzantine so that, as Clark and Pye (2000: 218) propose, it conveys "a sense of cultural and/or political commitment to certain beliefs, practices and material representations." Pool (2007: 13–14) notes that Clark and Pye's definition – and their examples of expansionary empires – are part of their interpretation that the inhabitants of San Lorenzo ruled an empire that (minimally) controlled a section of the Soconusco coast.

My use of the term Olmec does not necessarily imply anything about the level of complexity of people who used it. Instead, Olmec is simply used here to refer to a set of recognizable artistic conventions. Shared material traits (in particular, artistic conventions) define many types of interaction spheres, including those that are not hierarchi-cal (e.g., Caldwell 1964; Hayden and Schulting 1997; Odess 1998). In Chapter 5, I define the term Olmec as a cultural aesthetic. If Olmec is not used to denote the inhabitants of the Gulf Coast, then discussing Olmec horizons should not distress Grove and other researchers who share his concerns (e.g., Flannery and Marcus 1994: 385–390). However, style horizons do indicate that interaction was occurring between regions – a point no one disputes. But, although communi-cation is inferred, the uses and meanings of Olmec imagery may have been employed in locally specific ways (Grove 1999; Lesure 2000). I assume that inter-regional contact was occurring and thus stylistic cross-dating is a valid chronological tool. The nature of such inter-regional contacts is the subject explored in this book, and those who have read Chapter 2 have some idea of my thinking on the subject.

I define an Initial Ceramic Period and three horizons that together comprise the Early and Middle Formative periods (see Table 3.1). Cognizant of previous Mesoamerican uses of South American ter-minology that did not catch on (e.g., Tolstoy et al. 1977), the use of

49

EARLY AND MIDDLE
FORMATIVE
MESOAMERICAN
STYLE HORIZONS
AND CULTURE
HISTORY OF THE
SOCONUSCO AND
THE GULF COAST

Table 3.1. Chronology chart with ceramic phases from across Formative Mesoamerica

Uncal. Years BCE	Horizon	Soconusco	Chiapa de Corzo	San Lorenzo	La Venta	Oaxaca	Maya Lowlands	Chalcatzingo	Basin of Mexico	Copan	Formative
100		Hato	Horcones			Monte Alban 2	Chicanel	Late Formative	Patlachique	Sebito	Late Formative
300		Guillén	Guanacaste	Remplás		Monte Alban 1b			Ticoman		
500	Horizon III	Frontera	Francesa	Palangana	Late La Venta	Monte Alban 1a		Late Cantera	Zacatenco	Bosque	Middle Formative
700		Escalón	Escalera		Middle La Venta	Rosario	Mamom	Early Cantera	Tetelpan	Uir	
800		Duende	Vista Hermosa	Nacaste	Early La Venta			Late Barranca			
900	Horizon II	Conchas	Dili			Guadalupe	Swazey/Bolay	Middle Barranca	Manantial		
1000		Jocotal	Jobo	San Lorenzo B			Cunil/Kanluk	Early Barranca		Gordon	
1150	Horizon I	Cuadros	Cotorra	San Lorenzo A		San Jose	Late Archaic	Late Amate	Ayotla		Early Formative
1250		Cherla		Chicharras						Plata	
1350	Initial Ceramic Period	Ocós	Ocote	Bajío	Barí	Tierras Largas		Early Amate	Nevada	Rayo	
1450		Locona		Ojochi		Espiridión					
1600		Barra									

Based on Clark and Cheetham 2005; Coe and Diehl 1980b; Drennan 1983; Fash 2001: 64–70; Flannery and Marcus 1994: 374–384; Grove 1987.

these terms is less cumbersome than double temporal qualifiers of the Formative periods when referring to the "initial Early Formative" and the "late Early Formative" as some authors do (e.g., Diehl 2004; Lesure 2000; Rosenswig 2000; but see Evans 2004: 100) as well as the "early Middle Formative" and the "late Middle Formative" as others have done (e.g., Love 2002a). These horizons infer no *necessary* assumption on the origins of aesthetic traditions or iconographic conventions, so I generically number them Horizons I through III. I refer to each of these horizons as Olmec based on similar artistic conventions that were due to a historical connection between those that crafted Early and Middle Formative period objects. The geographic extents over which objects from each epoch are found may vary, but each is meaningful in the Isthmian area that encompasses the Soconusco and Gulf Coast. As noted in Chapter 2, most of the Maya area cannot be considered to have had an Initial Ceramic Period at all. Furthermore, outside the Isthmian area the reality of Horizon III is debatable. However, the four epochs I define later in this chapter are simply chronological tools that I employ to address specific questions in the Soconusco. Defining the variability in the timing of Mesoamerican culture history is beyond the scope of this book.

The date ranges for these four epochs are presented in Table 3.1 and reported as uncalibrated radiocarbon years BCE. Phase and horizon limits are based on the Soconusco chronology, but are basically consistent with stylistic changes in other regions. As I discuss elsewhere (Rosenswig 2005: Appendix 3; 2007: 2), any of these phase or horizon division dates can be moved forward or backward 50, 75 or even 100 years without changing interpretations of a sequence of cultural events. Phase limits similarly can be adjusted through calibration to calendar years without affecting the relative sequence of developments (see Pool 2007: Figure 1.4).

One advantage of using the horizon concept to establish contemporaneity is that slightly different local phase limits (often based on idiosyncratic interpretations of radiocarbon dates by investigators) can be stretched or compressed to fit when making inter-regional comparisons. A second advantage of putting greater weight on stylist cross-dating than the specifics of local phase limits is that anomalous dating of ceramic complexes become obvious and little weight need be given to outlying dates (see discussion in Flannery and Marcus 1994: 373). A third advantage of dividing archaeological time into horizons (that sometimes encompass numerous local phases) is that

51

EARLY AND MIDDLE
FORMATIVE
MESOAMERICAN
STYLE HORIZONS
AND CULTURE
HISTORY OF THE
SOCONUSCO AND
THE GULF COAST

this division facilitates comparisons between regions that employ coarser and those that use finer grained chronologies. The use of Formative Mesoamerican chronologies of different resolutions presents one of the largest obstacles to making meaningful diachronic comparisons between regions.

Relying on horizons created using stylistic cross-dating results in some interpretive limitations, the most significant of which is the appearance that changes occurred simultaneously and in tandem across all of Mesoamerica. This is, of course, not the way in which cultural change occurs. Change is often continuous and, by creating temporal units, archaeologists make it appear that all change occurs only at the phase (or horizon) limits (O'Shea and Barker 1996; Plog 1974: 43–45). Within one region this archaeological fact of life does not affect the relative sequence of change. However, when making comparisons between sequences, the way each one has been constructed can affect the perceived relationship between regional developments. Horizon styles did not spring fully formed into existence across large areas of Mesoamerica simultaneously as Table 3.1 would make it appear. Innovations developed in different areas and spread at different rates during different times. The problem is that our temporal units of analysis cannot document change occurring at the rate of years or decades, and even change at the rate of a century is often difficult to document. Rather than assume a greater level of accuracy than our temporal measuring tools can provide, it is better to incorporate an appropriate level of temporal inaccuracy into our interpretations.

Initial Ceramic Period

The earliest epoch during which ceramics were used across much of Mesoamerica is called the Initial Ceramic Period, which extends from the first use of ceramics to approximately 1,250 BCE (Table 3.1). Similarly, Evans (2004: 99–126) calls this the Initial Formative period. Ceramic styles were not uniform across Mesoamerica, but certain basic similarities among people using ceramics during this period can be productively contrasted with the changes that define Horizon I. The Initial Ceramic Period combines the Locona and the Red-on-Buff interaction spheres (Clark 1991: 24; Flannery and Marcus 2000: 9–11) at their broadest spatial and temporal extents. In the Maya lowlands, the Initial Ceramic Period corresponds to a continued preceramic adaptation in this corner of Mesoamerica (Lohse et al. 2006; Zeitlin and Zeitlin 2000). In the Soconusco, the Initial Ceramic Period encompasses the Barra, Locona and Ocós ceramic phases. At San Lorenzo this epoch is called the Ojochi and Bajío phases, Early Amate phase at Chalcatzingo, Barí phase at La Venta, Nevada phase in the Basin of Mexico, Espiridión and Tierras Largas phases in Oaxaca and Rayo phase in the Copán Valley (see Demarest [1989: 311–313] for other examples in southern Mesoamerica and Joyce and Henderson [2001] for important recent work from Honduras).

During the Initial Ceramic Period, the ceramic assemblages in most areas across Mesoamerica were dominated by thin walled vessels and the most common slip color was red. The shape of vessels sometimes imitated the gourds that they were replacing and suggests that food-processing practices were changing slowly (Clark and Gosser 1995). Figurines were relatively naturalistic, and those depicting humans often made the sex of the individual evident (e.g., Lesure 1997b; Marcus 1989: 157). It was during this time that many of the people in Mesoamerica adopted a sedentary lifestyle and began to experiment with more intensive forms of plant use (see Rosenswig 2006a).

SOCONUSCO

The Soconusco is one of the best known islands of complexity in lowland Mesoamerica during the Initial Ceramic Periods, largely due to work carried out in the Mazatán zone, which has some of the earliest evidence of political complexity documented among a network of interacting elites during the Locona phase (Blake 1991; Clark 1991, 1994; Clark and Blake 1994). Blake and Clark (1999: 56) outlined seven lines of evidence for the emergence of these rank societies: "(1) a two-tiered hierarchy settlement pattern comprised of small villages and hamlets centered around large villages, (2) elite domestic architecture, (3) differential mortuary practices, (4) unequal access to sumptuary goods, (5) presence of patronized craft specialization centered around elite house mounds, (6) clues of increased public feasting, and (7) evidence of redistribution within each large village community . . . " However, recent analyses of household data from Paso de la Amada call into question whether numbers 4 and 5 above are born out with larger samples (Lesure and Blake 2002). After presenting still more household data from this site, Blake et al. (2006: 207–208) conclude "that although architectural differences were

53

EARLY AND MIDDLE
FORMATIVE
MESOAMERICAN
STYLE HORIZONS
AND CULTURE
HISTORY OF THE
SOCONUSCO AND
THE GULF COAST

significant, there were few notable differences in wealth-related artifacts or trade items between the households at the site during the
Locona and Ocós phases." Therefore, although there seems to have
been political hierarchy during the Initial Ceramic Period, this does
not appear to have translated into economic differentiation.

Clark (1994) has conducted a 50 sq km systematic survey within
the Mazatán zone. His results indicate that overall population levels
were low during the Barra phase, but increased dramatically during the Locona phase; then dispersed settlements were absorbed
into established centers during the Ocós phase. The Initial Ceramic
Period villages documented by Clark in the Mazatán survey zone
were located on the coastal plain, and the larger centers were located
near swamp margins and away from the Coatán River.

Paso de la Amada, the largest of these polity centers, contained a
stratigraphically superimposed series of elite residences at Mound 6
and a ballcourt at Mound 7 (Blake 1991; Blake et al. 2006; Hill et al.
1998; Hill and Clark 2001; Lesure 1997b, 1999a; Lesure and Blake 2002)
(see Figure 3.1). These two architectural features fell into disuse by
the end of the Ocós phase, a century before the site was abandoned
(Blake et al. 2006; Lesure 1997b). Clark (2004: 53–54) has recently
proposed that, during the Locona phase, " . . . Paso de la Amada was
planned and constructed as a formal center . . . " that " . . . reached its
maximum extent of about 140 ha." In this new interpretation of the
site, the previous size estimate of 50 ha corresponds to what Clark
now interprets as the planned ceremonial core of the site (see Clark
2004: Figure 2.5; Clark et al. 2006).

Paso de la Amada is thus reconstructed as the largest and most
planned community in Mesoamerica of the time. The long axis of the
ballcourt (Mound 7) is oriented northeast–southwest, and the long
axis of the Locona and Ocós phase elite residences (Mound 6) are
oriented northwest–southeast (Blake et al. 2006: 198). These mounds
are thus perpendicular to each other and create a courtyard between
them (Figure 3.1).

In Clark and Blake's (1994) much-cited model for the emergence
of hereditary inequality, the elite at Mazatán polities are modeled
as ambitious aggrandizers engaged in behavior such as sponsoring
feasts and betting on ballgames (Hill and Clark 2001) to gain prestige. The unintended result of such competitive behavior would have
been to create social divisions within society. From early in the Initial Ceramic Period, the Soconusco is precisely the sort of center of

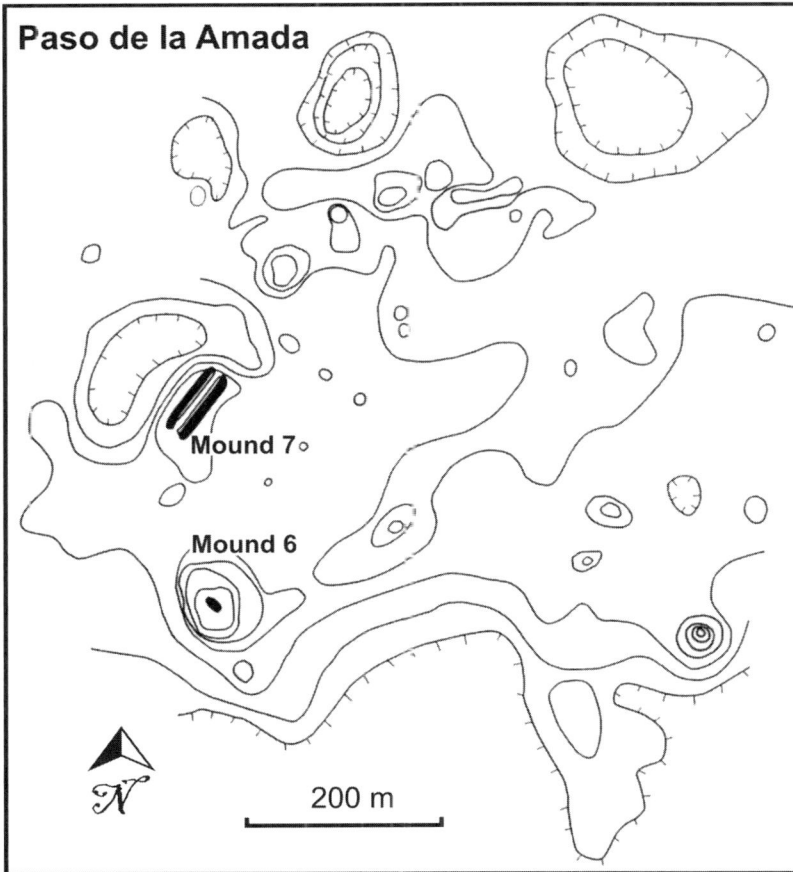

55

EARLY AND MIDDLE
FORMATIVE
MESOAMERICAN
STYLE HORIZONS
AND CULTURE
HISTORY OF THE
SOCONUSCO AND
THE GULF COAST

Figure 3.1
Paso de la Amada
site map with an elite
residence (Mound 6) and
a ballcourt (Mound 7)
indicated (after Clark
2004: Figure 2.5).

complexity I discussed in Chapter 2. In fact, Blake and Clark (1999: 63) note, in terms reminiscent of Braudel's, that across Mesoamerica at this time "There were a few exceptional areas, such as Mazatán. We are persuaded that demographic hot spots such as this were socially created or induced by aggrandizers competing for followers."

GULF COAST

On the Gulf Coast, there was a generally low population level during the Initial Ceramic Period. The La Venta area was sparsely populated during the entire Early Formative period (Rust and Sharer 1988). The results of a systematic survey in the lower Coatzacoalcos drainage indicate that population levels around San Lorenzo were also low (relative to subsequent times) during the Initial Ceramic Period (Symonds et al. 2002: Figure 4.1). From the 400 sq km lower Coatzacoalcos drainage survey area, 165 ha of occupation were reported for this 300-year epoch (Symonds et al. 2002: Table 4.4). A total of 105 sites have been documented, 81 of which were clustered around the San Lorenzo plateau (Symonds et al. 2002: 56). Therefore, by the end of the Bajío phase, San Lorenzo was a local center surrounded by a large proportion of the population in the region. The San Lorenzo site measured approximately 20 ha at this time and is known from a number of habitation surfaces documented below subsequent Horizon I construction.

In the lower Coatzacoalcos area, there are a number of natural factors that would have favored population aggregation. First, in this dynamic fluvial environment high ground is scarce. What high ground there is, elevates habitations above the flood plain (which can deposit as much as 3 m of silt in a single year) and is also the location of fresh water from natural springs (Symonds et al. 2002: 56). On the flood plain when seasonal lakes dry up, large quantities of aquatic resources are reliably available for harvest. As Arnold (2000: 129; also see Coe and Diehl 1980a: 107–120) notes, such brief concentrations of food provide a context for important leadership roles to develop as abundant resources must be acquired and processed in a short time period. The natural environment around San Lorenzo is thus structured so as to concentrate population in certain areas, and provides an incentive for resources to be intensively exploited by groups at particular times of the year. The natural environment would have been conducive to certain individuals directing the labor of others. However, this local, Northwest Coast–inspired explanation provides only half of the picture. San Lorenzo is also situated at the juncture of several rivers that would have made it an ideal location when traveling to and/or trading with distant regions (Symonds et al. 2002: 54). Therefore, the leaders that may have initially emerged to more efficiently exploit local resources could then have turned their attentions outward in search of exotic goods and further enhanced their prestige.

Initial Ceramic Period data from the Gulf Coast generally, and from the San Lorenzo area specifically, remain poorly understood relative to their importance. Nonetheless, it is clear that San Lorenzo was a center of complexity early on. As Clark and Blake (1989; Clark 1990, 1997) have long argued, these two islands of complexity had been intensively interacting, and this interaction is partially responsible for the maintenance of the Locona interaction sphere (Clark 1991: 24; Evans 2004: 106; Flannery and Marcus 2000: 9–11).

Horizon I

The cultural significance of Mesoamerica's first artistic horizon is contested (Blomster et al. 2005; Clark 1997; Diehl and Coe 1995; Flannery and Marcus 2000; Flannery et al. 2005; Neff et al. 2006a, 2006b; Sharer et al. 2006; Stoltman et al. 2005). However, a shared set of iconographic conventions as well as innovative ceramic and figurine styles demonstrate shared concepts and regular communication during the period from 1250 to 900 BCE. This is Lowe's Early Olmec Horizon and Coe's San Lorenzo Horizon (see Grove 1993: 88–95). Pool (2007: 181) has similarly opted to call this period simply the "Early Horizon," following Flannery and Marcus (1994: 390). Although I am in agreement with these scholars' recognition of Mesoamerica's first style horizon, the traits I use here to define Horizon I most closely resemble those employed by Tolstoy (1989b; Tolstoy et al. 1977) and Grove (1989: 278) and are summarized in Table 3.2. In the Soconusco, Horizon I is divided into the Cherla, Cuadros and Jocotal phases.

57

EARLY AND MIDDLE
FORMATIVE
MESOAMERICAN
STYLE HORIZONS
AND CULTURE
HISTORY OF THE
SOCONUSCO AND
THE GULF COAST

Table 3.2. Ceramic and figurine characteristics of Mesoamerica's Initial Ceramic Period and first three style horizons

	Ceramics	Figurines
Horizon III	— Orange and red wares become popular — Wide everted rims are distinctive — Post-slip incision elaborated on exterior of wall	— Punched pupils shrink in size — Clothing and facial hair more popular — Sex is less ambiguous
Horizon II	— Dominance of white wares — Post-slip incision is employed primarily on rim interior — Double-line-break motif is very popular — Composite silhouette vessels used for the first time — Grater bowls used for the first time	— Large punched pupils — Round heads are predominant — Sex and age are still usually ambiguous — Slanted eyes, downturned mouths and fat cheeks — Olmec facial features transferred to greenstone
Horizon I	— Dominance of black wares — White-rimmed black ware serving dishes are popular — Flat bottom, outflaring dishes dominate the serving assemblages — First use of abstract iconography	— Representation is abstract and stylized — Heads are oval and pupils small or nonexistent — Slanted eyes, downturned mouths and fat cheeks — Sexless and ageless imagery made of ceramic
Initial Ceramic Period	— Dominance of red wares — Some vessels imitate gourds — Tecomates are popular	— Representation is naturalistic — Small pupils represented — Sex is obvious and emphasized

At San Lorenzo, it is called the Chicharras, San Lorenzo A and San Lorenzo B phases, Late Amate and Early Barranca phases at Chatcatzingo, Ayotla phase in the Basin of Mexico, San Jose phase in the Oaxaca Valley,[1] and the Gordon phase in the Copán Valley. Flannery and Marcus (1994: 377–382) provide a detailed comparison of specific ceramic types from many regions during this epoch. In the lowlands of northern Belize and the Yucatan, ceramic objects were still not used during this epoch (see Iceland 1997; Lohse et al. 2006; Rosenswig and Masson 2001; Rosenswig 2004, 2006b). The well-known presence of such nonsedentary, non-ceramic-using inhabitants of much of the Maya area during Horizon I underscores the point I raised in Chapter 2 (and see Rosenswig n.d.) that many more people with Archaic adaptations likely existed around the ceramic-using villagers that formed an archipelago of islands of complexity.

Where they were used, Horizon I ceramics are most easily identified by the widespread use of a black and white color scheme – a dramatic visual change from the red wares that previously had been dominant. Best known are the white-rimmed black ware, flat bottom dishes that are differentially fired in a controlled manner (see Coe and Flannery 1967: 33). These include Pino Black and White and Pampas Black and White in the Soconusco (Clark and Cheetham 2005) as well as Perdida Black and White in the Chicharras and San Lorenzo phases (Coe and Diehl 1980b: 156, 184–185 and see other examples in Cruz and Guevara 2002). The iconography used to decorate ceramic vessels changed in most regions from a naturalistic tradition to a set of stylized and repetitive elements such as the so-called Olmec dragon (Joralemon 1971, 1996: 54).[2] Flannery and Marcus (1994: 377) note that "From the Basin of Mexico to Copan, Honduras, the Pan-Mesoamerican motifs carved and incised on pottery are so widespread that one can literally see Mesoamerica emerge for the first time as a cultural area." Although the extents (and sometimes the traits) that define this horizon are debated (Demarest 1989: 322), its existence is not.

Figurines changed from naturalistic local traditions created during the Initial Ceramic Period to depictions of individuals frequently depicted naked and seated during Horizon I. A distinctive group of figures made at this time have oval heads and slanted eyes without pupils (sometimes called plowing stroke), downturned mouths and fat cheeks (see Lesure 2000). These solid and hollow figurines can be described as having infantile features with age and especially sex left quite ambiguous. These jowly, slant-eyed figurines with downturned (and often open) mouths are similar in many regions, and calling them by a single name seems justified, especially when compared to earlier local traditions in each area. Unlike during the following Middle Formative period, the use of greenstone (and particularly carved greenstone figurines and masks with these Olmec facial features) was not common during the Early Formative period (Grove 1993).

GULF COAST

During Horizon I, San Lorenzo emerged as the center of an organized polity with two secondary centers that contain monumental sculpture (see Figure 3.2). These secondary sites were each located approximately 4 km from San Lorenzo along the route leading both out to the Gulf Coast and into the Isthmus of Tehuantepec where one has to travel to reach the Pacific coast of Chiapas and Oaxaca (Symonds 2000: 62). Population levels within the Coatzacoalcos survey zone rose by an order of magnitude during Horizon I with 1,627 ha of occupation documented. Of this, 500 ha are recorded for San Lorenzo and another 530 ha divided between the two secondary centers of Loma del Zapote (which includes Azuzul and Potrero Nuevo) measured as 400 ha and El Remolino measured as 130 ha. Together these three sites account for 63% of the

59

EARLY AND MIDDLE
FORMATIVE
MESOAMERICAN
STYLE HORIZONS
AND CULTURE
HISTORY OF THE
SOCONUSCO AND
THE GULF COAST

Figure 3.2
The lower Coatzacoalcos River survey area with Horizon I site hierarchy indicated and Horizon I stone monuments from first and second tier sites (after Diehl 2004).

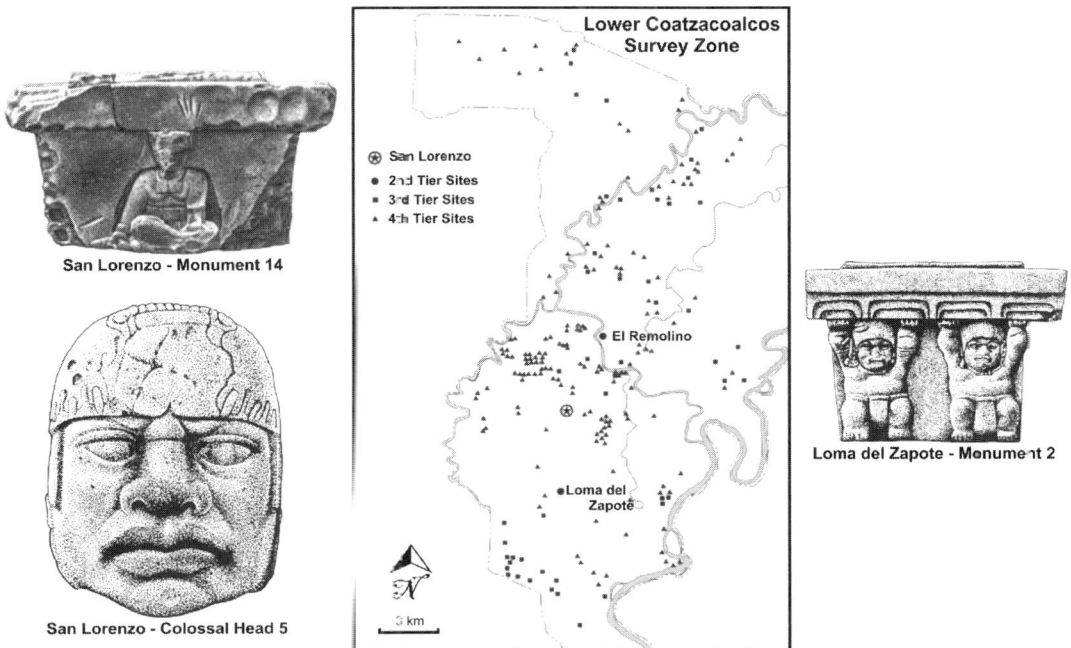

San Lorenzo - Monument 14

San Lorenzo - Colossal Head 5

Lower Coatzacoalcos
Survey Zone

⊛ San Lorenzo
● 2nd Tier Sites
■ 3rd Tier Sites
▲ 4th Tier Sites

El Remolino

Loma del
Zapote

3 km

Loma del Zapote - Monument 2

area occupied in the lower Coatzacoalcos survey zone at this time (Symonds et al. 2002; Figure 4.4). Furthermore, 126 of the 226 sites are located in the immediate vicinity of San Lorenzo providing a population density almost 20 times higher than in the rest of the survey area (Symonds et al. 2002: 65–66).

Recent work by Carl Wendt (2005a, 2005b) at El Remolino has produced evidence inconsistent with the interpretation of that site as a secondary center. The 130 ha size estimate assumes that the area currently covered by a modern river was part of the site that has been washed away. El Bajío, the northeastern part of El Remolino where Wendt documented stratified Horizon I deposits, today measures only 1.5 ha (Wendt 2005b: 166–167). Furthermore, although stone monuments were reported when the site was first documented (Stirling 1955: 7, Plate 4a, 4b), subsequent investigations have been unable to relocate them or find any others (Coe and Diehl 1980b: 373; Wendt 2005b: 167). However, even if El Remolino is not a secondary center as Symonds et al. (2002) interpret it to be, Loma del Zapote was. This site, built around a plateau a few kilometers from San Lorenzo, both covered a large area and contained many stone sculptures. Pool (2005: 232) notes that if Potrero Nuevo is not lumped with the rest of Loma del Zapote then each site (with its own monumental stone sculpture) could be considered a second-order site in its own right. Furthermore, 20 km west of the Coatzacoalcos survey zone, the site of Estero Rabón measured 140–160 ha during Horizon I and contained a number of monuments (including a throne) and is thus a likely candidate to be another secondary center (Borstein 2001: 158, 163). In a synthetic reanalysis of published data, Clark (2007: note 2) proposes seven potential secondary centers for the San Lorenzo polity during Horizon I measuring between 50 and 200 ha as well as nine potential tertiary centers measuring between 10 and 40 ha.

The recent surge in the quantity of survey and excavation work conducted at and around San Lorenzo is still in the process of being analyzed and published. These data will one day provide us with a much more detailed understanding of the San Lorenzo polity. Currently, it is clear that the San Lorenzo polity was organized in a complex hierarchical manner with a four-level settlement system. Whether this was a four-tier administrative hierarchy (and thus a state as Clark [2007] argues) or not (and therefore a complex chiefdom as Spencer and Redmond [2004] argue), will need to await future work before a consensus is likely to emerge. The crucial point, as far as I am concerned, is that the San Lorenzo polity had a much more complex and hierarchically integrated system than did other Gulf Coast peoples (as discussed later in this chapter) or the inhabitants of any other region in Mesoamerica during the Early Formative period. There simply was no precedent or contemporary in Mesoamerica for the political phenomenon at San Lorenzo during the latter part of the Early Formative period.

61

EARLY AND MIDDLE
FORMATIVE
MESOAMERICAN
STYLE HORIZONS
AND CULTURE
HISTORY OF THE
SOCONUSCO AND
THE GULF COAST

Initial estimates of the size of San Lorenzo employed a figure of 52.9 ha (Coe and Diehl 1980b: 119). However, that is now interpreted as the ceremonial core of the site (Cyphers 1997a: 67; 1997b: 108). The plateau on which San Lorenzo is located was artificially raised as much as 6.5 meters over previous Bajío and Chicharras-phase deposits (Coe and Diehl 1980b: 106–109). However, the depth of Horizon I age deposits are variable across the plateau (see Cyphers 1997b: 106–107). Substantial quantities of earth were moved to create a series of five evenly spaced terraces that run down the sides of the San Lorenzo plateau (Cyphers 1997b: 108). The labor invested in remodeling this plateau alone far surpassed anything that was previously attempted in Mesoamerica (Cyphers 1997b: 110; Diehl 1981: 74). There may also be a number of features at San Lorenzo and Azuzul that Cyphers (1997b: 113) interprets as causeways measuring up to 600 m long, 60 m wide and 2 m high. Despite all of this earth moving, the building of large pyramids at the center of the site (which define centers of later Mesoamerican civilization) had not been invented at this time.

The multiton colossal heads made of basalt, for which the Formative period residents of the Gulf Coast are most famous, were transported as much as 100 km from the Tuxtla mountains and represent a tremendous quantity of organized labor expenditure. Ten of the colossal heads and a number of thrones (such as those pictured in Figure 3.2) were aligned facing north–south in rows on the west side of the San Lorenzo plateau (Diehl 2004: 35; Grove 1999). Based on detailed stratigraphic excavations, colossal heads are securely documented from San Lorenzo A phase contexts, and a fragment broken off of a head or other large monument is documented in a Chicharras-phase context (Coe and Diehl 1991: 33) To date, the lower Coatzacoalcos is the only area in Mesoamerica where such huge stone carvings are documented dating to Horizon I.

There appears to have been a system of residential segregation with ceremonial precincts and elaborate dwellings located at the highest points of the plateau and more modest dwellings located on the terraces below (Symonds 2000: 56). Basalt columns and large limestone slabs were used to construct a number of monumental structures atop the San Lorenzo plateau, including the so-called Red Palace that Ann Cyphers (1997b: 101) interprets as an elite residence (but see Flannery and Marcus 2003: 6). Areas of the Red Palace's floor were covered with red sand (thus the name), and its walls were built of packed earth 40 cm thick (Cyphers 1997b: 98–99). A massive central basalt column measuring almost 1 m in diameter supported the roof. The Red Palace also contained a number of stone benches, and a system of basalt drains were built beneath the floor.

Another 12-m-long apsidal structure was built nearby on a 2-m-high platform that measures 50 m by 75 m (Cyphers 1997c: 265). In this area, elite workshops were documented for making (and reworking) basalt monuments. The carving of monumental stone sculptures for public use and architectural features such as support columns and drains for use in a restricted number of structures appears to have been a form of elite craft specialization on the San Lorenzo plateau.

The inhabitants of San Lorenzo were actively involved in acquiring goods from afar. Obsidian was transported to the site from numerous sources in both central Mexico and highland Guatemala (Cobean et al. 1971, 1991). In addition, perforated iron-ore cubes from Plumajillo, Chiapas have been found in large numbers at San Lorenzo (Agrinier 1984: 75–80; Di Castro 1997). Also, basalt used to carve the monumental sculpture was brought in from the Tuxtla mountains (Williams and Heizer 1965). Recent studies of population density and carrying capacity indicate that the inhabitants of San Lorenzo would have had to import food from outside the 90 km inner hinterland region of the site (Symonds et al. 2002: 47–50 and see Pool 2007: 202). The only documented exports are ceramic objects produced from clays originating in the San Lorenzo area that have been documented in numerous parts of Mesoamerica – 23 of which were documented in the Mazatán zone of the Soconusco (Blomster et al. 2005). Therefore, obsidian, iron ore and basalt were imported from distant regions, and food was possibly brought in from nearby whereas ceramic vessels and figurines are the only documented export.

To the west of San Lorenzo, a 400-sq-km area of systematic survey in the Tuxtla mountains indicates that, based on a lack of settlement hierarchy and low population densities, there was "... minimal sociopolitical complexity and subsistence based on hunting/

collecting, silviculture, and horticulture may have been the Early Formative norm" (Arnold 2000: 125; and see VanDerwarker 2005, 2006). Storage/fire pit features and other artifact patterns from La Joya further support this interpretation, and Arnold (1999; 2000: 128) notes that the presence of ceramic remains are the only evidence incongruous with a foraging lifestyle. South of Matacapan, in the Hueyapan survey zone, the population began to expand during Horizon I and a wider range of environmental zones were occupied by peoples using ceramic vessels very similar to those at San Lorenzo (Killion and Urcid 2001: 5). This zone is west of Llano del Jícaro, where another stone sculpture workshop has been documented (Gillespie 1994). In contrast, in an area of the San Juan basin on the east side of Llano del Jícaro and approximately halfway to San Lorenzo, settlement density increased and also expanded into upland areas in the course of Horizon I (Borstein 2001). In this area, during the San Lorenzo A phase, Laguna de los Cerros covered 150 ha, and Borstein (2001: 168–171) argues that it was established as the result of the San Lorenzo elite's interests in Llano del Jícaro sculpture.

This intra-regional variability helps to define the San Lorenzo polity and neighboring regions as forming an island of complexity of the sort I discussed in the previous chapter. While the San Lorenzo polity rose and fell during Horizon I, a few dozen kilometers to the west in areas of the Tuxtla mountains people may not have been living in permanent villages. The Tuxtla data provide support for a view of San Lorenzo as an island of cultural activity that transformed the landscape among a sea of very low population density and no political hierarchy (Pool 2007: 212–213).

A number of small polities were established to the east of San Lorenzo during Horizon I. The site of La Venta, if it was occupied at this time, would have been a local center with smaller sites surrounding it along the Bari River (Rust and Sharer 1988). In the Grijalva delta, the site of Zapata was also established as a local center surrounded by small hamlets during this period (von Nagy 1997: 267). The eastern part of the Gulf Coast was different than the parts of the Tuxtla mountains where no settlement hierarchy was present as well as the precociously hierarchical organization of the San Lorenzo polity. The Grijalva delta zone of the Gulf Coast appears to have been occupied in a similar manner as most of Mesoamerica during the Early Formative period with modest central places surrounded by dispersed villages. This variation in Gulf Coast organization – with a two-tier

63

EARLY AND MIDDLE
FORMATIVE
MESOAMERICAN
STYLE HORIZONS
AND CULTURE
HISTORY OF THE
SOCONUSCO AND
THE GULF COAST

settlement hierarchy in the Grijalva delta and no central places in the Tuxtla mountains – emphasizes how San Lorenzo was the type of cultural island of complexity that would have dazzled visitors just as Braudel (1992: 30) describes Medieval European towns.

SOCONUSCO

In the Mazatán zone of the Soconusco, white-rimmed black ware ceramics were first used during the Cherla phase when figurine styles also began to change (Clark and Blake 1989; Clark and Pye 2000; Lesure 2000, 2004). At Paso de la Amada, platform mounds occupied by the traditional elite were abandoned at the end of the Ocós phase (Blake 1991; Blake et al. 2006) and new mounds were built during the Cherla phase (Lesure 1997b). After the Cherla phase, Paso de la Amada and the other Mazatán polities were abandoned (Clark and Blake 1989; Clark and Pye 2000). During the following Cuadros and Jocotal phases, the political center in the Mazatán zone shifted from the swamp margins to the shores of the Coatán River at the sites of Cantón Corralito and then Ojo de Agua (Cheetham 2006, 2007; Clark 1997; Clark and Blake 1989: 391; Clark and Hodgson 2004; Clark and Pye 2000; Hodgson 2006; Peréz 2002).

In contrast to the Initial Ceramic Period, Horizon I was relatively poorly understood in the Soconusco until recently. The Cuadros and Jocotal phases were long ago defined by Coe and Flannery (1967) but are today the least published phases of the 800 years examined in this book. This is unfortunate as these two phases are essential to understanding Soconusco society at the time when San Lorenzo reached its apogee. Based on high densities of carved ceramics and greenstone objects, the sites of Cantón Corralito and Ojo de Agua have been proposed as the regional centers during the Cuadros and Jocotal phases, respectively (Clark 1990, 1997; Clark and Blake 1989; Clark and Hodgson 2004; Clark and Pye 2000).

Cantón Corralito was a small center during the Initial Ceramic Period, expanded during the Cherla phase, and reached its largest extent during the Cuadros phase. Tomás Pérez (2002) excavated six test pits at Cantón Corralito and documented carved pottery and Olmec figurines with distinctly infantile features. More extensive excavations carried out by David Cheetham (2006, 2007) for his doctoral dissertation sheds further light on this important site. Cheetham documented that the Horizon I component of the site covers at least 30 ha and that ceramic vessels and figurines were very similar to those made at San Lorenzo (Cheetham 2007). Twenty-three Horizon I ceramic sherds from the Mazatán zone have been chemically sourced as being made of clays from the San Lorenzo region (Blomster et al. 2005). Cheetham (2006) also documented a juvenile burial surrounded by fifteen plain greenstone axes during this field season.

The full extent and layout of Cantón Corralito are not known as it was abandoned after being covered by more than a meter of river silt deposited by the Coatán River. This site is the largest known in the Soconusco from this period and the one with the highest proportion of Olmec style artifacts. Clark's (1994) Mazatán survey documents fewer hectares of occupation during the Cherla and Cuadros phases than during the previous or subsequent Early Formative phases. Clark (1997: 228, 2007: 21) interprets the larger Cherla-phase sites in the Mazatán zone as the centers of simple chiefdoms and proposes that Cantón Corralito then emerged as the seat of complex chiefdom that united the area into a single polity during the Cuadros phase.

After Cantón Corralito was buried under river silt, Ojo de Agua became the largest site in the Soconusco during the Jocotal phase. Ojo de Agua, located on the opposite shore of the Coatán river, is likely where residents relocated after Cantón Corralito was destroyed. Excavations have just begun, but preliminary results indicated that the Jocotal component of Ojo de Agua measured as much as 100 ha and contained two 7-m-high mounds and numerous stone sculptures (Clark and Hodgson 2004; Hodgson 2006; Pinkowski 2006). The Jocotal phase is also when the most hectares of occupation were documented in the Mazatán survey zone of any Early Formative phase (Clark 1994). However, this demographic expansion was short-lived, and the end of the Jocotal phase marks the collapse and abandonment of both the Ojo de Agua polity and the entire Mazatán zone (Blake and Clark 1999: 64; Clark and Pye 2000).

At the end of the Cuadros phase and during the Jocotal phase, a number of sites were built across the Soconusco in the estuary next to large rivers. Lesure (1993, 2008; Pérez and Lesure 1998) has documented the site of El Varal in the estuary near the Mazatán zone. This site contains a small quantity of Cuadros material under extensive Jocotal phase deposits. Olmec style figurines, a life-size ceramic mask and a low ceramic stool are among the many spectacular finds from this site. A full understanding of the occupation history and political importance of this site awaits full publication of excavated materials. On the Guatemalan side of the border, Coe and Flannery (1967) first

65

EARLY AND MIDDLE
FORMATIVE
MESOAMERICAN
STYLE HORIZONS
AND CULTURE
HISTORY OF THE
SOCONUSCO AND
THE GULF COAST

defined the Cuadros and Jocotal phases at the site of Salinas la Blanca
on the northwest side of the Guamuchal/Manchón swamp. This site
was located on the south bank of the Naranjo river and, like El Varal,
was also built around a large, low mound that was constructed in the
course of the Jocotal phase. Pye and Demarest (1991; Pye 1995) have
documented the site of El Mesak, another Jocotal phase mound on
the southeast side of this swamp. They note that the artifacts found at
El Mesak are more elaborate and contain many more prestige goods
than would be expected at a simple resource extraction locale (Pye
and Demarest 1991). Each of these estuary sites may have been part
of a new transportation network at the end of the Early Formative
period, as described by Carlos Navarrete (1978). The network could
have connected Oaxaca to El Salvador through the Pacific coast estuary (discussed further in Chapter 7).

The Jocotal phase was a volatile period in the Soconusco, as I
discuss further at the end of Chapter 8. The regional importance of
San Lorenzo seemed to have been waning at this time, and influences
from other areas, such as the Basin of Mexico, were evident in the
Soconusco. Clark (2007: 23; Clark and Pye 2000: 241; and see Pool
2007: 181) views these changes as so significant that he combines the
Jocotal and subsequent Conchas phases in the Soconusco and refers
to this period as the Manantial Horizon based on the Basin of Mexico
phase name.[3]

Stylistic conventions used during the Jocotal phase derived from
those used during the Cuadros phase and, in turn, Conchas styles
derived from those used during the Jocotal phase. However, the
Jocotal ceramic assemblage is much closer to that of the preceding
Cuadros than to the following Conchas assemblage.[4] My reasoning
for including both the Cuadros and Jocotal phases in Horizon I goes
beyond stylistic similarities and also includes settlement and adaptive similarities – all of which contrast the following Conchas phase. A
dramatic regional demographic and political reorganization occurred
after the Jocotal phase when the Mazatán area was abandoned and
the La Blanca polity emerged at the other end of the land between
the large Soconusco swamps, as I outline in the next section and
describe in more detail in Chapter 4. Another significant transition
is that the Conchas phase was when the residents of the Soconusco
markedly intensified their reliance on food production compared to
any previous time (see Chapter 5). Based on the current state of our
knowledge, no such adaptive change occurred in the transition from

Cuadros to Jocotal. What did occur at the end of the Cuadros phase was that a natural event wiped out the regional center of Cantón Corralito, and the new center of Ojo de Agua was immediately set up across the river in a place safe from future flooding. Rebuilding your capital in a nearby but safer locale seems a reasonable response for the descendants of the Cantón Corralito elite to continue the existing political order.

67

EARLY AND MIDDLE
FORMATIVE
MESOAMERICAN
STYLE HORIZONS
AND CULTURE
HISTORY OF THE
SOCONUSCO AND
THE GULF COAST

Horizon II

Horizon II marks the beginning of the Middle Formative period. One of the most dramatic developments of the Middle Formative period was that large conical pyramids were built at the center of Mesoamerican sites for the first time. Pyramid mound construction occurred very early at La Blanca polity (Love 1991, 1999a, 1999b; Rosenswig 2007, 2010) and shortly thereafter at many other islands of complexity across Mesoamerica (e.g., Grove 2000: 139; Joyce 2004a). The beginning of the Middle Formative period is also when greenstone carvings (such as figurines and masks) and stone monuments began to be used in unprecedented quantities across much of Mesoamerica (see Grove 1993: 97–98, 1996).

During Horizon II, post-slip incision became a very common method of decorating ceramic vessels, especially on the interior lips of outflaring dishes where the double-line-break motif was often represented (e.g., Coe and Diehl 1980b: 195–198; Love 2002a: 95, 104).[5] In fact, Tolstoy et al. (1977: 98) proposed that the first part of the Middle Formative period be termed the "Double Line Break tradition." Post-slip incisions were also commonly employed on the interior of vessels at this time to highlight painted designs such as the cleft motif. White-rimmed black wares were no longer used in most parts of Mesoamerica (the Gulf Coast being a notable exception), and monochrome white wares became more common than black wares (Henderson 1979). This period corresponds most closely to Lowe's (1989: 55) Intermediate Olmec Period (and see discussion in Note 3 of this chapter).

I define Horizon II based on the Conchas phase in the Soconusco. At San Lorenzo, Horizon II is called Nacaste, and although people continued to occupy the plateau, surrounding areas were abandoned (Coe and Diehl 1980b: 188; Symonds et al. 2002: 88–90). The dissolution of the San Lorenzo polity at approximately 900 BCE and the apogee of the La Venta polity dating to 700–400 BCE supports the interpretation of a hiatus in political centralization in the region immediately after the collapse of San Lorenzo. Horizon II can be identified in the Middle Barranca phase at Chalcatzingo and the Guadalupe phase in the Etla arm of the Valley of Oaxaca.[6] Love (2002a: 89–146) provides a detailed comparison of Horizon II ceramic types from around Mesoamerica.

A new and distinctive punched eye figurine style is first documented in the Soconusco during Horizon II (see Arroyo 2002: 206–224; Coe 1961) and is found in many other areas of Mesoamerica (e.g., Lowe 1989: Figure 4.4b; Marcus 1989: Figure 8.23). Instead of the long oval faces with closed or barely open (aka ploughing stoke) eyes, figurines were predominantly made with round heads and deeply punched pupils that stare out and engage the observer's attention. This new figurine style is documented at San Lorenzo (Coe and Diehl 1980b: 277) and La Venta (Drucker 1952: Plate 26, 27a-c), in Oaxaca (Marcus 1998: Chapter 16) and the Belize Valley (Awe 1992, Cheetham 1998), among other areas of Mesoamerica. In the Soconusco, more detail was placed on modeling hair, jewelry and clothing out of clay during Horizon II – but the majority of figurines were still depicted naked. Whereas most Horizon I figurines were chubby, certain Horizon II figurines were truly obese. As noted earlier in text, greenstone is recorded in greater quantities during the Middle Formative period and carved greenstone figurines appear for the first time. Although Horizon II ceramic figurines were no longer depicted with closed, slanted eyes, human representations carved into greenstone at this time often maintained this distinctive trait. Therefore, this distinctive Olmec imagery seems to have been transferred from ceramic to stone in the Middle Formative period, thus further differentiating between the individuals depicted using each raw material.

SOCONUSCO

In the Soconusco, La Blanca abruptly rose to prominence during the Conchas phase in an area near the Guamuchal/Manchón swamp that had had a small population during the previous Jocotal phase. The site quickly grew to cover a minimum of 100 ha (Love 2002a: 55) and perhaps as much as 200 ha (Love and Guernsey 2007: 923). During the Conchas phase at La Blanca, the 25-m-high central Mound 1 was constructed, and I have previously estimated it would have contained

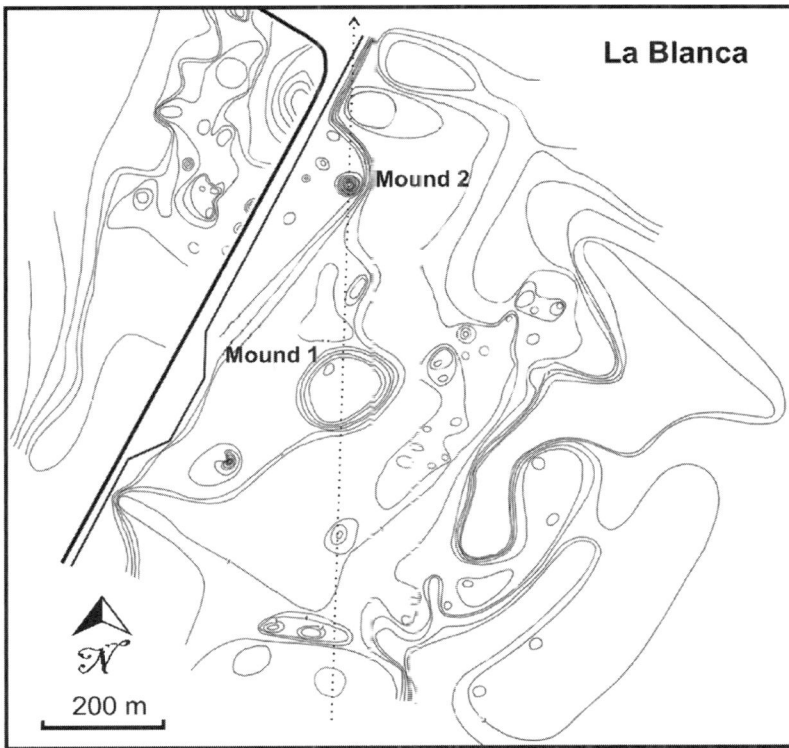

69

EARLY AND MIDDLE
FORMATIVE
MESOAMERICAN
STYLE HORIZONS
AND CULTURE
HISTORY OF THE
SOCONUSCO AND
THE GULF COAST

Figure 3.3
La Blanca site map with
mound numbers indi-
cated (after Love 2002a:
Figure 15).

at least 140,000 cu m of fill (Rosenswig 2000: Table 3). This made it the
largest mound built in Mesoamerica at the time (Love 1999a, 1999b).
The orientation of the mounds at La Blanca was roughly north–south
(Love 1999b: 138) with Mound 1 at the center of the site (see Figure 3.3). There were at least forty-three house mounds at La Blanca,
and the site was at the center of a multitiered settlement system that
includes fifty-six documented sites in the Naranjo river zone (Love
2002a).

The La Blanca polity contained at least three administrative tiers
during the Conchas phase. The sites of La Zarca and El Infierno were
second-tier centers built around mounds measuring 20 m and 18 m,
respectively (Love 2002a). Although no excavation has occurred at
either site, these are the largest mounds documented at the time after
La Blanca. Izapa also may have been a second-tier center in this polity
(Love 1999b: 137). Cuauhtémoc, with its 5-m-high central mound
and evidence of social differentiation (Rosenswig 2007), represents
a third-tier center in the La Blanca polity, and data from this newly
excavated site are the subject of the next four chapters of this book
(also see Rosenswig 2006a, 2009, 2010). There are a few other sites

documented thus far that measure 1 to 2.5 ha and had no mounds. I have excavated at two such sites – San Martin (measuring 2.5 ha) and Las Palmas (measuring 1 ha) (Rosenswig 2002, 2005). The only other excavation of a Conchas phase site was carried out at La Victoria (Coe 1961) – which measures 2 ha. There are also many smaller Conchas-phase sites covering less than 0.7 ha, thirty-five of which were documented in the Cuauhtémoc survey zone (Rosenswig 2008). These last two classes of site size are likely villages and hamlets that comprise the lowest tier in the settlement system.

The Conchas phase corresponds to a dramatic reorganization of the land between the two large Soconusco swamps. Due to the virtual abandonment of the Mazatán zone to the northwest (Clark 2004) and the Jesús River zone to the southeast (Pye 1995; Pye and Demarest 1991), the leaders of the La Blanca polity appear to have attracted the surrounding populations to this newly emerging polity (Blake and Clark 1999: 64; Love 1999a: 90). The Soconusco island of complexity that extended from one side to the other of the land between large Soconusco swamps during the Initial Ceramic Period and Horizon I shrank to half of this extent during Horizon II (see Figure 2.1). The population concentration around La Blanca is similar to what occurred around San Lorenzo during Horizon I when the population density was 20 times higher in the vicinity of that site compared to the rest of the lower Coatzacoalcos survey area (see discussion earlier in text). The concentration of population may therefore be the single most important factor for the establishment of both of these early Mesoamerican centers. With no apparent ecological explanation, the nucleation of population at both of these precocious centers can best be explained in political terms.

During the Conchas phase, manos and metates replaced mortars and pestles as the most common grinding tools in the Soconusco (Coe and Flannery 1967: 126; Rosenswig 2006a). In the Soconusco as well as northern Veracruz, grater bowls also became popular during this time and then abruptly fall out of use (Coe 1961: 67–68; Ekholm 1944; Love 2002a: 97; MacNeish 1954; also see example from the Basin of Mexico in Flannery and Marcus 1994: Figure 19.2). Obsidian prismatic blades are first documented at most sites in the Soconusco during the Middle Formative period (Clark 1987; Jackson and Love 1991), although a few are documented at Cantón Corralito from the Cuadros and Jocotal phase deposits (Clark and Pye 2000). The Conchas phase is also the time when data suggest that maize was used as a staple crop for the first time, as I discuss further in Chapter 5 (and see Blake 2006;

Blake et al. 1992b; Rosenswig 2006a). Initial faunal analysis from La Blanca suggests that the range of species consumed changed from a broad based combination of swamp and forest species to predominantly dog, deer and turtle (Wake and Harrington 2002). These demographic and technological transformations that occurred during the Conchas phase indicate a fundamental reorganization of the economic base on which Soconusco society was built.

71

EARLY AND MIDDLE
FORMATIVE
MESOAMERICAN
STYLE HORIZONS
AND CULTURE
HISTORY OF THE
SOCONUSCO AND
THE GULF COAST

GULF COAST

In the lower Coatzacoalcos, the beginning of the Middle Formative period marks a dramatic decrease in the number of sites that surrounded the San Lorenzo plateau as this site fell from prominence in the Gulf Coast region. This change in political fortunes may have been due to shifting river courses as a result of geologic uplift (Ortiz and Cyphers 1997). In the 400-sq-km lower Coatzacoalcos survey zone, there were only 206 ha of occupation during the 300-year Middle Formative period, or just slightly more area was settled than during the Initial Ceramic Period Ojochi and Bajío phases (Symonds et al. 2002: Figure 4.4). Furthermore, the largest site in the area was Peña Blanca (Symonds et al. 2002: 89). The Nacaste phase is not well understood at San Lorenzo, and Ann Cyphers (personal communication 2003) has found only scattered pockets of material from this phase despite intensive work since 1990. One thing is certain – San Lorenzo was no longer a regional center and whatever elevated position the elite of this polity enjoyed had crumbled by 900 BCE.

The ceramic chronologies in other areas of the Gulf Coast are not fine-grained enough to divide Horizon II from Horizon III. Instead, a single Middle Formative phase is reported in most areas (e.g., Pool and Ohnersorgen 2003; Rust and Sharer 1988; Santley and Arnold 1996). In particular, the chronology of La Venta is problematic and does not permit the sort of fine-grained analysis that is possible in other regions (Gonzalez 1996: 73). However, recent work by Christopher von Nagy (2003: Table 6.4; von Nagy et al. 2002) documents a Horizon I hiatus at San Andrés near La Venta and then four Middle Formative phases that correspond to my Horizon II and III.

Horizon III

During Horizon III, monumental architecture was built around plazas and formal architectural plans became more complex than before (see Joyce 2004a: 23; Lowe 1977: 222). On the Gulf Coast, this is most well-known at the new center of La Venta (see Figure 3.4). In the Soconusco, this horizon corresponds to the Escalón and Frontera phases. At San Lorenzo, Horizon III corresponds to the Palangana phase while at La Venta it encompasses the Middle and Late La Venta phases. Traditional wisdom holds that La Venta replaced San Lorenzo as the dominant Gulf Coast center (e.g., Tolstoy 1989b). This would place La Venta and La Blanca as coeval and the political centralization part of a contemporary phenomenon. Unfortunately, the chronology at La Venta is poorly understood (see Demarest 1989: 323–324; Gonzalez 1996: 73; Grove 1997: 72–73; Tolstoy 1989b: 287–289). The interpretation that I follow in this book relies on stylistic cross-dating, which opens a gap between the fall of San Lorenzo and the apogee of La Venta (see Clark and Pye 2000; Demarest 1989: 332; Love 2002a). The implication of this proposal is that the demise of San Lorenzo may have resulted in a power vacuum that corresponds to the emergence of numerous centers across Mesoamerica during Horizon II. It was into this new system of interacting centers that La Venta emerged a century or two later (see Andrews 1986: 40–41; Demarest 1989: 333–335). Horizon III forms the majority of Lowe's Late Olmec and Coe's La Venta Horizon (see Grove 1993: 95–99). This horizon corresponds to the Cantera phase at Chalcatzingo, the Rosario and Early Monte Albán I phases in the Valley of Oaxaca, and Uir and Bosque phases in the Copán Valley (and see Urban et al. 2002). In the Maya region, this horizon is contemporaneous to, yet distinct from, the Mamom complex.

Post-slip incised decoration continued to be the defining characteristic of ceramic decoration during Horizon III. However, rather than single or double (or occasional triple and quadruple) lines around vessels' rims and bases, or highlighting painted iconography, Horizon III incisions were more often on the exterior of dishes, vases and composite silhouette vessels and employed to create geometric and other designs (e.g., Diehl 2004: Figures 52, 53; Lowe 1989: Figure 4.9). Punched eye figurines continued to be produced during this time, but pupil diameters were dramatically smaller and not punched as deeply (e.g., Diehl 2004: Figure 57; Drucker 1947: Plate 4; Ekholm 1989). In addition, facial hair was represented regularly and clothing was much more frequently molded in clay.

GULF COAST

In the La Venta area, a three-tiered settlement hierarchy has been reported by the second half of the Middle Formative period (Rust

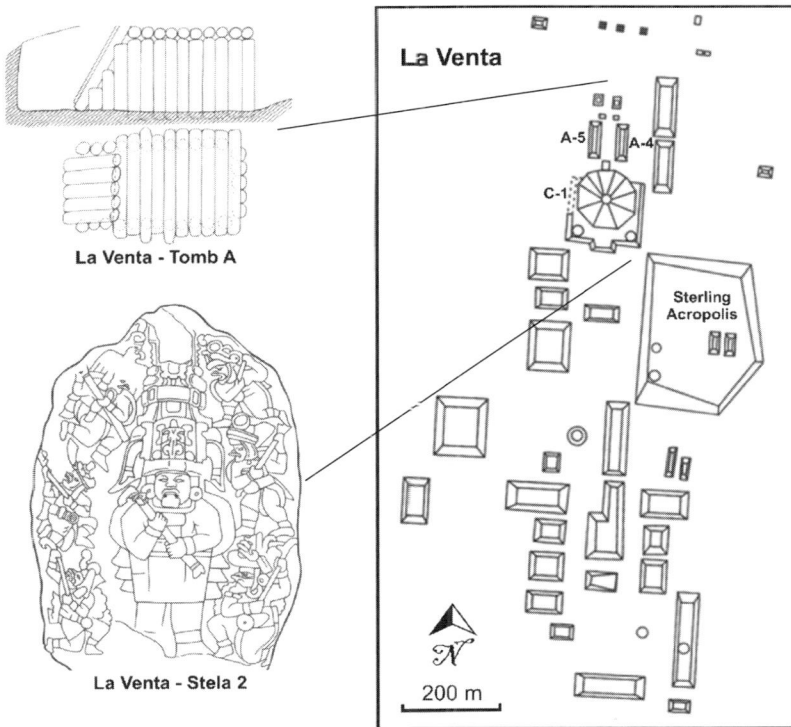

73

EARLY AND MIDDLE
FORMATIVE
MESOAMERICAN
STYLE HORIZONS
AND CULTURE
HISTORY OF THE
SOCONUSCO AND
THE GULF COAST

La Venta

A-5   A-4

C-1

Sterling
Acropolis

La Venta - Tomb A

La Venta - Stela 2

N

200 m

Figure 3.4
La Venta site core with
Tomb A and Stela 2 inset
(after Diehl 2004).

and Sharer 1988). The beginning of residential occupation at La
Venta dates to 800–700 BCE when the site covered 200 ha (Rust 1992:
125). Thus, as just discussed, there appears to have been a political
hiatus between the collapse of the San Lorenzo polity by 900 BCE
and the emergence of the La Venta polity after 800 or 700 BCE. La
Venta emerged along with yet another pan-Mesoamerican iconographic tradition (Reilly 1990, 1995; Taube 1995, 2000). Iconography
was obviously derivative of that from Horizon I but was transferred
to new media such as jade (Grove 1993: 98). La Venta has been called
Mesoamerica's first urban settlement due to its organized program
of carved stone monuments, buried drains and courtyards formed by
monumental architecture with a 30-m-high central mound (Gonzalez
1989: 84; 1996). Whereas the area was occupied during most of the
Middle Formative periods, the mounds at La Venta were built during
Horizon III. In addition, thousands of serpentine blocks were placed
in numerous caches in the site core, and elaborate burial tombs were
constructed during the second half of the Middle Formative period
(Drucker et al. 1959). Therefore, Horizon III construction at La Venta
represented an unprecedented level of massive scale conspicuous
consumption of resources in Mesoamerica.

Elsewhere on the Gulf Coast, settlement was modest. In the Grijalva delta, a two-tier settlement system persisted from the Early Formative period (von Nagy 1997: 269–270). In the Tuxtla mountains, Tres Zapotes emerged as a regional center measuring 80 ha at this time (Pool and Ohnersorgen 2003). As mentioned earlier in text, in the lower Coatzacoalcos survey zone, there were only 206 ha of Middle Formative occupation forming a two-tiered settlement system with Peña Blanca being the largest site in the area (Symonds et al. 2002: 89).

SOCONUSCO

As abruptly as La Blanca sprang into existence at the beginning of the Conchas phase, the site was abandoned by the end of this phase. During Horizon III, Izapa rose to prominence in the land between the two large Soconusco swamps (Figure 3.5). The initial accession of Izapa as a political center postdates the collapse of La Blanca and was thus likely contemporary with the rise of La Venta on the Gulf Coast. At both sites, formal plazas were laid out and large conical mounds built. The presence of more than 200 stelae that used complex narrative scenes to legitimize rulership at Izapa is attributed by Lowe et al. (1982; also see Guernsey 2006; Guernsey Kapelman 2003, 2004; Justeson and Mathews 1983) to the Guillén phase at the beginning of the Late Formative period. However, the construction of stone monuments began during Horizon III when Misc. Monument 2, depicting a crouching individual emerging from a niche, was erected northeast of Mound 30 (see Figure 3.5). This figure is reminiscent of the individuals emerging from the stone thrones recovered from San Lorenzo and La Venta. Izapa was then occupied until the Early Postclassic period (Lowe et al 1982: 139).

In addition to Izapa, major Middle Formative settlements on the Pacific piedmont of Guatemala were built at sites such as Takalik Abaj, El Baúl and Chocolá (Kaplan 2008; Kaplan and Valdés 2004; Miles 1965; Parsons 1981). Each of these centers were located on the piedmont, a zone that receives as much as four times the rainfall of coastal plain below. Other centers were also built at this time on the coastal plain at sites such as Ujuxte (Love 1999b: 146, 2002b; and see Rosenswig 2008: 403–405). The construction of large sites on the piedmont during Horizon III marks a major settlement shift as after nearly a millennium, political centers were no longer located exclusively on the coastal plain. The rise of La Venta and Izapa during

Horizon III, along with the changes to Pacific Coast settlement focus, also marks a time beyond that examined in this book.

THE "OLMEC PROBLEM"

In documenting the first 800 years of settled life in the Cuauhtémoc zone of the Soconusco, I evaluate this local population in relation to their interaction with people living in the Mazatán zone as well as those inhabiting Mexico's Gulf Coast. Did a new level of socio-political complexity coalesce in the Soconusco as a result of contact with, and borrowing of ideas and institutions from, distant peoples? Did the rulers of San Lorenzo (or their emissaries) actually make incursions into the Soconusco? Alternatively, is the impact of Gulf Coast peoples overemphasized in understanding Early Formative Mesoamerican society? Longstanding debate has surrounded these questions (see Grove 1997; Pool 2007: 15–17, 179–181). Wilk (2004: 85) notes that "There is no question that the area over which objects with distinctive 'Olmec' iconography are found is vast . . . The question of how the objects or styles got there and what they signify remains one of the most contentious issues among Mesoamerican

Figure 3.5
Formative site core of Izapa (after Lowe et al. 1982) with Misc. Monument 2 inset (photo by author).

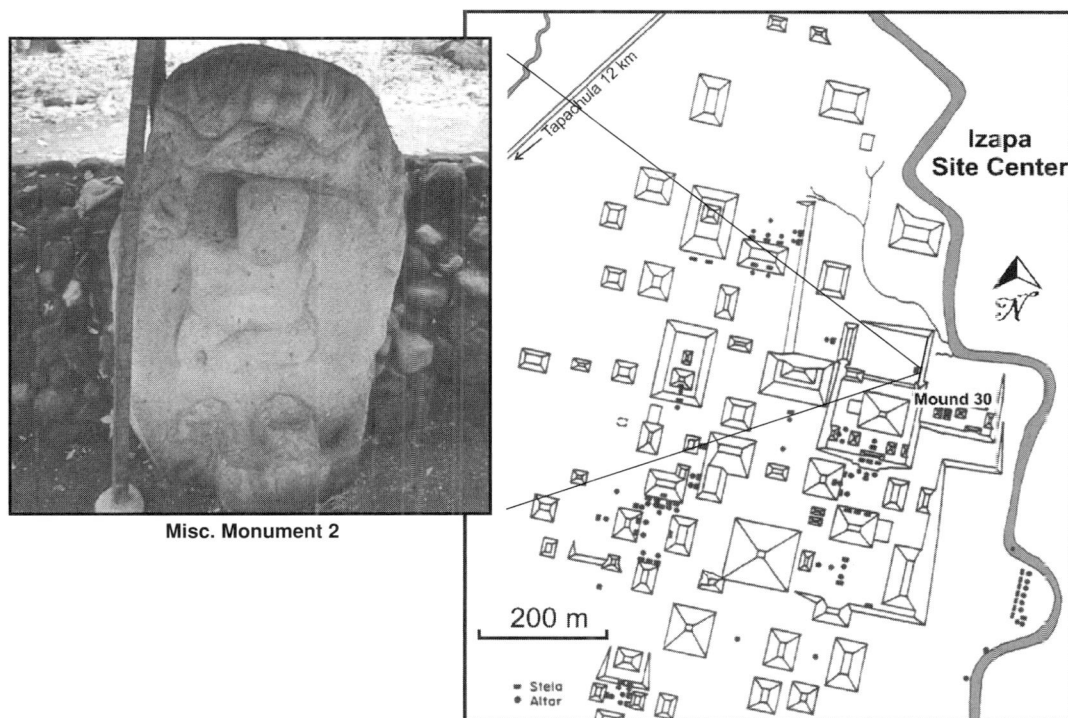

Misc. Monument 2

Izapa
Site Center

Mound 30

200 m

• Stela
• Altar

archaeologists." At least three distinct models have been proposed to account for pan-regional similarities across Mesoamerica that define Horizon I.

In the remainder of this chapter, I present each model as a hypothesis of the nature of inter-regional interaction from which archaeological expectations are derived (see Odell 2001: 684). The first step in systematically evaluating archaeological evidence is to explicitly lay out each of these three models in turn and explore the material expectations of each. To frame each model as contrastive of the others, I may be stereotyping the position of the authors I cite by quoting their most extreme claims. This is done only to create hypotheses that are as mutually exclusive as possible and not to disregard the nuances of the thinking of these scholars.

The first model I call the Peer Polity Model (PPM) where a pan-regional ideological system is posited to have not been centered in the Gulf Coast,[7] or anywhere else (e.g., Grove 1989; Hammond 1989a; Marcus 1989; Marcus and Flannery 1996: 118–120, 138). Instead, a number of distinct yet equal polities are said to have evolved, or inherited, a united iconographic system and developed sociopolitical complexity at approximately the same time. Changes that occurred during Horizon I were influenced by developments at San Lorenzo as much as at any other island of complexity in Mesoamerica. In fact, Flannery and Marcus (2000; Flannery et al. 2005; Stoltman et al. 2005) have gone to lengths to downplay any uniqueness of the achievements at San Lorenzo. Proponents of the PPM propose that cultural changes between the Initial Ceramic Period and Horizon I were not dramatic, so no special explanation is required to account for what was occurring at San Lorenzo. Furthermore, the relationship between the San Lorenzo elite and other elites was not particularly different than that between the inhabitants of any of these other regions of Mesoamerica at the time. In typological evolutionary terms, proponents of this position interpret the most complex Early Formative Mesoamerican societies as chiefdoms at various yet comparable levels of organization. The key difference between this model and the next two is that San Lorenzo is not seen as having been qualitatively different than other Early Formative polities.

The second model I refer to as the Elite Emulation Model (EEM) whose advocates propose that less developed polities in various areas of Mesoamerica borrowed ideas and styles of material culture from the more advanced San Lorenzo polity (e.g., Blomster 1998, 2004;

Flannery 1968; Tolstoy 1989b: 292–300). This model proposes a system of socially complex societies with the elite at San Lorenzo leading the political innovations occurring at the time. The fundamental motivation driving change according to proponents of the EEM were symbiotic political needs of the rulers both at San Lorenzo and in other Early Formative islands of complexity such as the Soconusco. Exotic goods and knowledge were employed to maintain prestige within all of the interacting polities in ways I explored at length in Chapter 2. In typological evolutionary terms, proponents of the EEM interpret San Lorenzo as some form of very complex chiefdom or possibly an archaic state and other Early Formative Mesoamerican centers of complexity as less complex chiefdoms.

The third model evaluated in this book I call the Aztec Analogy Model (AAM). Proponents of this model interpret San Lorenzo as the seat of an Early Formative empire whose elite conquered and administered the Soconusco, located hundreds of kilometers from the Gulf Coast. This is said to have occurred in much the way that the Aztec invaded and extracted tribute from their distant Xoconusco province (Coe 1965b: 123) or a number of variants that employ imperial analogies (e.g., Clark 1997: 229; 2007; Clark and Blake 1989; Coe 1989). Clark (1990, 1997, 2007; Clark and Blake 1989; Clark and Pye 2000; Clark and Hodgson 2004) proposes a multistep model where elite emulation during the Cherla phase was followed by a Gulf Coast invasion of the Mazatán zone of the Soconusco at the beginning of the Cuadros phase. Therefore, despite the use of the EEM for the Cherla phase, the second step of Clark's scenario proposes a Gulf Coast invasion and conquest of at least a portion of the Soconusco, so his model is included with the AAM. Clark has characterized the elite from San Lorenzo as being responsible for "an aggressive takeover of the Mazatán region" (Clark 1997: 228) after which "an Olmec king controlled the Mazatán region by dispatching a contingent of elites and bodyguards to govern in his name" (Clark 1997: 229). In evolutionary terms, proponents of this position interpret San Lorenzo as the capital of an imperial state powerful enough to colonize and govern distant lands. The crucial difference between the EEM and the AAM is therefore not simply the degree of complexity evident at San Lorenzo but the ability of this polity's rulers to organize the conquer and control of other regions of Mesoamerica.

These three hypotheses differ in the cultural interpretations given to Mesoamerica's first style horizon and our understanding of

Gulf Coast–Soconusco relations. Was Olmec imagery the expression of a long-standing tradition shared by distant peoples? Was it borrowed from the inhabitants of the Gulf Coast by local elites for their own aggrandizement? Or, was Olmec imagery part of an imperial ideology mandated by colonial masters and imposed on colonized subjects? The core issue is thus to understand the nature of relations between distant regions of Mesoamerica at this time. Such discussions are sometimes framed as whether the inhabitants of the Gulf Coast during Horizon I were Mesoamerica's "mother culture" or whether there were a number of early "sister cultures" (Hammond 1989a). Recently, Diehl and Coe (1995), Clark (1997) and Blomster et al. (2005) have advocated the mother scenario whereas Flannery and Marcus (2000; Flannery et al. 2005) disagree strongly with this characterization and champion the sister scenario. However, the questions I am more interested in pursuing are where, why and how Horizon I iconography was used and if it supported a political ideology that allowed for a greater degree of hierarchy to be achieved in each area that employed it. Specifically, in this book I ask what affect such pan-Mesoamerican iconography had on the inhabitants of the Cuauhtémoc zone of the Soconusco. I briefly return to the mother/sister characterization of Mesoamerica in the final chapter of this book but devote most of my efforts to differentiating among the three models presented above.

The "Olmec style" (incorporating artifacts from at least Horizons I, II and III) is distinctive and incorporates black and white ceramics, distinct iconography featuring supernatural creatures (such as the Olmec Dragon) at various levels of abstraction, as well as depictions of humans with infantile features (as well as fat cheeks, closed eyes and downturned mouths) as I define in more detail in Chapter 6. The term Olmec is used here only to refer to this style regardless of where or when it is found, as Lesure (2004) has aptly argued. Classical architecture was built in ancient Greece and in postcolonial Washington DC. Although there is a historical relationship between these uses of the Classical architectural style, local reasons for the use of aesthetic conventions can only be understood at one place and in one time.

Employing the term Olmec to refer to an art style over the many centuries of use runs the risk of obscuring the dynamism of the generations of people who employed and redefined the iconographic elements that are so easy to recognize. However, the persistence of certain iconographic images and stylistic conventions over centuries, and their transference between different media, is not accidental (see Pool 2007: 110–112). Such continuity demonstrates historical connections, with each generation carrying on certain aspects of their parents' and grandparents' traditions and simultaneously making them their own. Olmec is not used here to refer to a group of people or a political phenomenon – however, the ease with which the Olmec aesthetic can be recognized could have facilitated the transmission of cultural ideas, and is unlikely to have been accidental.

Rather than dwelling on debates of either the mother versus sister culture or chiefdom versus state, the research presented in this book simply documents the evolving social, political and economic organization of people inhabiting one small region of the Soconusco. Local developments in the Cuauhtémoc region are framed in terms of the timing of changes in other parts of the Soconusco as well as developments on the Gulf Coast. The inhabitants of the Cuauhtémoc site were never the most powerful rulers in the Soconusco, and, likely because of this, the site was occupied much longer than was Paso de la Amada, Cantón Corralito, Ojo de Agua or La Blanca.

Most regions of Mesoamerica have relatively coarse ceramic chronologies that divide time into phases that each last for a few centuries. In Soconusco there are seven ceramic phases to work with for the period in question (Blake et al. 1995; Clark and Cheetham 2005). Therefore, due to the hard work of researchers who have labored on the archaeology of the Soconusco during the past half century, the data patterns presented in this book can evaluate the hypotheses discussed in this chapter on almost a century-by-century basis from 1600 to 800 BCE – before, during and after the apogee of San Lorenzo during Horizon I.

EXPECTED PATTERNS FOR THREE MODELS OF INTER-REGIONAL INTERACTION

To evaluate the three models presented in the previous section, I explore Horizon I society in diachronic terms. A certain part of the "Olmec Problem" revolves around the nature of the San Lorenzo site, but more controversial is to what degree the inhabitants of other regions were affected by this Gulf Coast polity. In the remainder of this chapter, I present the three models in terms of a series of hypotheses of what can be expected during the Initial Ceramic Period when San Lorenzo was a modest local population center, Horizon I when San Lorenzo reached the apogee of its power and Horizon II after San Lorenzo had collapsed. Expected patterns are organized within each of these three epochs in terms of settlement/political organization, local economy, representational systems and foreign economy patterns. Data from Cuauhtémoc, informing on each of these categories in turn, are then presented in the next four chapters.

Rather than looking for material correlates of particular synchronic states of political organization (e.g., Creamer and Haas 1985; Peebles and Kus 1977; Renfrew 1973), I attempt to understand the evolution of society by the way in which changes occurred through time (see Blake 1991: 31). Flannery's (1968) model of Oaxaca–Gulf Coast interaction is functional in that it provides only a synchronic *description* of the role of interaction between various regions of Mesoamerica during Horizon I. Much of the published literature follows Flannery's approach by describing data from only Horizon I. This synchronic perspective has resulted in less attention being paid to how evidence from the preceding or the subsequent periods can shed light on the final centuries of the Early Formative period. In the following sections, direct quotations of predicted material patterns are included from proponents of each model. I elaborate a number of other expectations based on archaeological treatments of different types of inter-regional interaction. In particular, I address definitions of interaction spheres relevant to the PPM and the definition of empires relevant to the AAM and make reference to the EEM as I have already discussed at length in Chapter 2.

There is no a priori reason to assume that any two regions of Mesoamerica will resemble each other during any of the time periods discussed here. Each model is neither correct nor incorrect in characterizing all of Mesoamerica. Instead, one of the three models outlined in this chapter can only said to be better (or worse) at describing the available data from a given region during a particular time period. The following expectations are presented as a preliminary attempt to list the material consequences for each model as they apply to the Soconusco. The most important result of assembling this somewhat pedantic set of expectations is to frame the debate in terms of competing hypotheses that can be evaluated using explicit criteria. This approach is more productive than is constructing polemical narratives (and counter-narratives) that attempt to justify entrenched positions that have changed little over the past quarter century.

Initial Ceramic Period: Hypothesis 1 (PPM) expectations

SETTLEMENT/POLITICAL ORGANIZATION

Each area should have a relatively low population with similar levels of political organization throughout Mesoamerica. Village leaders might be present, but not hereditary inequality (Marcus and Flannery 1996: 88–92).

LOCAL ECONOMY

Presumably each area exploited resources at a similar level of intensity (Demarest 1989: 310). Although specifics are rarely addressed, the assumption is that sedentary, early agriculturalists emerged in most areas of Mesoamerica during the Initial Ceramic Period.

REPRESENTATIONAL SYSTEMS

Similar iconographic themes in most areas are evidence of a shared "...basic ideological complex (of unspecified origins)" (Grove 1989: 12) during the Initial Ceramic Period. Common ideological themes were presumably painted or carved in wood or gourds but not on ceramics or other nonperishable materials (Grove 1993: 91). Then, during Horizon I, their "...transfer to pottery took place essentially simultaneously over the entire area from the Basin of Mexico to Copan..." (Flannery and Marcus 1994: 389). If each region of Mesoamerica that later had evidence of Olmec imagery used this iconography during the Initial Ceramic Period then one might also expect them to share other forms of representation during this early time. Some level of interaction is inferred by the Red-on-Buff and Locona interaction spheres discussed earlier in this chapter. Widespread distribution of material culture styles (and presumably the ideas they materialize) is the case for any interaction sphere regardless of the subsistence strategy any particular group pursues or the degree of political organization present (e.g., Caldwell 1964; Hayden and Schulting 1997; Odess 1998).

Grove (1989: 12) further proposes that such shared ideas may account for similarities between Olmec and Chavín art, thus presumably dating to a time before the South American continent was colonized. Trigger (1991: 558) has also proposed that there are some pan-American ideas shared by most New World peoples that date back to the late Pleistocene colonization from northeast Asia. Such primordial themes could have contributed to Olmec iconography and this explains why, when "the motifs first appeared on ceramics, they were already stylized and had regional variants" (Flannery and Marcus 2000: 13). Whereas this scenario is certainly possible, a convincing case is difficult to make with negative evidence. However, although the scholars cited propose a united ideology with no material manifestation until Horizon I, this is not *necessarily* a requirement of a PPM.

FOREIGN ECONOMY

Presumably inter-regional exchange was occurring at levels sufficient to allow the Locona and the Red-on-Buff interaction spheres to be maintained as two internally similar yet distinct areas persisting for a few centuries (Flannery and Marcus 2000: 9–11).

Initial Ceramic Period: Hypothesis 2 (EEM) expectations

SETTLEMENT/POLITICAL ORGANIZATION

The areas that will be most intensively interacting with each other during Horizon I can be predicted by those areas that are most politically developed and have the highest population levels during the Initial Ceramic Period (Flannery 1968: 80). These are the islands of complexity described in Chapter 2. Each region is expected to have its own settlement organization at this time based on local political criteria. Each of these areas is expected to have a higher population density than the immediate surrounding areas.

LOCAL ECONOMY

Islands of complexity with the greatest evidence of feasting and other forms of competitive display are those whose elite will most want to interact with the San Lorenzo elite during Horizon I (see Flannery 1968: 80). Furthermore, as population levels rise and people centralize in each region, forms of subsistence intensification might be expected to occur so that more people can be supported by less land.

REPRESENTATIONAL SYSTEM

The Gulf Coast develops ideas and/or practices (reflected in iconography or other media that leave material remains) that later will be imitated by other societies. Such ideas and associated imagery could have been based on shared pan-regional cultural principles during the Initial Ceramic Period. In fact, a common set of principles would have allowed new variants on these ideas to be more easily adopted across Mesoamerica during the following Horizon I. However, each island of complexity in Mesoamerica is expected to have had local traditions and ideologies that account for distinct Initial Ceramic Period representational systems. Olmec imagery is expected to have developed first in the Gulf Coast island of complexity.

FOREIGN ECONOMY

Relatively little long-distance exchange is expected to have been occurring at this time compared to what follows in Horizon I as San Lorenzo emerged as a polity that the elite in less developed regions want to interact with. However, some exchange was occurring for the Initial Ceramic Period interaction spheres to have been maintained, as is also assumed by the PPM.

Initial Ceramic Period: Hypothesis 3 (AAM) expectations

SETTLEMENT/POLITICAL ORGANIZATION

The Initial Ceramic Period organization of a region that was later colonized by San Lorenzo is less important than the presence of desired resources (or other motivating factors) that will attract Gulf Coast colonizers to that region during Horizon I. Therefore, contrary to the EEM, Initial Ceramic Period islands of complexity were no more likely to be colonized than were less developed regions.

LOCAL ECONOMY

Subsistence details are not generally specified for the Initial Ceramic Period. As with settlement/political organization, details of the local economy will not predict which areas are more likely to be colonized by the San Lorenzo polity. This expectation of the AAM is also in contrast to the EEM expectation.

REPRESENTATIONAL SYSTEM

Olmec symbolism should have been developed first on the Gulf Coast and have been absent in other regions during the Initial Ceramic Period. The AAM shares this expectation with the EEM, so both contradict the manner in which the PPM is often cast. Olmec symbolism should be well developed on the Gulf Coast by the end of the Initial Ceramic Period and exported during Horizon I as a coherent representational system. Each area of Mesoamerica is expected to have employed a distinct symbolic system and set of customs during the Initial Ceramic Period that the Gulf Coast colonizers would have replaced in areas that were conquered. However, the AAM also allows that imitation of Olmec symbolism could occur in regions not under direct imperial control and employed as prestige objects. In areas distant from direct imperial control, use of imperial iconography would be similar to the elite emulation described in Chapter 2 for the Germanic tribes using Roman objects. Therefore, documenting elite emulation in one region does not preclude colonial relations in another, nor complete disengagement from pan-Mesoamerican imagery and customs in yet other areas. In fact, each of these three types of relations (and others as well) could coexist and vary from region to region.

FOREIGN ECONOMY

Some elements of the San Lorenzo elite were receiving the resources they desired from the area in question by the end of the Initial Ceramic Period. It was only when the flow of goods did not keep up with demand (or that the Gulf Coast elite wanted a more advantageous exchange arrangement) that the San Lorenzo armies would have been sent to invade (Clark 1997, 2007). Therefore, resources are expected to have already been arriving on the Gulf Coast by the end of the Initial Ceramic Period from some of the areas that were later invaded. The other two models predict some exchange of goods during the Initial Ceramic Period, but the AAM expects a markedly higher intensity by the end of this epoch. Here, I make the materialist assumption that the ultimate motivation for empire is economic.

Horizon I: Hypothesis 1 (PPM) expectations

SETTLEMENT/POLITICAL ORGANIZATION

There is no reason to expect changes in the location or size of settlements from the Initial Ceramic Period as the two preexisting interaction spheres simply grew to incorporate more people (see Hayden and Schulting 1997). Changes in local political organization should be explainable in terms of local developments.

LOCAL ECONOMY

Expectations are never specified but presumably patterns of subsistence continued relatively unchanged from the Initial Ceramic

Period, and when changes did occur they spread through each inter-action sphere.

REPRESENTATIONAL SYSTEM

Olmec iconography (or at least the ideas it represents) was not new at this time; it was simply applied to durable media for the first time. Iconography is expected to have been derived logically from preexisting local traditions with distinctive regional variation (Flan-nery and Marcus 2000: 14). Furthermore, Flannery and Marcus (2000: 29) propose that, when Olmec motifs are more numerous and show greater variability in a particular area, it indicates where they orig-inated. Olmec baby face figurines are expected to have appeared everywhere in Mesoamerica at the same time (Flannery and Marcus 2000: 16).

FOREIGN ECONOMY

Flannery and Marcus (2000) contend that during Horizon I the two interaction spheres continued separately from the Initial Ceramic Period. If the intensity of this exchange did increase, there is no reason to expect that significantly more goods arrived on the Gulf Coast than in other areas. Furthermore, if the Gulf Coast was not the principal destination of exchange, then a distance-decay pat-tern should account for the inter-regional distribution of goods. Each region would thus be expected to have a proportion of foreign goods as a function of its distance from the location of origin. Although there were local centers in each interaction region, from a Mesoamerica-wide perspective there should be no core areas. This expectation is in contrast to both the EEM and the AAM, which posit San Lorenzo as the core area in a newly emerged regional exchange system.

Horizon I: Hypothesis 2 (EEM) expectations

SETTLEMENT/POLITICAL ORGANIZATION

The most dramatic changes in local settlement location and over-all political organization are predicted in islands of complexity with the most intensive interaction with the San Lorenzo polity. How-ever, changes are expected to have been the result of local elite self-interest geared to facilitating access to their counterparts at San Lorenzo. Among many examples, this pattern is evidenced among the contact period Cuna (Helms 1979: 39), Early Horizon Chavín (Burger 1992: 129) and Bronze Age Cycladic (Broodbank 2000: 237–244) societies. As reviewed in Chapter 2, leaders who derive their power from long-distance exchange locate their principal centers on transportation arteries.

LOCAL ECONOMY

Increased interaction would not be expected to significantly alter the basic subsistence patterns of the inhabitants in a given region (Flannery 1968: 79). Increased feasting activity might be expected in association with foreign derived (and/or inspired) objects as local leaders employ exotic objects and ideas to bolster their position in the established prestige systems. Change in feasting patterns could occur as successful leaders transform local social relationships to their advantage. Some increase in the production of prestige goods is expected to be used locally as well as to be exported to San Lorenzo.

REPRESENTATIONAL SYSTEM

Symbols of distant power and authority are expected to have been adopted rapidly and quickly copied locally. New symbols associated with distant and more sophisticated elites are expected to have spread to areas where existing local elites would have benefited from their use. Initial emulation is expected to have been rapidly followed by whole-scale replacement as the once novel ideas became internalized in everyday life. Local elites can only effectively employ foreign symbolism if they can convince their followers of its usefulness/power, so Olmec imagery should have been accepted by all segments of the population and objects bearing such imagery used by everyone.

As the result of local pragmatic manipulation of foreign symbolism by local chiefs, the ostentatious elaboration of motifs would be greater in peripheral areas than at San Lorenzo (contra both Grove 1989 and Flannery and Marcus 2000: 29). A modern parallel is the hammer and sickle image and the red star of the communist international that, during the twentieth century, were used in a standard canonical manner within the Soviet Union, whereas, for example, in Latin America these symbols were sometimes playfully incorporated into folk traditions by local leftist groups. Similarly, the Angola flag substitutes a machete for the sickle and a factory gear for the hammer, adapting the twentieth-century African reality from its late-nineteenth-century Russian origins. Such an iconographic transformation maintains the basic concept of a unified industrial and agricultural proletariat but uses locally relevant imagery. However, in Mesoamerica the canonical Olmec symbols and iconographic conventions (discussed at greater length in Chapter 5) should occur on the Gulf Coast earlier than elsewhere in Mesoamerica.

FOREIGN ECONOMY

Elites from each island of complexity were the "entrepreneurs who facilitate exchange" (Flannery 1968: 79), and interacting elites would have attempted to parlay exchanged objects (and associated knowledge) to their advantage within their respective societies. The overall quantity of exchanged objects is expected to have increased during Horizon I. Foreign objects, technologies, symbols and so forth would have been in high demand in each island of complexity as the prestige of local leaders provided the impetus for their acquisition. The overall quantity of goods entering and leaving the Gulf Coast might have been similar to that in other areas such as the Soconusco, but their nature would have been different. Consistent with both Flannery's (1968) and Rathje's (1972) models, ideologically charged objects would have tended to move from the Gulf Coast to other areas in greater quantities and raw materials would have tended to flow in the opposite direction.

Horizon I: Hypothesis 3 (AAM) expectations

SETTLEMENT/POLITICAL ORGANIZATION

San Lorenzo was the first "stratified society in Mesoamerica ruled by kings" (Clark 1997: 215) with secondary centers administered by princes (Clark 1997: 217). Both the EEM and the AAM propose that the San Lorenzo polity was significantly more complex than other polities in Mesoamerica at the time. Clark (2007) has recently laid out the most detailed argument to date as to why San Lorenzo should be considered a state and counters Spencer and Redmond's (2004) argument that it was not. However, both Clark (1996: 196, 2007) and Spencer and Redmond (2004: 174) conflate the archaeological identification of states and empires.[8] Whereas empires are by definition states, the opposite is not necessarily true, and San Lorenzo could have been some form of archaic state but not an empire. As far as this last statement is true, evidence for San Lorenzo being a state will not help differentiate between the EEM and the AAM. Instead, evidence of an empire is only to be had from a purported colony such as in the Soconusco.

Clark (1997: 228) has proposed that Gulf Coast intervention in the Soconusco resulted in "All the formerly independent simple chiefdoms [being] consolidated into one complex chiefdom directed from a new regional center established in the middle of the region..." This could be because imperial rule frequently results in a reorganization of colonized territories "... in order to better control them, to lessen chances of revolt, or to achieve particular economic ends" (Smith and Montiel 2001: 249).

For Stark (1990: 257), territorial empires that directly administer their colonies (e.g., the Romans or Inca) are expected to reorganize the local settlement system. In contrast, hegemonic empires such as the Aztec, which indirectly administer their colonies, are expected to replace and/or co-opt local elites. Therefore, the co-option of an existing regime would result in traditional locations of power being maintained by the conquerors (Stark 1990: 258) and if San Lorenzo is interpreted as a hegemonic empire then no dramatic change in the local power structure would be expected. Alternatively, if San Lorenzo were a territorial empire then a reorganization of the local power structure instituted by the colonial power might be expected. The EEM might also predict changes in local settlement systems due to the expectation that competing elites who were more focused on distant exchange partners would have an advantage over those who were more committed to local strategies of prestige acquisition.

LOCAL ECONOMY

The level of local agricultural and craft production are expected to have increased to meet tribute demands after colonial administration was established (Smith 1987; Stark 1990: 257). Agricultural intensification could result in evidence of terracing or irrigation, and craft production could have been intensified (Smith and Montiel 2001: 249). Feasting might have been reduced as new colonizers imposed their will through violence (or the threat of violence) and enforced a higher level of social or political differentiation than the local population was used to. In general, colonization should result in a lowering of the local standard of living (Smith 1987; Smith and Montiel 2001). A lowered standard of living would have been the case for both elites and commoners as "... the net effect of prolonged imperial rule would have been to undermine local leadership economically by eroding its base in labor and other assets without effectively entraining local elites in the central system of wealth and prestige . . . " (Stark 1990: 259).

New technology could be expected to spread and convey new symbolism. However, the distribution of such objects might have been found in a more discrete pattern if they arrived with, and were used primarily by, local representatives of colonial masters (Stark 1990: 258). Clark and Pye (2000: 234) posit that differentially fired white-rimmed black wares were imitated during the Cherla phase using local technology and that the correct technical knowledge did not arrive in the Soconusco until the following Cuadros phase. Furthermore, during the Cuadros phase "all serving wares had been transformed from red wares to black and white wares. Olmec dragon designs were carved or painted on pots, and storage and cooking vessels had gone from thin tecomates to thick, brushed tecomates" (Clark and Pye 2000: 234).

REPRESENTATIONAL SYSTEM

Iconographic discontinuity from earlier and later periods would be expected for the duration of imperial occupation. Foreign symbols (preserved as distinct iconography or artifacts, clothing, etc.) can be expected to have been brought with conquerors, and so, to have arrived rapidly and been maintained for the duration of the time that the occupying forces resided in an area. Specifically, Clark (1997: 223) argues that Gulf Coast kings were being depicted as ballplayers or warriors (rather than shamans or gods); these depictions evoke their physical prowess and a greater role of coercion being reflected symbolically. Generally, an "imperial ideology" would be expected that involved explicit reference to militarism and violence as well as glorification of kings or the state as one of the clearest indicators of an empire (Smith and Montiel 2001: 248). Although violence and warfare exist in almost all societies, their use as part of an imperial ideology is usually materialized in public art and elite objects (Marcus 1983; Spencer 1982). The only way that relatively small invading armies can maintain control is through terror – this is as true from cases as disparate as Late Formative Oaxaca (Spencer and Redmond 1997: 24) to the Roman conquest of Europe and North Africa and a similar attempt by the Nazi empire two millennia later (Luttwak 2007). The protracted implementation of terror by invading colonial armies should leave some traces in their art, sculpture or other objects used in public ritual.

Imperial symbols would have been concentrated in the newly formed colonial capitals or administrative outposts. The range of Olmec motifs would be expected to have been roughly the same on the Gulf Coast and in the Soconusco as the canonical use of such symbols would indicate that the new Mazatán polity of Cantón Corralito was directed from San Lorenzo (Clark 1997: 229). In the case of ceramics, two traditions might be expected to coexist with utilitarian, domestic wares changing very little and maintaining indigenous norms whereas elite wares suddenly changing after the area was invaded. There also would have been distinct spatial limits of the use of such elite ceramics (or other foreign objects) at the edge of the region under direct control of colonial forces. Distinct foreign objects and imagery are expected to have arrived rapidly and been used in public ritual, whereas indigenous rituals carried out in private contexts would have maintained traditional local symbolism (Stark 1990: 249). Consumption of foreign goods beyond the new colonial outpost would be expected to have been dramatically lower (Clark 1997: 228).

FOREIGN ECONOMY

Exchange levels could be expected to have increased dramatically with the establishment of a colonial regime as the acquisition of goods was the reason the region was invaded in the first place. Warfare and plunder can be a part of any form of inter-regional interaction, but colonization is distinct as subjugated territory is maintained and administered from the distant imperial center. The economic relationship should be extractive, and goods are expected to have flowed out of the Soconusco and into the Gulf Coast. Both territorial and hegemonic empires build storage or transshipment facilities to help in the extraction of resources from their colonies (Stark 1990). The lack of evidence of such facilities due to the vagaries of preservation and limited quantities or excavation is not convincing evidence against colonization, but their presence would certainly add strength to documenting a colony.

Horizon II: Hypothesis 1 (PPM) expectations

SETTLEMENT/POLITICAL ORGANIZATION

Local settlement patterns, and the political fortunes of the elite at centers in any given region, should be the result of local processes and not show temporal correspondence to events occurring on the Gulf Coast. Local settlement patterns and political organization would not have been affected by collapse on the Gulf Coast if San Lorenzo was no more important to local political organization than "a sack of sawdust" (Marcus 1989: 194).

LOCAL ECONOMY

There is no reason to expect any significant changes to have corresponded with the collapse of San Lorenzo if this polity had not occupied a defining role in the Horizon I inter-regional system as either a colonial master or a core polity the elite of which were emulated.

REPRESENTATIONAL SYSTEM

Stylistic changes between Horizon I and Horizon II are explained as being the result of local changes resulting in increased social stratification. Marcus (1989: 196) proposes that, after Horizon I in the Valley of Oaxaca, the:

> . . . explanation for the disappearance of "Olmec" motifs, therefore, would have nothing to do with diffusion or the collapse of the Olmec. I suggest that the San Jose phase "sky" and "earth" motifs were referents to large, valley-wide descent lines that had existed since egalitarian times and did not carry information on ranking. Their Early Formative medium for representation had to be abandoned when Oaxaca society went through an escalation of ranking in which the elite came to be identified with sky (lightning) while low status people were not. Once the evolution to stratification had begun, "lightning" could reemerge as a more naturalistic depiction of a supernatural associated with the ruling class.

Therefore, Marcus argues that increased rank distinctions during Horizons II and III resulted in more naturalistic iconographic standards compared with the more abstract iconography of Horizon I. The situation in other areas of Mesoamerica could have been different, but this model predicts that local factors will explain changes (if any) after the dissolution of the San Lorenzo polity.

FOREIGN ECONOMY

Trade is not expected to have been significantly affected at this time as San Lorenzo was simply one among many exchange partners. The collapse of the San Lorenzo polity would not have affected inter-regional exchange patterns any more than the collapse of any of the other island of complexity in Mesoamerica at the time.

Horizon II: Hypothesis 2 (EEM) expectations

SETTLEMENT/POLITICAL ORGANIZATION

Local political organization (and possibly settlement location) is expected to have been disrupted as local elites had to redefine their legitimizing ideology or be replaced by other elites. Those centers whose elites had relied on their relationship with the San Lorenzo elite to bolster local power and prestige would be likely to have collapsed, and those who could find alternative sources of power would be likely to increase their local political position.

LOCAL ECONOMY

As with the PPM, no change is expected to the overall standard of living of local residents after the collapse of San Lorenzo. Feasting might be expected to intensify as local hierarchy was redefined after the foreign source of prestige disappeared. The surviving elites would have had to work harder and/or change the basis of the local prestige system to make up for the disappearance of the traditional external sources of status. A reinvented structure of status generation could have been based on new forms of local craft products. Local elites also could have cultivated new foreign exchange partners. However, for this latter possibility to have been effective, the new exchange partners would have had to be (or at least be perceived) as desirable as those at San Lorenzo had been.

REPRESENTATIONAL SYSTEM

The collapse of San Lorenzo at the end of Horizon I might be expected to leave a local elite in the Soconusco without its primary exchange partner as well as source of cultural inspiration and esoteric knowledge. Such a disruption in exchange patterns could have resulted in a recombination of Olmec iconography in new and creative ways as local elites redefine and manipulate the iconography they have inherited from their predecessors. In contrast to Marcus's proposal for the PPM quoted earlier in this chapter, the range of Olmec iconography could be expected to have expanded at this time as there was no longer a source of distant authority maintaining ideological canons and their artistic depiction. Remember that Olmec is employed to describe an artistic style that persisted through Horizons I, II and III.

FOREIGN ECONOMY

A lack of San Lorenzo as a source of prestige goods would be expected to result in a reorientation of exchange activities. The need of local elites for foreign goods (and valued knowledge) would have remained high, so they would have been motivated to establish new exchange networks. This might have resulted in imported goods arriving from a wider range of areas and Soconusco goods to have been found in greater quantities in other areas than had previously been the case. Increased exchange between various islands of complexity immediately following the collapse of San Lorenzo is a distinct expectation of the EEM as demand for exotic goods remained high (in contrast to expectations of the AAM) when the most important exchange partner and source of esoteric knowledge was removed (in contrast to the PPM). This scenario is comparable to the Cuna example (Helms 1979) if the Ecuadorian elite were suddenly removed from the equation.

Horizon II: Hypothesis 3 (AAM) expectations

SETTLEMENT/POLITICAL ORGANIZATION

The political system at San Lorenzo and administrative colonial capital in the Soconusco would all be expected to have collapsed. If foreign political rulers – Clark's (1997: 223) "contingent of elite and bodyguards" dispatched by the king of San Lorenzo to govern the Soconusco – were removed from the local system, then less political centralization would be expected compared to that which had existed before (similar to, e.g., Europe after the fall of the Roman Empire). In the scenario described at the end of Chapter 2 by Wells (1992, 1999), areas under the control of Rome collapsed whereas more distant lands not under direct colonial control continued as they had before.

LOCAL ECONOMY

If the standard of living of the inhabitants of the Soconusco had fallen during the period of colonization due to tribute burdens, the situation is expected to have rebounded after Gulf Coast tribute was no longer being extracted from the region. Storage facility and transshipment facilities, if they had ever existed, would no longer have been necessary. Public ritual would be expected to have changed as

Table 3.3. Summary of expectations for three models of inter-regional interaction

Initial Ceramic Period	PPM	EEM	AAM
Settlement/Political Organization	Level of political complexity is similar in numerous regions of Mesoamerica.	Islands of complexity with the most developed polities are those that will interact most intensively during Horizon I.	Local political organization does not predict Horizon I interaction; proximity to desired resources does.
Local Economy	Not specified	Larger centers with more public rituals and prestige goods are those that will interact most intensively during Horizon I.	Local economic organization does not predict Horizon I interaction; proximity to desired resources does.
Representational System	Shared ideology that Olmec imagery is part of is found across many areas of Mesoamerica.	Local distinct traditions and Olmec imagery develop exclusively on the Gulf Coast.	Local distinct traditions and Olmec imagery develop exclusively on the Gulf Coast.
Foreign Economy	Exchange occurred at high enough levels to maintain internal cohesion within two interaction spheres.	Exchange occurred at high enough levels to maintain internal cohesion within two interaction spheres. Islands of complexity share more with each other than with immediate surrounding areas.	Increased quantities of goods flow into the Gulf Coast by the end of this period. Regions invaded are not predicted by degree of local development.

Horizon I	PPM	EEM	AAM
Settlement/Political Organization	Any changes should be explainable in terms of local developments.	Local elite are those people most able to associate themselves with distant exchange partners, and political centers are located on transportation arteries.	*Hegemonic*: local elite co-opted and their existing capital is used to administer colony *Territorial*: colonial elite installed to administer colony and location of local capital changed to break ties with previous regime.
Local Economy	No change to local economy specified but any technological development is expected to spread to all areas in each interaction sphere.	Overall, little change to the local subsistence economy but increase in production of prestige items for local use is to be expected.	Local production significantly increased to supply San Lorenzo's tribute demands; excessive tribute demands could lower local standard of living.

Horizon I	PPM	EEM	AAM
Representational System	Long-standing pan-Mesoamerican ideas materialized for the first time using nonperishable media (e.g., ceramics) by all members of society.	New foreign imagery employed by local elite to demonstrate their ties to distant power; foreign styles adopted, rapidly copied locally and used by all members of society.	Imperial ideology represents violence and is limited to elite and public contexts in colonies. Traditional symbolism is maintained in private and domestic contexts. This expectation differs from both the PPM and EEM.
Foreign Economy	Two interaction spheres continue from earlier times; no core area of pan-regional exchange.	Elite items were exchanged with greater frequency overall. More symbolically charged items would have left the Gulf Coast and more raw materials would have arrived there. Gulf Coast was the core area in the pan-regional exchange system.	In colonized regions, few foreign objects or those employing colonial symbolism were found outside of colonial outposts. Gulf Coast was the core area of pan-regional exchange system with the power to impose its interests above those of local elites.

Horizon II	PPM	EEM	AAM
Settlement/Political Organization	Local affairs were not impacted by events on the Gulf Coast. Changes must be explained locally.	Significant reorganization as those elites that employed ties with San Lorenzo to bolster local standing no longer had this source of prestige.	Significant reorganization as colonial regime is withdrawn and tribute demands removed.
Local Economy	Change should not necessarily occur at this time and must be explained in terms of local developments.	Increase in feasting and other means of creating local cohesion such as new forms of craft production and/or the establishment of new exchange partners.	Increased local prosperity results from the end of tribute demands.
Representational System	Any temporal correspondence in changes at this time is coincidental.	Reinvention of Olmec iconography due to lack of San Lorenzo as the center of ideology.	Either a resurgence of precolonial aesthetic or reconstitution of imagery in a secondary state context.
Foreign Economy	Not affected by the collapse of San Lorenzo; no reason to expect changes in inter-regional exchange patterns to occur at this time.	Increase in the number of exchange partners to fill the void left by the collapse of the San Lorenzo polity.	Exports decrease as tribute is no longer extracted by foreign masters (think of Mediterranean Europe after the fall of Rome).

foreign masters were no longer there to enforce colonial standards and rituals.

REPRESENTATIONAL SYSTEM

If imperial masters were removed from the system, then certain "folk traditions" and symbols might be expected to have been revived. Indigenous rituals using symbols from an earlier epoch (i.e., the Initial Ceramic Period) that had been practiced only in private during Horizon I could reemerge to be practiced in public contexts after the colonial masters had withdrawn or been driven out. Alternatively, foreign customs could have been maintained by surviving local elites and adapted to local conditions (e.g., India after British rule or Algeria after the French withdrawal). Postcolonial ideology can be conceived of as a secondary state situation where ideas and imagery of past hierarchy persist even if the political organization no longer does. Therefore, iconographic recombination and elaboration could be expected in a similar manner as described for the EEM earlier in text.

FOREIGN ECONOMY

The level of inter-regional exchange is expected to have dropped significantly if the San Lorenzo tribute demands were a driving force in increasing the Soconusco production and acquisition of goods. The local economy would have been focused on providing basic utilitarian goods in higher relative proportions than before. It might have taken some time in the postcolonial era to develop new exchange relationships with peoples in areas that were not previously in direct contact.

Summary

A number of arguments and expectations from each of the three models during each of the three epochs have been presented. Many of the expectations presented here could be expanded and explored in more detail. Also, other models could be evaluated. This is an initial step in laying out competing hypotheses; the basic differences between each are summarized in Table 3.3.

CREATING MUTUALLY EXCLUSIVE HYPOTHESES

As mentioned previously, I have chosen the most polemical authors who have published on Horizon I inter-regional interaction with the intention of producing three distinct models that can more easily be differentiated. Furthermore, I have cited some of their most controversial claims. However, in their quieter moments, most of the authors cited in this chapter do allow for less extreme positions. Diehl and Coe (1995: 23–24) state that, during Horizon I, a Gulf Coast "... military conquest and mass religious proselytization can be ruled out ... " and that "... Olmec leaders or merchants may have forced these changes on Mokaya chiefs or ... the Olmec did not actively encourage the changes, but instead local leaders were inspired by Olmec examples." This latter option is fully consistent with the EEM rather than the AAM. For his part, despite the strong AAM opinions quoted, Clark and Pye (2000: 244) have described Flannery's 1968 EEM as "One of the more plausible explanations of the social dynamics of the time." Blake et al. (1995: 177), citing Flannery's 1968 article, state that they " .. think of the Cuadros phase as the culmination of a long trend of local adoption, emulation, and importation of elite styles and goods found in many regions of Mesoamerica, rather than as a product of Olmec intrusion." Clark (1997: 228) has referred to the Cantón Corralito polity as a complex chiefdom and more recently acknowledged a lack of compelling evidence that the elite of San Lorenzo carried out an aggressive takeover of the Mazatán area (Clark 2007: 23).

For their part, Flannery and Marcus (2000: 2) state that "We would not describe the Olmec as 'no more advanced' or 'contributing little.' Their contribution has simply been exaggerated ... " They clearly state that the inhabitants of the Gulf Coast were more politically complex than the inhabitants of neighboring regions when labeling them, following Goldman (1970), as a " ... paramount chiefdom ... in a landscape of traditional and open chiefdoms" (Flannery and Marcus 2000: 2). This statement could be read as withdrawing from their earlier rejection (Flannery and Marcus 1994: 389) of Flannery's 1968 EEM model. This return to the 1968 position is further suggested by the description of San Lorenzo's political complexity as being comparable to that of Tonga or Hawaii (Flannery and Marcus 2000: 5) and stating that as such they " ... look impressive relative to their contemporaries" (Flannery and Marcus 2000: 6). This quote seems consistent with Flannery's (1968: 75) original formulation of the EEM to describe Gulf Coast–Oaxaca relations during Horizon I. However, given their most recent article (Flannery et al. 2005), such a conciliatory turn seems less likely. For his part, Demarest states that

"Given the impressive development at San Lorenzo at this time and the wide scattering of Olmec motifs in Chiapas, it is probable that Olmec heartland contact was an important factor during this period . . . [however] . . . evidence does not demonstrate Olmec political control or colonization" (Demarest 1989: 308). Demarest's position is therefore consistent with the EEM and only rejects the AAM (also see Demarest 2004: 65–66).

The authors cited all leave open the possibility of more consensus than is first apparent in their more polemical passages. However, the reason for defining the three models in as distinct terms as possible is to allow data to be more easily evaluated. To be upfront about my position (and not hide behind a false pretense of deductive objectivity), I favor the EEM as the best explanation of our current knowledge of the Soconusco data. As outlined in Chapter 2, I propose that a number of islands of complexity developed during the course of the second millennium BCE and that elites from these areas exchanged goods and ideas. Gulf Coast society around San Lorenzo formed the most developed of these islands during the second part of the Early Formative period that I term Horizon I. The AAM may turn out to have some truth in the Soconusco (if nowhere else!) during the Cuadros phase, but this has not been convincingly demonstrated yet, as even its most vocal proponent concedes. The PPM, however, is simply not a tenable way to interpret the Soconusco data.

In the next four chapters, I present data from the Cuauhtémoc zone of the Soconusco but hold off formally evaluating the three hypotheses until Chapter 8. The lack of reference to these models in Chapters 4 through 7 is done primarily to leave open the interpretation of what is an admittedly small amount of fragmentary evidence from a site that was never more than a local center.

NOTES

1. Flannery and Marcus (2000: 12–14) reject the distribution of ceramics from this period as a single horizon and claim that the two ceramic spheres of the Initial Ceramic Period continue into Horizon I. However, my use of the horizon concept seems justified as an approximate definition of the limits of inter-regional interaction at the time, first of all, because of the distribution of white-rimmed black ware dishes employed at this time as well as distinct closed-eye, open-mouth, jowly figurines with oval heads and certain abstract (aka Olmec) symbols found across the entire region at this time. Second, these stylistic traits have both northern and southern limits during the second part of the Early Formative period that have basically defined the extents of Mesoamerica ever since. For example,

two Cuadros phase, Guamuchal brushed utilitarian storage jar fragments from the Soconusco had been reported from San Jose Mogote, which indicates to me that the intensity of interaction justifies the horizon label (see Flannery and Marcus 1994: Figure 12.161). However, if we restrict the geographic extents of Horizon I to the lowland Isthmian zone and use it solely to explore Gulf Coast–Soconusco interaction, none of my following arguments need be altered; the size of the interaction sphere would then simply be smaller.

2. This style is composed of a limited set of readily identifiable motifs that form a coherent subject matter that can be expressed at various levels of abstraction (Lesure 2004: 74–75). Technically Olmec stone carving "often contains forms which recall line engravings on close-grained wood, and ribbed planes of relief as in wood-carvings" (Kubler 1990: 121). Examples from the Soconusco are presented in Chapter 6, and the Olmec style is discussed in more detail there.

3. Based on my analysis of the Cuauhtémoc ceramics, there are closer stylistic and technological ties between the Cuadros and Jocotal phases than between the Jocotal and Conchas phases. Clark and Pye (2000: 241) state that "The designs on Jocotal ceramics have always been identified as Olmec and doubtlessly will continue to be so in the future. But it is important to stress that they are not Olmec in the same sense as their predecessors . . . " They also note that " . . . the Jocotal complex was a clear derivative of the preceding complex of strong Olmec presence and influence" (Clark and Pye 2000: 241). In the quotes above, the term Olmec refers to a people or an ethnicity, so "Olmec presence and influence" means direct contact with inhabitants of San Lorenzo. My use of Olmec in this book solely as a style allows us to separate the identification of Olmec traits from any implication as to the form of inter-regional interaction. Clark and Pye (2000: 218–219) acknowledge this distinction and agree that an Olmec style can be identified from the Cherla through Duende phases (i.e., 1100–700 BCE uncalibrated), which corresponds to my Horizon I and II. Therefore, Clark and Pye would not appear to dispute my identification of the Cherla, Cuadros, Jocotal (and Conchas) phases as sharing an Olmec decorative style.

   The Manantial phase from the Basin of Mexico is problematic to use as the basis for defining a horizon style, as Clark and Pye (2000) do. The incised designs on the base of Manantial phase grater bowls at Tlapacoya (e.g., Niederberger 1987: 569–590) as well as the double-line-break motif around the interior of white wares (e.g., Niederberger 1987: 568) certainly seem more similar to Conchas-phase decorations than to that used during the Jocotal phase in the Soconusco. However, that such double-line-break motifs are found on white-rimmed black ware dishes (Niederberger 1987: 633) is not consistent with most regions. In the Soconusco, such differentially fired decorative techniques are limited to ceramic vessels from the Cherla, Cuadros, and Jocotal phases and are one of the criteria used to define Horizon I. Some Manantial-phase figurines from Tlapacoya (Niederberger 1987) resemble those from the Jocotal phase in the Soconusco. In contrast, few such late Early Formative figurines are known from the Gulf Coast (but see references in Clark 2007: 24). Nacaste figurines (Coe and Diehl 1980: 277) are definitely similar to those of the

Conchas phase, and neither resemble the Manantial or Jocotal phase figurines. It is, however, important to remember that figurines were used as grave goods in the Basin of Mexico which is incongruous with the rest of Mesoamerica at this time (Blomster 1998; Coe and Diehl 1980b: 260; Cyphers 1988, 1993: 217; Hammond 1989b: 111; Lesure 1997a; Marcus 1996: 286, 1998). As Basin of Mexico figurines filled a unique functional role it is probably not a good idea to employ them as a horizon marker, especially as Tolstoy (1989b: 102, 105; Tolstoy et al. 1977: 98) also notes differences between burial and domestic ceramic vessel assemblages at Tlatilco. Furthermore, it is at least possible that Soconusco figurine styles were copied by the residents of the Basin of Mexico rather than vice versa. This would make sense if the Ayotla-Manantial transition is dated too early. If this phase limit were nudged forward a century or so, it would then line up with my Horizon I–Horizon II transition (see Table 3.1). Unfortunately, the radiocarbon dates used to define the Manantial phase are of little help to distinguish it from the previous or subsequent phase due to their expansive error ranges (Tolstoy 1989b: Figure 12.2). Trying to line up the Manantial phase with the Jocotal and Conchas phases in the Soconusco and with the San Lorenzo B and Nacaste phases at San Lorenzo highlights problems with using stylistic cross-dating between regions with finer and coarser chronologies. If the Manantial phase could be divided into an earlier and a later component, then the former might fit more comfortably within Horizon I and the latter within Horizon II. Later, in Note 6 of this chapter, I discuss a similar problem of the coarse-grained sequence in the Valley of Oaxaca chronology also blurring this temporal divide.

4. Basic storage, cooking, and serving wares show clear continuity from the Cuadros to the Jocotal phase and marked contrast with the following Conchas-phase assemblage. Following Coe and Flannery's (1967) definition of the Cuadros and Jocotal phases, I employ the similarities of tecomates and flat-bottom serving dishes between these two phases as the primary reason to link these phases based on ceramic wares. Acknowledging the commonality of Cuadros and Jocotal tecomates, Clark and Cheetham (2005) have combined the Suchiate Brushed and Guamuchal Brushed ceramic types that Coe and Flannery (1967) used to distinguish between the plain tecomates produced during the Cuadros and Jocotal phases. In contrast, Conchas-phase Alamo Red tecomates (Love 2002a: 119–120) are markedly different and could never be lumped with the preceding periods. Flat-bottomed, outcurving-walled serving vessels also show clear similarities during the Cuadros and Jocotal phases, especially the white-rimmed black wares – called Pampas Black and White in both phases. No such differentially fired vessels were used during the Conchas phase when the principle serving vessels were monochrome black or white wares and red-on-white Meléndrez wares (Love 2002a: 89–118 and see Chapter 6). Based on the least fancy and most abundant ceramics, the Cuadros and Jocotal phase assemblages are much more closely related to each other than either is to the Conchas phase. Working (as I do) in a region of the Soconusco where the Jocotal- and Conchas-phase remains are the most abundant of any in the Early or Middle Formative

periods, there is never a problem distinguishing between the two ceramic assemblages. This is equally the case when dealing with ceramics from excavated contexts or from the much more eroded surface finds. In contrast, when dealing with remains from the southeast end of the Soconusco (i.e., distant from the Mazatán area where the finest Cuadros-phase serving wares are found), the Cuadros and Jocotal can be more difficult to differentiate. I have repeatedly examined the collections from Salinas la Blanca held at Yale's Peabody Museum in the course of my field work and analysis of remains from Cuauhtémoc, and it is clear that the Cuadros phase is defined in this area without the spectacular pottery of the sort found at Cantón Corralito (Cheetham 2007).

5. Post-slip incision (including the double-line-break motif) does occur during the Jocotal phase, so the simple presence or absence of this trait cannot be used to define Horizon II. However, the occurrence of both post-slip incision and the double-line-break motif are present in relatively low proportions during the Jocotal phase, and this changed dramatically during the Conchas phase when it was ubiquitous. Furthermore, the Jocotal-phase double-line-break motif, when it does occur, is most often found on Xquic Red dishes.

6. Flannery and Marcus (1994: 377–382; 2000: 24–25) include their post-slip incised double-line-break motif ceramic types with the San Jose phase which combines Horizon I and the beginning of Horizon II. I suspect that the ceramics with double-line-break motifs are primarily from the very end of their 300-year-long phase. The same is the case with a Cesto White grater bowl that they report (Flannery and Marcus 1994: Figure 12.160). The very end of this phase and the following 50-year-long Guadalupe phase (that they have so far only identified in the Etla arm of the valley) together correspond to my Horizon II. In fact, four dates are attributed to San Jose/Guadalupe transition contexts (see Drennan 1983: 364), so they may have stratigraphic evidence of Horizon II as well. This is an example of the sort of problem that can arise when areas with coarser phase division, like the Valley of Oaxaca, are compared with regions like the Soconusco that have more finely divided phases. Flannery (1968: 70) originally defined the most typical Guadalupe phase type as the Atoyac Yellow White flat-bottomed bowls with slanting walls and double-line-break motif (Marcus 1989: 194; and see Demarest 1989: 322). White ware dishes with outflaring walls and the double-line-break motif are the most distinctive ceramic indicator of Horizon II.

7. My use of the term peer polity is simply descriptive and not a reference to Renfrew's (1986a) much cited model. Although it shares some characteristics, Renfrew's model is more apt for interacting city states as the examples of the Greek and Classic period Maya demonstrate (Renfrew and Cherry 1986).

8. Here I must respectfully disagree with scholars who conflate states and empires and use evidence of the former as proof of the latter (e.g., Clark 1996: note 4, 2007; Spencer and Redmond 2004: 174). Spencer and Redmond (2004: 175) claim that primary states can be identified archaeologically "according to three diagnostic criteria: (a) the emergence of a four-tier regional settlement-size hierarchy; (b) the appearance of royal palaces

and specialized temples; and (c) the conquest/subjugation of distant territories." Clark (2007: 12–13) reduces the criteria for identifying a state to the four-tier settlement hierarchy and control of distant provinces. I see no reason to assume a priori that all states will be predatory and expansionary – especially not primary states for which we have no ethnographic or historical analogies. Furthermore, an important distinction must be made between hegemonic and territorial empires as each will produce different material patterns (see Smith and Montiel 2001; Stark 1990). In the Valley of Oaxaca, Spencer and Redmond (2003, 2004: 178) propose that there were three states during the Late Monte Albán I period: Monte Albán itself as well as the Tlacolula and Ocotlán–Zimatlán polities. As they claim these latter two polities were secondary states, we can infer that Monte Albán emerged as a primary state during the Early Monte Albán I phase before there is evidence of an empire which can be dated to Late Monte Albán I, if conquering neighbors within a valley constitutes an empire of Monte Albán II – if more distant conquest (e.g., Cuicatlan Cañada) is the criterion. Likewise, although Clark dates the San Lorenzo empire to the San Lorenzo A phase, he proposes that the San Lorenzo polity was organized as a state during the preceding Chicharras phase (Clark 2007: 41). In both cases, evidence of predatory invasion and administration of a distant region is taken as proof of the existence of state-level organization, and then it is assumed that some form of nonimperial state must have preceded the empire. However, the existence of a state-level society has not been independently documented during either the Early Monte Albán I phase in the Valley of Oaxaca or the Chicharras phase at San Lorenzo.

SECTION II

ARCHAEOLOGICAL DATA

4

Settlement Patterns and Architecture

> If the capital city of a world-economy fell, it sent ripples through-
> out the system to the periphery. And it is indeed in these
> marginal regions . . . that one can often best observe what is hap-
> pening.
>
> Braudel 1992: 34

The southeastern half of the Soconusco is approximately 60 km long, 30 to 40 km wide and is framed on all sides by a geographic barrier (Figure 2.1). To the southwest is the Pacific Ocean, to the northeast is the Sierra Madre and to both the northwest and the southeast are two enormous estuary–lagoon systems: La Cantileña and Guamuchal/ Manchón (see Voorhies 2004: 6–13, 20–21). This relatively small area in between has the greatest concentration of fertile land on the Pacific coast of Mexico and Guatemala and today is used to grow many crops including banana, mango, papaya, sesame seed and cacao. The area to the northwest of the Cantileña swamp system contains poor gravelly soils with lower rainfall and thus relatively unproductive agricultural lands (Lowe 1977: 202). In fact, the area between Pijiji-apan and Tonalá was called the *despoblado del Soconusco* in colonial times (Orellana 1995: 11). Today, the area is still sparsely populated and primarily used to graze cattle. To the southeast of the Soconusco, beyond the Guamuchal/Manchón swamp system, the coastal plain becomes wider and the piedmont is further from the ocean. In this region of the Guatemalan coast, estuary swamp systems do not form behind the beaches, and the soils contain so much clay that maize is not grown (Neff et al. 2006c: 299). It is thus not surprising that some of the most significant Early and Middle Formative period developments to have occurred on the Pacific coast of Mesoamerica transpired between these two large swamp systems.

The land between these two swamps is cut by four major rivers that, from north to south, are the Coatán, the Cahuacán, the Suchiate and the Naranjo (see Figure 2.1). These rivers originate on the piedmont and drain the watersheds of the Tacaná and Tajumulco volcanoes. A number of smaller streams originate on the coastal plain and form a series of mangrove swamp systems parallel to the ocean where water flow is insufficient to break through the barrier beaches (see Coe and Flannery 1967; Lowe et al. 1982). These rivers create a dynamic set of microenvironments that have likely changed dramatically since prehistoric times. An example of how dramatic this can be is the 1902 eruption of the Santa Marta volcano that produced enough discharge to raise the nearby Salama river bed (located 30 km southeast of the Guamuchal/Manchón swamp) by 15 m (Love 2002a: 10). The area between the two swamps is the southern half of the Aztec Xoconusco province, which extends northwest to the tribute town of Mapastepec on the San Nicolás river in modern Mexico and extends to the Tilapa river on the Guatemalan side of the border (Voorhies 1989a). In this book, the area between these two swamp systems is the local region within which I discuss the developments in the Cuauhtémoc zone. A basic assumption is that this geographically circumscribed region was the type of island of complexity described in Chapter 2 (and see Rosenswig n.d.).

In the remainder of this chapter, I present the Early and Middle Formative period results from a 28-sq-km survey in the Cuauhtémoc zone. Then, I introduce the Cuauhtémoc site, describe its natural and cultural formation, as well as outline the excavations undertaken there. Finally, I discuss the significance of changing architectural patterns at Cuauhtémoc culminating in the Horizon II novelty of building conical mounds.

EARLY AND MIDDLE FORMATIVE SETTLEMENT PATTERNS IN THE CUAUHTÉMOC ZONE

In 2002, a full coverage, pedestrian survey was undertaken that covered 28 sq km in the Cuauhtémoc zone of the Soconusco[1] (Figure 4.1). This survey produced data with which to document the demographic and political history of the area (Rosenswig 2008). There are many methodological problems associated with interpreting the results of

107

EARLY AND MIDDLE
FORMATIVE
SETTLEMENT
PATTERNS IN THE
CUAUHTÉMOC ZONE

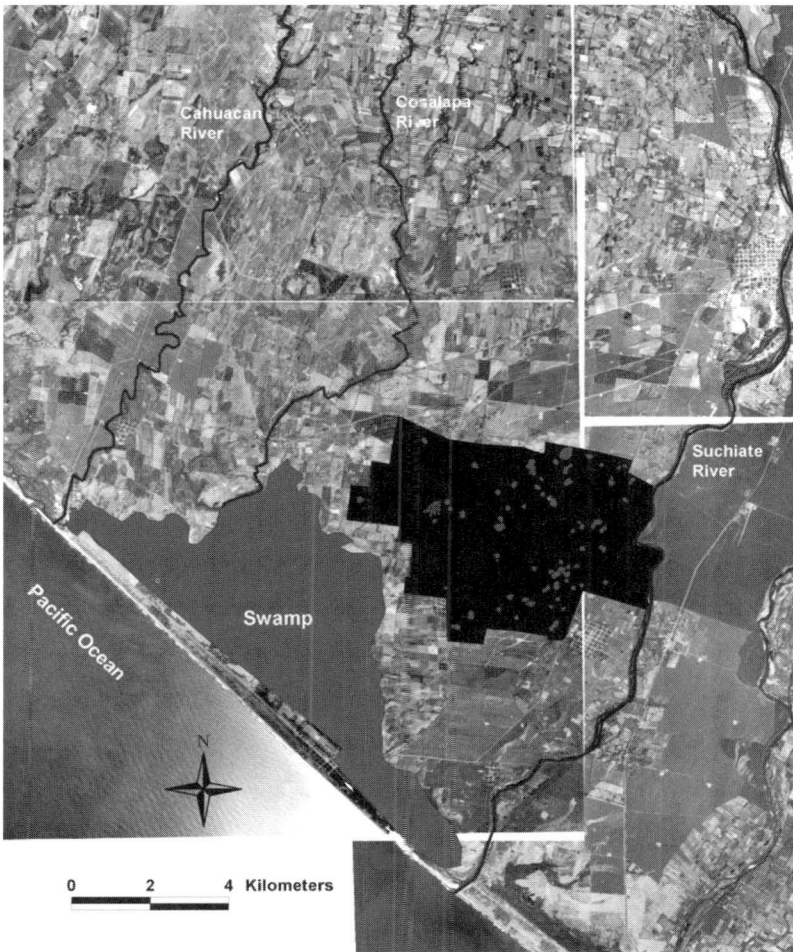

Figure 4.1
Aerial photo of
Cuauhtémoc survey
zone (*black area*) and all
documented sites (*gray
dots*).

surface surveys (e.g., Curet 1998; Dewar 1991; Kintigh 1994; Schacht 1981, 1984). However, the data produced by such studies provide fundamental conclusions on pre-Hispanic Mesoamerican political evolution, agricultural intensification and ecological systems, among other issues (Nichols 1996). The survey results presented below are not interpreted using complex assumptions or mathematical calculations. However, larger sites are interpreted as local centers when there are no comparably sized sites in the vicinity. This interpretation is based on the assumption that when access to productive land (for farming, foraging or a combination of the two) is not a limiting factor due to low population levels, then population is expected to be near resources. In environments of abundant, evenly distributed resources, the concentration of people is explained in cultural terms based on the political organization of the region (see Rosenswig

2000: 422). However, as the Cuauhtémoc survey zone does not encompass a complete political system, my use of these survey data reflects general demographic trends. In the following discussion I review how relative population levels (measured as the number of hectares covered by ceramics attributable to each phase) changed over time.

Survey methods

The Cuauhtémoc survey zone is located between the major Suchiate and Cahuacán rivers, not far from the smaller Cosalapa river (Figure 4.1). Two months of systematic survey were carried out that covered a 28-sq-km area and documented eighty new sites (see Rosenswig 2008 for complete results). Of these, forty-two sites date to the Early and Middle Formative periods and inform the following discussion. During a preliminary field season in 2001, reconnaissance was conducted in three of the environmental zones: swamp, coastal plain and low hills below the piedmont and documented eleven other Early and Middle Formative sites (Rosenswig 2001) to bring the total to fifty-three documented by the Soconusco Formative Project thus far. Sites from many time periods were located in each zone, but on the coastal plain, drainage canals for banana plantations provide a unique opportunity to collect reliable diachronic settlement data from surface deposits. As all areas surveyed in 2002 had been trenched, subsurface materials were spread across the surface and thus provide an exceptionally reliable indicator of subsurface remains (see Ashmore 1984, 1991). Due to these conditions, it is much easier to assume that there is a correspondence between surface and subsurface remains than for most surface surveys (Downum and Brown 1998; Dunnell and Dancey 1983; Simmons 1998; Tolstoy and Fish 1975).

The well-known highland surveys in the valleys of Mexico and Oaxaca began with extensive survey coverage (Blanton et al. 1982; Kowalewski et al. 1989; Sanders et al. 1979). A number of lowland surveys also followed this strategy on the Gulf Coast of Mexico (Santley et al. 1997; Santley and Arnold 1996: 226; Symonds et al. 2002). The main advantage of this approach is that large areas are quickly covered at relatively low cost (Kowalewski 1990). However, the disadvantage of this method is that site boundaries and the extents of temporal occupation of sites are generally determined in the field and are therefore not replicable in a laboratory setting (contra Beck and Jones

1994). In addition, the consistency of results can be biased by survey or familiarity with ceramic types, weather conditions and ground visibility (Cowgill 1990; Orton 2000: 103). I opted for a more intensive approach for the Soconusco Formative Project survey. Although the survey proceeded more slowly, it provides replicable, quantitative data on both the temporal assignments of site components and the artifact density falloff at site limits. An intensive collection strategy assures that the temporal results produced by the fine-grained Soconusco chronology will not be offset by coarse recovery methods (Cowgill 1986; Redman 1987).

109

EARLY AND MIDDLE
FORMATIVE
SETTLEMENT
PATTERNS IN THE
CUAUHTÉMOC ZONE

The Soconusco banana plantations have regularly spaced drainage canals every 100 m and perpendicular ditches every 30 m. Each survey team walked at 15-m intervals to maintain visual contact. Survey teams consisted of five people – and, with a survey intensity of 15 m between participants, coverage can be said to be total for sites larger than 0.1 ha (Orton 2000: 71) with 100% *detectability* of these sites (Shennan 1997: 390–393).

In the trenched environment of the banana plantations, sites are easily recognized by a dramatic increase in surface artifact density. After a site was identified based on the presence of artifacts on the ground surface, collections were taken at 30-m intervals. A stake was driven into the ground and a 3-m rope defined a circular area measuring approximately 28 sq m. All cultural materials from within these areas were collected and machetes were used to cut vegetation and increase visibility when necessary. Next, each stake's location was recorded with a handheld global positioning system (GPS) unit that provided 4- to 6-m error readings. Surface collections were taken beyond the limit of artifact scatters to document the site edges. This method is more economical than documenting all "non-site" areas as advocated by Dunnell (1992; Dunnell and Dancey 1983) and others yet still provides a quantitative basis to determine site limits.

The GPS coordinates of all surface collections were downloaded onto a laptop computer. Temporal designations of ceramic sherds from each collection context were linked to their respective GPS coordinates using ArcView 3.2. The Cuauhtémoc site provides an example of how this methodology works. Figure 4.2 shows the site represented as a series of dots plotted as the GPS coordinates of each collection context stake. Each dot was linked to a table of sherd density values and used to create a polygon with ArcView's Assign Proximity function. This function groups each cell with the closest

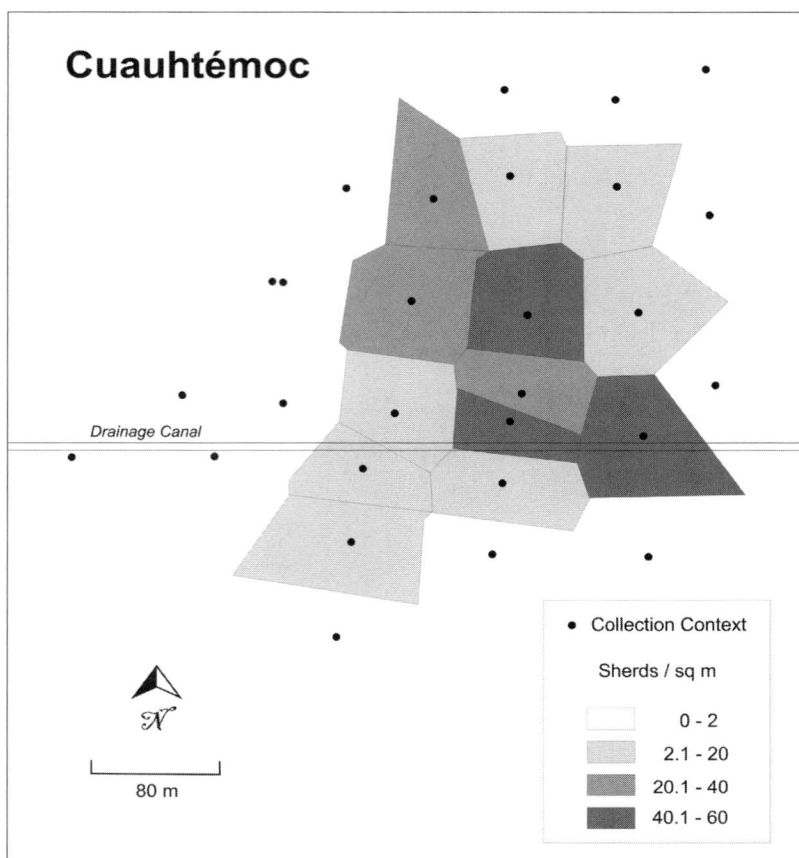

Figure 4.2
The Cuauhtémoc site's
limits as determined on
regional survey.

dot and treats the resulting polygons the same as the data linked to
the dot. Therefore, the collection results from each dog leash area are
projected to represent the entire polygon. Those collection contexts
with fewer than two sherds per square meter were eliminated from
further analysis and represented as white. This methodology provides a consistent and quantitative manner with which to establish
the site's limits.

Figure 4.3 represents the temporal associations of each collection
context's corresponding polygon. In this manner, changing site size is
quantitatively documented as hectares of occupation for each phase.
Based on two seasons of excavations, we know that the polygon
missing in the middle of the site during the Conchas phase is the
result of bulldozer activity scraping away the final phase of occupation. In addition, the three collection contexts in the southeast of the
site contain Jocotal- and Conchas-phase material but do not meet the
two-sherds-per-square-meter cutoff, and so, were eliminated from

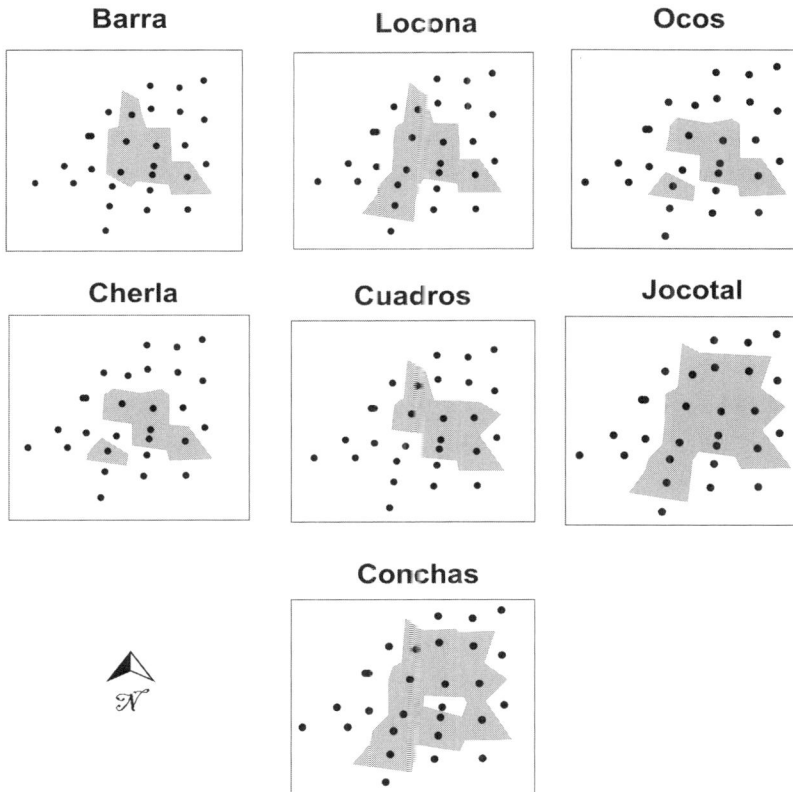

Barra

Locona

Ocos

Cherla

Cuadros

Jocotal

Conchas

Figure 4.3
The Cuauhtémoc site's
occupation by phase as
determined by surface
collection.

further consideration. However, from knowledge gained through excavation, we know that this was an artificially raised area of the site. Sherd density from this construction fill is considerably lower than from habitation and midden deposits, and so fell below the cutoff point (Rosenswig 2008). At the site level, after extensive excavation, these issues can be addressed (e.g., Rosenswig 2009), but it is unrealistic to tackle site-based formation processes at a regional scale based on survey data alone. The recovery method described thus produces survey results that err on the side of being conservative in their estimate of site size.

SURVEY RESULTS

In the tropical environment of the Soconusco, it is often difficult to determine with any degree of confidence whether discrete artifact scatters located near each other should be considered a single site. In an attempt to deal with this issue, Clark (2004: 54) defines "analytical" and "natural" sites and groups the former together when they are located closer than 200 m from each other to define a natural site. An additional aspect of analytic ambiguity is introduced by trying to convert the number of hectares of occupation into the number of people. Although this step is necessary to explore issues such as whether the population surpasses the carrying capacity of available land, this is an unnecessary step if one is simply trying to document general population trends in one region or between regions in *relative* terms. Any universally applied conversion figure used to transform hectares of artifacts to numbers of people will not alter relative patterns. Therefore, for the following discussion I present survey results as the number of hectares per phase. In addition, I do not adjust the number of hectares of occupation by different phase lengths. This lack of adjustment was due to each phase's rough equivalence in length (i.e., 100 to 150 years) as well as the somewhat arbitrary basis required to determine phase limits from radiocarbon dates as discussed in Chapter 3. The resulting hectares reported for each phase correspond to those collected in the fields, as determined by ceramic phase designations (Figure 4.4).

From the beginning of the Initial Ceramic Period, the Cuauhtémoc site forms the greatest part of the occupation in the area, making it the demographic center within the 28-sq-km survey zone. The Locona-phase increase in hectares of occupation is significant at both the Cuauhtémoc site and the surrounding area. This increase could reflect a general rise in population and/or suggest that the site, as a local center, attracted increasing numbers of people to its political orbit. Excavation data from the Cuauhtémoc site support the interpretation that this was a political center based on a concentration of prestige and specialized craft objects – these patterns are presented in the following chapters.

Of the three phases from the Initial Ceramic Period, the most hectares of occupation were documented during the Locona phase, which is consistent with the Mazatán zone where a network of interacting polities established some of the first rank societies in Mesoamerica (Clark 2004; Clark and Blake 1994). Survey evidence coupled with excavation data from the Cuauhtémoc zone indicate that virtually identical material culture was used across the Soconusco (see Chapters 5, 6 and 7) beginning in the Initial Ceramic Period and that subsequent changes occurred in tandem.

During Horizon I, there was a slight decrease in population in Cherla and Cuadros times followed by a marked increase during the Jocotal phase. This pattern is also similar to that observed in the Mazatán survey zone (Clark 1994, 2004). Clark (1997; Clark and Pye 2000) postulates that the center of political activity shifted out of his 50-sq-km Mazatán survey zone during the Cuadros and Jocotal phases to the sites of Cantón Corralito and Ojo de Agua on the Coatán River (Figure 2.1). In the Cuauhtémoc zone in general, and at the Cuauhtémoc site in particular, there was little demographic change between the Ocós-phase occupation at the end of the Initial Ceramic Period and the Cherla and Cuadros phases. Horizon I was the time during which the San Lorenzo site reached its maximal extents (Coe and Diehl 1980b; Symonds et al. 2002). It is significant that the hectares of occupation in both the Mazatán and Cuauhtémoc survey zones increased dramatically only at the end of Horizon I during the Jocotal phase.

In addition to the inland occupation around Cuauhtémoc, I have also documented a Jocotal-phase site (Ponce el Estero Mound 2) on the north side of the Cahuacán River (Rosenswig 2001) along the estuary transportation route described by Navarrete (1978). This site, along with at least seven others, including El Varal and El Mesak, located in the estuary or on rivers leading to the estuary (see Clark and Pye 2000: 236), hint at the importance of this transportation route for travel up and down the Pacific coast. The significance of this settlement focus during the Jocotal phase is discussed at greater length in Chapter 7.

Figure 4.4
Graph of total hectares of occupation for the ten Early and Middle Formative phases.

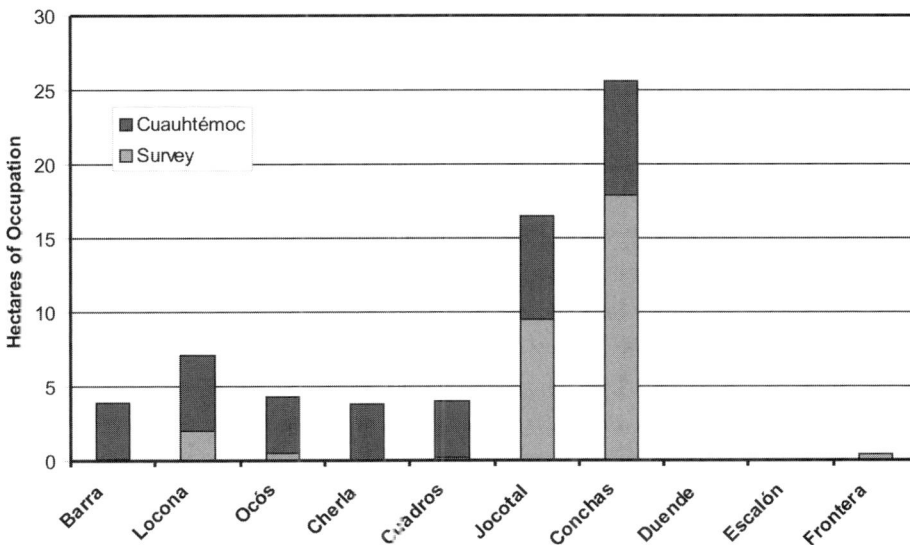

During the Horizon II Conchas phase, population increased yet again in the Cuauhtémoc survey zone. The La Blanca polity was the largest in the Soconusco at this time, and Cuauhtémoc appears to have been a third-tier center incorporated into the La Blanca polity (see Rosenswig 2007). This increase in settlement hierarchy contrasts with the pattern in both the Mazatán (Blake and Clark 1999; Clark 2004) and the Jesús river zones around the site of El Mesak (Pye 1995) where no Conchas-phase sites have been documented despite intensive survey. Clark and Blake (1989; Blake and Clark 1999) interpret this regional pattern as representing a time when virtually all of the inhabitants of the Soconusco were drawn to the political phenomenon at La Blanca (see Love 2002a). The previously dispersed Jocotal-phase settlement system was consolidated into a single highly centralized system that focused population at sites in a much smaller area (see Rosenswig 2007, 2008, 2009). Blake et al. (1995: 180) note that 56 of the 70 Conchas-phase sites known at that time were located in the Naranjo survey zone. Another two dozen Conchas-phase sites are now documented in the Cuauhtémoc zone, between 10 and 15 km from La Blanca. The Cuauhtémoc survey results add more evidence of the population concentration between the Cahuacán and Tilapa rivers during the Conchas phase.

Not a single site was encountered in the 28-sq-km Cuauhtémoc survey zone during the following Duende or Escalón phases. During the Frontera phase, only two small settlements were documented. It was during Horizon III that Izapa began to emerge as a major center on the nearby piedmont (Clark and Pye 2000; Lowe et al. 1982). Therefore, whereas the majority of people in the Soconusco relocated to the Naranjo and Cuauhtémoc zones during the Conchas phase, during the rest of the Middle Formative period a significant quantity of the population appears to have moved onto the piedmont around Izapa. In the Mazatán zone, the site of Huanacastal was occupied at this time (Clark and Pye 2000) as was El Ujuxte (Love 2002b) and Takalik Abaj to the southeast in Guatemala. Although the entire coastal plain was not abandoned, these survey results suggest that some people from the surrounding area were drawn to the emerging Izapa polity during the second half of the Middle Formative period.

Comparisons between Soconusco and San Lorenzo settlements

To make quantitative comparisons with the Mazatán and lower Coatzacoalcos regions, the total number of hectares of occupation from these survey zones was standardized by the 28–sq-km area of the Cuauhtémoc survey zone (see Table 4.1). Furthermore, to compare the Soconusco results with results from the lower Coatzacoalcos survey zone, phases were lumped into their respective epochs. Although it is unfortunate that full advantage cannot be taken of all the Soconusco phases, meaningful comparisons cannot be made as at San Lorenzo the Ojochi and Bajío phases were lumped to form a single Initial Ceramic Period epoch and the Chicharras, San Lorenzo A and San Lorenzo B phases were combined to form one Horizon I epoch (Symonds et al. 2002). To make this comparison as simple as possible, I have used the most extensive Initial Ceramic Period and Horizon I (i.e., Locona and Jocotal) phases from the Soconusco to represent them. The assumption is that if the more subtle phase distinctions were not made then these would be the number of hectares recorded for each of the longer epochs.

During the Locona phase, there were 7.12 ha of occupation in the 28-sq-km Cuauhtémoc survey area. In the 50-sq-km Mazatán survey zone, 589 ha of occupation are reported during the Locona phase. Standardized by my 28-sq-km area, this produces 329.8 ha of occupied area. Compared in this quantitative manner, the Mazatán zone appears to have been much more densely populated than the Cuauhtémoc zone. Although the magnitude of the difference may be exaggerated due to different methods of determining site area, I do not doubt that the Mazatán zone was more densely occupied during the Initial Ceramic Period than was the Cuauhtémoc zone.

The 165 ha of Initial Ceramic Period occupation documented by Symonds et al. (2002: Figure 4.4) in their 400-sq-km survey zone around San Lorenzo was also standardized by my 28-sq-km area surveyed to make meaningful comparisons. When this calculation is done, the results are 11.55 ha of standardized occupation in the lower Coatzacoalcos during the Ojochi/Bajío period. Therefore, in relative terms, the lower Coatzacoalcos zone had one and a half times as many hectares of occupation during Initial Ceramic Period as did the Cuauhtémoc zone during the Locona phase. Clark's Mazatán zone results dwarf both these other results. This finding suggests that the political phenomenon occurring at Paso de la Amada and surrounding sites in the Mazatán zone was not only unique in Mesoamerica at the time but also localized in a single zone of the Soconusco.

During Horizon I, the lower Coatzacoalcos survey zone was considerably more intensively occupied than the Cuauhtémoc area with almost ten times as many hectares of occupation (Table 4.1). This

Table 4.1. Comparison of the Cuauhtémoc, Mazatán (John Clark, personal communication 2004) and San Lorenzo (Symonds et al. 2002: Figure 4.4) survey zones (total hectares of occupation)

	Cuauhtémoc zone (28 sq km)	Mazatán zone (50 sq km)		Lower Coatzacoalcos zone (400 sq km)	
	Hectares	Hectares	Standardized by 28 sq km	Hectares	Standardized by 28 sq km
Initial Ceramic Period	7.12	589	329.8	165	11.55
Horizon I	16.56	650	364	1627	113.89
Horizon II	24.68	0	0	206	14.42

Results are standardized by the Cuauhtémoc survey area of 28 sq km. Note that the 206 ha for the lower Coatzacoalcos zone survey zone in Horizon II includes results from Horizon III.

is not surprising due to the nature of the polity at San Lorenzo. The hectares of occupation documented in the Mazatán survey zone seem high compared to San Lorenzo (given the cultural interpretation from the two areas) and suggest that differences in site recovery may play a significant role in these results. The difference between the two regions is even more dramatic if the results can be assumed to be even higher around the site of Ojo de Agua, the regional capital during the Jocotal phase, than in Clark's survey zone around Paso de la Amada. Soconusco population densities from both the Mazatán and Cuauhtémoc survey zones would be lower if the Cherla- or Cuadros-phase patterns were used. This comparative exercise makes evident the loss of nuance caused by lumping the Soconusco phases into the three epochs.

During Horizon II, there was a dramatic decrease in the hectares of occupied land in both the Mazatán and lower Coatzacoalcos survey zones whereas the Cuauhtémoc zone reached its greatest population density. Located only 15 km from the La Blanca site, these relative population numbers provide a quantitative estimate of the La Blanca polity's demographic explosion during the Conchas phase.

I would be interested to know how many of the 206 ha documented in the lower Coatzacoalcos zone from the Middle Formative period date to the Nacaste period (i.e., Horizon II) and how many are from Palangana times (i.e., Horizon III). Unfortunately, these phases were not differentiated on survey. Therefore, Nacaste-phase occupation of the area likely had an even lower population level than these numbers indicate. The 14.42 ha (see Table 4.1) might be halved to account for the two phases it represents. Regardless, a dramatic demographic collapse is apparent in both the lower Coatzacoalcos and the Mazatán zones during Horizon II.

From 2001 through 2003, excavations were undertaken at the site of Cuauhtémoc (Figure 4.5). The data produced by these excavations complement the survey data presented in the previous section and provide detailed economic, symbolic and trade data with which to evaluate the competing hypotheses presented in Chapter 3. In this section, I introduce the Cuauhtémoc site in terms of its natural and cultural formation. The history of architecture documented at the site is described, and the social function of building conical mounds during the Conchas phase is explored.

At its maximal extents, Cuauhtémoc covered 10 ha (7.68 ha measured on survey) and contained three mounds: one 3 m high, one 5 m high and a third linear platform that measured approximately 100 m by 25 m by 1 m high. The latter two mounds have recently been flattened by heavy machinery when the area was prepared for banana production in 1996. In addition, the site was exposed by 3-m-deep trenches (drainage canals cut for the banana plantation) that are several kilometers long and spaced 100 m apart. Furthermore, every 30 m there is a 1-m-deep drainage canal running perpendicular to

Figure 4.5
The Cuauhtémoc survey zone with all Early and Middle Formative sites indicated.

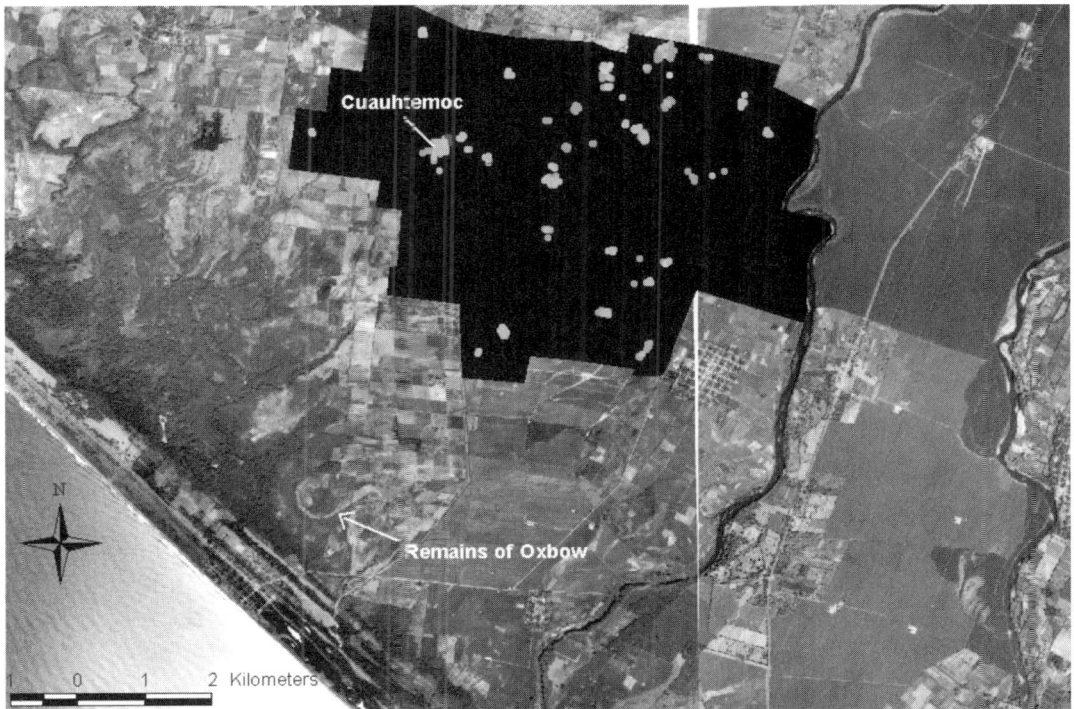

the main trenches (see Figure 4.6). These trenches expose cultural deposits down to the sterile clay substratum and allow this early village to be documented in cross section. Although the damage to the site is unfortunate, it provides a remarkably extensive subsurface view of the cultural deposits. During the 2001 season, the site was systematically surface collected and a 220-m section of the profile shown in Figure 4.6 was mapped. The trench profile revealed a 100-m-long section of Initial Ceramic Period remains flanked by middens descending from the edges of the village that contained superimposed remains from Horizons I and II. During the 2002 and 2003 field seasons, fifty-seven units covering 123.5 sq m were excavated and four additional 50-m-long sections of drainage canals were profiled.

These excavations and profiles have allowed for a detailed reconstruction of the site's formation and growth over time (Figure 4.7). The natural and cultural formation of Cuauhtémoc is outlined in greater detail elsewhere (Rosenswig 2009). The local bedrock is a thick gray clay found 2 to 4 m below the current ground surface. On top of this, an ancient river deposited a large quantity of sand in an area that was up to 100 m wide and more than 300 m long. This

Figure 4.6
The site of Cuauhtémoc looking east along Trench 1, a 3-m-deep drainage canal profiled in 2001.

sand horizon was documented in the 220-m-long profile of Trench 1 and many of the other canals. Furthermore, during the 2003 season, bananas had not yet been planted but all vegetation was removed, which allowed the sand horizon exposed by plowing to be documented through the center of the site.

Above the sterile white sand, a layer of yellow sand contains all of the Barra, Locona and Ocós deposits documented at the site. The existence of both sand layers was documented across much of the site and was likely the reason that this location was initially favored for habitation as it raised the community above the seasonal floods in this alluvial environment (see Blake 1991: 32). This high ground would have been particularly desirable to remain above the flood level during the rainy season. Even today, during the rainy season many of the inhabitants of the area are evacuated for a few months as their houses are under water.

The river that used to run by Cuauhtémoc continued to the swamp, and the ancient oxbow that formed when this river reached the coast is indicated on the aerial photo in Figure 4.5. Such oxbows often form locally when sandbars block rivers from emptying into the ocean. These rivers form a system of inland estuaries and canals that run parallel to the coast (see Navarrete 1978). Similar oxbows can be seen in Figure 4.1 where the Cahuacán and Suchiate rivers are blocked from entering the Pacific Ocean today. Before the Cuauhtémoc site was bulldozed, a seasonal stream flowed along the northwest edge of the site.

Above the sand layer, there is a dark brown layer that has a markedly higher clay content and contains Horizon I and Horizon II materials. The extents of the site expanded during the Jocotal phase, and then the site limits were expanded more significantly during the

Figure 4.7
Stratigraphy at Cuauhtémoc as documented in the north profile of Trench 1. The horizontal axis is exaggerated to make the stratigraphic history of the site more apparent. Actual height of profile is 3 m and actual length is 220 m.

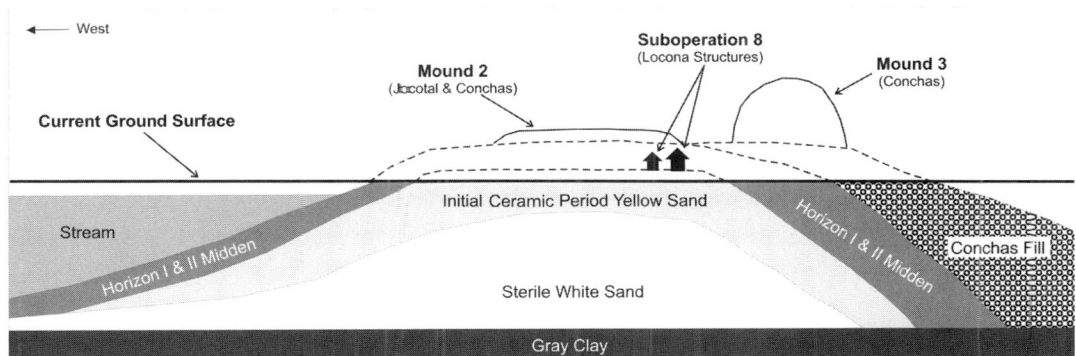

Conchas phase (see Figures 4.3 and 4.7). I describe cultural developments at the site in the following section.

ARCHITECTURAL DEVELOPMENT AT CUAUHTÉMOC

Architecture quite literally encloses human behavior and so creates a built environment within which activities occur at the village and household levels (Lawrence and Low 1990). In Rapoport's (1990) terms, "systems of settings" structure "systems of activities," so architectural form and layout reflect and reinforce cultural norms and values. The construction of impressive architecture can embody political power and reflect unequal social structures (Rapoport 1982, 1988). Smith (2003: 32) has recently defined landscapes in similar terms as "encompassing not only specific places and moments but also the stretches between them: physical, aesthetic, and representational." He then observes that:

In spatial terms, landscapes are not simply built out of a collection of practices but simultaneously constrain the possibilities for practice. By remaining within a given set of spatial parameters, practices reproduce not only the spaces themselves but also the social structures and political regimes that these spaces support (Smith 2003: 72).

The built environment (or built landscape) thus both reflects and determines social and political relationships that can be at the same time maps of the cosmos and "political and propagandistic tools" (Ashmore 1989: 272). Together, the political and cosmological use of architecture creates a "political aesthetic" (*sensu* Smith 2000) with appeal to the population at large. From a diachronic perspective, changes in architectural form therefore can be expected to reflect changing social and political norms (Low 2000: 105–118; Rosenswig and Masson 2002). Changing architectural practices thus provide a productive point of entrance to both physical and political changes that occurred in the past.

At Cuauhtémoc, two Locona-phase structures were documented from post hole patterns and associated features (Figure 4.8). These structures measured approximately 11.5 m by 5 m and 8.5 m by 4 m, respectively. These domestic structures are associated with trash/storage pits, hearths and burials. The structure to the east was more completely documented and contains a hearth next to two central post holes, a pit filled with Locona trash 1 m to the east as well

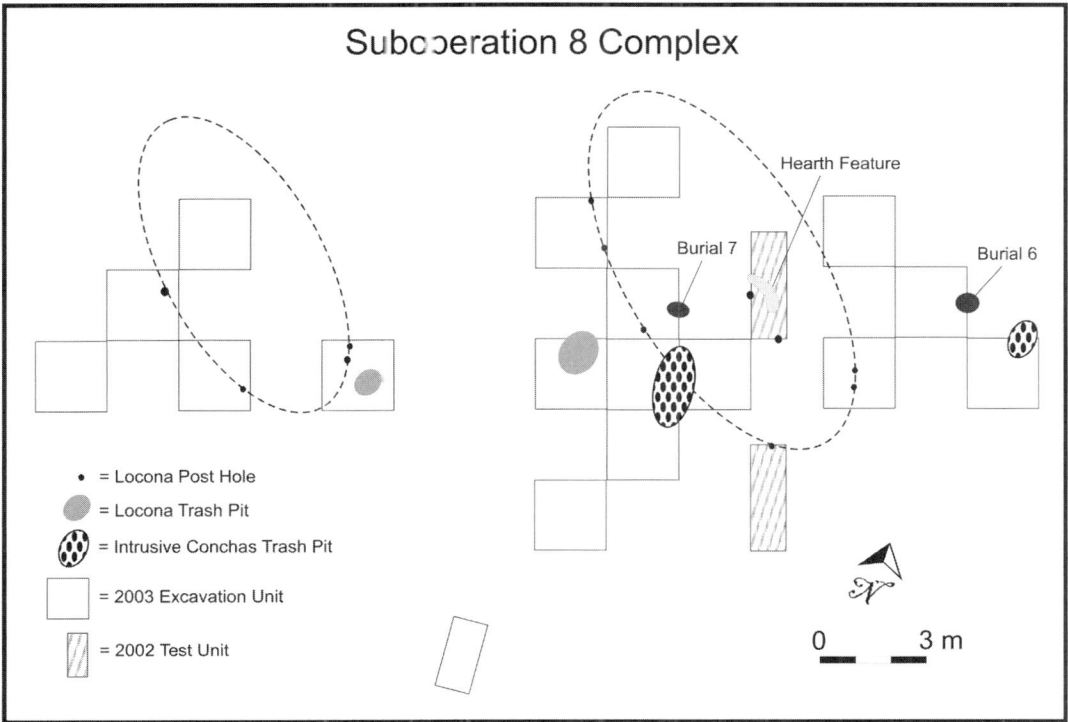

Suboperation 8 Complex

Hearth Feature

Burial 7

Burial 6

• = Locona Post Hole

⬤ = Locona Trash Pit

⬤ = Intrusive Conchas Trash Pit

☐ = 2003 Excavation Unit

⬚ = 2002 Test Unit

0   3 m

as one subfloor burial (see Figure 4.9) and another burial 3 m to the west. Although there certainly could have been a larger structure at Cuauhtémoc during the Initial Ceramic Period, analogous to Mound 6 at Paso de la Amada (Blake 1991), nothing of the sort was encountered during excavations in 2002 and 2003. Due to extensive Horizon

Figure 4.8
Suboperation 8 complex at Cuauhtémoc where two Locona-phase structures were documented

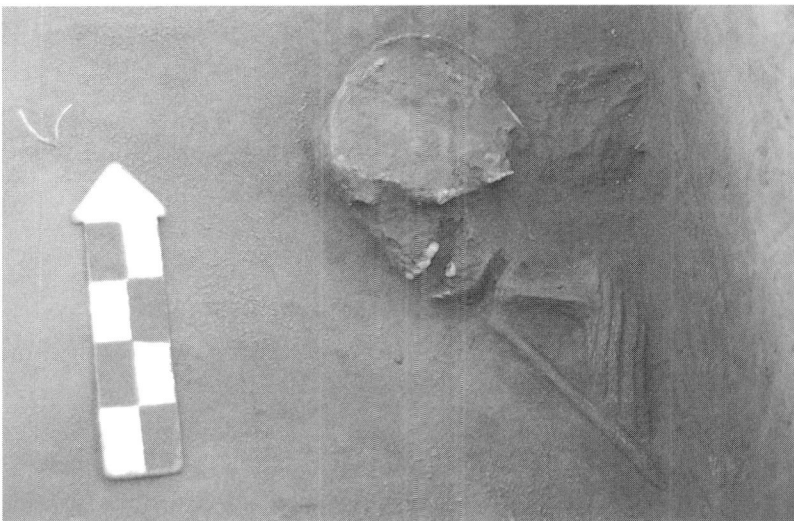

Figure 4.9
Burial #7 from Cuauhtémoc dates to the Locona phase.

I and Horizon II occupation of sites in the Cuauhtémoc zone, Initial Ceramic Period house mounds are not visible on the surface as they are in the Mazatán area. However, despite differences in structure size and the presence of platforms with certain structures at Paso de la Amada (Lesure 1997a, 1999a), artifact patterns are similar from all documented residences (Lesure and Blake 2002). The Initial Ceramic Period artifact patterns documented at Cuauhtémoc are also comparable to those from Paso de la Amada and other Mazatán zone sites.

One of the most significant facts about the two Locona-phase structures at Cuauhtémoc is their orientation. Both structures' long axes align northwest–southeast, which orients their long axis in the same direction as Mound 6 at Paso de la Amada (see Figure 3.1). Measuring a little more than 5 ha in extent during the Locona phase, Cuauhtémoc was a modest center at this time. However, such a correspondence in architectural alignment from both ends of the Soconusco suggests that Initial Ceramic Period architectural orientation was laid out with regard to some shared point of reference. This glimpse of architectural orientation does not provide a sufficiently large view to determine if Cuauhtémoc structures were laid out around plazas as Clark (2004) has recently identified at Paso de la Amada.

The similarity in architectural orientation in both the Mazatán and Cuauhtémoc zones during the Initial Ceramic Period (as well as the demographic patterns just described and similarities in ceramic and figurine iconography described in Chapter 6) demonstrates a tightly knit system of representation and expression across the Soconusco. I argue throughout this book that the degree of material culture similarity from the coastal plain between the Cantileña and Guamuchal/ Manchón swamps indicates that these geographic barriers also acted as cultural boundaries from people further to the northwest and southeast and created an island of cultural complexity.

Evidence from the site of Cuauhtémoc indicates that the precocious developments in the Mazatán zone (Clark and Blake 1994) provide only part of the picture of political evolution occurring in the Soconusco at this time. While more people were living in the Mazatán zone at larger sites, parallel developments were under way in the Cuauhtémoc zone. Villages in these areas may have been linked to each other during marriage or funeral rituals and to have competed with each other in such activities as playing the ballgame (see Hill and Clark 2001). Sponsoring events such as competitive sports along with associated feasts and gambling would have provided the context for competitive and ongoing interaction as described by Mauss (1990) in relation to gift giving (also see Rosenswig 2007). Gifts must be repaid but so too must gambling debts and the loss of village honor if one's team loses. As Hill and Clark (2001: 339) report for the Acaxee of Nayarit, Mexico:

> stakes rose even higher for intercommunity games . . . A challenge by one village could not be refused by another . . . If the host team won, everyone dined on a luxurious feast. However, if they lost, the host did not share their feast with the victors who had just made off with their possessions.

Preparing to compete in festivities associated with the ballgame provides similar integrative community spirit as the preparation for kula voyages discussed in Chapter 2. Furthermore, skill at playing the ballgame and knowledge of associated ritual would be the important factors in such competitions. Therefore, the ballgame provides an example of the type of social interaction that would have motivated people to make the one-day journey between the Cuauhtémoc and Mazatán zones. Such intraregional trips and competitive activities over a distance of 40 km would have preadapted the Soconusco elite for future expeditions over greater distances such as the 400 km to the Gulf Coast. Competitive events such as playing the ballgame, along with marriages and funerals, would be the types of gatherings where ideas and technological innovations would have been shared and/or traded.

Unfortunately, no evidence of Ocós-, Cherla- or Cuadros-phase architecture has been documented at Cuauhtémoc to date. However, as cultural remains from each of these phases have been recovered from the site, future excavations could expand this fragmentary architectural sample. During the Jocotal phase, Mound 2 – the 100-m-long, 25-m-wide and 1-m-high platform – was built through the center of Cuauhtémoc (see Figure 4.10). This long, low mound is similar to other Jocotal-phase mounds documented at El Varal (Lesure 2009), Salinas la Blanca (Coe and Flannery 1967) and Ojo de Agua (Clark and Hodgson 2004; Pinkowski 2006). All of these Jocotal-phase mounds appear to have been long, low platforms on which houses were built. Although Mound 2 was razed before my excavations began, Clark mapped its size and orientation in 1996. I have subsequently documented Jocotal- and Conchas-phase middens and features off its southern edge which date its occupation (see Rosenswig 2007). The construction and use of such a mound during the Jocotal phase likely represented a reorganization of the social structure at the community. By creating a large raised platform, a limited segment of the inhabitants of Cuauhtémoc would have had their residences segregated from the rest of the community.

Furthermore, Mound 2 was not oriented northwest–southeast as the Initial Ceramic Period residences at Cuauhtémoc and Paso de la Amada had been. Instead, the long axis of the mound was oriented east–west. Such a change in architectural orientation along with the residential elevation of a limited segment of the community provide two lines of evidence that indicate that a change in the structure of the built environment occurred at some point between the Locona and Jocotal phases. Furthermore, the alignment of this platform on cardinal directions recalls the north–south orientation of stone monuments at San Lorenzo (discussed in Chapter 3) and marks a change from the Locona northwest–southeast orientation.

Mounds 1 and 3 were built north and south of each other during the Conchas phase (Figure 4.10). This architectural alignment continues the Jocotal phase pattern of building mounds aligned on cardinal directions. At La Blanca, there was also a north–south orientation of architecture during the Conchas phase with a small mound built directly north of that site's impressive 25-m-high central Mound 1 (see Figure 3.3). Therefore, during the Conchas phase, at both sites a small mound was built to the north and the largest mound at the site was built to the south. A north–south orientation is also consistent with the Horizon III architecture built at La Venta (among other sites), which is oriented 8 degrees west of north. Therefore, although elaborated during Horizon III, the north–south orientation that structured subsequent architectural planning in Mesoamerica appears to have been in place in the Soconusco by at least the Conchas phase.

Mound 1 at La Blanca and Mound 3 at Cuauhtémoc are examples of large, conical, nondomestic mounds establishing a single focal point at these sites that could have been seen for quite a distance on the flat coastal plain. The construction of Mound 3 required more labor input than anything previously built at Cuauhtémoc and for the first time created an elevated location from which rituals could be enacted. The creation of a 5-m-high mound could have allowed greater numbers of people to view rituals than before. However, at the same time as increasing the integrative, inclusive nature of such ritual, it would have also raised the rituals enacted by certain individuals in the community above where the majority of residents lived their lives. These elite individuals were presumably the same as those living on the nearby raised residential platform (Mound 2). These individuals would therefore have been raised above the rest of the inhabitants of Cuauhtémoc in both a domestic as well as ritual contexts.

The labor required to build the 5-m-high Mound 3 is greater than it first appears, as the levee on which the site was initially built was artificially extended with construction fill by approximately 30 m on the east side of the site before mound construction began (see Figure 4.7). This added labor expenditure would have at least quadrupled the quantity of earth that was moved to build Mound 3 (Rosenswig 2010). The construction of this extension to the site means that very little area of Jocotal-phase site was covered to erect this new ceremonial structure. A continuity in the political regime from Jocotal to Conchas times at Cuauhtémoc is suggested as the residences of established village families who occupied the site prior to

Figure 4.10
Limits of the Cuauhtémoc site with documented structures indicated.

Figure 4.10 Limits of the Cuauhtémoc site with documented structures indicated.

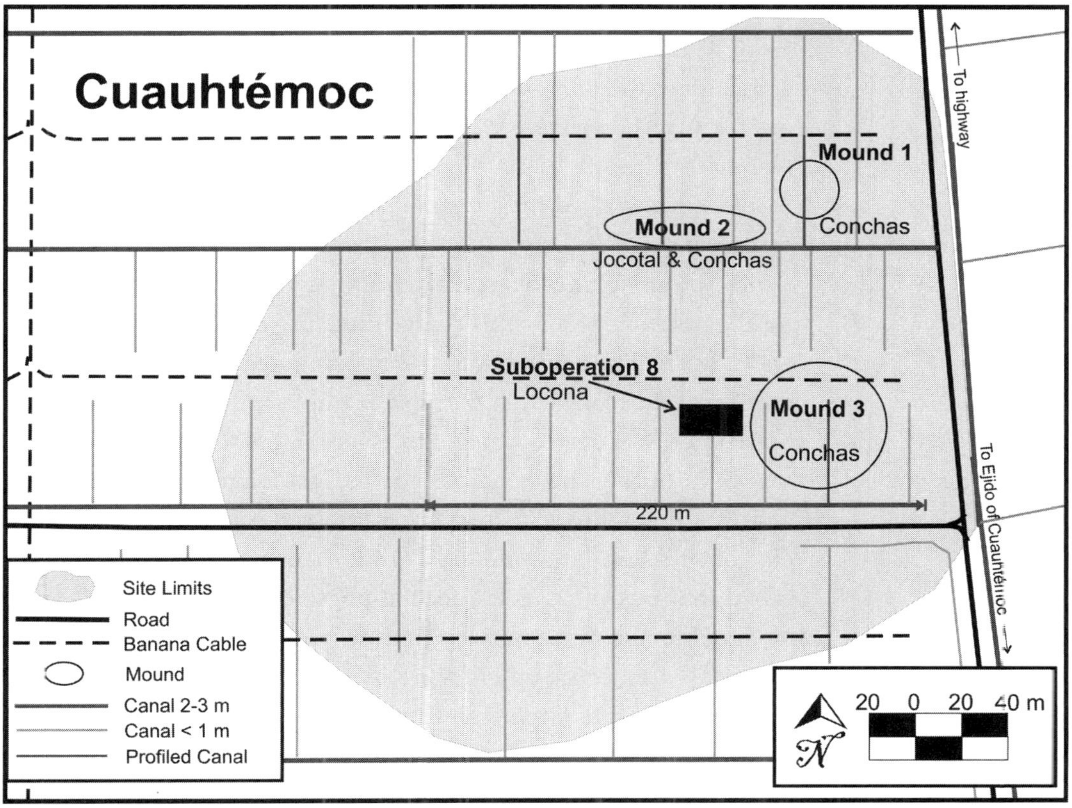

the emergence of La Blanca were not disturbed by Conchas-phase architectural innovations. Furthermore, the residential continuity at Mound 3 (based on superimposed middens with features from both phases) indicates that the collapse of Horizon I political organization of the Mazatán zone (and abandonment of the Ojo de Agua site) did not adversely affect Cuauhtémoc (Rosenswig 2008). The Cuauhtémoc elite appear to have forged an alliance with (or been conquered by) the rulers of La Blanca and to have adopted a new way of life (see discussion in Rosenswig 2006a, 2007; and see Chapter 8). Details of the subsistence and iconographic changes that occurred at Cuauhtémoc are presented in the following chapters.

Although the 25-m-high mound at La Blanca was substantially larger than the 5-m-high mound at Cuauhtémoc, the former site was inhabited by ten to twenty times as many people (based on the number of hectares of occupation). I have previously estimated that Mound 1 at La Blanca would have contained 140,000 cu m of fill (Rosenswig 2000: 438). In comparison, I have recently calculated that building Mounds 1 and 3 would have required just less than 4,000 cu m of fill, and extending the east side of Cuauhtémoc would have required an additional 13,500 cu m of fill to build (Rosenswig 2010). If the labor required to extend the east side of Cuauhtémoc is included, then an estimated 17,500 cu m of fill was moved during the Conchas phase. With a population one-tenth (or even one-twentieth) the site of La Blanca's, the inhabitants of Cuauhtémoc would have worked for at least the same length of time on mound construction.

The most significant aspect of building monumental architecture for the first time is how this changed the use of a community's labor and how the built environment was permanently altered. The 25-m mound at La Blanca was the first example of this phenomenon in Mesoamerica (Love 1999b) and the 5-m-high mound at Cuauhtémoc was built during the same period, and presumably for similar reasons. Recently, Joyce (2004a) has addressed the effects of the novelty of building large mounds in Honduras. She argues that low broad mounds, such as the Jocotal-phase construction of Mound 2 at Cuauhtémoc, were initially built to raise certain activities above everyday occurrences. Achieving greater visibility, these platforms could incorporate larger numbers of people in "... feasts, dances and games ... then the builders of early monumental platforms can be understood as acting within traditional structures of technical, ritual, and domestic productive and reproductive practices" (Joyce 2004a: 24). However, after these modest structures turned out to be durable, it was then only a small step to build larger mounds and raise certain activities even higher above the level of the mundane. Large mounds, the hallmark of all later Mesoamerican civilizations, mark sites on the regional landscape and establish focal points within sites. Reilly (1999) suggests that the large, conical earthen mound at La Venta may have represented the mountain of creation and served as a ritual stage for political performances (also see Grove 1999). La Venta's central axis runs through its central Mound C-1 that was 30 m high. This central mound commands a view of the entire site which means that it would have also been visible from everywhere in the site. La Venta's main occupation was during Horizon III and its architecture was more elaborate at that time than anything built at La Blanca and Cuauhtémoc – but likely functioned in a similar manner as its Horizon II Soconusco predecessors.

It is productive to review a diachronic example of how architectural construction functioned politically in Hawaii. Archaeologically documented monumental construction on the island of Maui from the fourteenth through eighteenth centuries, combined with oral history, provides evidence of the interplay between political instability and building episodes at temple mounds (Kolb 1994). During the Formative period, small pavements were built at political centers across the island. During the following Consolidation period, two larger polities emerged, one on the east and the other on the west side of the island (Kolb 1994: 527–528). Members of genealogically distinct chiefly lines ruled each polity and were regularly at war with one another. During this time, the amount of labor invested in temple mound construction per year increased by 56 times compared with the previous Formative period (Kolb 1994: 527). During the sixteenth-century Unification period, east and west Maui merged into a single polity and the annual labor investment in temples dropped to half that of the previous period. During the following Annexation period, Hawaii conquered the east half of Maui and labor investment in temple construction fell. In contrast, on the still-independent west side of Maui, labor investment in temple construction increased over Unification period levels. The intensity of labor invested into architectural construction thus appears to be correlated with periods of political instability. For the early historical Consolidation period, Kolb (1994: 531) explains that:

The use of labor obligations rather than foodstuffs as a means of taxation during this period of political instability bespeaks an attempt to stabilize social relationships by involving both chiefs and commoners in a coordinated effort... their direct involvement would have demonstrated that success in temple construction both required cooperation and promised prosperity for the entire polity... [and then]... after unification, large amounts of temple labor seem to have been no longer necessary for the assertion of chiefly political power.

Therefore, the act of building large mounds, and the social unity produced by such coordinated labor projects, may have been as important as the ultimate function that such newly erected structures were put. In the Soconusco, the first system of large mounds was built during the Conchas phase when populations from the Mazatán and Jesús river zones were drawn to the area surrounding La Blanca. One way to integrate people at these newly congregating centers could have been through the coordinated labor projects that transformed the built environment and left a permanent reminder of these founding events in the form of impressive central mounds that literally raised public rituals above the level of everyday events. Architectural landscapes and political relations changed in tandem in a reinforcing synergy. In other words, the authority that created Conchas-phase architecture also can be said to have been created by it (Smith 2003). At Cuauhtémoc, the labor required to extend the high ground on which the site was built as well as the construction of a 5-m-high mound would have united the site's inhabitants in a communal work project. Relative to the number of inhabitants at Cuauhtémoc, this labor project would have required a comparable amount of time as it took the inhabitants of La Blanca to build Mound 1.

SUMMARY OF SETTLEMENT PATTERNS AND ARCHITECTURE

One limitation of the Cuauhtémoc zone survey is that only a small area of the coastal plain was systematically surveyed, so it provides an incomplete picture of demographic changes in the area. In addition to the relatively small area, the Cuauhtémoc survey zone never contained an entire political system or a site that attained regional dominance. Therefore, the demographic changes documented by this survey are the results of political forces at work elsewhere that are reflected, perhaps obliquely, in local changes. However, as Braudel observes at the beginning of this chapter, it is often in peripheral regions such as the Cuauhtémoc zone that a fuller understanding of long-term political processes can be gained than by directly observing the changing fortunes of large (and often short-lived) political centers.

Initial Ceramic Period demographic patterns in the Cuauhtémoc and Mazatán zones are similar and peak during the Locona phase. The Locona phase corresponds to the time when a network of interacting polities in the Mazatán zone emerged as some of the earliest rank societies in Mesoamerica (Clark and Blake 1994). Measuring a little more than 5 ha, the Cuauhtémoc site appears to have been the center of another small, Locona-phase polity some 40 km down the coast. Although architectural evidence from the Cuauhtémoc site is incomplete, it provides some tantalizing hints of the larger cultural processes at work in the Soconusco. The orientation of two Locona-phase structures documented at Cuauhtémoc, along with Mound 6 at Paso de la Amada, suggests that the inhabitants of the Soconusco built their architecture based on a standard plan or oriented toward some common point of reference that is yet to be determined. The area between the large swamp systems of La Cantileña and Guamuchal/Manchón thus appears to have functioned as an integrated island of complexity.

The Mazatán and Cuauhtémoc zones continued to have similar demographic histories through Horizon I. In both zones, population levels were low during the Cherla and Cuadros phases and then increased significantly during the Jocotal phase. In the Mazatán zone during Horizon I the center of power shifted first from Paso de la Amada to Cantón Corralito on the Coatán River and next across the river to Ojo de Agua. In fact, there is virtually no occupation at Paso de la Amada after the Cherla phase. Although there was a change in the center of power in the Mazatán zone during the Initial Ceramic Period to Horizon I transition, the site of Cuauhtémoc continued to be occupied and grew during the Jocotal phase. The east–west alignment of the long axis of Cuauhtémoc's Mound 2 indicates that, at least by the end of Horizon I, the inhabitants of this site ceased building their structures according to the previous Initial Ceramic Period standard and instead were guided by consideration of the cardinal directions. Furthermore, Mound 2 is a raised, 100-m-long, residential platform that segregated a limited sector of the site's population and raised these residents above everyone else in the community.

Cuauhtémoc then benefited from La Blanca's rise to regional dominance at the beginning of Horizon II. The site increased in size again, and more area was occupied in the 28-sq-km survey zone than at any point previously. The continued occupation of Cuauhtémoc's Mound 2 during the Conchas phase suggests that successive generations of the site's elite survived the political collapse and abandonment of the Mazatán zone. In fact, the extension of the east side of the site along with the construction of two new mounds demonstrates that there was an increased emphasis placed on public works projects that left a permanent mark on the landscape. The construction of large conical mounds during Horizon II began a tradition in Mesoamerica that persisted until Spanish contact. These architectural features marked sites on the flat coastal landscape and elevated rituals above the level of the quotidian. The north–south alignment of the two Cuauhtémoc conical mounds, with the larger one to the south, mirrors the arrangement and orientation of mounds built at La Blanca. Such an alignment is the earliest known evidence of a pattern that was expanded during Horizon III when the architecture at La Venta was built oriented 8 degrees west of north on the Gulf Coast.

The rhythm of settlement change in the Cuauhtémoc zone appears to have been responsive to the political fortunes of Paso de la Amada and Cantón Corralito/Ojo de Agua in the Mazatán zone as well as La Blanca in the nearby Naranjo zone. Population levels in the Cuauhtémoc and Mazatán zones rose and fell in tandem during the Early Formative period. However, the Cuauhtémoc polity was not a major political center during the Initial Ceramic Period and was spared the Horizon I abandonment of Paso de la Amada and other centers in the Mazatán zone. The dramatic increase in hectares of occupation in the Cuauhtémoc survey area during the Conchas phase and the lack of occupation during the Duende and Escalón phases further reflect the meteoric rise and fall of La Blanca. However, as Cuauhtémoc was then more centrally engaged in the political phenomena of the La Blanca polity, these two sites, and the entire area, were abandoned as Izapa emerged as the new political center on the piedmont 25 km inland. Cuauhtémoc's peripheral position during the Initial Ceramic Period and Horizon I appears to have allowed it to survive the collapse of Paso de la Amada and Ojo de Agua. In contrast, as it was more tightly integrated in the La Blanca political system, this connection appears to have resulted in its ultimate downfall.

NOTE

1. Five previous systematic surveys have been conducted in the Soconusco, and all targeted the estuary and coastal plain. These are, from northwest to southeast: the Acapetahua zone, northwest of the Huixtla river, surveyed by Voorhies (1989b) and a number of her students. A river survey of the west half of the Soconusco was undertaken by Voorhies and Kennett (1995). The Mazatán zone, around the site of Paso de la Amada, was surveyed by Clark (1994). A survey of the Naranjo river zone was carried out by Love (2002a). Finally, the Jesús river zone, around the site of El Mesak, was surveyed by Pye (1995). Earlier, nonsystematic reconnaissance in the area included work by Drucker (1948), Lorenzo (1955), and Ceja (1985) in Chiapas as well as Shook (1948, 1965) and Coe (1961; Coe and Flannery 1967) in Guatemala.

5

Diet, Food Processing and Feasting

> It is not the unity of living and active humanity with the nat-
> ural, inorganic conditions of their metabolic exchange with
> nature...which requires explanation...but rather the separa-
> tion between these inorganic conditions of human existence and
> this active existence...
>
> Marx 1973 [1857–1858]: 489

Using the well-known architectural analogy, it is the economic base
that supports society's political and ideological superstructure.
Defined in these terms, the economic base combines the means of
production (based on the fertility of land, technology for extracting
and producing food, as well as systems for its redistribution) with
social (particularly property) relations to form the mode of production. Among small-scale societies, the majority of economic activity
consists of people nourishing themselves and supplying the other
basics to sustain life. In such societies, satisfying the need for food
limits a number of demographic factors. For example, the environment (given a constant level of technology) sets limits on the number
of people that can be sustained in a particular location and, therefore, the size of social groups and concentration of people. Therefore,
foragers would not live in cities of millions of people nor would
they develop state apparatus to manage such concentrations of population. The means of production (which subsumes environmental
factors) also set limits on the ideological realm of society. For example, it would be impossible for vegetarian dietary taboos to develop
in the Arctic where animal products are the only food available.[1]

The ability (in environmental, technological and social terms)
to produce surplus food can expand the labor available for

nonsubsistence activities. Developments in the technology of food production as well as knowledge of plant and animal domestication increase the level of output of the means of production. Therefore, changes in foods eaten and the tools used to process food can redefine the parameters of cultural developments. Furthermore, a dependence on agriculture, with intensifiable and storable products, created the first stages of the metabolic rift that changes the way that people understand their world (Childe 1950). A limited segment of society employing such surplus for their own ends marks the emergence of differential property/class relations and, strictly speaking, for the first time one can speak of the mode of production.[2] At its most extreme (i.e., with capitalist agriculture), a complete metabolic rift is created by separating most people from personally fulfilling any of their subsistence needs (Patterson 2003: 27–29). However, among early agriculturalists with incipient social differentiation the elite are often still negotiating their liberation from having to meet their subsistence needs (i.e., receiving tribute).

The anthropological literature is rife with definitions of precapitalist modes of production (see Roseberry 1989: 145–152). The wide range of such definitions is likely due to the fact that Marx himself was not particularly concerned with the dynamics of prefeudal societies for most of his career, and his discussion of these societies' mode of production was vague. However, as Wolf (1982: 76) points out, the utility of the mode of production "... concept does not lie in classification but in its capacity to underline the strategic relationships involved in the deployment of social labor by organized human pluralities." Rather than try to redefine the mode of production for early sedentary Mesoamerica, I follow Wolf's (1982: 88–100) well-known definition of modes of production to describe the economic organization of the inhabitants of Cuauhtémoc. The acquisition/production of food, its preparation, consumption, and the social uses it serves dominate all other human activities. This is true of the time devoted to carrying out such activities as well as the cultural practices involved in anticipating and later reminiscing about hunting expeditions, harvests, feasts, and so forth. Not surprisingly, over the past fifty years cultural anthropologists from all theoretical positions have devoted much energy to the study of food and eating (see Mintz and Du Bois 2002). Particularly relevant to scholars who explore culture diachronically from its material remains is how the political and economic changes that occur in society affect food (e.g.,

Lentz 1999; Mintz 1985). Archaeologists have long been interested in subsistence and, more recently, in studying a broader range of issues related to food and the social context of its production and use (Gerritsen 2000; Gosden and Hather 1999; Gummerman 1997). Feasting is one of the most socially charged contexts of food consumption (e.g., Dietler 1996; Dietler and Hayden 2001; Rosenswig 2007; Turkon 2004). Competitive feasting has been explored as the fulcrum of cultural change from a range of perspectives that emphasize the political (Clark and Blake 1994), economic (Hayden 1990, 1995) or ritual (Spielman 2002) aspects of small-scale and incipiently hierarchical societies. Such perspectives posit that the self-interest of past peoples provides the mechanism that drives change and results in an intensification of economic productivity.

In this chapter, I present data that document what the inhabitants of the Cuauhtémoc zone ate, how they prepared and served food as well as how these things changed over time. First, I define the ecofact and artifact samples from which analyses are undertaken. Next, dietary reconstructions are inferred based on Cuauhtémoc faunal and macrobotanical maize remains as well as previous isotopic results from the Soconusco. Changes to food preparation techniques are inferred by comparing relative quantities of unslipped tecomates, their wall thickness as well as changing quantities of ground stone, fire-cracked rock and obsidian. Then, food-serving practices are explored by tracking changes in the proportions of serving-to-cooking vessels, the size of slipped tecomates for serving liquids, the proportion of decorated dishes for serving food, and the range of sizes of such vessels.

These analyses build on those undertaken in the Mazatán zone both in terms of the refined ceramic chronology and many of the variables explored. My goals in reconstructing aspects of the Cuauhtémoc domestic economy are threefold. My first goal is to track changes in artifact patterns from a site that was occupied throughout the turbulent Early and Middle Formative periods in the Soconusco. The Cuauhtémoc data provide evidence from a small local center in a consistently politically peripheral area. My second goal is to track changes from a single site across the Initial Ceramic Period, Horizons I, and Horizons II. Whereas the Mazatán zone was abandoned at the end of the Jocotal phase and La Blanca was not occupied until the Conchas phase, the Cuauhtémoc data extend from Barra through Conchas times. As all the data used in the following

Table 5.1. Summary of volume (in cubic meters) for temporally secure excavation lots from which detailed ceramic analysis was carried out (see Appendix 1), as well as temporally secure lots from which ceramic variables were not coded (see Appendix 2)

Phase	Lots with detailed ceramic variables	Other temporally secure lots	Total volume
Barra/Locona	1.429	5.87	**7.295**
Locona	7.345	14.31	**21.650**
Ocós	3.949		**3.949**
Cherla	3.091		**3.091**
Cuadros	3.256		**3.256**
Jocotal	2.444		**2.444**
Conchas	10.591	14.01	**24.599**
Total Volume:			**66.183**

analyses are drawn from the same site (which was a minor center for the period investigated), geographic location and regional political standing are both held constant when documenting changing artifact patterns. My third objective is to assess the degree to which changes previously documented in the Mazatán zone can be generalized across the Soconusco. Although early work in the Soconusco was undertaken at the sites of La Victoria (Coe 1961) and Salinas la Blanca (Coe and Flannery 1967) in the Naranjo zone, the majority of Initial Ceramic Period and Horizon I economic data has been generated more recently from the Mazatán zone (e.g., Blake et al. 1992a, 1992b; 2006; Clark 1994; Clark and Blake 1994; Clark and Gosser 1995; Lesure 1995, 1998). Therefore, the following analyses will explore the degree to which the economy of the land between the two Soconusco swamps developed in tandem. Documenting similarities between the Mazatán and Cuauhtémoc zones provides the empirical reality of this region as an island of cultural complexity.

THE CONTEXT OF SAMPLES

The data presented in this chapter and the next were recovered from the most temporally secure excavation contexts at Cuauhtémoc from just over 66 cubic meters of excavated deposits (see Table 5.1). These contexts provide temporally unmixed samples from each phase except the Barra. These Barra-phase deposits were documented with some Locona types in two large midden areas and so represent either mixed deposits or else date to late in the Barra phase. These

Barra/Locona contexts are included in the following analysis to provide the most complete temporal breadth possible.

As described in Chapter 4, two sets of Locona-phase post molds as well as one long mound and two Conchas-phase conical mounds were the only architectural features documented at Cuauhtémoc by my excavations. Therefore, it is not possible to compare individual houses to each other and make inferences about relative status (except for during the Conchas phase; see Rosenswig 2007). The strength of the Cuauhtémoc data is instead its time depth, and in this chapter I track developments in the domestic economy of the site's inhabitants. As Cuauhtémoc was built on high ground in an environment prone to flooding, and was occupied quite intensively during many centuries, a number of stratified village middens developed around the edges of the site (Figure 4.7). Such village middens (and a number of trash pits) represent secondary refuse (Schiffer 1972) from which to generalize about the overall economy of the community (see Rosenswig 2009).

Interpretations based on these analyses require the assumption that secondary refuse from village middens and trash features at different locations across the site and from different time periods do not systematically reflect functional differences, different disposal practices or differential postdepositional processes. Therefore, I assume that relative breakage rates for each class of artifacts remained constant from phase to phase (Mills 1989). An advantage of comparing village middens is that whereas refuse disposal can produce assemblages that vary among households irrespective of social status (Hayden and Canon 1983) and change in composition through a household's life cycle (Deal 1998:123–129), such variability is minimized where artifacts accumulate from multiple social groups over a number of generations. In other words, the deposits employed for the following analyses are assumed to be comparable to each other and to reflect the range of activities engaged in by the village's inhabitants through time (Rosenswig 2009). To expand Smith's (1992: 30) concept of a household series " . . . as the sequence of households that successively inhabit a given structure or house over a span of more than one generation," these contexts could be said to form a *village series*. Such a village series incorporates the four to six generations that make up each 100- to 150-year ceramic phase, and the resulting artifact patterns documented below from secondary context are a modal reflection of the activities carried out during each phase (see discussion in Rosenswig 2007: 5–6; Rosenswig and Masson 2002: 219–220).

CUAUHTÉMOC DIET

I explore changing diet using three lines of evidence: vertebrate faunal remains and macrobotanical maize density from Cuauhtémoc as well as the results of isotopic analysis published by Blake et al. (1992a). A total of 4,757 bone fragments were recovered from the two years of excavation. Of these, 3,078 bones were excavated from the temporally secure lots listed in Appendixes 1 and 2. Although faunal remains provide an indirect measure of the meat consumed, I assume that the relative proportions of species documented archaeologically do not differ significantly from the proportions actually consumed.

Maize densities were determined by Amber VanDerwarker at the University of California, Santa Barbara. Fifteen flotation samples from pit features and middens dating to the Locona through Conchas phases produced macrobotanical samples. Changing densities of the maize remains from domestic trash contexts provide a relative gauge of the importance of this crop for the inhabitants of Cuauhtémoc over time.

To approach the diet of people who lived at Cuauhtémoc from another angle, bone samples were analyzed for carbon and nitrogen isotope levels by John Krigbaum at the University of Florida, Gainesville. Initially, eight human and seventeen dog and deer samples were tested. When these samples did not produce results, samples of the eight individuals were run again with larger bone samples and tooth samples as well. Unfortunately, the collagen content of all but one bone sample was insufficient to provide results.

Faunal remains

Coe and Flannery (1967: 113–117) produced an expected list of game mammals and reptiles from the "Ocós Transect" of the lagoon, estuary and costal plain of Guatemala just on the other side of the modern border from the Cuauhtémoc zone (see Table 5.2). This list was based on species they collected in 1962 supplemented by published collections taken from both sides of the border during the 1940s and 1950s. In 1962, Coe and Flannery (1967) report sightings of both tapir and jaguar in the Ocós and Tilapa areas. Such incidents are now unheard of, and there are no longer any such large, forest-dwelling mammals in the Soconusco as virtually all forests have been converted into farmland with small, interspersed areas of dense secondary growth. Table 5.2 lists the mammals and reptiles that could potentially be present in a prehistoric faunal assemblage, assuming that the environment has not changed significantly from the first half of the twentieth century.

Vertebrate faunal remains were quantified as the Number of Identified Specimens Present (NISP) and the Minimum Number of Individuals (MNI) (Grayson 1984; Lyman 1994). The former is a count of all identified bone ascribed to a particular taxa whereas the latter is the minimum number of individual animals that could be represented by the recovered bones. This latter statistic was calculated using the most common element accounting for both the side and size of each element. The single most important analytic decision for the following analysis is one of aggregation. To achieve meaningful sample sizes it was necessary to combine faunal data into Initial Ceramic Period, Horizon I, and Horizon II aggregated assemblages. Sample sizes were deemed representative once relative percentages of MNI and NISP corresponded (Grayson 1984: 49–85). In addition to temporal aggregation, MNI was calculated by combining adjacent excavation lots that contain ceramics from the same phase and treating all lots from features together. Therefore, excavation decisions do not artificially inflate MNI calculations. A total vertebrate MNI of 266 was produced from the NISP of 3,078 recovered from all temporally secure contexts (Appendixes 1 and 2). This sample is not large, especially when divided into the various time periods. Therefore, the following discussion should be viewed as suggestive rather than conclusive. Furthermore, results are presented as %MNI values, which do not reflect the contribution of meat to the diet in absolute terms. As %MNI does not account for animals of different sizes, changing proportions of species are interpreted as reflecting relative changes to the diet.

There were few surprises from the analysis of Cuauhtémoc fauna. All recovered mammal remains are found in Table 5.2 but, among others, no tapir, peccary or jaguar bones were documented. In fact, tapir has never been documented archaeologically in the Soconusco from any time period (Wake and Harrington 2002: 250). This means that either the inhabitants of the Soconusco did not venture into the forests to hunt (Wake 2004: 221) or that other large mammals such as deer

Table 5.2. List of game mammals and large reptiles from the Soconusco coastal plain recorded by Coe and Flannery (1967: 113–117)

Mammals order	Family	Species	Common name	Spanish name
Marsupialia	Didelphidae	Didelphis marsupialis Philander opossum Marmosa mexicana	Common opossum Gray-masked opossum Mouse-opossum	Tacuazín Comadreja
Edentata	Myrmecophagidae	Tamandua tetradactyla Dasypus novemcinctus	Collard anteater Nine-banded armadillo	Oso hormiguero
Lagomorpha	Leporidae	Sylvilagus floridanus Sylvilagus brasiliensis	Eastern cottontail rabbit Tropical forest rabbit	Conejo Conejo
Rodentia	Sciuridae Geomyidae Erethizontidae Dasyproctidae	Sciurus variegatoides Orthogeomys grandis Coendou mexicana Cuniculus (Agouti) paca Dasyprocta punctata	Variegated squirrel Pocket gopher Mexican porcupine Spotted cavy Agouti	Ardilla Tuza Puerco espín Tepescuintl Cuautuza
Carnivora	Canidae	Canis familiaris Urocyon cinereoargenteus	Domestic dog Gray fox	Perro Zorra
	Procyonidae	Procyon lotor Nasua narica Potos flavus Bassariscus sumichrasti	Raccoon Coati Kinkajou Ring-tailed cat	Mapache Pisote Mico de noche Cacomistle
	Mustelidae	Mustela frenata Galictis allamandi Mephitis macroura Lutra annectens	Weasel Grison Hooded skunk River otter	Coadreja Zorillo Perro de agua
	Felidae	Felis onca Felis yagouaroundi	Jaguar Jaguarundi	Tigre Onza
Perissodactyla	Tapiridae	Tapirella bairdii	Tapir	Danta
Artiodactyla	Tayassuidae	Tayassu tajacu Tayassu pecari	Collard peccary White-lipped peccary	Jabali Senso
	Cervidae	Odocoileus virginianus Mazama americana	White-tailed deer Brocket deer	Venado Temazate
Large Reptiles				
Chelonia	Cheloniidae	Chelonia mydas	Green sea turtle	Parlama
Crocodilia	Crocodylidae	Crocodylus acutus Caiman fuscus	Crocodile Cayman	Lagarto Lagarto
Squamata	Iguanidae	Iguana iguana Ctenosaura similis	Green iguana Black iguana	Iguana Giota

have always been more abundant and far easier to kill. In addition to those reptiles listed in Table 5.2, snake remains were also recovered. Bird remains were relatively rare and were not identified to species in this study. Steadman et al. (2003: Table 1) provide a list of sixty bird species identified from the Paso de la Amada fauna that likely reflect the same range of birds available to the residents of Cuauhtémoc. Fish remains from the Cuauhtémoc assemblage were identified as catfish, gar, a lumped category of perciformes and an unidentified category of other fish species. Voorhies et al. (2002: Table 3) provide a detailed list of fish species documented from the Archaic period site of Cerro de las Conchas in the Acapetahua zone (also see Cooke et al. 2004). The fauna from six other sites in the Acapetahua zone document a similar overall range of species as those documented at Cuauhtémoc but with no Early or Middle Formative period occupation at any of the sites (Hudson et al. 1989). For the following analysis species are lumped into the taxonomic classes of fish, bird, reptile and mammal, and then mammals are further subdivided into dog, deer, small mammal and other unidentified mammal.

Overall, faunal remains indicate a mixed economy during each time period with species exploited from the swamp, estuary and coastal plain environments (Figure 5.1). In fact, the overall proportion of different faunal classes is virtually identical during the Initial Ceramic Period and Horizon II (compare Figure 5.1A and Figure 5.1C) with half of the MNI from mammals and the remainder divided among reptiles, birds and fish. The fish remains and reptiles like iguana, turtle and cayman indicate that the swamps were important sources of animal protein and that the inhabitants of Cuauhtémoc would have regularly entered the nearby swamps to procure them.

The comparatively low proportion of mammal remains from Horizon I deposits (Figure 5.1B) is partly due to a large Cherla-phase pit feature (Suboperation 3c) that contained 71% fish remains. This feature, documented in the wall of an irrigation canal, measured 1.85 m in diameter and contained layers of burnt rock, fauna and shell (Figure 5.2). In addition, this feature produced thousands of clam shells and 185 crab claws (MNI = 47), indicating an even greater use of aquatic foods than results based on vertebrate remains alone. It would thus appear that this feature represents the remains of fish, clams and crabs roasted in an open pit. A wide range of sizes of catfish bones, including some very small specimens, suggests that these fish were procured using nets. The maize remains from this

Cherla-phase feature are also anomalous, as is discussed in the following section. However, even when this Cherla-phase feature is removed from the sample, the assemblage still contains relatively more fish and fewer mammals than during the Initial Ceramic Period or Horizon II (Figure 5.1D). It is thus possible that, during the Cherla phase (and perhaps more generally during Horizon I), there was an increased exploitation of aquatic resources. Similar Cherla-phase features were documented in the Mazatán zone at Aquiles Serdán (Blake et al. 1992a), where 81.5% of the species MNI were fish (Clark 1994: Figure 69) and preliminary results from another Cherla-phase pit at Paso de la Amada indicate 64% (84 of 131) of the vertebrate MNI were fish (Wake 2004).

A number of interesting patterns are suggested when the relative proportion of different mammal remains are examined (Figure 5.3).

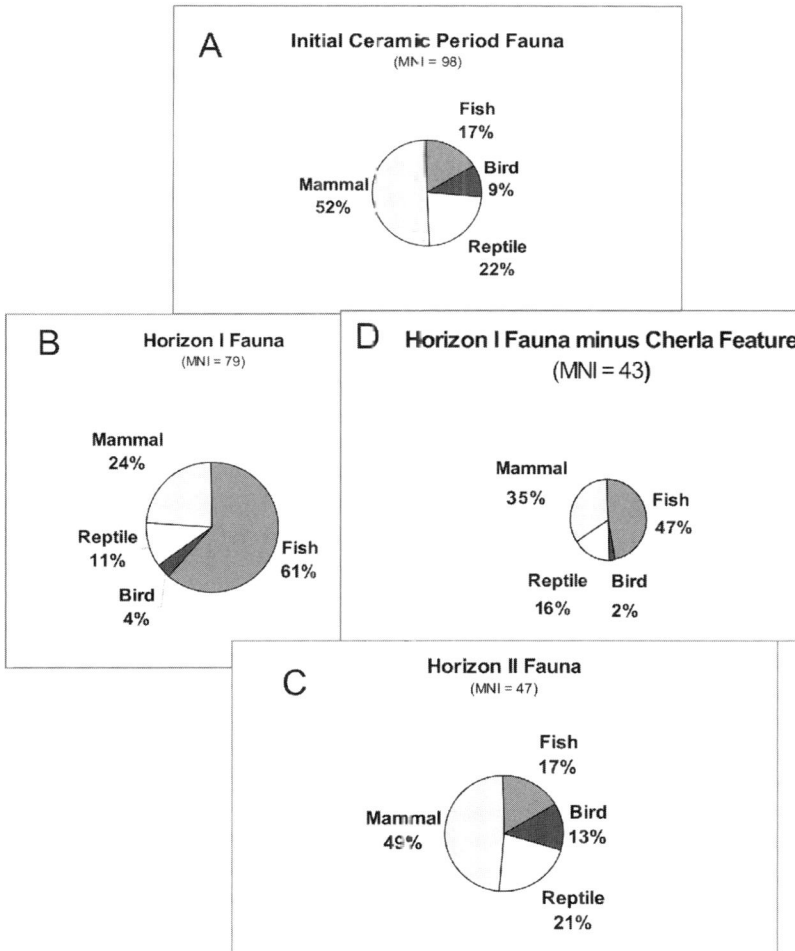

Figure 5.1
Relative proportion of classes of fauna from village midden contexts at Cuauhtémoc.

First, from all time periods there was a mix of dog, deer and a range of small mammals with gopher, opossum and armadillo being the most common. This finding indicates that hunting expeditions into the surrounding forests were not a significant activity as all of these species could have been found near the site. Furthermore, deer cranial, axial and limb elements were all well represented in the faunal assemblages, which suggests that the animals were killed relatively close to the site and that differential transport of meat-bearing elements was not a factor in determining the makeup of refuse, as Wake and Harrington (2002) also argue was the case at La Blanca.

Second, these results indicate a relatively lower proportion of dog remains and a relatively higher proportion of small mammals during Horizon I (Figure 5.3B). This pattern may be attributed to small sample size (MNI = 19), but combined with the overall dominance of fish (Figure 5.1, B or D), it suggests that the composition of Horizon I faunal assemblage may have been different than that during earlier and later times.

Third, there appears to have been a significant change in the use of mammals during the Horizon II Conchas phase (Figure 5.3C). Together, dog and deer account for almost 80% of the mammal remains recovered from deposits dating to this time, considerably

Figure 5.2
Cherla-phase trash pit in Suboperation 3c before being excavated.

more than ever before. This Conchas-phase narrowing of the mammal species consumed is consistent with the faunal assemblages recovered from three house mounds at La Blanca that are dominated by dog, deer and turtle remains (Wake and Harrington 2002).

Dogs were an extremely important source of food across Mesoamerica during the Formative period. After documenting that dog remains were the most abundant terrestrial species present at four sites on the Gulf Coast, Wing (1978: 39, 41) proposed that human dependence on dog in Mesoamerica was comparable to Old World dependence on domestic animals. Elsewhere, I argue that dogs

Figure 5.3
Relative proportion of mammals recovered from village midden contexts at Cuauhtémoc.

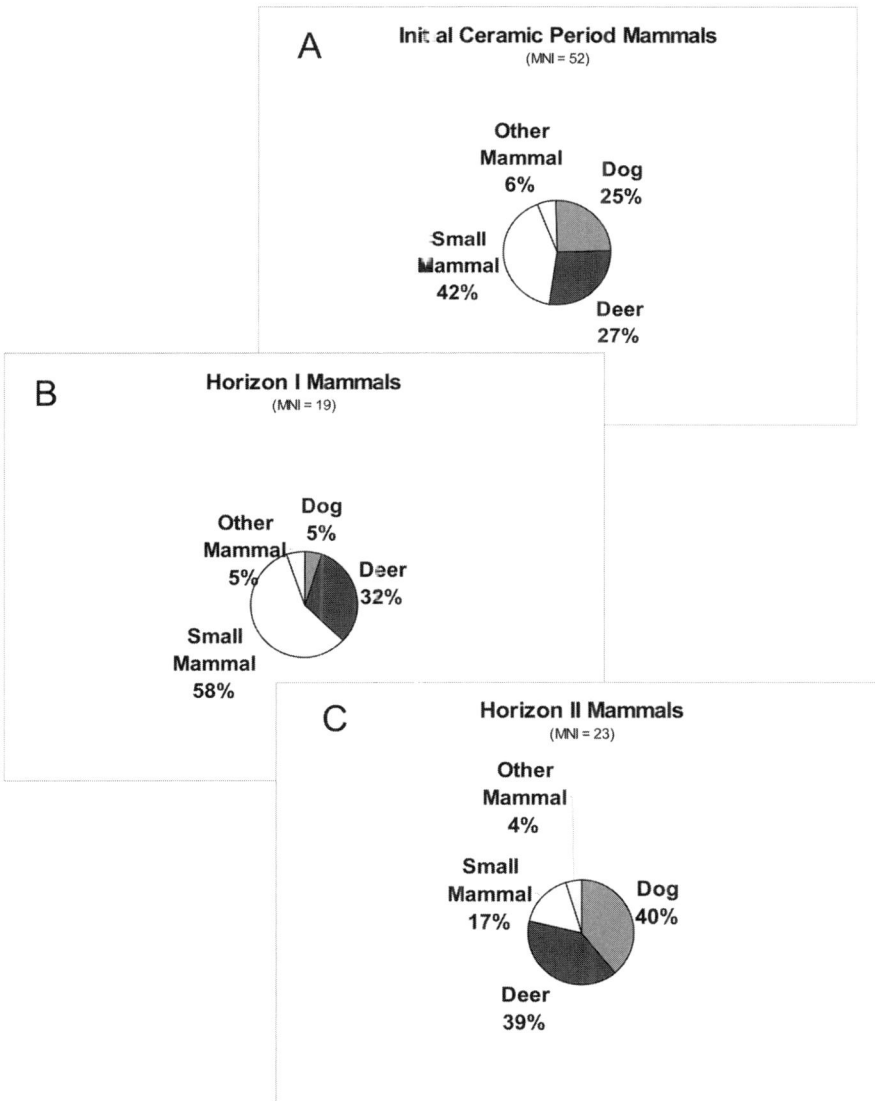

A — **Initial Ceramic Period Mammals** (MNI = 52)
Other Mammal 6% · Dog 25% · Deer 27% · Small Mammal 42%

B — **Horizon I Mammals** (MNI = 19)
Dog 5% · Other Mammal 5% · Deer 32% · Small Mammal 58%

C — **Horizon II Mammals** (MNI = 23)
Other Mammal 4% · Small Mammal 17% · Dog 40% · Deer 39%

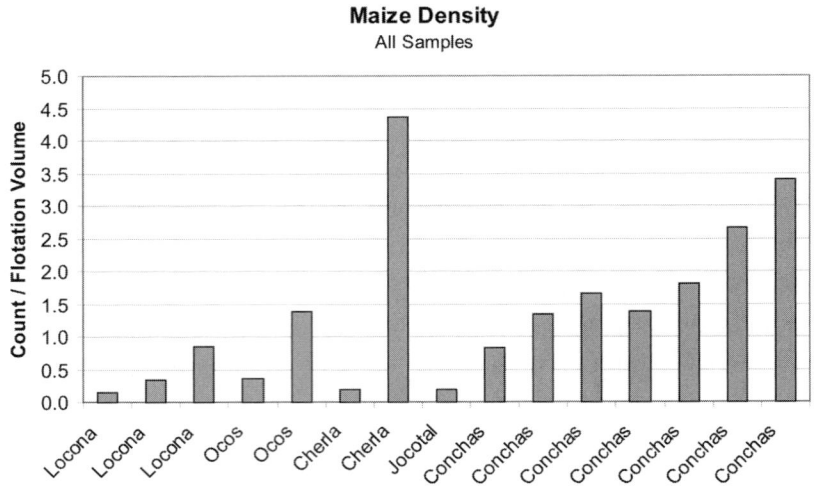

Figure 5.4
Early and Middle Forma-
tive maize density from
Cuauhtémoc.

were used in elite contexts as a feasting food at Cuauhtémoc during the Conchas phase (Rosenswig 2007: 19–23). The Cuauhtémoc data demonstrate that, during the Conchas phase, there was a significantly higher proportion of domestic dog recovered from elite trash than from village middens (see Rosenswig 2007: Figure 18, Table 4). The use of dog at Cuauhtémoc during the Conchas phase could have been similar to that of pig in the Pacific by being tended and then given away live at feasts (e.g., Sahlins 1992: 28; Strathern 1971). As a controlled and intensifiable species, dog populations could have been kept and eaten at feasts and other special occasions sponsored by village elites.

Maize density

Maize is only one of many plants used as food by Mesoamerican peoples. However, it became one of the most important New World domesticates due to its high caloric content. Macrobotanical maize remains were identified from fifteen contexts at Cuauhtémoc and quantified as the number of remains standardized by the volume of flotation samples (Figure 5.4). In general, Initial Ceramic Period and Horizon I maize densities were lower than those from Horizon II contexts. This finding provides intriguing evidence for the increase in relative importance of this crop at the beginning of the Middle Formative period. The one exception was the Cherla-phase pit that had the highest maize density of any sample analyzed (see Figure 5.4). This sample was from Suboperation 3c (Figure 5.2), the

TP-1 SOP 7d-108-12/13

Figure 5.5
Complete Locona-phase
Chilo Red dish recovered
upside down on a dog
burial.

same pit feature that also has an anomalously high proportion of fish remains (see Figure 5.1).

Bone isotopes

Carbon isotopes provide a direct measure of the quantity of maize in the diet of the individual whose bones are analyzed. As I have recovered only eight human burials at Cuauhtémoc, isotope samples were initially supplemented by both deer and dog bones. As well as constituting a source of food, dogs may have been pets during the Initial Ceramic Period, as two Locona-phase dog interments have been recovered from Cuauhtémoc and seven others have been recovered from Paso de la Amada. In fact, one of the Locona-phase dog burials recovered from Cuauhtémoc was interred with a complete ceramic dish (Figure 5.5) covering its skull. Certain dogs were thus receiving burial accoutrements similar to those of humans during the Initial Ceramic Period. Dogs living at Cuauhtémoc at this time were undoubtedly scavenging and/or being fed whatever humans were eating (Schulting and Richards 2002; VanDerwarker 2006; White et al. 2001). Therefore, changing canine carbon and nitrogen isotope levels could reflect the quantity of C_4 plants (such as maize) and aquatic animals being consumed at the site by their human masters. Deer thrive when forests are cleared for planting crops as this clears more grazing land for them (Flannery 1969: 211). In addition, as opportunistic edge browsers, deer are notorious scavengers of maize fields (Emery et al. 2000; VanDerwarker 2006: 148–149; White et al. 2001, 2004). Therefore, increased presence of maize fields could show up as increased C4 levels in deer bone. Dogs scavenge at the village level, and deer scavenge in the field where crops are grown, so the diets of both are tied to those of humans. Therefore, dog and deer C4 levels can be used as proxy measures of human reliance on maize.

Unfortunately, no results were generated by the initial twenty-five samples. Subsequent analysis of the eight human interments produced only enough collagen from one individual from the Locona phase who was not consuming high levels of C4 plants ($d13C = -14.65$ and $d15N = 12.49$). A previous isotope study of Soconusco burials indicates that Early Formative inhabitants of the Mazatán zone did not rely on maize as a staple crop but that, during the Conchas phase, inhabitants of La Blanca did (Blake et al. 1992b). The single result from Cuauhtémoc is consistent with this pattern of low C4 levels during the Early Formative period.

Summary of dietary evidence

Faunal data suggest a relatively stable, broad-based diet throughout the occupation of Cuauhtémoc. As Coe and Flannery (1967: 82–83) have observed, hunting birds, reptiles and mammals seems to have occurred in an opportunistic manner to animals that wandered into human habitats (also see Linares 1976; VanDerwarker 2006: 148–149). The only organized procurement of fauna appears to have been fishing using nets. This activity is indicated by the wide range of sizes of fish, crab and clam remains. These faunal patterns are supported by the ubiquity of ceramic sherds with two notches that were apparently reused as fishing weights (Figure 5.6).

During Horizon II, the inhabitants of Cuauhtémoc continued to exploit fish, birds and reptiles in similar proportions as before. However, among the mammals exploited, approximately 80% were dogs and deer, significantly more than ever before. The vertebrate fauna from Cuauhtémoc thus indicate a persistent broad base during the Conchas phase with an increased focus of mammals that could be domesticated. Evidence from elite Conchas midden contexts further suggest that dog may have been a highly prized meat or at least a meat consumed in higher frequencies in elite contexts during special events such as feasts.

Figure 5.6
Initial Ceramic
Period notched sherd
fish weights from
Cuauhtémoc.

Macrobotanical maize remains have been documented in the Soconusco from throughout the Early Formative period. Maize is documented at Paso de la Amada dating to the Initial Ceramic Period (Blake et al. 1992b; Feddema 1993) and at the site of Salinas la Blanca from Horizon I (Coe and Flannery 1967). At Cuauhtémoc, maize remains also have been documented beginning in the Locona phase through to the Conchas phase. However, with the exception of one Cherla-phase feature, Cuauhtémoc data indicate lower relative density during the Initial Ceramic Period and Horizon I with a significant increase during Horizon II. The carbon isotope evidence published by Blake et al. (1992a) is consistent with these macrobotanical data as C_4 plants were not consumed at levels high enough to indicate a staple crop until Horizon II. Blake (2006; Smalley and Blake 2003) proposes that alcohol production could have been one initial motivation for planting maize. Another, complementary effect of clearing fields and planting maize is that deer are attracted to browse on sweet maize stalks and leaves and could then have been killed with minimal effort. The initial impetus to cultivate maize by the inhabitants of the Soconusco was likely varied, but maize does not appear to have significantly contributed to the nutritional base of Soconusco society until Horizon II.

The Conchas phase represents a time when deer, dog and maize were more intensively exploited at Cuauhtémoc than they had been during the Initial Ceramic Period or Horizon I. In fact, it is only during the Conchas phase that agriculture (*sensu* Rindos 1984: 101) truly emerged in the Soconusco (see discussion in Rosenswig 2006a: 332–335). This shift in the economy to domesticated, and thus intensifiable and controllable, floral and fauna occurred concurrently with the building of Mesoamerica's first coordinated system of mounded architecture. This cannot have been a coincidence as I discuss further elsewhere (Rosenswig 2006a, 2007, 2010). Public building projects would have required surplus to provision people while they worked (Saitta 1997). Although public building projects were undertaken during the Initial Ceramic Period at Paso de la Amada (Clark 2004), as discussed in Chapter 4, large conical mounds at the center of sites (which became a fundamental characteristic of later Mesoamerican society) did not become a common practice in the Soconusco until the Conchas phase. The cultural implications of monumental construction projects were explored at greater length at the end of Chapter 4, where comparisons are made to similar patterns in Hawaii (Kolb 1994).

FOOD PREPARATION AT CUAUHTÉMOC

In this section, I move from evidence of the food consumed at Cuauhtémoc to changes in the implements used to process and prepare food. To do so I present six lines of evidence. First, I document changing relative proportion of the ceramic assemblage made up of unslipped tecomates. These plain tecomates were likely used both to steam food (Clark and Gosser 1995: 215; Coe and Flannery 1967: 28–30, 80–81) and to store it (see Arnold 1999). Clark and Gosser (1995: Figure 17.3) use the increase in plain tecomates and decrease in fire-cracked rock through the Initial Ceramic Period to argue for a change in food-preparation technique from roasting in pits to boiling in pots (but see Voorhies 2004: 357–366).

Second, I document changing average wall thickness of these unslipped tecomates. Wall thickness is one way to indirectly measure the overall size of a tecomate. Volume would be the best measure of overall size but is not possible to reliably calculate from fragmentary sherds. Large body sherds could be used to generate horizontal and vertical diameters and (assuming that tecomates are round – which we know not to be the case) provide an estimated volume. The most significant problem with such a measure is how then to provide a reliable minimum number of vessels (MNV) statistic from the masses of body sherds. The admittedly imperfect solution I employ here is to use tecomate wall thickness from rim sherds that provide the tecomate size and MNV. As far as thicker walls of ceramic containers correspond to larger vessels (see Braun 1983; 1995: 275–278), an increase of this measure corresponds to larger groups of people being cooked for and more food and drink being stored. Alternatively, thicker tecomate walls could indicate more intensive use of vessels as thicker walls are more resistant to thermal stress and less likely to break when moved. Either way, thicker walls of undecorated, utilitarian tecomates signal an increase in the scale of food preparation.

Third, the relative quantity of fire-cracked rock is presented. As noted, Clark and Gosser (1995: Figure 17.3) report that an increase in the quantity of plain body tecomates inversely corresponded to the decrease in quantity of fire-cracked rock throughout the Early Formative period. Lesure (1995: Figure 6.13) also notes a steady decrease in fire-cracked rock from Locona to Cherla times at Paso de la Amada. Together, changing quantities of fire-cracked rock and plain tecomates may indicate the replacement of one food preparation technique by another.

Fourth, the overall density of ground stone is presented. Clark (1994: 244–246) presents ground stone data from the Barra through Jocotal phases in the Mazatán zone that indicate a gradual increase in the frequency of manos during the Early Formative period. Increased numbers of manos indicate more intensive grinding activities being carried out through time. Clark (1994: Figure 70) plots the inverse relationship between fire-cracked rock (decreasing) and manos (increasing) as another indication of changing food preparation techniques. Later in this chapter, I document the overall quantity of ground stone as a more generalized measure of the amount of grinding activity undertaken by the inhabitants of Cuauhtémoc. The relative quantity of grinding implements recovered from middens of different phases reflects changes in the quantity of grinding that was carried out by the inhabitants of Cuauhtémoc. Ceramic grater bowls and round pestles from the Conchas phase are also discussed, and I argue that their use to grind condiments, pigments, temper and so forth further expanded the range of grinding tools used during Horizon II.

Fifth, the relative proportion of manos and metates to mortars and pestles is presented. Overall, there is little ground stone from the Early Formative Soconusco. Lowe (1967: 58–60; and see Davis 1975) used the lack of manos and metates, and abundance of obsidian chips, to suggest that manioc was being used as a staple crop (see also DeBoer 1975). In describing Initial Ceramic Period ground stone technology, Clark (1994: 236) states that " . . . data on early grinding implements indicate that they were (1) present in limited numbers, (2) designed for small grinding tasks and probably a range of tasks, and (3) generally little worn. From the perspective of later developments in grinding technology, Early Formative tools appear unspecialized, inefficient, and light weight." The proportion of manos and metates to mortars and pestles is another way to look at changing food preparation techniques. Manos provide more grinding surface than pestles, and thus an increase in their use indicates an increase in the quantity of materials being ground. Furthermore, experimental studies indicate that metates are more efficient to produce fine flour through wet-grinding soaked maize seeds whereas mortars function better for grinding dry substances (Adams 1999).

Sixth, I present the relative density of obsidian. As just mentioned, Lowe (1967) and Davis (1975) used the abundance of obsidian chips (along with a lack of manos and metates) to argue that manioc rather than maize was a staple crop. However, noting the lack of wear on most obsidian, Clark et al. (1989) argue that the high quantities of this shiny lithic material can be explained as gifts distributed by aggrandizers to their followers at competitive feasts during the Barra through Cherla phases (Clark and Blake 1994). Changing relative quantities of obsidian may partially reflect their distribution at feasts but also can be attributed to the more utilitarian uses of this sharp cutting material.

I quantify each of these variables at Cuauhtémoc and extend the analysis temporally beyond that undertaken in the Mazatán zone to incorporate Conchas-phase patterns. In a number of cases, data from combined Barra-/Locona-phase contexts were omitted from discussion due to small sample size that produced unreliable results. However, results from these early deposits do not differ greatly from those produced by pure Locona-phase contexts, so their omission does not impact the overall assessment of changing artifact patterns between epochs. As I am ultimately attempting to evaluate the effects of the San Lorenzo polity on the Soconusco during Horizon I, it is first the transition from the Ocós to the Cuerla phase and then the change from the Jocotal to the Conchas phase that are most significant.

Ceramic data

Style/decoration and function are basic criteria used to analyze archaeological ceramic remains. The style and decoration of pottery vessels is often the basis for tracking chronological change. Function (inferred by form) often provides information on technological developments that reflect the adaptive use of these objects. Of course, technological change can be effectively employed as temporal markers, and stylistic change is far from passive within society as it is often the result of purposeful social strategies (Hodder 1982b; Wobst 1977). Therefore, changing style may be an important aspect of the way ceramic vessels function within society. However, the basic distinction between style and function is a useful analytic division. In this chapter, I examine the changing function of ceramic containers within Cuauhtémoc society and leave their evolving stylistic information to be explored in Chapter 6.

In two years of excavation, a total of 94,224 ceramic sherds were recovered and 11,224 of these were rims. From this sample universe, the most secure contexts (Appendix 1) were chosen and all refits glued back together. The resulting subsample consists of 4,381 refitted rim sherds. Small rim sherds with less than 5% of their circumference intact were further eliminated as accurate measurements on most variables were either not possible or else not reliably replicable. The resulting sample used for the following analyses consists of 2,972 refitted rims more than 5% complete from the most secure contexts at Cuauhtémoc. Twenty-three variables were coded for each of these rim sherds. When type, decoration and metric dimensions were identical for various sherds within an excavation lot, they were counted only once to produce the MNV statistics. Therefore, two sherds that could be refitted were counted only once, but so were rims of the same type and size that could have been from the same vessel. The MNV reduces the chance that vessels with large orifice diameters will produce higher counts (than will those with smaller openings) simply due to their size. MNV values are used in each of the following ceramic analyses to gauge the relative importance of different vessel types (Love [2002a: 88] calculates ceramic MNV slightly differently).

Proportion of undecorated tecomates

The proportion of undecorated tecomates (to the total number of vessels) at Cuauhtémoc shows a progressive increase through the three phases of the Initial Ceramic Period (Figure 5.7). Therefore, following Clark and Gosser's (1995) logic outlined earlier in this chapter for the Mazatán zone, steaming food in pots appears to have become more common at Cuauhtémoc during the course of the Initial Ceramic Period. During Horizon I, there was a reversal in this trend and the relative proportion of undecorated tecomates decreased. However, instead of indicating a decrease in steaming food (i.e., the reverse of the Initial Ceramic Period interpretation), this decrease is likely due to an overall increase in the number of dishes used at this time (Rosenswig 2005: Appendix 5) rather than a return to earlier cooking techniques. A decrease in undecorated tecomates during Horizon I is also documented in the Mazatán zone by Clark and Gosser (1995: Figure 17.3) – although not discussed by these authors. Such a decrease in the relative proportion of undecorated tecomates in both zones of the Soconusco during Horizon I is likely explained by an increased importance of serving food in public contexts such as feasts, as I argue later in this chapter.

Figure 5.7
Proportion of undecorated tecomates to total
MNV.

These Cuauhtémoc data further indicate that the Cherla- and Cuadros-phase assemblages resemble assemblages from the Initial Ceramic Period phases more than either resemble the Jocotal or Conchas phase assemblages, suggesting a gradual introduction of

Proportion of Undecorated Tecomates

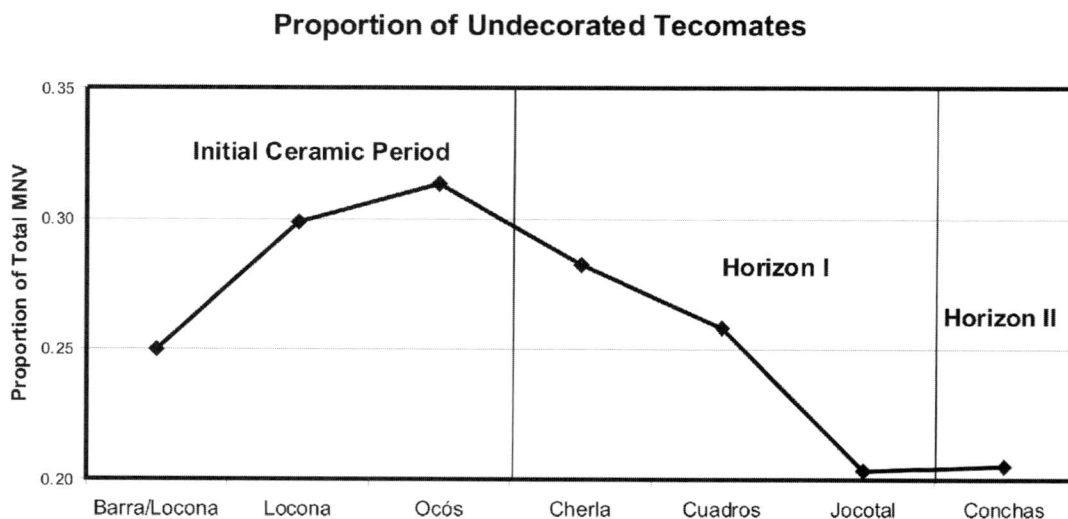

new practices. In contrast, there is no change from the end of Horizon I to Horizon II in the proportion of undecorated tecomates, which suggests a stable practice of food preparation.

Wall thickness of undecorated tecomates

Although Figure 5.7 indicates that relatively fewer undecorated tecomates were in use over time at Cuauhtémoc, the average size of these tecomates increased during Horizon I and II (Figure 5.8). This finding provides quantitative data on a long-noted pattern. Initial Ceramic Period tecomate patterns from Cuauhtémoc show a slight decrease in wall thickness for each phase from 0.74 cm to 0.69 cm during the Ocós phase. This slight decrease is followed by an increase in average wall thickness during the Cherla phase to 0.77 cm and a more significant increase documented by Cuadros (0.93 cm), Jocotal (0.92 cm) and Conchas (0.97 cm) samples. The small Cherla-phase change from the previous Initial Ceramic Period patterns suggests that the Horizon I increase in wall thickness was a gradual change at Cuauhtémoc. Then, relatively thicker tecomates from the Cuadros, Jocotal and Conchas assemblages suggest that relatively less technological change occurred during the Horizon I to Horizon II transition. As I argue later in this chapter, decrease in MNV and increase in size

Figure 5.8
Average wall thickness of undecorated tecomates.

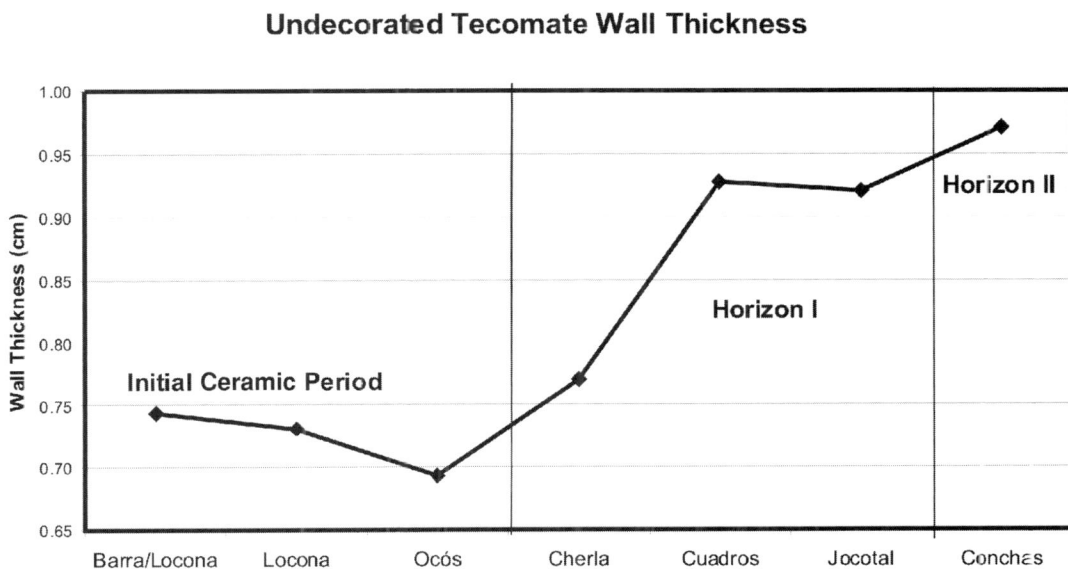

Undecorated Tecomate Wall Thickness

Table 5.3. Counts and weights of fire-cracked rock, ground stone and obsidian from temporally secure contexts

	Fire-cracked rock		Ground stone		Obsidian	
	#	Kg	#	Kg	#	Kg
Barra/Locona	130	8.035	2	0.320	752	1.196
Locona	288	16.000	15	2.710	2126	3.089
Ocós	74	6.160	2	0.170	702	1.133
Cherla	26	2.015	3	0.330	499	0.411
Cuadros	5	0.180	0	0.000	168	0.163
Jocotal	6	0.245	1	0.030	239	0.208
Conchas	197	13.705	46	12.596	2021	1.864
Total:	**726**	**46.340**	**69**	**16.156**	**6507**	**8.064**

(wall thickness) indicate that fewer, larger tecomates may have been used at Cuauhtémoc to prepare food for larger groups of people.

Fire-cracked rock density

Fire-cracked rock density is presented as both counts and weights standardized by excavated volume (see Table 5.3). There seems to be considerably less fire-cracked rock during the Cuadros and Joco-tal phases than during the preceding Initial Ceramic Period phases (Figure 5.9). Again, changes during the course of Horizon I did not occur suddenly. The density of fire-cracked rock in Cherla-phase contexts is only slightly less than in contexts dating to the Locona phase. The high Ocós-phase density may be the result of the relatively small Ocós sample providing anomalous results. Although not as tidy as the results presented from the Mazatán zone (Clark and Gosser 1995: Figure 17.3; Lesure 1995: Figure 6.13), the Cuauhtémoc data demonstrate roughly the same pattern. That is, considerably more fire-cracked rock during the Initial Ceramic Period, less during the Cherla phase and even less for the rest of Horizon I.

The density of fire-cracked rock increased at Cuauhtémoc during the Conchas phase when levels were just slightly below those of the Cherla phase. This finding may suggest an increase in the practice of pit roasting during Conchas times. Alternatively, it could indicate more intensive occupation of the site (i.e., higher population density or longer occupation) during the Conchas phase as compared to Horizon I. Overall, from the perspective of the entire occupation of

Fire-Cracked Rock Density

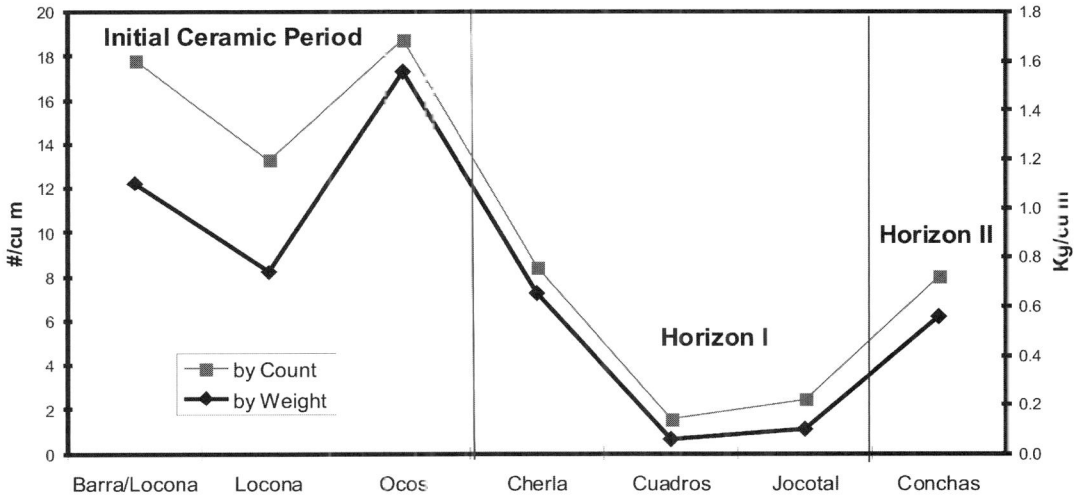

Cuauhtémoc, the low density of fire-cracked rock during the Cuadros and Jocotal phases is the most striking pattern.

Figure 5.9
Count and weight of fire-cracked rock per cubic meter excavated.

Ground stone density

Due to a relatively small sample size (see Table 5.3), ground stone data were lumped into the three epochs when presented in Figure 5.10. The results are temporally coarser than other measurements,

Figure 5.10
Count and weight of ground stone per cubic meter excavated over time.

Ground Stone Density

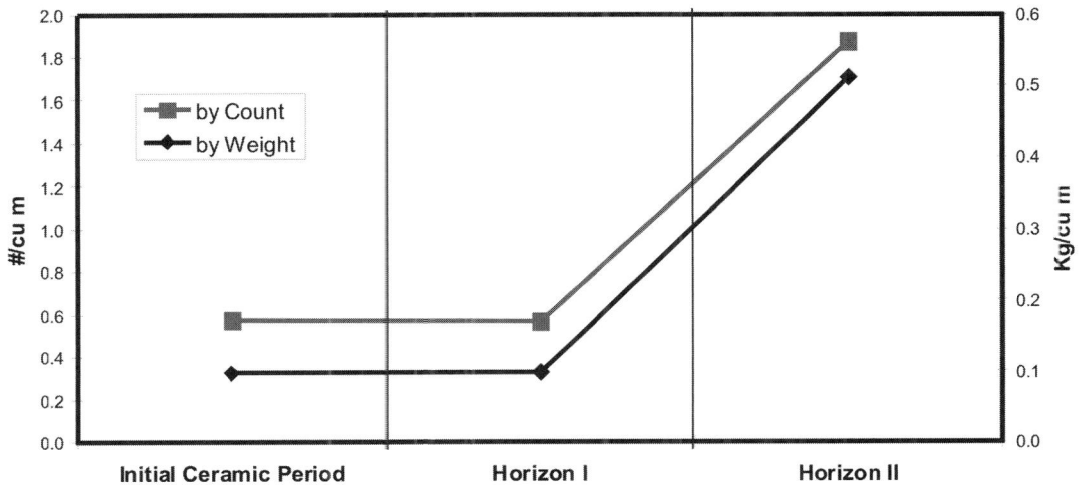

but, as discussed for faunal patterns, more reliable due to increased sample size. These data indicate, that, calculated by either count or weight, a similar overall quantity of ground stone tools was in use during both the Initial Ceramic Period and Horizon I. Furthermore, there was a significant increase in the relative quantity of ground stone used at Cuauhtémoc during Horizon II. This increase is not surprising due to the maize density and isotopic results discussed earlier in this chapter that indicate a greater reliance on maize during the Conchas phase. The use of maize as a staple crop would have required grinding tools if this grain was to be consumed as tortillas or other forms of bread. Therefore, the results in Figure 5.10 provide an independent line of evidence for the use of maize as a staple crop only during Horizon II at Cuauhtémoc (Rosenswig 2006a; and see Morris 1990).

Coe and Diehl (1980b: 223–234) recovered 101 manos and 290 metate fragments, 28 mortars and 7 pestles from San Lorenzo. No Ojochi-phase ground stone was recovered, and only one mano fragment was recovered from Bajío-phase contexts (Coe and Diehl 1980b: Tables 5.1 and 5.2). Furthermore, the majority of ground stone was recovered from San Lorenzo B–phase contexts and the second greatest quantity from Nacaste-phase contexts. Although the exact numbers are not available, considerably fewer cubic meters were excavated from Nacaste contexts compared to San Lorenzo B–phase contexts. A relative increase in ground stone may thus be indicated from Horizon I to II contexts at San Lorenzo. Therefore, at San Lorenzo, maize also may not have been used as a staple crop until Horizon II (and see VanDerwarker 2006: 195). A Middle Formative date for the first intensive use of maize is also consistent with iconographic changes (Taube 2000, 2004: 25–29) and is discussed at greater length in Chapter 6.

Ground stone form

We have just seen that, compared with earlier times, there was a significant increase in the overall quantity of ground stone during the Conchas phase. The type of ground stone tools also changed at this time, and more manos and metates were used relative to mortars and pestles (Figure 5.11). The fact that manos and metates tend to weigh more than mortars and pestles accounts for the ratio being almost twice as great when assemblage counts are compared

Manos & Metates : Mortars & Pestles

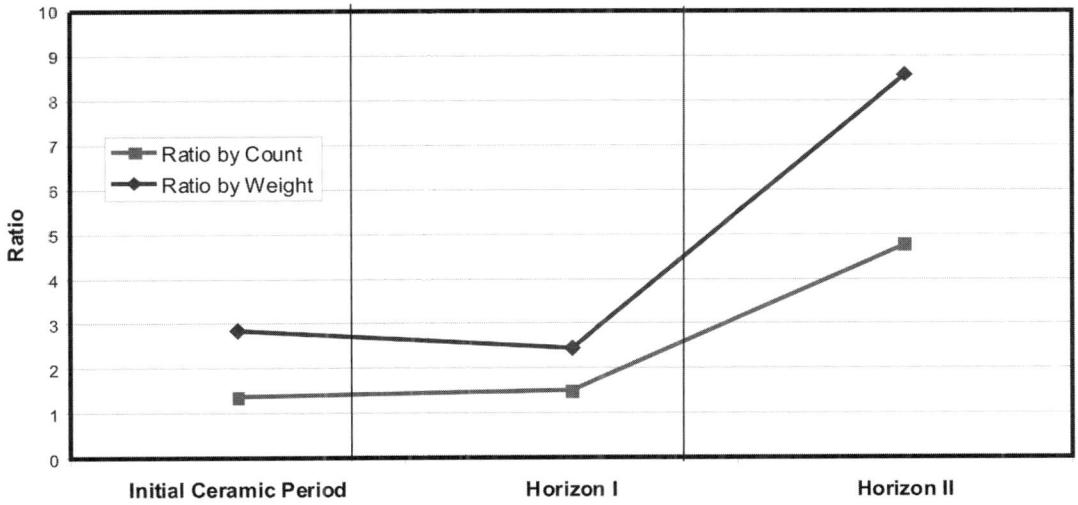

to weights (e.g., Horizon II is 4.8:1 by count and 8.5:1 by weight). However, a significant increase is indicated by either measure during Horizon II. A parallel pattern is documented at La Joya in the Tuxtla mountains on the Gulf of Mexico, where only mortars and pestles were recovered from Early Formative contexts and then manos and metates dominated the ground stone assemblage in later periods (Arnold 2000: 127).

Figure 5.11
Ratio of manos and metates to mortars and pestles over time.

Conchas-phase grater bowls

Due to their sudden appearance during the Conchas phase and dis-appearance after the phase, grater bowls are a very useful Horizon II marker in the Soconusco.[3] These vessels are complex silhouette dishes with either three or four supports and incised lines cover-ing the base of their interior surface (Figure 5.12 and see Coe 1961:

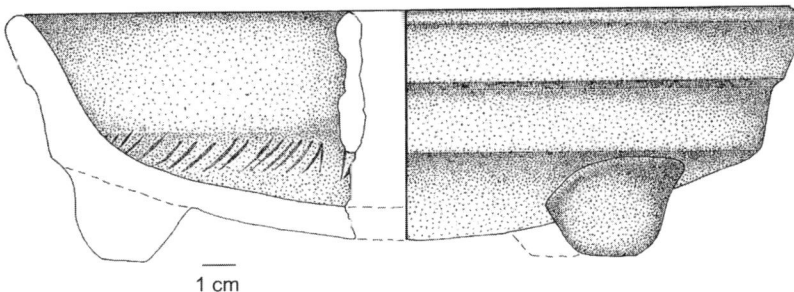

1 cm

Figure 5.12
Conchas-phase grater bowl from Cuauhtémoc (Suboperation 7, Lot 48). Drawing by Wilberth Cruz.

Figure 26, 52q-s, 53; Love 2002a: Figure 51). Conchas-phase grater bowls can be fancy, slipped vessels with fine and intricate patterns of incisions or only slightly burnished with crude incisions. They often show evidence of extensive use to the point where the interior incisions were completely worn away except where the vessel base meets the wall (Figure 5.13). The incisions from this small area were only preserved because the grinding implement used with this class of vessels could not reach all the way into the corner. Note, for example, in Figure 5.13B where slip has been worn away from the interior base as well as from the bottom of the wall (indicated by arrow).

Conchas-phase grater bowls were first reported from the Soconusco at La Victoria (Coe 1961) and Love (2002a: Figure 51) also illustrates a number of examples from La Blanca. Grater bowls can be best understood functionally as expanding the range of grinding implements to include a new media of manufacture. As we have just seen, the appearance of grater bowls during the Conchas phase corresponds to the time when maize was first used as a staple crop. Furthermore, the Conchas phase was when both the overall quantity of ground stone (Figure 5.10) and the proportion of manos and metates (Figure 5.11) used at Cuauhtémoc increased dramatically. Manos and metates are used to grind a wide array of materials including corn, cacao, clay and tempers for pottery production as well as chilies and other spices (Clark 1988: 91). Chilies, as well as other spices and soft vegetable matter, would be ideal to grind on ceramic grater bowls. As they provided a deep container, grater bowls would have been an ideal tool to grind such dry substances (Adams 1999). If ceramic grater bowls were used to grind soft materials, then a larger proportion of stone tools could be used to process maize. Therefore, the increase in overall quantity of ground stone, the increase in the proportion of manos and metates, as well as the novel use of grater bowls all appear to be part of a reorganization of food preparation technology during Horizon II.

Another tool that became popular during the Conchas phase was the small, round stone pestle (Figure 5.14). These pestles fit comfortably into most grater bowls, and their diameter generally corresponds to the unworn area of incisions at the edges of the grater bowl bases. Together, grater bowls and round pestles form a tool kit that is functionally analogous to the mortar and pestle. Along with a reliance on maize during the Conchas phase there was, not surprisingly, an increased use of the lithic tools to grind it. As no

5 cm

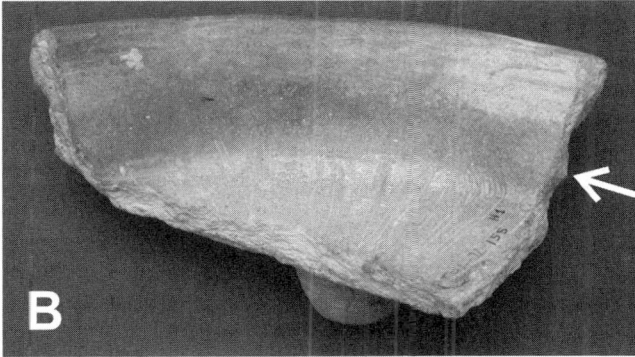

Figure 5.13
Photo of grinding dam-
age on interior of grater
bowls. Examples from
Suboperation 7, Lot 48
drawn in Figure 5.12.

such lithic material is available on the coastal plain of the Soconusco, the increased demand placed on the available ground stone may have encouraged people to fulfill some of their grinding needs with ceramic vessels that could be made from locally available clays.

Complex silhouette vessels are also a significant component of the following Horizon III Duende-, Escalón- and Frontera-phase assemblages. However, none of the complex silhouette vessels from Horizon III were grater bowls. The sudden disappearance of grater bowls after the Conchas phase hints at the possibility that increased ground stone exchange may have allowed people to return to using stone tools to fulfill all of their grinding needs. The closest source of stone to make manos and metates is Tajumulco, which is also a source of obsidian (Clark 1988: 130).

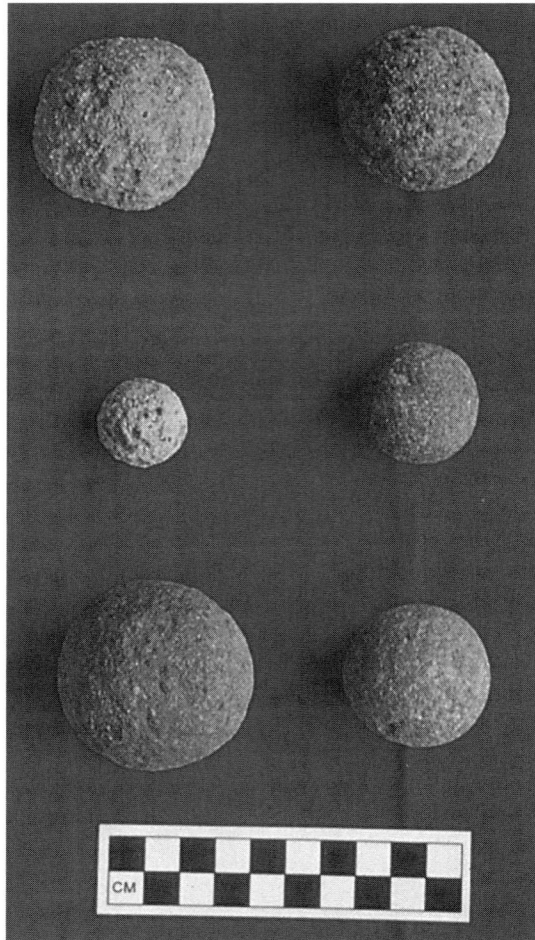

Figure 5.14
Conchas-phase round
stone pestles from
Cuauhtémoc.

Obsidian density

The density of obsidian was relatively higher from deposits dating
to the Initial Ceramic Period than from those dating to the later two
horizons through which Cuauhtémoc was occupied (Figure 5.15).
This pattern is especially evident if we rely on changing obsidian
density measured by weight. As with fire-cracked rock (Figure 5.9),
the density of obsidian during the Ocós phase seems quite high.
Although elevated levels of these two materials may be due to some
bias of the deposits sampled, overall patterns are still discernable.

There is a marked decrease in the density of obsidian from
deposits dating to after the Cherla phase. Cuadros-phase deposits
contain approximately one-third the quantity of obsidian of Cherla-
phase deposits when measured by either count (51.6 and 161.4

pieces/cu m = 31.97%) or weight (0.050 and 0.133 Kg/cu m = 37.59%). In the Mazatán zone, obsidian density during the Cuadros phase fell to 20% that of earlier times (Clark et al. 1989: 278). Although the decrease at Cuauhtémoc was not as dramatic, its timing during the Cuadros phase (especially when documented in terms of count) suggests that similar changes in the use of obsidian were occurring from one end to the other of the land between the Soconusco swamps. The decrease in obsidian density at Cuauhtémoc is thus consistent with the interpretation by Clark et al. (1989) that by the Cuadros phase obsidian was no longer employed as a gift to be given away by aggrandizers.

Of course, obsidian also has the utilitarian function of providing an effective cutting edge. A certain amount of the Initial Ceramic Period obsidian recovered from Cuauhtémoc was undoubtedly being used for cutting purposes. However, as obsidian densities remained constant from the Jocotal to the Conchas phase, the Horizon I to Horizon II transition does not appear to reflect a major change. The timing of change in obsidian density instead occurs after the Initial Ceramic Period.

Summary of food preparation evidence

Based on the evidence presented earlier in this chapter, food preparation tools changed twice during the occupation of Cuauhtémoc. The

Figure 5.15
Count and weight of obsidian per cubic meter excavated over time.

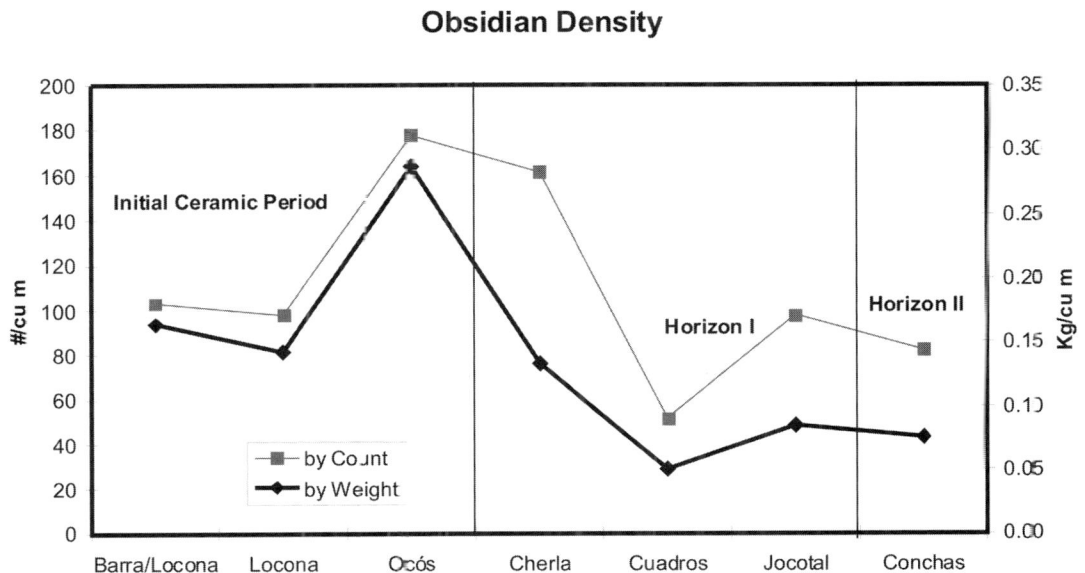

Obsidian Density

first change occurred during the transition from the Initial Ceramic Period to Horizon I. This change is documented by the increased proportion of plain tecomates and the increase in their size as well as decreases in the quantity of both fire-cracked rock and obsidian. In each of the four cases, Cherla-phase patterns indicate a gradual transition between the Initial Ceramic Period and the Cuadros- and Jocotal-phase patterns. Furthermore, little change in three of these variables is documented into the following Horizon II. This continuity suggests that the changes in food preparation that occurred at the beginning of Horizon I became stable practices retained by the residents of Cuauhtémoc until the site was abandoned. The one exception was fire-cracked rock, which, after almost completely falling out of use during the Cuadros and Jocotal phases, increased again during the Conchas phase.

A number of the technological changes documented at Cuauhtémoc during Horizon II relate to an increase in tools required to process maize. There was an overall increase in the amount of ground stone used at this time as well as an increase in the relative proportion of manos and metates compared to mortars and pestles. I also have argued that ceramic grater bowls were used at this time to further expand the quantity of grinding tools available. Together, these three lines of evidence support macrobotanical (Figure 5.4), isotopic (Blake et al. 1992b) and iconographic (Taube 2000) data that maize became a staple cereal crop for the first time only at the beginning of the Middle Formative period (see Rosenswig 2006a).

FEASTING AT CUAUHTÉMOC

Feasting is a realm of behavior that, although based in the biological function of eating, also serves political and ritual functions. Not always strictly economic, feasts do provide an occasion when resources are amassed to exchange them, give them away, gamble with them and so forth. Feasts provide a cross-culturally relevant form of social interaction that brings people together in a dynamic context of eating and drinking (see Rosenswig 2007: 1–3). Feasts also provide a competitive forum where social norms can be challenged and subverted. Dietler (2001: 66) contends "...both that feasts are inherently political and that they constitute a fundamental instrument and theater of political relations." Furthermore, (following Appadurai [1981]), "...as public events, in contrast to daily activity, feasts provide an arena for the highly condensed symbolic representation of social relations" (Dietler 1996: 89). Feasts are thus an archaeologically visible social context where the economic, political and ideological dimensions of society intersect (Rosenswig 2007: 22–23).

Ceramics can be used as an indirect measure of the presentation side of feasting behavior. Again, I am not excavating at Pompeii or Cerén, and so, do not attempt to reconstruct particular feasts and ascribe to them specific meaning. Instead, the "festive landscape" will form a palimpsest of different types of feasts (Dietler 2001: 93), and the residue from these events will be averaged (over the multiple generations that constitute each ceramic phase) and be deposited as secondary refuse in the village middens at Cuauhtémoc (Rosenswig 2009). The previous two sections of this chapter have addressed the food eaten and tools used to prepare food. In this section, I explore evidence of food presentation.

The first variable I quantify is the proportion of serving vessels relative to the number of cooking vessels (see Welch and Scarry 1995: Figure 6). Feasting has been inferred from the presence of a high proportion of fancy serving vessels from a range of archaeological contexts (e.g., Clark and Blake 1994; Dietler 1990; Junker 2001: 289–294; Pauketat et al. 2002: 269–270; Turkon 2004: 236–237; Welch and Scarry 1995: 410–415). An increase in the relative quantity of serving to preparation vessels implies a shift in emphasis to the presentation of food over its preparation for simple nutritional purposes.

Second, I present changing average wall thicknesses of decorated tecomates through time. Fancy tecomates were presumably used for serving liquids, so changing size of such vessels is relevant to feasting. As in the previous section, wall thickness is employed as an admittedly imperfect proxy measure of overall tecomate size. Larger vessels used for preparing and storing food imply that larger groups of people were being prepared for as is the case at feasts. As the size of decorated tecomates relative to undecorated tecomates is also relevant, wall thickness of plain tecomates is presented again from Figure 5.8 and compared to their decorated counterparts.

Third, the proportion of decorated dishes is calculated relative to all dishes. Although related to the first variable, fancy dishes form a functionally distinctive subset of all serving vessels. A higher proportion of fancy serving dishes implies the importance specifically of food presentation. Plain dishes fulfill utilitarian roles whereas the energy and attention required to decorate dishes emphasize the social and/or symbolic role that these vessels also fulfill.

The fourth variable I quantify is the changing average size of serving dishes through time. Average rim diameters provide an approximate measure of the size of a dish. As with tecomates, a more accurate measurement would be the volume that a dish could hold. However, the sample size of sherds with rim diameter, base diameter (for outsloping and outflaring dishes), as well as wall height is quite small (as in the case of most midden assemblages). Rim diameter is thus used as a proxy measure of dish size. Feasting in politically charged contexts has been inferred by archaeologists based on the presence of large serving dishes (e.g., Blitz 1993; Henrickson and McDonald 1983; Junker 1999: 331–333; Lesure 1995: 275–277; Potter 2000: Figure 6). Such vessels in elite contexts suggest that this small segment of society sponsored events such as feasts where large numbers of people were served. However, a more general increase in the size of fancy dishes used by society at large indicates a change in the festive landscape to bigger groups of people being served.

Fifth, the distribution of decorated dish rim diameters is presented from each phase. The distribution nuances the average diameter measurements and allows for the investigation of different size classes of serving vessels. There is ethnographic evidence to support the contention that larger serving vessels are used at feasts. To mention two recently published examples of people using two or more distinct serving vessel size ranges, DeBoer (2003) has reported this pattern among the Shipibo of Peru and Adams (2004) has done so among the Sulawesi of Indonesia.

For each of the five variables discussed, I assume that secondary refuse provides a conglomerate of all types of garbage, including that from feasts (see Rosenswig 2007: 6). If more feasts were held, then fancier and/or larger vessels would have been used, broken and eventually deposited in trash contexts. As the aggregated village midden assemblages from each phase have similar depositional histories, no complex simplifying assumptions are required as is the case when comparing multiple household assemblages to each other. Diachronic comparisons provide a village level average of serving vessels at Cuauhtémoc over the course of the site's occupation.

Proportion of serving-to-cooking vessels

For this analysis, serving vessels consist of decorated dishes and tecomates, whereas cooking vessels are unslipped tecomates (Figure 5.16). The slight decrease in the proportion of serving vessels from the Locona to Ocós phases may reflect a diversification of vessel forms. As already discussed, Barra-phase fancy tecomates were some of the earliest ceramics used in Mesoamerica, and the novelty of making containers of this new medium was harnessed by village leaders as prestigious feasting paraphernalia (Clark and Gosser 1995: 216). The Locona- and Ocós-phase introduction of dishes used to present and display food was accompanied by an expanded range of functions filled by ceramic vessels. Gourds, baskets and/or wood vessels could have been used to hold and process food during Late Archaic and Barra times. The expansion of ceramic forms to include utilitarian types would account for the apparent decrease in the proportion of serving vessels during the course of the Initial Ceramic Period (Figure 5.16).

The subsequent increase in the relative proportion of serving vessels from Cuadros-phase contexts suggests an increased emphasis on serving activities. However, changes are slight, especially between Ocós and Cherla assemblages, so any such interpretation must be made cautiously. Figure 5.16 does indicate a higher proportion of serving vessels during the Cuadros, Jocotal and Conchas phases than during Locona and Cherla times.

Figure 5.16
Proportion of serving-to-cooking vessels over time.

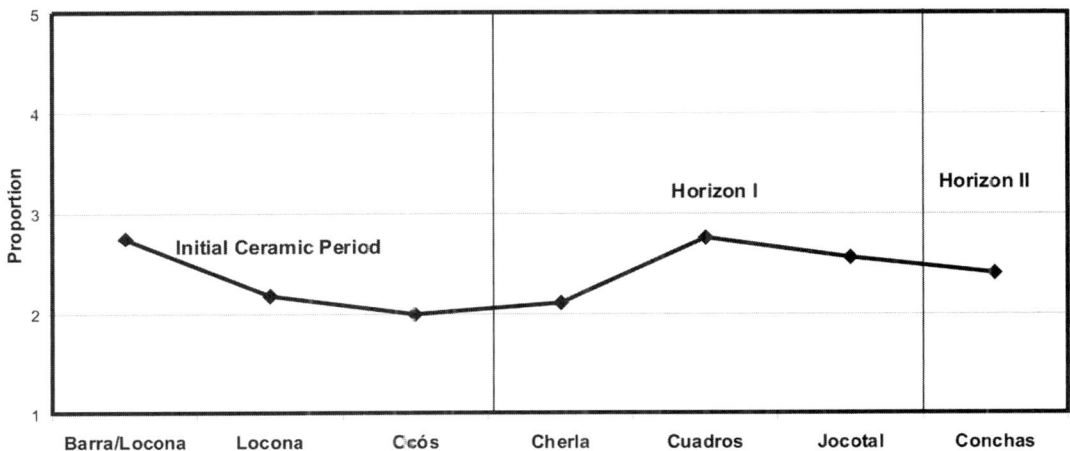

Proportion of Serving-to-Cooking Vessels

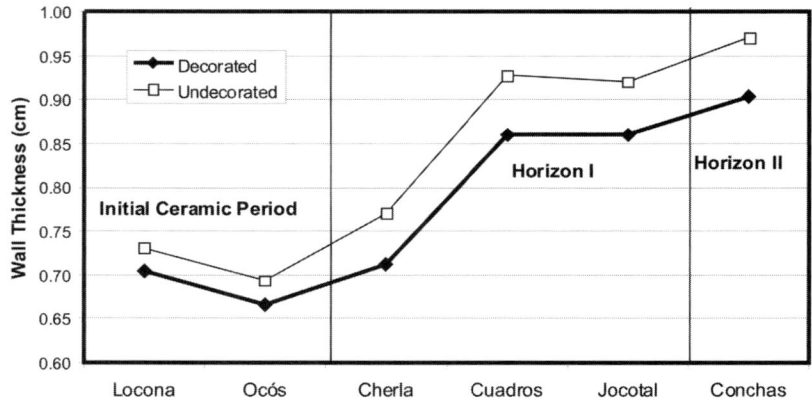

Figure 5.17
Wall thickness of deco-
rated and undecorated
tecomates.

There is a dramatically higher proportion of serving vessels from the elite Conchas-phase contexts than from village middens at this time (see Rosenswig 2007: Figure 16). Serving-to-cooking vessel ratios have been used by a number of analysts as an index of status (e.g., Costin and Earle 1989; Drennan 1976b: 117; Welch 1991: 56–58). The residents of Mound 2 were of a higher status than the other residents of Cuauhtémoc during the Conchas phase, as I argue at length elsewhere (Rosenswig 2007).

Wall thickness of decorated tecomates

Beginning during the Cherla phase, there was a progressive increase in the wall thickness of tecomates decorated with slip or incisions (Figure 5.17). This increase was small from the Ocós to the Cherla phase but was significantly higher when the Locona, Ocós and Cherla phases are considered together and compared to the Cuadros, Jocotal and Conchas phases. This pattern suggests an increase in the average size of groups being served liquids at events such as feasts, where decorated tecomates would have been used.

Decorated tecomates increased in size less through time than their undecorated counterparts did (Figure 5.18). Average decorated teco-mate wall thicknesses were 0.03 and 0.02 cm thinner than those of undecorated tecomates during the Locona and Ocós phases, 0.06 cm thinner during the Cherla and Jocotal phases and 0.07 cm thinner during Cuadros times (Figure 5.18). Although this difference is not statistically significant, it may nonetheless suggest that, as all tecomates were increasing in size, slipped tecomates increased proportionally less through time. For each phase, the average decorated tecomate walls were thinner than those of undecorated ones (Figure 5.17), so these size/decoration classes became more pronounced over time.

Proportion of decorated dishes

The proportions of decorated dishes relative to the total MNV of all vessels are presented in Figure 5.19. The overall proportion of all dishes (combined decorated and undecorated) increased significantly at Cuauhtémoc during the Cherla phase (Rosenswig 2005: Appendix 5). Figure 5.19 indicates that the proportion of decorated dishes also increased at Cuauhtémoc beginning during the Cherla phase. Overall, there was a relatively low proportion of decorated dishes in Initial Ceramic Period assemblages followed by a marked increase in the relative proportion of decorated dishes during each of the three Horizon I phases. Such an increase in the proportion of decorated dishes during the Cherla phase contrasts with the slight overall increase in serving-to-cooking vessel proportions documented in Figure 5.16. Such a discrepancy may suggest that, at the beginning of Horizon I, serving food in decorated containers occurred more frequently, so it was an increasingly more important social event than during the Initial Ceramic Period.

Figure 5.18
Difference in wall thickness between decorated and undecorated tecomates.

Decorated vs. Undecorated Tecomate Wall Thickness

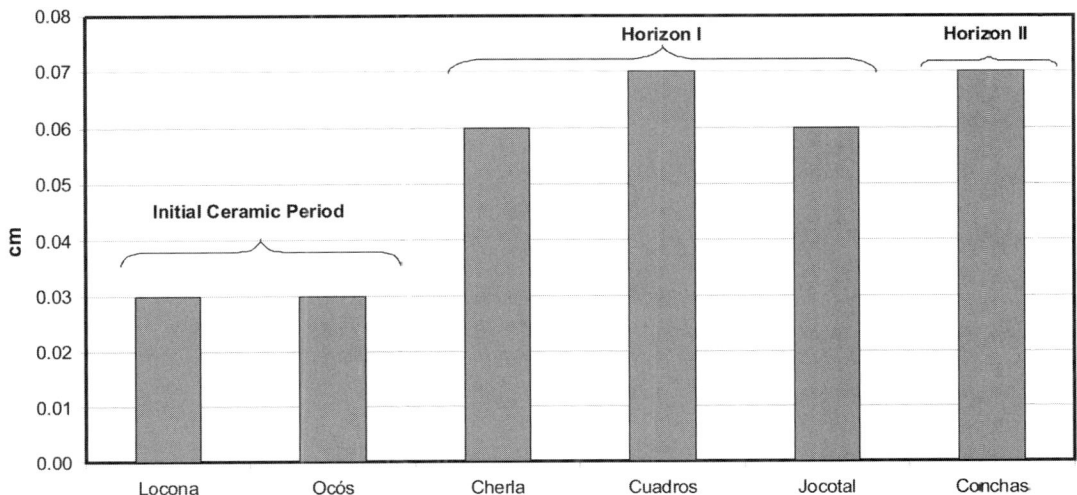

Table 5.4. Average rim diameter of decorated dishes from village middens at Cuauhtémoc

Phase	Sample size (MNV)	Rim diameter of decorated dishes			
		Average (cm)	Median (cm)	Mode (cm)	Standard deviation
Barra/Locona	12	**19.75**	21	21	5.58
Locona	153	**20.52**	21	21	6.53
Ocós	40	**20.65**	20.5	27	6.15
Cherla	69	**23.17**	24	26	6.08
Cuadros	83	**24.18**	24	20	7.89
Jocotal	64	**24.53**	25	23	5.49
Conchas	342	**23.87**	23	21	6.65

Average rim diameter of decorated dishes

The average rim diameter of decorated dishes was lower during the Initial Ceramic Period (at approximately 20 cm) and higher during Horizon I and II (at 23 or 24 cm) (Table 5.4). This pattern is not surprising as I have already qualitatively characterized the Initial Ceramic Period pottery assemblage as consisting of small bowls. These summary data provide quantitative confirmation of the smaller size of Initial Ceramic Period decorated dishes. More significant than this overall summary pattern is when the distribution of rim diameters of decorated dishes is presented from each phase (Figures 5.20 and 5.21).

Figure 5.19
Proportion of decorated dishes by phase as a proportion of MNV over time.

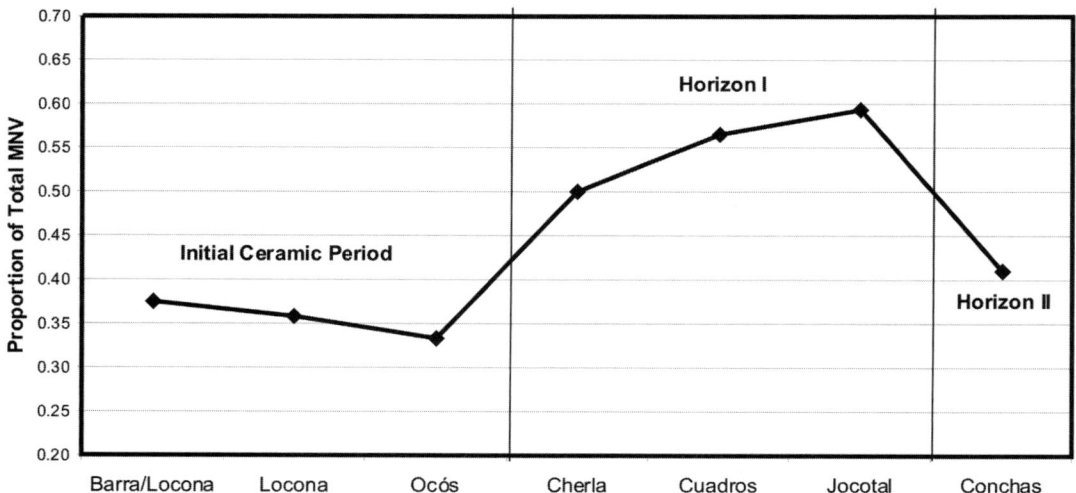

Proportion of Decorated Dishes

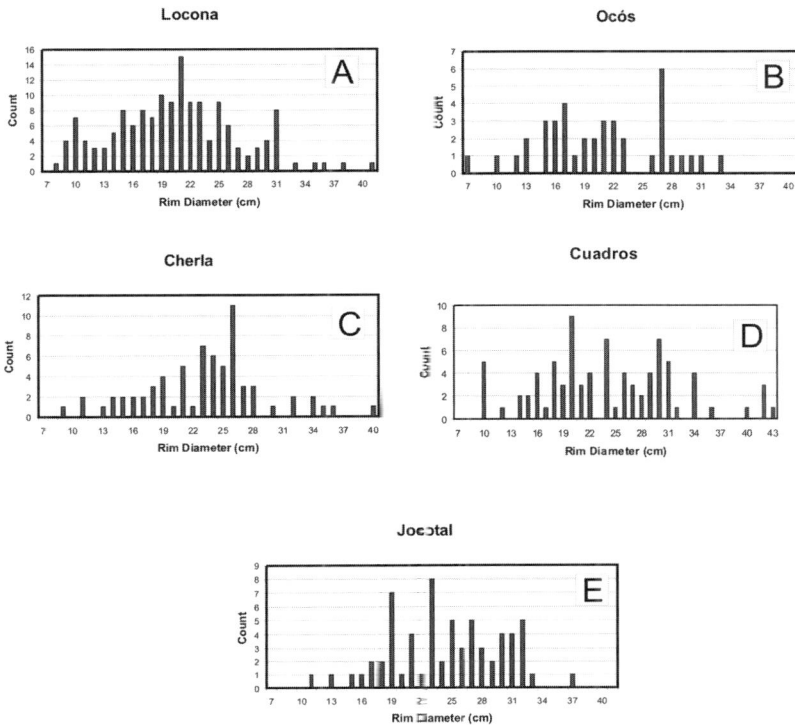

Figure 5.20
Rim diameters of deco-
rated dishes for Initial
Ceramic Period and
Horizon I assemblages.

Rim diameters of decorated dishes

The distribution of rim diameters of Initial Ceramic Period decorated dishes shows a number of size classes (Figure 5.20). The Locona phase sample suggests one size class less than 13 cm, one approximately 14 to 28 cm and a third larger than 28 cm (Figure 5.20A). During the Ocós phase, the distribution is roughly equivalent with small vessels less than 17 cm, medium vessels between 17 and 24 cm and large vessels bigger than 25 cm. Due to a relatively small sample size, the Ocós-phase pattern should be interpreted cautiously.

During Horizon I, rim diameters are larger on average than before, and three vessel size ranges can be discerned. There are a few Cherla-phase vessels smaller than 12 cm, the majority fall between 13 and 30 cm and there are a few larger vessels measuring 32 to 40 cm in diameter (Figure 5.20C). Cuadros-phase dishes can be separated into those smaller than 13 cm, those 14 to 28 cm, those 28 to 36 cm and those measuring 40 cm or larger (Figure 5.20D). Similarly, Jocotal-phase dishes can be separated into those smaller than 20 cm, those measuring between 20 and 29 cm and those larger than 29 cm (Figure 5.20E).

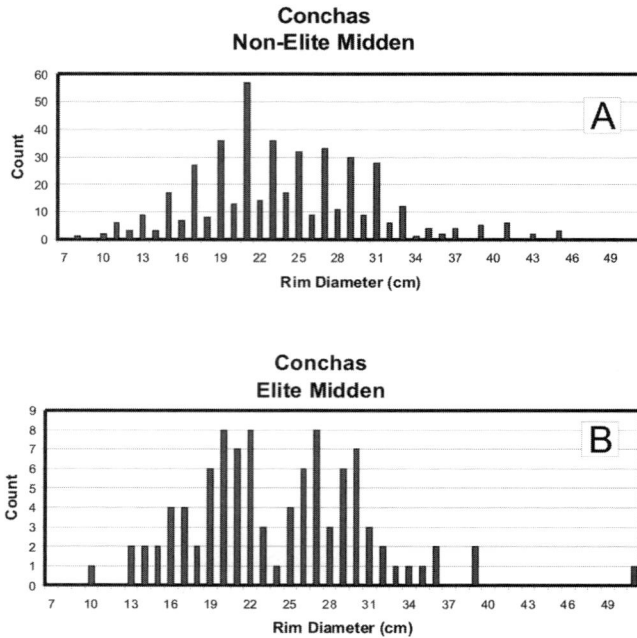

Figure 5.21
Rim diameters of decorated dishes from Horizon II non-elite and elite midden contexts.

During the Conchas phase, the range of rim diameters varied between contexts of different social standing (Figure 5.21). The distribution of decorated dishes from non-elite midden contexts at Cuauhtémoc is normal with a slight skew to the right (Figure 5.21A).[4] In contrast, the distribution from elite midden contexts at this time shows a clear bimodal pattern (Figure 5.21B). Approximately half of the vessels are smaller than 24 cm and the other half are larger. A third size range could be designated for vessel from this assemblage that are larger than 34 cm, but relatively few vessels are included in this range. The largest decorated dish recovered is a Cuca Red-on-Buff serving dish that measured 51 cm in diameter.

As mentioned, the presence of larger vessels for serving larger groups of people corresponds to the pattern described ethnographically for feasting assemblage (e.g., Adams 2004; DeBoer 2003). Although different size classes could be arbitrarily set for the Conchas-phase village midden assemblage, clear peaks are not obvious. This finding is especially relevant as, with an MNV of 342, this assemblage has the largest sample size of any assemblage presented here (see Table 5.4). Assemblages of decorated dishes from earlier phases have discernable size classes and this makes the lack of size classes in village middens during the Conchas phase especially significant in light of clear size classes documented in contemporary elite deposits (see discussion of depositional contexts in Rosenswig 2009). This discrepancy in the distribution of decorated dish sizes provides another measure to document that a distinct set of material culture was used in elite contexts at Mound 2, dating to the Conchas phase. These contrasts and others between elite and non-elite contexts from the Conchas-phase occupation of Cuauhtémoc are explored at greater length elsewhere (Rosenswig 2007, 2009).

Summary of feasting evidence

Much has been written on feasting patterns during the Initial Ceramic Period in the Mazatán zone (e.g., Clark and Blake 1994; Lesure 1995, 1998). However, compared to residents in later times, the Initial Ceramic Period residents of Cuauhtémoc used proportionately fewer serving vessels and considerably fewer decorated dishes. Initial Ceramic Period decorated dishes were also smaller on average, so they appear to have been used for smaller groups of people.

During Horizon I, changes in serving technology developed gradually in the proportion of serving-to-cooking vessels as well as in terms of the increasing size of decorated tecomates. However, the proportion of decorated dishes and the size of these food presentation vessels increased markedly at this time. These measures suggest that, unlike changes in diet and food preparation, the Cherla phase was a time of significant change in the practice of serving food. In all variables documented in this section, changes in food-serving practices began during the Cherla phase and became more marked during the Cuadros and Jocotal phases.

The subsequent Jocotal-to-Conchas-phase transition does not indicate significant changes in patterns of food presentation. There were similar proportions of serving-to-cooking vessels, similar differences in the average size between slipped and unslipped tecomates and a similar average size of decorated dishes. However, there was a dramatically lower proportion of decorated dishes deposited in Conchas-phase village middens than was the case during the preceding Jocotal phase. So, although serving practices may have been similar, the Conchas-phase elite appears have been able to influence feasting practices to a degree not previously achieved.

SUMMARY OF THE CUAUHTÉMOC DOMESTIC ECONOMY

The Initial Ceramic Period was a time when the inhabitants of Cuauhtémoc consumed a broad range of plant food and many terrestrial as well as aquatic vertebrate animal species. Middens from this period contained a relatively high proportion of obsidian and fire-cracked rock. There was a relatively low proportion of ground stone compared to later times, and what ground stone there was consisted mostly of mortars and pestles. The ceramic assemblage was dominated by small tecomates, fewer serving dishes were used than at later times, and those that were used tended to be smaller. Therefore, smaller groups of people were served during the Initial Ceramic Period relative to patterns documented in Horizon I and Horizon II contexts at Cuauhtémoc.

During Horizon I, the Cuauhtémoc diet continued to be as broad as during the Initial Ceramic Period in terms of the plants and animals consumed. The one exception was a Cherla-phase pit feature (see Figure 5.2) packed with fish, clam and maize remains. Fire-cracked rock was found in lower frequencies during the Cuadros and Jocotal phases than in any other phase examined. Ground stone was still only present in low frequencies, and mortars and pestles continued to be relatively more common than manos and metates, in contrast to the following Horizon II patterns. However, Horizon I food preparation and storage tecomates decreased in relative frequency as they increased in average size. Decorated serving dishes also increased in size during this time. This finding indicates that the changes documented in food preparation and serving practices were not caused by changes in diet. Instead, I propose that the ceramic assemblages were changing as the result of a new scale of feasting activities. This new scale of feasting activities is most convincingly documented by increases in both the relative proportion of decorated dishes and the size of these vessels during the Cherla phase.

Beginning in Horizon II there was a fundamental change in the inhabitants of Cuauhtémoc's diet. Such changes include a narrowing of mammal exploitation to mostly dog and deer as well as a reliance on maize as a staple crop for the first time. Mortars and pestles were significantly replaced by manos and metates at this time. In addition, grater bowls expanded the range of grinding tools in use and compensated for the increased demand on stone tools to process maize.

However, the size of ceramic food preparation, storage and serving vessels generally remained the same as during Horizon I. The proportion of plain tecomates and the proportion of serving-to-cooking vessels was also the same as during the previous Jocotal phase. The quantity of fire-cracked rock at Cuauhtémoc in Horizon II contexts was higher after being almost absent during the Cuadros and Jocotal phases. The major economic changes at this time were the increased use of domestic plants and animals and the tools needed to process the former. However, given these dietary changes, other aspects of the Cuauhtémoc economy show a surprising level of consistency from Horizon I.

The emergence of agriculture is not explicitly dealt with by the three models outlined in Chapter 3, as most authors assume that maize agriculture was the basis of society. However, isotope evidence indicates that maize did not become a staple until the beginning of the Middle Formative period in the Soconusco (Blake 2006; Blake et al. 1992a) or on the Gulf Coast (Arnold 2000: 118–120; VanDerwarker 2006: 182–192). This finding has profound implications because it means that the changes occurring in Mesoamerica during Horizon I were not the result of the metabolic rift discussed at the beginning of this chapter (Rosenswig 2006a).

Overall, the economic base of Cuauhtémoc was transformed only during Horizon II. At that time, the diet changed to one in which maize was a staple crop and dog and deer meat was consumed in ever greater proportions. The overall quantity of ground stone increased as did the relative proportion of manos and metates that were used. Horizon II was also the time when many novel ceramic forms (including grater bowls) were introduced. In contrast, most of the Horizon I changes documented in this chapter correspond to a new host of feasting behaviors and, thus, relate to the superstructure. The economic base of Cuauhtémoc's residents during Horizon I shows remarkable continuity from their Initial Ceramic Period ancestors. Marx's metabolic rift, which generally corresponds to Rindos's (1984: 101; and see Rosenswig 2006a: 333–335) definition of agriculture, is only documented at Cuauhtémoc during the early Middle Formative Conchas phase.

NOTES

1. My point here is that the means of production sets limits on political structure and ideological content, not that they are determined by

the environment or the level of technology. The environment and level of technology structure what can occur in a nondeterministic manner in the sense of the possibilism that Trigger (2003b: 7–8) borrows from geography.

2. Marx spent most of his time defining the capitalist mode of production and contrasting this with the feudal mode of production that was still present in parts of Eastern Europe during the nineteenth century. Earlier modes of production (i.e., Slavonic, Germanic) were vaguely modeled after Morgan's idea of primitive communism and were poorly and inconsistently defined (Wolf 1982: 75; Roseberry 1989: 155). Marx's own definitions of prefeudal modes of production are thus not particularly helpful.

3. Relevant to the discussion in Chapter 3 (and see notes 3, 4, and 5 from that chapter) regarding the Manantial phase, it is worth pointing out that the grater bowls from the Basin of Mexico (Niederberger 1987: 569–590) do not have supports but are instead flat-bottomed like the serving dishes. The Conchas-phase grater bowls are more similar to those from the area of Panuco in northern Veracruz (e.g., Ekholm 1944: Figure 5:U, V, X; Figure 13:M, N; MacNeish 1954: Figure 14:6,10; Figure 16:17). This area also has deeply punched-eye figurines similar to the Conchas/Nacaste type (e.g., MacNeish 1954: Figure 21: 5, 8, 9; Figure 22:9).

4. The saw-toothed pattern evident in Figure 5.21A is not the result of measurement bias but is a real pattern that I have also documented in the Conchas-phase dish assemblage at San Martín. Such standardized vessel sizes approximately 2 cm different may have a functional purpose related to the volume of the vessel's contents. Alternatively, such vessels would have stacked one within the other, and this would have facilitated transport.

6

Representation and Aesthetics

> In the case of the arts, it is well known that certain periods of
> their flowering are out of proportion to the general development
> of the society, hence also to the material foundations, the skeletal
> structure, as it were, of its organization.
>
> Marx 1973 [1857–1858]: 110

The other side of the historical materialist dialectic "...includes
social, religious, legal, and aesthetic institutions, beliefs, and conventions" (Childe 1946: 250). On first reading the epigraph above, one
notes that Marx does not appear to attribute a causative role to artistic expression. Rather, he is puzzled by the lack of correspondence
between such development and society's material foundations during certain periods. He does note, however, that the elaboration of
artistic expression (and by extension the superstructure more generally) can operate independent of society's economic base. Although
it is possible to marshal passages in Marx's writing to support their
position that the superstructure is epiphenomenal, such a simplification ignores the nuances of his thinking (Roseberry 1989: 37–42).
Marx viewed the human brain, and ability for abstract thought, as
distinguishing humans from other organisms. He famously stated in
Capital that:

A spider conducts operations which resemble those of the weaver, and a
bee would put many a humble architect to shame by the construction of his
honeycomb cells. But what distinguishes the worst architect from the best of
bees is that the architect builds the cell in his mind before he constructs it in
wax. At the end of every labor process, a result emerges which had already
been conceived by the worker at the beginning, hence already existed ideally.

Marx 1977 [1867]: 284

Humans are therefore qualitatively different from bees and spiders due to their capacity for abstract thought and strategic planning. Although human cognitive abilities create the possibility of purposeful innovation, they also provide the weight of previous generations (aka cultural heritage) that structures what is possible to think or do. Following Marx, Childe (1949: 6–8) noted that humans adapt to the world not as it is but as they perceive it to be, filtered though their cultural beliefs. However, human perceptions and cultural traditions that do not largely correspond to the real world will not endure long, so are irrelevant in the long term (see Trigger 2003a: 9–10). As a result, the material and the ideological aspects of society intersect in ways that, although culturally specific, are at the same time grounded in largely objective reality as well as local social and ecological conditions.

Art objects provide the most accessible routes of access into *prehistoric* cognition but generally provide distorted glimpses of cultural norms. Fortunately, the material nature of archaeological data results in numerous such points of access to the creative world for those peoples without writing. The historical materialist perspective provides a framework from which to decouple developments in the economic base from those that transpire in the ideological (or political) superstructure. This decoupling results in a series of interesting questions. When does the flowering of artistic expression (or political organization) become more developed than would be predicted by the economic organization of society, and conversely, when is it less developed? When such periods are identified, how might they be explained? Also, more generally, what role do the objects we view as artistic fulfill in society and why might aesthetic standards change over time?

In this chapter, I return to the distinction between style and function, discussed in Chapter 5 – and address the former. Style is conceived of here as an inseparable side of a cultural coin that generally cannot be understood apart from its functional side (Carr 1995: 166; Cunningham 2003: 35; Wiessner 1990: 106–107). The style/function dialectic parallels that of the base and superstructure to a degree as neither exists without the other. Furthermore, both dichotomies are artificial products of dividing the forbidding complexity of human culture into more manageable analytic units. Stylistic analysis has a long history in archaeology. During the late nineteenth century, Montilius used changing styles of metal artifacts to divide the European

Bronze, Neolithic, and Iron Ages into twenty periods (Trigger 1989: 158). Style was employed for much the same purpose in the Americas to establish ceramic types to divide time into the basic building blocks of cultural reconstruction (Willey and Sabloff 1993: 164–169). More recent treatments of style have emphasized the social strategies that result in stylistic changes and continuities (e.g., Carr and Neitzel 1995; Conkey and Hastorf 1990; Hodder 1982b; Miller 1982; Robb 1998; Wobst 1977, 1999).

Shared styles are the basis on which interaction spheres and archaeological horizons are defined and chronologies are built. Therefore, the data discussed in this chapter inform a number of different subjects. Chronological cross-dating is the first use to which style is put. When ceramic phases are refined beyond the point where radiocarbon dating can distinguish between them, stylistic cross-dating must take precedence (Rosenswig 2005: Appendix 3). Second, shared styles of material culture are used to infer the geographic extents, and level of intensity, of interaction between regions. These two "functional" aspects of style were introduced in Chapter 3 and will be taken up again in Chapter 8, where I attempt to evaluate the competing hypotheses. Both these uses of style address synchronic relationships (i.e., questions of contemporaneity and intensity of interaction) over large distances. In this chapter, I focus on local aspects of representational data within the Soconusco and how they change over time. Therefore, for much of the following discussion, style is interpreted diachronically from a single locale.

The term style possesses historical disciplinary "baggage" in archaeological discourse (see Cunningham 2003), so instead I employ the concept of aesthetics. The aesthetic quality of an object is used here to mean simply its "sensory impact" (Gosden 2001: 165). Defined in this way, the aesthetic qualities of archaeological data are more amenable to anthropological consideration because the aesthetic qualities of mundane objects can be evaluated alongside more obviously artistic objects (Carr 1995: 164–167). Not only does the concept of aesthetics, thus defined, lend itself to cross-cultural inquiry but it also opens up the possibility that certain qualities (based on contrasts perceived by the human eye and processed by the human brain) are universal and thus allow archaeologists to infer prehistoric perception (Hovers et al. 2003). For example, some quality of obsidian appealed to pre-Hispanic and colonial societies as well as to modern tourists (Saunders 2001). In addition, certain qualities of gold seem to give it cross-cultural appeal (Renfrew 1986b: 148–150). Certain cognitive predispositions hardwired into the human brain could account for cross-cultural behavioral convergences more convincingly than claims of similar environmental adaptation (see Trigger 2003a: 3–4, 12–13; Whitehouse 2001). At the most basic level, the capacity for language and abstract thought have resulted in a relatively high degree of adaptive similarity when humans are compared to other species. I will not take this biologically based mode of inference particularly far. All I intend to argue here is that the dominant color of ceramic vessels and the manner in which human and animal forms were molded in clay were significant and that change in aesthetic norms requires cultural explanation. Rather than focusing on specific meaning, the following analyses explore the effect that changes in the aesthetic qualities of objects had on social relationships (Appadurai 1986).

In this chapter, three lines of quantitative data are presented as well as qualitative patterns of changing figurines, effigy pots, and iconographic representations. First, I quantify the change in color used to decorate pottery vessels. This quantification is easily done and provides absolute numbers to describe impressions of increasing and decreasing popularity of the colors used to decorate pots. Second, the distribution of color schemes on different sized Horizon I decorated dishes are presented. These results provide a clue as to the social use of the new Horizon I black-and-white color scheme. Third, anthropomorphic figurine fragments are quantified over time to provide an estimate of the relative importance with which the human form was recreated in clay and thus how common rituals that employed such objects were during different periods. The evolution of figurine style and subject matter are explored. The discussion of changing anthropomorphic figurine styles is complemented with a description of contemporaneous developments in the manner in which zoomorphic effigies adorned ceramic vessels. The use of abstract iconography was a novelty adopted during Horizon I – this transformation is also described and its significance explored.

THE COLOR OF CERAMICS

The overall color scheme of ceramic vessels is approached here as a basic level of expressive data that contains aesthetic information. Changes in the dominant colors used to decorate pottery provide one avenue through which to enter the prehistoric cognitive world. The

Figure 6.1
Cherla-phase Pino Black
and White dishes from
Cuauhtémoc.

Initial Ceramic Period to Horizon I change from an assemblage dominated by small red tecomates to one that consisted predominantly
of black and white dishes is assessed. In Chapter 5, I documented
changes in the size and shape of these vessels. In this chapter, I
approach the color characterization quantitatively and then explore
the effect this change may have had on the residents of Cuauhtémoc.

I quantify two color-related variables: 1) the overall proportion of
vessels made of different colors and 2) the distribution of Horizon I
decorated dish rim diameters by color. For both variables, refitted rim
sherd MNVs (minimum number of vessels) were used to determine
the relative proportion of vessels attributed to each color category. By
using the MNV of sherds recovered from secondary midden contexts,
the contextual and deposition biases that plague ceramic stylistic
studies are minimized (see Skibo et al. 1989). Six color categories
were coded: 1) red; 2) red rim; 3) black to white (including shades of
gray); 4) white-rimmed black; 5) orange to brown; and 6) unslipped.
Categories such as black to white and orange to brown were used to
minimize the subjective nature of such assessments as these colors
tended to grade from one to the other. Furthermore, from an overall
visual perspective, a ceramic assemblage dominated by red vessels is
very different from one dominated by black, white, and gray vessels –
the exact proportion of the former three shades being less important
for my purposes than that they are visually very different than red
(for a similar perspective, see Pool and Britt 2000: 154–155). White-
rimmed black wares (Figure 6.1) were reported separately due to their

significance as a marker for Horizon I. However, they are subsumed in the black to white category when assessing the aesthetic impact of overall assemblage color scheme.

Quantitative changes in ceramic color scheme

Changes in the overall color of pottery vessels used from the Initial Ceramic Period to Horizon I were dramatic (Figure 6.2). Both the Locona and Ocós phase assemblages contain 65% red or red rim ceramics, and fewer than 20% were black to white or unslipped. These proportions were reversed during the Cherla phase, when 20% of the ceramics were red or red rim and 66% were black to white, white-rimmed black wares or unslipped. These findings demonstrate an aesthetic disjuncture in Horizon I that contrasts the Initial Ceramic Period patterns at Cuauhtémoc. By the Jocotal phase, more than 50% of the ceramics were still black to white, white-rimmed black wares or unslipped, but red and red-rimmed vessels had increased in popularity. The temporally diagnostic, flat bottom, outleaning or outflaring, white-rimmed black ware serving vessels constituted 21%, 14%, and 16% of the overall assemblage, respectively, during the Cherla, Cuadros, and Jocotal phases. These distinctively decorated vessels were not recovered from Cuauhtémoc during the preceding Initial Ceramic Period or during the subsequent Conchas phase. As well as providing a straightforward style marker for Horizon I, these distinctively decorated serving vessels also created an aesthetic statement of change from the Initial Ceramic Period – also evident in other classes of data (discussed later in this chapter).

During the Conchas phase there was a subtle but significant change in the color scheme used to decorate pottery. Unslipped vessels with red rims constitute only 21% of all vessels, so more ceramic vessels than ever before were decorated. Furthermore, black to white ceramics constituted more than 50% of the entire Conchas-phase assemblage. As white-rimmed black ware vessels were no longer produced at Cuauhtémoc during the Middle Formative period, these were monochrome black, white or gray wares. However, whereas the overall color scheme of Conchas-phase ceramics shows continuity from Horizon I, the range of vessel forms expanded (Rosenswig 2005: Appendix 5). The expanded range of ceramic forms (such as the adoption of grater bowls and other composite silhouette vessels, as discussed in the previous chapter) indicates an elaboration in the functions that pottery fulfilled. Color was therefore not employed as a novel form of aesthetic expression on pottery vessels during Horizon II as it had been at the beginning of Horizon I. Instead, vessel form and an expanding range of iconography (discussed later in this chapter) appear to have provided a forum for more elaborate information to be conveyed.

Black and white ceramics on the Gulf Coast

The black and white ceramics that are so distinctive of Horizon I began to increase in popularity at the end of the Initial Ceramic Period during the Bajío and Ocós phases. The Rompido Black and White type (Coe and Diehl 1980b: 145–148) did not consist of white-rimmed black wares, but the black and white fire-clouded vessels pictured in the color plate in front of Coe and Diehl's (1980b: between pages 22 and 23) San Lorenzo monograph anticipate the early Horizon I (i.e., Chicharras phase) pottery aesthetic. In the Soconusco there are also some Ocós-phase black wares such as Alba Gris (Clark and Cheetham 2005: 309) that can be fire clouded. However, overall, vessels

Figure 6.2
Proportion of differently colored ceramics at Cuauhtémoc.

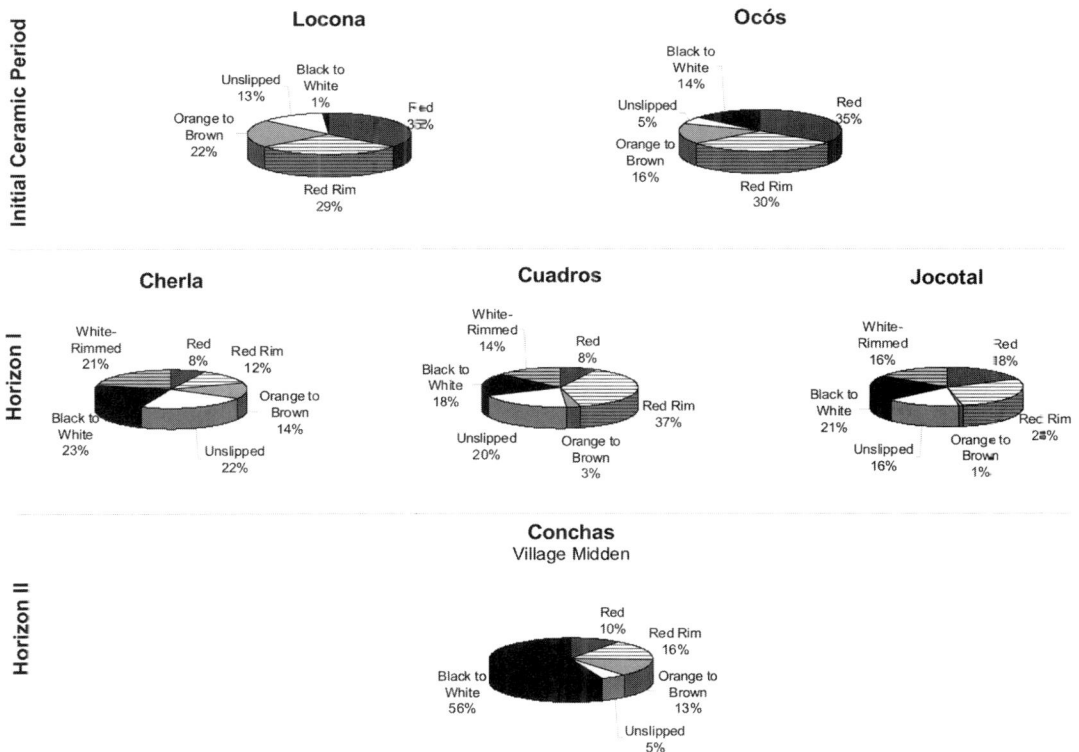

decorated with black and/or white are relatively rare in the Ocós-phase assemblage at Cuauhtémoc (14%) compared to the Cherla (44%), Cuadros (32%), Jocotal (36%) or Conchas (56%) assemblages (Figure 6.2).

By the Conchas phase, white-rimmed black ware dishes were no longer used at Cuauhtémoc (Figure 6.2), at La Blanca (Love 2002a) or elsewhere in the Soconusco. In contrast, on the Gulf Coast this stylistic and technological tradition continued throughout the Middle Formative and into the Classic period. During Horizon II, Tular Black-and-White continues the white-rimmed black ware tradition of the Nacaste phase at San Lorenzo (Coe and Diehl 1980b: 200). Pool and Britt (2000) report that differentially fired vessels continue to be produced in the Tuxtla mountains until the Early Classic period. Late Classic examples of white-rimmed black wares from the Gulf Coast include the Copilco complex (AD 600–700) with Jiménez Black-and-White from the San Andrés collection (von Nagy 2003: 638–639). Related black and white types from the Late Classic period are also found in adjacent areas of Chiapas at San Isidro and Chiapa de Corzo, areas that were always closely tied to the Gulf Coast (Lee 1978). As we have seen, monochrome white, black, and gray are the most common colors for vessel slip during Horizon II, but red (and especially orange to brown) wares began to be used in greater relative frequencies than before.

Based on the continued use of white-rimmed black wares on the Gulf Coast through to the Classic period, this color combination (and the technology required to produce it) was evidently a long-standing Gulf Coast tradition. The use of this distinctive color scheme to decorate ceramic vessels thus likely began on the Gulf Coast and spread to other areas to become the distinctive pan-Mesoamerican Horizon I style marker. Current temporal units are not fine-grained enough to determine if Gulf Coast examples predate their use in the Soconusco (or elsewhere). However, the continued use of this decorative aesthetic during Horizon II and into the Classic period suggests that it was a persistent, indigenous Gulf Coast aesthetic. In contrast, after being adopted during the three ceramic phases that make up Horizon I, white-rimmed black ware vessels ceased to be used by the inhabitants of Cuauhtémoc, the Soconusco, and the rest of Mesoamerica.

The contrast between red and black appears to be a cognitive universal and may have a physiological basis in the way humans perceive color. The colors red and black were used as far back as Plio-Pleistocene to Upper Paleolithic times and, by the Middle Paleolithic, red ochre is found in contexts that suggest its symbolic use almost one hundred thousand years ago (Hovers et al. 2003: 491–492). Cross-cultural ethnographic (Sagona 1994: 10–26; Turner 1967), linguistic (Berlin and Kay 1969; Kay et al. 1997),[1] as well as prehistoric (Scarre 2002) surveys indicate that the triad of red, black, and white forms fundamental cognitive categories into which societies worldwide divide colors. Furthermore, neurophysiological characteristics of the human eye may result in these three colors being perceived as maximally different (Mollon 1997). For the following discussion, I assume that the change from red to black and white pottery vessels was perceived by the Cherla-phase inhabitants of Cuauhtémoc to be as different as it is to me analyzing the sherds from their refuse. The use of black and white to decorate Horizon I ceramics was therefore as contrastive as it could have been compared to the reds used to decorate Initial Ceramic Period ceramics. This aesthetic contrast must have been the intention of the people who employed these vessels. This color replacement was part of a larger aesthetic change that began during the Cherla phase and transformed the way in which the inhabitants of the Soconusco created material objects.

White-rimmed black ware decorated dishes

White-rimmed black wares represent a technological innovation of differential firing first adopted by the residents of Cuauhtémoc during the Cherla phase. As I have just argued, white-rimmed black wares and the technological knowledge associated with their production was a Gulf Coast decorative aesthetic that persisted there until the end of the Classic period. In this section, I document the proportion of white-rimmed black ware dishes and their rim diameter relative to other colors employed to decorate vessels during Horizon I (Rosenswig et al. 2007).

The bar graphs in Figure 6.3 of decorated dish rim diameters are the same as those presented in Figure 5.20 but with stacked bars used to represent the number of vessels from each color class. Each graph shows three dominant color categories: 1) white-rimmed black wares; 2) black to white ceramics; and 3) red, orange and brown vessels. For the Jocotal phase, orange and brown vessels constitute a small proportion of the assemblage (see Figure 6.2) and so are labeled simply as red.

The most significant pattern documented in Figure 6.3 is that during the Cherla phase white-rimmed black ware dishes (and a few black ware dishes without white rims) constitute the largest size category (i.e., those larger than 28 cm). This finding means that not only did the overall color scheme of the Cherla-phase pottery assemblage change dramatically from the Initial Ceramic Period but that the replacement was complete for the largest serving dishes. Furthermore, no Cherla-phase Pino Black and White dishes had a rim diameter smaller than 18 cm. If we assume that the largest dishes were used to serve food to the largest groups of people, and that larger groups of people tended to be served at special events (such as feasts), then during the Cherla phase the newly dominant black-and-white color scheme was associated with public events and served a political functions. The change from a pottery assemblage (in particular, one used to serve food) dominated by red wares to one that was predominantly black and white represents a change in aesthetics that requires cultural explanation. That the new Cherla-phase black-and-white color scheme corresponds to a distinctive size class of serving dishes indicates the social contexts of this aesthetic change. That is, large decorated vessels that created an aesthetic break from the past were used to serve food to larger groups of people than was previously the case.

There is evidence from the Americas from which to infer specific meanings associated with various colors (e.g., Helms 1993b). However, I make no claims here to the *specific* meaning of the Initial Ceramic Period to Horizon I change in ceramic decoration aesthetic. My argument is instead that the change from an assemblage of ceramic vessels dominated by red to one dominated by black and white was purposeful to create as dramatic an aesthetic disjuncture as possible. The use of such vessels signaled a change that was associated with serving larger groups of people than was previously the case.

In the Mazatán zone, 24% of serving dishes were adorned with incised/carved Olmec iconography at Cantón Corralito during the Cuadros phase compared with 4% to 7% at other sites in the Mazatán zone of the Soconusco (Lesure 2004: 83). This finding suggests that this site was important in the Soconusco during the apogee of San

Cherla

Cuadros

Jocotal

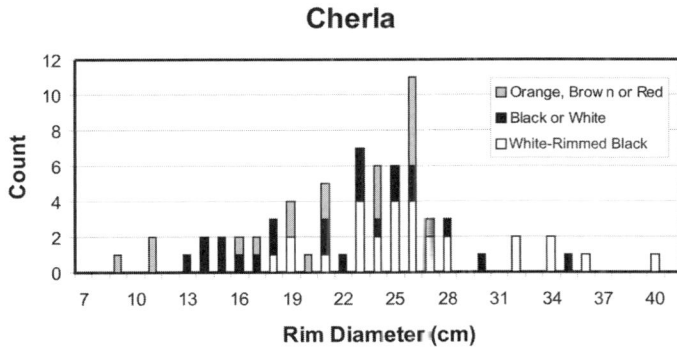

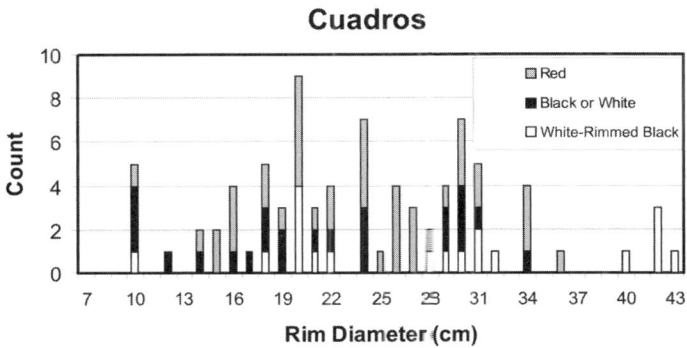

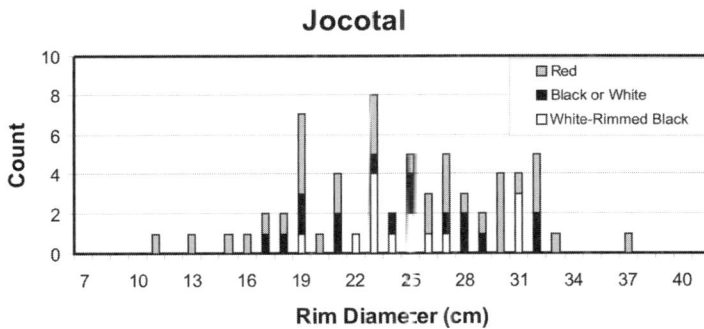

Figure 6.3
Horizon I decorated dish
assemblages by vessel
size and color.

Lorenzo (see Cheetham 2007: Figures 6-49, 2010). However, prior to
the onslaught of new iconographic information on vessels during the
Cuadros phase there was an aesthetic revolution during the Cherla
phase. Just as the pan-Mesoamerican distribution of Olmec iconography was part of its symbolism (Lesure 2004: 91), so too was the
widespread replacement of red wares by black ware vessels. Black
ware vessels, and more so white-rimmed black wares, appear to have
signaled a break with the past. Furthermore, this local change in decoration was occurring in numerous areas of Mesoamerica, so it linked

the residents of the Soconusco to other Early Formative islands of complexity.

A comparative example of changing ceramic color symbolism is provided by Ramey Incised pottery used in the American Southeast during the eleventh and twelfth centuries CE. Pauketat and Emerson (1991: 922) argue that Mississippian Ramey Incised pottery conveyed an ideology of authority as they, among other things, "are well made... have broad simple designs that are highly visible from a distance... [and]... lack stylistic antecedents." This description could as easily be applied to Cherla-phase white-rimmed black dishes from the Soconusco (Figure 6.1). Furthermore, they argue that the spread of such distinctive Ramey Incised vessels (through trade as well as imitation) reflected exchange networks of Cahokia and Mississippian elites. Interestingly, the bodies of Ramey Incised vessels were slipped black and had lighter colored lips whereas all other vessels were slipped red (Pauketat and Emerson 1991: 936). This synchronic contrast of red and black ceramics in the southeastern United States parallels the contrast I argue occurred from Ocós- to Cherla-phase ceramics in the Soconusco – both resulted in maximum aesthetic contrast. Pauketat and Emerson's (1991) discussion of Ramey Incised pottery provides another archaeological example of black vessels being aesthetically and technologically distinguished from red vessels and the meaning of this contrast inferred by the context of their use.

ANTHROPOMORPHIC FIGURINES

Another cross-culturally relevant route through which to enter prehistoric cognition is the manner in which people chose to represent human facial expressions, body postures, and so forth. There is no better medium to document human self-representation than the handmade ceramic figurines that are so ubiquitous in Formative Mesoamerica. As was the case with most Formative Mesoamerican figurines (e.g., Blomster 1998; Coe and Diehl 1980b: 260; Cyphers 1988, 1993: 217; Hammond 1989b: 111; Lesure 1997a; Marcus 1996: 286, 1998), those at Cuauhtémoc were recovered from domestic contexts (Rosenswig n.d.). In contrast, monumental scale objects (e.g., stone sculpture) recovered in limited numbers from public contexts reflect the political ambitions of society's elite. Therefore, figurines

Figurine Density

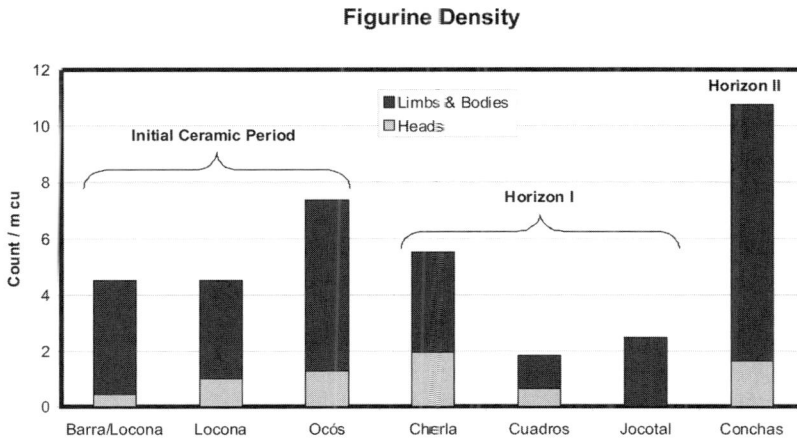

Figure 6.4
Density of figurine
fragments recovered
at Cuauhtémoc.

recovered in much greater numbers from domestic contexts reflect more pervasive social norms. It then becomes an empirical matter to document whether the style of iconography from the public and domestic realms corresponds.

In this section, I first document the relative quantity of anthropomorphic figurines recovered from midden deposits at Cuauhtémoc. This is done to estimate the frequency of figurine use over time. Next, I describe and discuss the changes in figurine style and subject matter from each period of the site's occupation. Lesure (1997a) and Clark (1994: 420–433) have previously discussed the Initial Ceramic Period and Horizon I figurines, and Arroyo (2002) has published many of the Horizon II figurine types discussed later in this chapter.

Quantitative changes

A total of 1,062 figurine fragments have been recovered from excavated and surface contexts at Cuauhtémoc. Of these, 518 (90 heads and 428 body and limb fragments) have been recovered from temporally secure contexts and form the basis of this quantitative assessment (Figure 6.4). There were roughly similar figurine densities during the Locona, Ocós, and Cherla phases, a marked decrease during the Cuadros and Jocotal phases, and then a significant increase during the Conchas phase. Extremely few figurines have been recovered from Barra-phase deposits in the Mazatán zone, and all are interpreted as dating to the very end of that phase. These findings are consistent with my interpretation that the deposits I label Barra/Locona at Cuauhtémoc are either mixed or date to the end of the Barra phase due to the relative frequency of figurine fragments. A relatively higher density of Ocós figurines also has been noted in the Mazatán zone and represents the most developed stage of this indigenous Soconuscan medium of expression. There were four to seven figurine fragments per cubic meter of excavation from Barra through Cherla phases and approximately two fragments per cubic meter during the Cuadros and Jocotal phases. From Conchas contexts there were more than ten fragments per cubic meter from village midden. Overall, the density of figurines falls during the Cuadros and Jocotal phases when abstract iconography is adopted for the first time (see below) only to reach a density not previously attained during the following Conchas phase.

Qualitative changes

During the Initial Ceramic Period most figurines were small, solid representations of human adults. A few large, hollow figurines have been encountered, but these are poorly understood as they have rarely been recovered sufficiently complete for a systematic analysis. Lesure (1999b: 216) interprets such large, hollow Naca Group figurines as props for public political discourse. These hollow figurines were generally much larger than Initial Ceramic Period solid figurines and were slipped. In addition, the occasional figurine depicts an animal, but these are rare; of the 1,062 figurines recovered from all time periods at Cuauhtémoc, only 17 are the heads of animals. What can be asserted with a high degree of certainty is that, by the late Barra or early Locona phase, the inhabitants of the Soconusco began to mold small, solid, anthropomorphic figurines in considerable numbers. These Initial Ceramic Period figurines from the Paqui Group were of two basic types: 1) seated individuals with large stomachs wearing masks and clothes and 2) young, naked females who were depicted standing. The Paqui Group was originally defined by Clark (1994: 426) and has been described in more detail by Lesure (1997b; 1999c).

The Paqui seated figurines are called the Xumay Type and generally depict individuals with large stomachs, many of whom wear clothing and/or elaborate masks (Figure 6.5). Some of these masks are of animals such as foxes and monkeys, and others are fantastic creatures that resemble 1940s Hollywood extraterrestrials. Special attention was paid to modeling headgear and eyes that stare intently

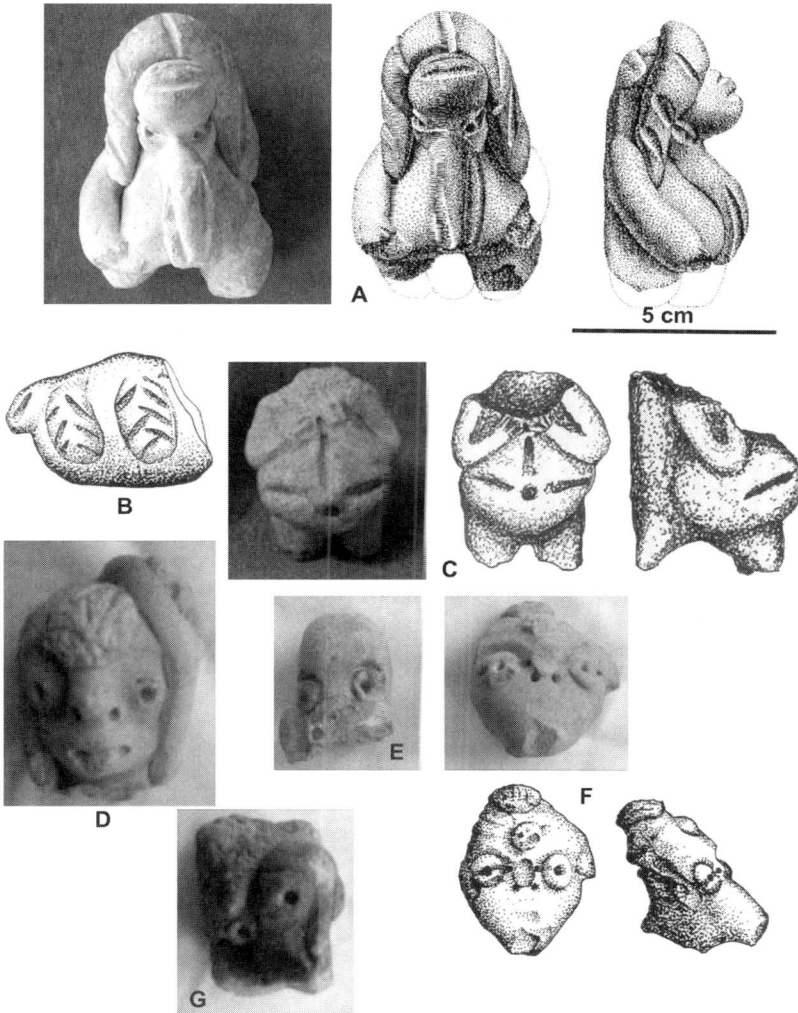

Figure 6.5
Initial Ceramic Period
seated Xumay figurines
from Cuauhtémoc.
Drawing A by Ajax
Moreno; B, C and F by
Willie Lowe.

out at the observer. Eyes are either punched appliqué (Figure 6.5, D,
F, and G) or the punched, double-stroke trough type (Figure 6.5A).
As the sample of Xumay figurines increases, it appears that there was
an elaborate set of standardized masks. Lesure (1997a: 240) defined
four mask types from the Mazatán zone. I have two others from
Cuauhtémoc, and using both assemblages together a seventh mask
type can be defined. Xumay figurines generally have fat stomachs
with ornamentation in the form of multiple tassels hanging on the
front of their stomachs (Figure 6.5B), a fur tunic, and/or a large pec-
toral. Xumay figurines also were generally modeled with their arms
resting on their jutting bellies (Figure 6.5, A and C). The characterization of these figurines as depicting old individuals is due to their large

bellies in contrast to the more slender (and thus young) female figurines described later in this chapter. Xumay figurines were depicted seated, and stools were often indicated with three legs descending from below the fat belly (see Figure 6.5, A and C). These Xumay figurines were made to stand by themselves in an upright position.

Lesure (1997a: 240) suggests " . . . that the fact that multiple representations of the same mask can be identified at different sites suggests that these were representations drawn from some sort of shared iconographic system rather than the sort of individualized masks we might expect of chiefly or other high-status offices in separate, independent villages" and further that "these were representations of people reenacting or recalling important mythological events" (Lesure 1997a: 241). Clark (1991; Clark and Pye 2000: 232–233) interprets Xumay figurines as "village shaman-chiefs." Regardless of which of these two interpretations is correct, a common set of standardized masks were used at the Mazatán sites as well as at Cuauhtémoc, 40 km to the southwest. The distribution of Xumay figurines indicates that during the Initial Ceramic Period this shared culture extended from one end of the land between the two large swamps to the other. Along with the unity of ceramic decoration in this area, the distribution of Xumay figurines supports my interpretation that these geographic barriers also correspond to cultural borders (Rosenswig n.d.).

The gender of Xumay figurines is not clear. They have been described as male by Clark (1994: 420), whereas Lesure (1997a) claims that there is not enough detail to consistently determine sex. The Cuauhtémoc figurine assemblage contains one example of a fat (and presumably old) seated woman who is not wearing a mask (Figure 6.6). This individual has a large, protruding stomach with distinct breasts. In contrast to most Initial Ceramic Period female Paqui figurines that appear to have carefully coifed hair (e.g., Figure 6.7, B and C), this individual has long hair flowing down her shoulders and back and is depicted in a manner normally reserved for animal hair (see Figure 6.14E). This figurine might be seen as the exception that proves the rule, and the lack of clear indication of breasts on most other masked Xumay figurines makes Clark's gender interpretation seem probable. This interpretation of Xumay figurines being male is further supported by the straightforward manner in which the sex of Paqui female figurines was depicted and the generally

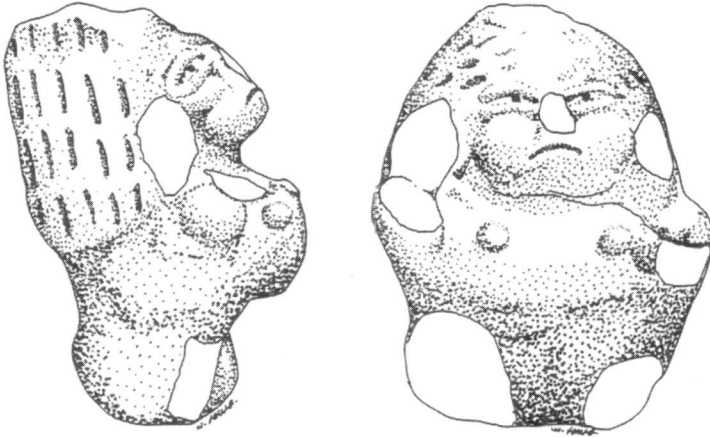

Figure 6.6
Seated female figurines
from Cuauhtémoc dating
to the Initial Ceramic
Period. Drawing by Willie
Lowe.

naturalistic manner of most Initial Ceramic Period representations in
the Soconusco – both of which are described later in this chapter.

The Paqui female figurines group is divided into the Muscu, Nicotaca, and Pama types that depict young naked women (Figure 6.7).
The three types distinguish different paste composition and certain
design characteristics but are the material expression of a single concept modeled in clay that persisted for quite a long time. Generally,

the Muscu type was earlier, poorly made, and progressively replaced by the Nicotaca type during the Ocós and Cherla phases. The Pama type was a slipped version of Nicotaca made during the Cherla phase. Quite a bit of attention was paid to depicting hair and facial features of all Paqui figurines, but their noses were often depicted anatomically incorrect as a long band of clay between the eyes (Figure 6.7, A and C). Eyes were typically the punched, double-stroke trough type, and heads were round.

These young, naked women were generally depicted standing, and attention was paid to molding their breasts, hips, and buttocks. Stomachs were often rounded but rarely appear pregnant. I recovered no definitely pregnant examples from the Cuauhtémoc zone, and only 8% of the larger sample from the Mazatán zone are said to obviously depict pregnancy (Lesure and Clark 2001; and see Ceja 1985: Figure 50a). In contrast to the detailed manner in which these body characteristics were depicted, most Paqui figurines have pointed stubs instead of arms (see Figure 6.7, A, E, and F). Their legs below the hips narrow to tiny feet or simply points that could not have been used to stand the objects up on a hard surface. However, these long pointed legs would have served well to stick into sand or loose soil. Although I have not recovered fat Paqui figurines, Ceja (1985: Figure 49h) reports one from Paso de la Amada with a large (nonpregnant) stomach similar to those depicted in Figure 6.5A and Figure 6.6 from Cuauhtémoc.

In sum, Initial Ceramic Period solid figurines depicted old, seated individuals and young, standing women and thus emphasized both their age and gender. These figurines could have been easily arranged into scenes with the women's legs stuck into the ground and the seated figurines placed around them. Equally as important as what was depicted by solid figurines during the Initial Ceramic Period is what was not depicted. These representations of the human body were portrayed in a natural manner and none depicted motion or activity which suggests that static events and/or iconic images were being depicted. Furthermore, young, fit men are conspicuously absent from the figurine assemblage as are the actual faces of old men (or any genitalia). Senior men thus appear to have been depicted not as individuals but instead fulfill standardized roles that, based on the correspondence of mask types between the Mazatán and Cuauhtémoc zones, were salient across the Soconusco. Although

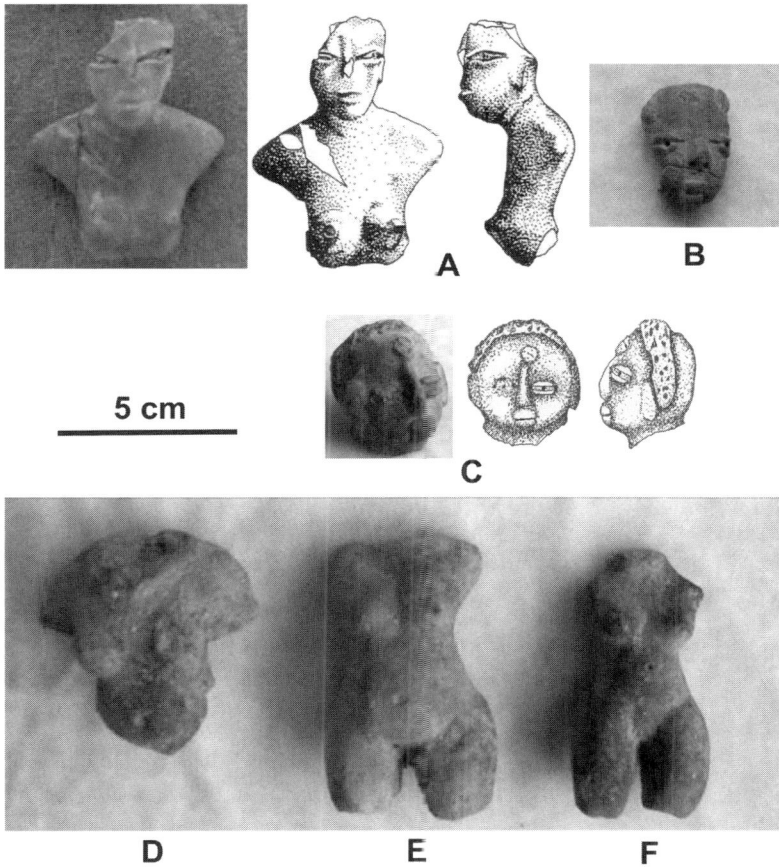

Figure 6.7
Initial Ceramic Period
standing female fig-
urines from Cuauhtémoc.
Drawing A by Willie
Lowe; C by Joseph
McGreevey.

seated figurines primarily depicted men, the fact that at least one
old, fat woman was depicted hints that age rather than gender
was the most important characteristic of these individuals. As for
the young, standing female figurines, most examples conspicuously
lack arms. The lack of arms combined with the detailed representation of breasts, hips, hair, and faces places the emphasis on young
women's sexuality and appearance. However, as very few are actually pregnant, women's fertility may not have been emphasized. We
will never know the precise meaning of Xumay and Paqui figurines,
but they do provide a clear complex of indigenous Initial Ceramic
Period Soconusco human representations that can be contrasted with
figurines produced during subsequent periods. These figurines are
found from one end of the land between the two large Soconusco
swamps to the other in virtually identical form and are unknown
beyond this cultural island (see Rosenswig n.d.).

Horizon I figurines demonstrate a clear break from the past (see Figure 6.8). Figurines from the Cherla, Cuadros, and Jocotal phases include both solid and hollow types. As with the Initial Ceramic Period assemblage, solid figurines were more common and better preserved during Horizon I – and are the focus of discussion here. The Poposac and Yacsas types were produced during the Cherla and Cuadros phases; the former was slipped white, gray or black (like the newly adopted ceramic types) and the latter was simply burnished (Figure 6.8, C and E). Yacsas figurines were more poorly made, and their crude facial features were sometimes not as obviously of the Olmec style (Lesure and Clark 2001), but the examples presented in Figure 6.8, D and F, are. The Toya type of solid figurine was produced primarily during the Jocotal phase from a coarser paste and was of both slipped and burnished varieties (Figure 6.8, A and B).

Although there is some variation, the typical Horizon I, solid figurine head shape was oval or rectangular and frequently curved backwards so that the individuals' faces would have been directed skyward. Eyes were usually slanted toward the nose; pupils were often not represented, and were small when they were depicted. Mouths were generally depicted open and downturned with thick lips, and tongues or teeth often represented. Cheeks were generally fleshy, and jowls were often represented (see Cheetham 2007: Figures 56 through 66, 2009). Ears were generally represented in some detail, minimally by a vertical appliqué fillet and maximally with earspools and detailed depiction of the outer ear. These figurines are sometimes referred to as having baby faces due to being fat with no clear indication of sex and many having open mouths that appear to have been representing crying or yelling. Horizon I solid figurine bodies were generally seated with arms resting on thighs or knees, and fat bellies were not depicted.

The facial characteristics of the figurines in Figure 6.8 are what I refer to as Olmec. Remember, I use the term Olmec as a stylistic label without any necessary implication of geographic origin. In fact, chemical-sourcing data discussed in the following chapter document the figurines presented in Figure 6.8, A and D, were made of clays from the southeastern part of the Soconusco. There is no evidence that I am aware of to suggest that Olmec figurines appeared earlier on the Gulf Coast than elsewhere, but their exchange seems to have been only from the Gulf Coast to the Soconusco (Cheetham 2009).

Jocotal Phase

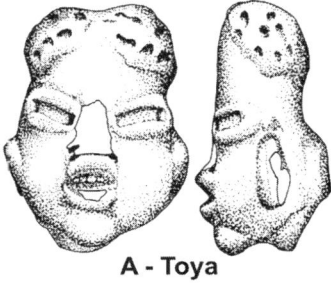

A - Toya

B - Toya

Cuadros Phase

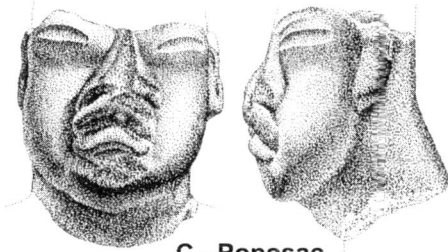

C - Poposac

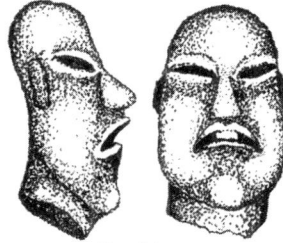

D - Yacsas

Cherla Phase

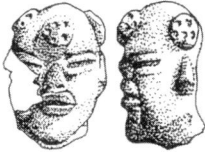

E - Poposac

5 cm

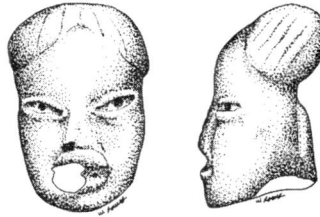

F -Yacsas

Figure 6.8
Cherla-, Cuadros- and
Jocotal-phase figurines
from Cuauhtémoc zone
(A, B, C, E and F from
the site itself; D from
~2 km to the southwest).
Drawings A and E by
Willie Lowe; B and C by
Ajax Moreno; D and F by
Joseph McGreevey.

Horizon I figurines hold together as a group when contrasted with either Initial Ceramic Period or Horizon II figurines. There are, however, chronological differences that make these solid figurine heads relatively easy to separate into each phase. During the Cherla and Cuadros phases, eyes were formed by a single or double slit cut into the clay that angles down toward the nose, whereas during the Jocotal phase the same effect was produced with an appliqué fillet creating the eye (Figure 6.8, A and B). Cherla-phase figurine heads tended to be smaller; their hair was usually depicted in a wide range of styles; and pupils, when present, were represented by small round punctation. During the Cuadros phase, pupils were almost never represented, and when hair was indicated it was a single strip running down the back of the head and neck. Jocotal figurines occasionally have small pupils depicted as vertical slits giving them a slightly feline look (see Figure 6.8B), and when hair is represented, it is often depicted as two large hair buns.

In sum, Horizon I figurines appear to have been ageless and sexless and therefore do not seem to depict biological aspects of the human condition. It is possible that age and sex were being depicted in a manner that we are simply not appreciating. However, given the clarity (from our twenty-first-century perspective) with which the age and sex of figurines was depicted during the Initial Ceramic Period, this is unlikely the case. Even if this were so, the change from the earlier Initial Ceramic Period representational system would have been that much more dramatic as it indicates a completely new manner in which the human body was represented. Furthermore, the angle of the head along with open mouths suggests that Horizon I figurines were depicted shouting, singing or making some other sort of noise. In addition, the detail given to forming these figurines' ears further emphasizes the noise that they appear to be producing. The vocal and auditory nature of Horizon I figurines contrasts with the Xumay and Paqui figurines on which no action, movement or sound appears to have been depicted. Also, the general lack of pupils and unnatural infantile features give these Horizon I figurines an appearance that seems to purposely not engage the observer. At least one example from the Mazatán zone in the collections of the New World Archaeological Foundation (NWAF) in San Cristobal and one from San Lorenzo (Coe and Diehl 1980b: Figures 326 and 351) lack any eye slits at all and appear to represent closed eyes. Finally, during the Cuadros and Jocotal phases, there was only a single class of solid figurine as there is no counterpart to the Initial Ceramic Period Paqui standing female depictions. Therefore, during these two phases, no contrast between different social personas was being made with figurines as was previously the case when old/young and male/female distinctions were evident.

As with many other classes of data, Cherla-phase solid figurines represented a transitional assemblage ushering in new Horizon I norms. As Clark (1990, 1994, 1997; Clark and Pye 2000) and Lesure (1997b; 1999c) have previously discussed, during this phase the female Paqui figurines continued to be produced while the seated Xumay figurines were replaced by those of the Olmec style. In his dissertation, Clark (1994: 420–433) interprets the change in figurine styles as being a process of homologous items replacing each other. Clark (1994: 420) states that "If one is dealing with a sequence of homologous types, and if the meaning of any one of the series can be determined, then one can extrapolate this general interpretation to the remainder." Clark (1994, 1997; Clark and Blake 1989; Clark and Pye 2000) uses this perspective to argue that Olmec style figurines replaced the seated Xumay figurines during the Cherla phase and that both depicted leaders. Building on this interpretation, Lesure (1999b: 218–219) posits:

If it is true that these two kinds of figurines were displayed or used together during the transitional period, then the stylistic dichotomy must surely have been a fundamental part of their meaning. . . . this fits into what we might expect for a developing chiefly ideology Chiefly nobilities sometimes make claims for distinct noble and commoner identities and origins. The nobility's links with external exchange networks are often a crucial element of such a system. In this case, these social processes may have been referenced in material culture during the Cherla phase by the adoption of a style of human representation drawn from pan-Mesoamerican contacts and the deliberate juxtaposition of this with the styles of a longer-standing local tradition.

During the following Cuadros phase the female figurines fell out of use and only the seated figurines persisted. Using the logic of homologous types, Cuadros figurines are interpreted as male leaders (Clark and Pye 2000: 234).

Clark's and Lesure's interpretation of homologous replacement of the representation of political leaders during the Cherla phase is quite plausible given our current understand of Soconusco figurines. This interpretation provides a synchronic explanation of the Cherla-phase figurine assemblage as integrating novel, pan-regional symbolism into the preexisting system of representation in the Soconusco. Furthermore, the functions of both the preceding Locona and Ocós and subsequent Cuadros and Jocotal assemblages are illuminated by the dynamic manner in which the former system was transformed into the latter. Solid clay figurines with Olmec features (described in text above) can be associated with leadership during the Cuadros and Jocotal phases partly because these figurines replaced Xumay elders during the Cherla phase. The implication of this interpretation is that, during the Cherla phase, it would have been the Olmec figurines that were arranged in scenes with young Paqui women. Age and sex were no longer the determinants of status for these new figurines; instead, pan-regional associations expressed through a novel aesthetic appears to have been.

Excavations from Cuauhtémoc provide a further nuance for the manner in which Olmec style figurines were integrated into the

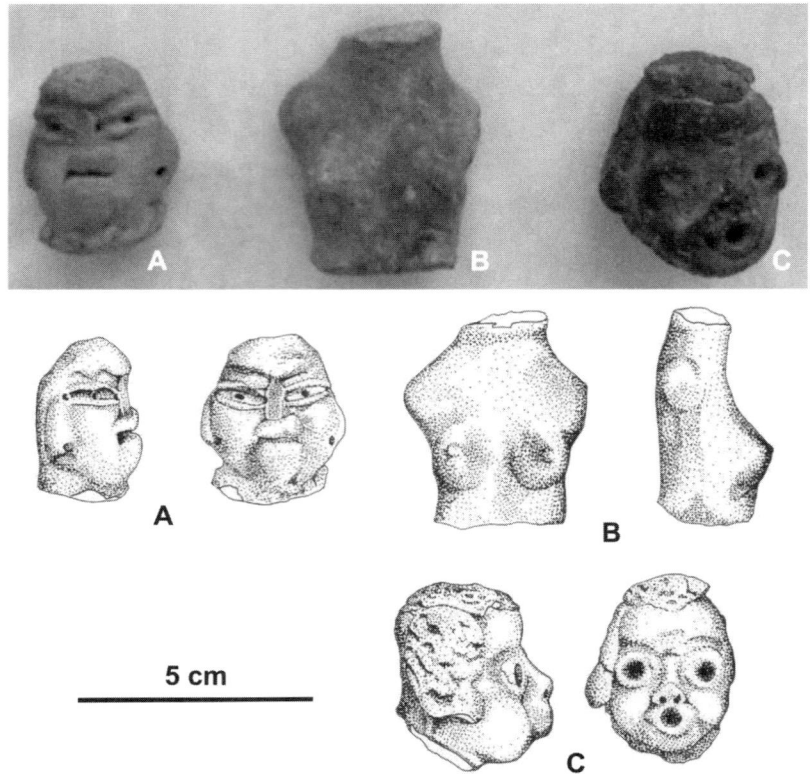

Figure 6.9
Figurines from a Cherla-phase pit feature at Sub-operation 3c (pictured in Figure 5.2). Yacsas head (A), Nicotaca body (B) and Xumay head (C). Drawings by Willie Lowe.

Soconusco assemblage. The fortuitous discovery of an intact Cherla-phase trash pit (shown in Figure 5.2) with no mixing of earlier period ceramics as well as three associated accelerator mass spectrometry (AMS) dates, one from the pit itself and two from below it (Rosenswig 2005: Appendix 3), provides a securely dated context. Along with a number of limb fragments, this feature contained two solid fig-urine heads and two bodies. As expected, a crude Yacsas head with slanted eyes and an open, downturned mouth with thick lips (Figure 6.9A) was recovered along with two armless Nicotaca bodies with well-formed breasts (the most complete example is presented in Fig-ure 6.9B). Not expected was that a Xumay type masked head was also recovered from this feature (Figure 6.9C).

It is possible that this Xumay figurine fragment was incorporated into the Cherla feature as part of Locona or Ocós trash at the site. However, given the intact nature of the feature and the lack of any ceramic mixing, this seems unlikely. The contents of the pit appear to consist of undisturbed Cherla-phase secondary refuse (Rosenswig 2009; Schiffer 1987: 58–59). Therefore, in at least this one case, a Xumay figurine appears to have been used during the Cherla phase.

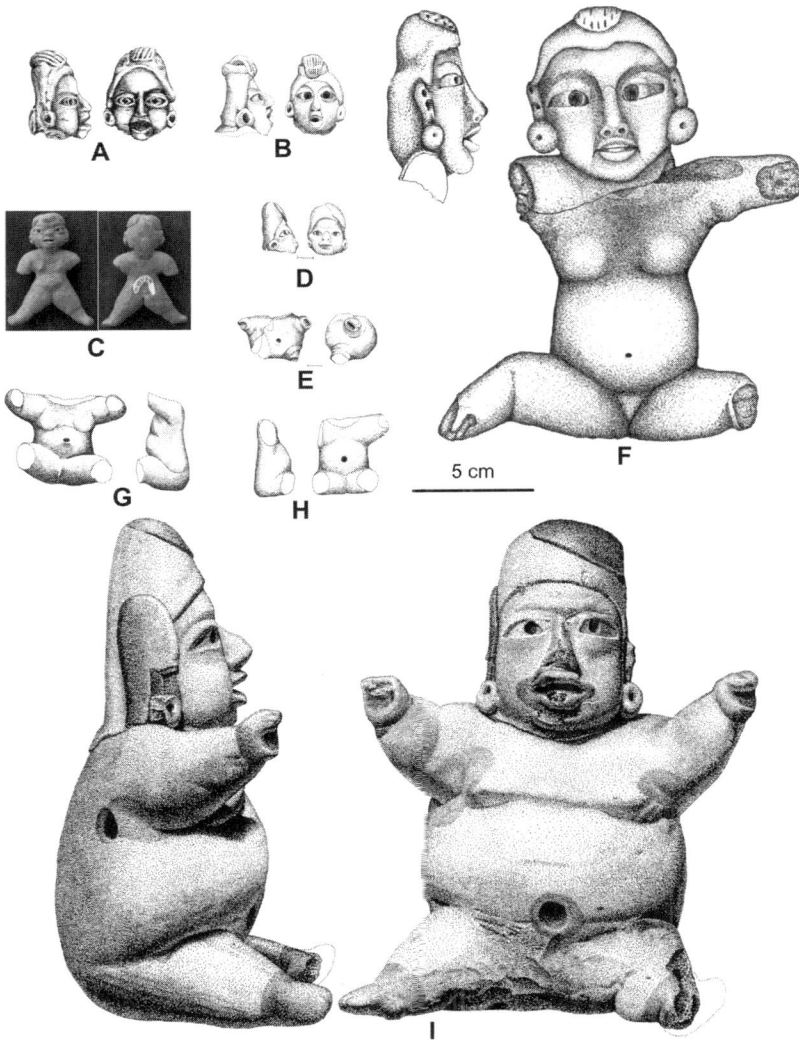

Figure 6.10
Conchas-phase Her-
nandez Group figurines
(Type 1 and Type 8) from
Cuauhtémoc. Heads:
A and D – Type 8 Solid
Variety; B and C – Type 1
Solid Variety; F – Type 1
Solid Variety I – Type 8
Hollow Variety. Bodies G
and H – Type 1 Solid Vari-
ety; E – Type 8 Solid Vari-
ety. Drawings A, B, D, E,
G and H by Willie Lowe;
F by Joseph McGreevy;
I by Ayax Moreno.

Therefore, at least at Cuauhtémoc, the adoption of Olmec figurines
may have been an even more gradual process than Clark and Lesure
propose for the Mazatán zone. It is perhaps not surprising that the
adoption of Olmec imagery took different forms in different parts of
the Soconusco and that new symbols of leadership were more gradually adopted in the peripheral Cuauhtémoc zone when compared
to the larger Mazatán polities that were presumably the centers of
more intensive inter-regional interaction during Horizon I.

Conchas-phase figurines represent an explosion in both the quantity (Figure 6.4) and variety (Figures 6.10, 6.11 and 6.12) of figurine types compared with those produced during the previous

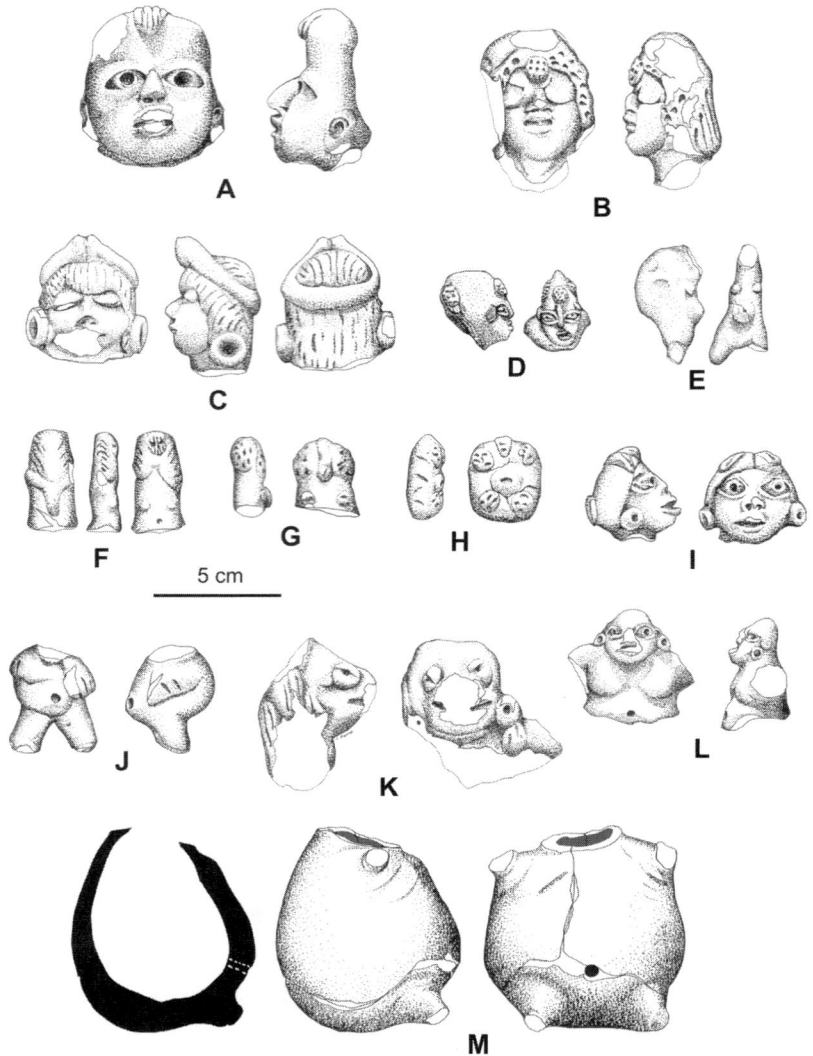

Figure 6.11
Less common Conchas-phase Hernandez Group figurine types from Cuauhtémoc. A – Type 4; B and C – Type 7; D and E – Type 11; F, G and H – Type 9; I and J – Type not determined; K and L – Type 10; M – Type 8 Hollow Variety. All drawings by Willie Lowe.

phases. Published comparative assemblages of Conchas-phase figurines come from the 915 figurine fragments recovered from La Victoria (Coe 1961: 91–94) and the 1,200 fragments recovered from La Blanca (Arroyo 2002). Ekholm (1989: Figures 1, f–i and 2, a–c) also published seven examples of Conchas-phase figurines from Izapa (that she misattributes to the Jocotal phase). I have developed a working typology of Conchas-phase figurine heads called the Hernandez Group and divided them into Types 1 through 12. So as not to introduce multiple classification terminologies, I follow Arroyo (2002) in her numbering of types as much as possible. Our types are not identical as hers focus on head shape whereas mine is an attempt to differentiate subject matter, or at least different types of representation.

The single most common figurine type was Hernandez Type 1 that are generally solid with a few hollow examples (Figure 6.10, A–C and F). Hernandez Type 8 was also common but usually hollow, and depicted wearing a fitted helmet and having short arms, legs and glovelike hands (Figure 6.10, D, E and I; Arroyo 2002: Figure 117). Most other characteristics are shared by these two figurine types (Figure 6.10). These are by far the most numerous Conchas-phase figurines and generally have round faces. Eyes were made by the double-triangle-punch technique. Large, deep, circular pupils stare out at the observer. These large pupils give Conchas-phase Hernandez Group Type 1 and Type 8 figurines an intensity of human connection that provides the biggest contrast with pupil-less figurines produced during Horizon I. Furthermore, many examples of these two figurine types are cross-eyed (see Figure 6.10, B and F), giving them an even more realistic, nonstylized appearance. However, similar to Horizon I figurines, these figurines have fleshy cheeks and jowls that also give them an infantile quality. Hernandez Types 1 and 8 are not the typically Olmec figurines but are nonetheless ageless and sexless as they had been during the preceding Cuadros and Jocotal phases. Earspools are always represented and, as during the previous horizon, much detail was involved in modeling mouths and ears. Mouths generally were depicted open, and teeth and tongues were often represented. However, unlike during Horizon I, lips are not thick and mouths are not downturned. The focus on open mouths and detailed ears provides another line of continuity with the past as they also appear to be making and hearing some sort of sound.

Figure 6.12
Conchas-phase greenstone figurine recovered at Cuauhtémoc. Drawing by Joseph McGreevy.

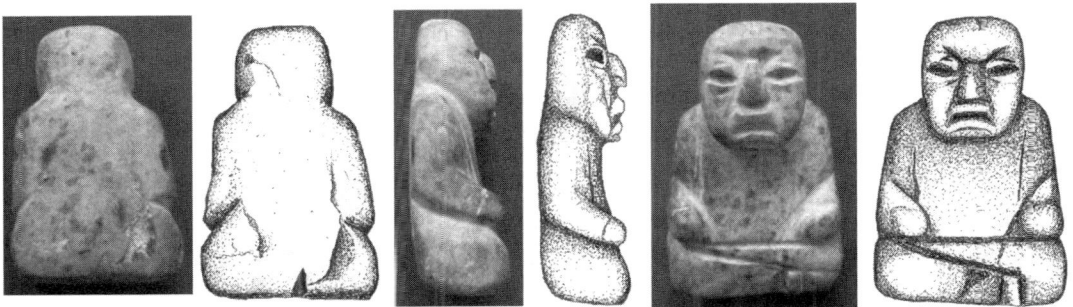

5 cm

Most Conchas-phase figurines are seated, their arms parallel with or higher than their shoulders. Stomachs range from flat to obese, and breasts range from nonexistent to large. However, the size of breasts often corresponds to the size of the stomach, so sex is still often not obvious as these could be fat males or fat babies. A few examples with flat stomachs and large breasts are obviously female. However, such examples make the ambiguity of the majority that much more evident. Navels are always represented. In fact, the depiction of ear-spools and navels are so ubiquitous with Conchas-phase figurines of all types that, given the variability of other characteristics, these two elements may well have been essential factors in depicting what it was to be human during the Conchas phase. Hernandez Group Types 1 and 8 figurines are often slipped white (and very occasionally black) with red pigment added to accentuate mouths, ears, navels, hands and sometimes underarms and crotches (e.g., the darker areas around the mouth, armpits, navel and feet of the figurine depicted in Figure 6.10I).

Hernandez Group Types 1 and 8 figurines come in a wide array of sizes and shapes, and yet share basic characteristics that make them easily identifiable. The Hernandez Type 1 figurine depicted in Figure 6.10A sits 19 cm high from buttocks to head whereas that depicted in Figure 6.10C is standing and measures only 5 cm from feet to head. The hollow Hernandez Group Type 8 figurine depicted in Figure 6.9 sits 24 cm high whereas a small, solid example is almost identical but measures only 3 cm from buttocks to where the head was broken (Figure 6.10E). Both have round bodies, unnaturally short legs and up-reaching arms with glove-like hands (see Arroyo 2002: Figure 131d). It is as if these are two types of people or two types of activities that can be represented at any size, hollow or solid, yet still convey the same information.

Although Hernandez Group Types 1 and 8 are by far the most common ceramic figurines, there are a number of other distinct Conchas-phase head types (see Figure 6.11). Some of these types have only a single example documented to date at Cuauhtémoc but are classified as distinct types based on other examples published from Michael Love's excavations at La Blanca (Arroyo 2002) as well as the extensive collection that I have reviewed (acquired by Edwin Shook while La Blanca's Mound 1 was destroyed) at the Universidad del Valle in Guatemala City (Ivic de Monterroso 2004). Examples of some of these types from Cuauhtémoc are presented in Figure 6.11 to provide an impression of the overall range of variability of Conchas-phase figurines.

Although a detailed description of these figurines will not be presented here, a number of observations are worthwhile. First, a closed-eye variety (Figure 6.11, B and C) shows continuity with the closed-eye, Cuadros-phase figurines mentioned earlier in text and also could be interpreted as the precursor to the potbellied stone monuments recovered further south on the Guatemalan Pacific pied-mont at Monte Alto and elsewhere (see Guernsey n.d.). This figurine type is defined by its closed eyes, detailed depiction of hair with a headband around it and either a pendant or some other marker at the front of the headband (Arroyo 2002: Figure 116). Second, an unusual figurine type (Figure 6.11, F and G) is made of a small ceramic tab with detailed hair, breasts and navel. Ironically, whereas the overall form of these figurines is vaguely phallic, the consistently depicted breasts indicate that they are female (Arroyo 2002: Figure 116; Coe 1961: Figure 58d). A related type (Figure 6.11, D and E) sometimes has the face molded. These are the only Conchas-phase figurines that are clearly gendered in my opinion. The figurine depicted in Figure 6.11H is a unique object that appears to represent a navel at the center of four hair buns at each corner and a fifth indicating hair on the forehead (as in Figure 6.11, F and G). Fourth, another type depicts individuals with no necks either wearing a mask or with a grotesque, deformed face (Figure 6.11, K and L; Arroyo 2002: Figures 124a and 125, g and h). This type generally has parts of the upper body attached, likely due to the lack of a neck, which is a weak point that breaks. Some types – such as one with obvious cranial deforma-tion (Figure 6.11A) and another that gives the impression of depicting a drunk, retarded or otherwise disheveled individual (Figure 6.11I; and see Arroyo 2002: Figure 106, b, e and f, 107b, 113, c and f; and 114b) – could be forced into Hernandez Type 1 but are distinctive and internally consistent enough that they appear to portray a different social role or character.

In sum, Conchas-phase figurines represented an elaboration in the variety and sizes of execution of human representation used in household ritual. The pantheon of Horizon II characters modeled in clay expanded – from the Initial Ceramic Period types (Paqui women and Xumay elders) as well as from the single Horizon I fig-urine type – to depict multiple distinctive characters that were made in a greater range of sizes than before. The quantity of figurines used at Cuauhtémoc increased during the Conchas phase at the same time as the number of different characters expanded beyond anything previously seen. As figurines continue to be found in domestic midden contexts, these changes suggest that villagers were involved in increasingly complex rituals that made some symbolic allusions to the past but expanded the range of characters depicted.

The use of greenstone to make figurines was another Horizon II innovation. At Cuauhtémoc, a complete Conchas-phase greenstone figurine has been recovered (Figure 6.12). This figurine's features more closely resemble those of a large stone statue than a Middle Formative ceramic figurine. The square body with incised lines to indicate hands, legs and feet focuses our attention to the square face. Unlike Horizon II ceramic figurines, this greenstone figurine's face is executed in the Horizon I style with slanted eyebrows and a downturned mouth with thick lips. The famous cache of greenstone figurines and axes recovered from La Venta, as well as the collection held at Dumbarton Oaks (see color photos in Benson and de la Fuente 1996: 204, 228–229), provides well-known Middle Formative examples of stone figurines that resemble Horizon I ceramic figurines in terms of their facial features (see Benson and de la Fuente 1996: 204–233 for many more examples of Olmec greenstone figurines). However, these figurines, along with a number of Middle Formative axes, all depict the Olmec facial features that had long fallen out of use for ceramic figurines being produced at that time. In addition to providing another symbolic continuity linking Horizon I and II, this greenstone figurine from Cuauhtémoc serves as an example of the expanding range of figurine style, subject matter and material of manufacture. A 65-cm-high greenstone figurine known as "Slim" or the "Young Lord" was recovered from the Guatemalan side of the Soconusco (Benson and de la Fuente 1996: 213–216). This object likely came from La Blanca when Mound 1 was carted away as road fill in the early 1970s, and has similar facial features to the example in Figure 6.12 from Cuauhtémoc.

EFFIGY POTS AND CERAMIC ICONOGRAPHY

Effigy pots are another class of material culture that provides insight into the changing cognitive world of the inhabitants of Cuauhtémoc. Due to the relative rarity of such effigies, quantitative comparisons of the frequency of occurrence failed to produce discernable changes through time. Therefore, all I can conclude is that this medium of expression was present at low frequencies during all periods. In addition, the overall frequency of abstract iconographic designs on ceramic vessels at Cuauhtémoc does not produce any clear patterns. As a result, both forms of expression are discussed qualitatively in this section. In addition, the effigies and abstract iconography described were recovered from domestic contexts and, to date, none are known from mortuary or other primary contexts at Cuauhtémoc or elsewhere in the Soconusco.

Initial Ceramic Period

During the Initial Ceramic Period, representations of animals from the Soconusco environment were modeled on ceramic vessels. The animals depicted reflect the range of wildlife that the inhabitants of Cuauhtémoc encountered on a daily basis in the estuaries and forests as well as the coastal grasslands that surrounded the site (Figure 6.13). Initial Ceramic Period effigies were executed in a naturalistic manner and so corresponds directly to what the people who made them observed. Such representations of animals were often depicted on the small, red serving dishes used at the time but also occasionally adorned unslipped tecomates. Lesure (2000: 202) documents that less than 1% of serving dishes in the Mazatán sample had effigies attached (but, because most effigy vessels' rims appear identical to rims of noneffigy varieties, he estimates that 2% to 4% of Initial Ceramic Period serving dishes actually had effigies). The Locona-phase fish executed on a Chilo Red dish presented in Figure 6.13D had a rim diameter of only 9 cm and shows signs of extensive wear on the interior. Therefore, this small, individual-serving dish was roughly treated through many meals before it was eventually broken and incorporated into the village midden.

Initial Ceramic Period effigy vessels were made in the same technical tradition as the figurines discussed earlier in text. For example, the punched, appliqué technique used to make some of the Xumay figurines' eyes (Figure 6.5, F and G) also were commonly used for animal effigies (Figure 6.13, A and C). Hair and fur were represented by groups of punctations (compare Figures 6.5F and 6.7, C and D, to Figure 6.13A), and hands or paws were depicted as two or three parallel lines (compare Figure 6.5C to Figure 6.13C).

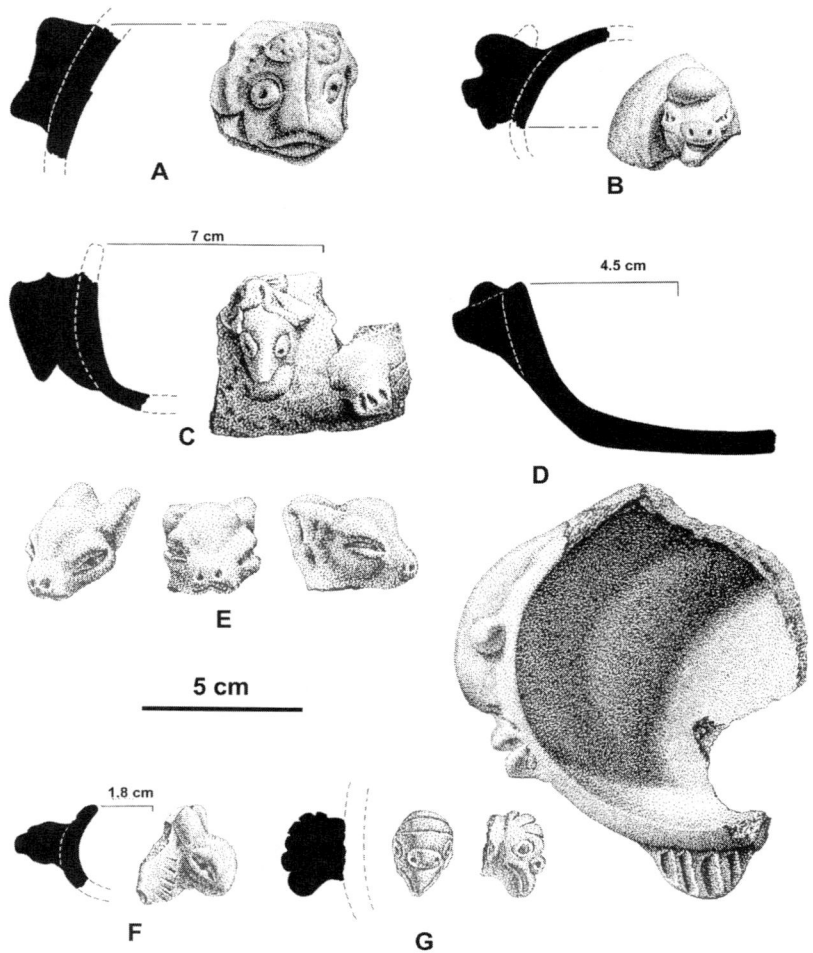

Figure 6.13
Initial Ceramic Period
effigy pots from
Cuauhtémoc: tapir (A),
dog with tongue hang-
ing out of mouth (B),
armadillo (C), fish (D),
deer (E), rabbit (F) and
bird (G). Drawings by
Ayax Moreno.

Some Initial Ceramic Period utilitarian vessels were given a
female gender. The supports of Michis tecomates sometimes resemble the hips and legs of the standing Paqui figurines (Figure 6.14, C
and D; and see Ceja 1985: Figurine 44b). The pointed feet of these tecomate supports would have held them securely in place on a sandy
or soft soil surface just as the figurines' pointed feet could have been
used to arrange them into scenes. Therefore, not only was the gender of these Initial Ceramic Period figurines explicitly portrayed but
other objects such as these tecomates appear also to have been given a
gender by forming the hips and legs of both figurines and tecomates
in the same way. The gender of these tecomates may have been the
same as the people who cooked and stored food in them. However,
female hips and legs were not the only representation on tecomates.
Animals were also depicted, such as the example of a peccary head

presented in Figure 6.14E. This zoomorphic Ocós-phase tecomate support has small appliqué ears and oval double-slash eyes, and the flat snout rests on the ground. Rows of punctations, representing fur, run from between the ears to the end of the snout. This peccary fur is depicted in a similar manner as the hair of the seated female figurine presented in Figure 6.6.

An additional, and rare, type of Initial Ceramic Period ceramic effigy vessel depicted humans wearing animal masks and provides further material manifestations of the cognitive world that the residents of Cuauhtémoc inhabited. The two examples presented in Figure 6.15 depict human faces wearing a duck bill mask covering the mouth and chin (on the left) and one half of a bivalve shell with the hinge placed just below the mouth and the rest of the shell covering the chin (on the right). Both effigy vessels depict detailed and realistic human facial features and contrast-raised orange areas with lower,

Figure 6.14
Locona-phase Michis tecomate supports (C and D) rendered in the same shape as female figurine legs (A and B) and an Ocós-phase Michis tecomate support (E) depicting the head of a peccary. Drawings by Ayax Moreno.

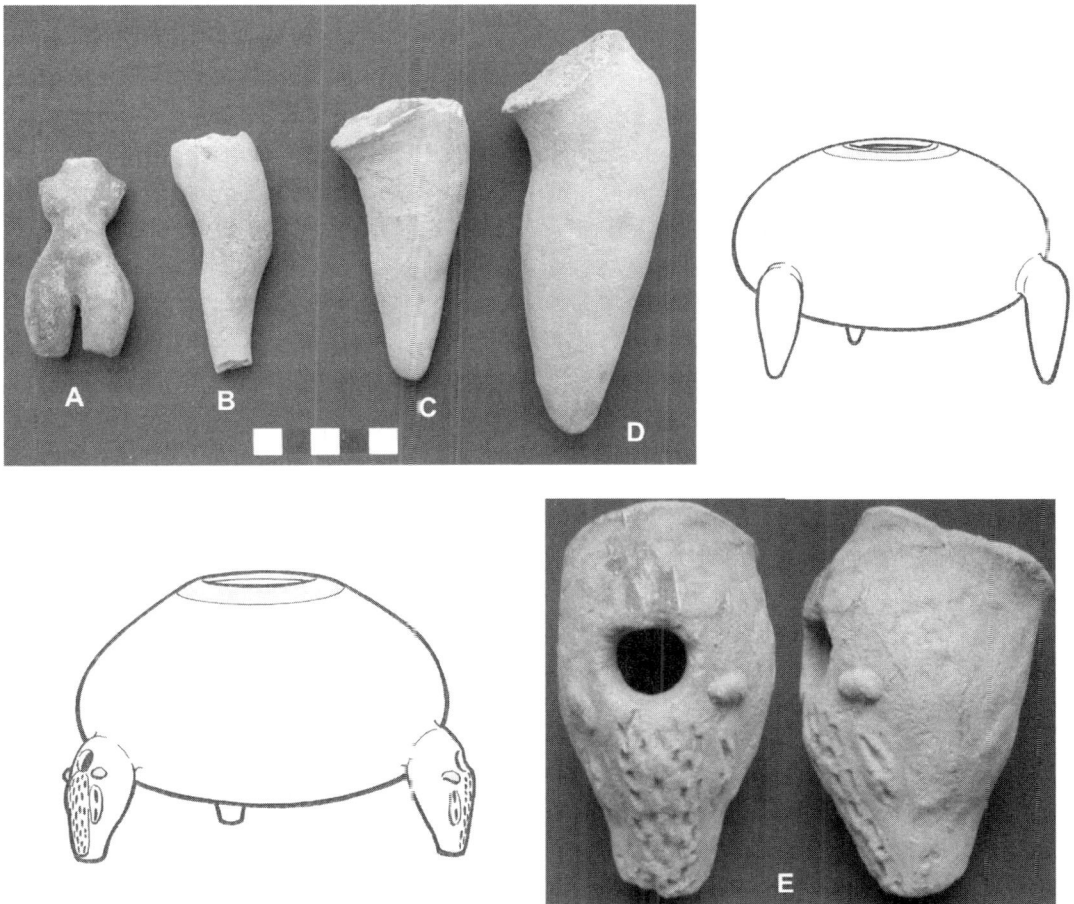

light gray areas to add further depth to these three-dimensional representations. I have previously noted that imagery of a human with a duck beak descending from below the nose is known from at least three Gulf Coast contexts dating to the Middle and Late Formative periods: the Epi-Olmec Tuxtla statuette as well as La Venta Altar 7 and Cerro de las Mesas Monument 5 (Rosenswig 2003). However, this sort of imagery was part of an Initial Ceramic Period tradition in the Soconusco represented in both figurines and effigy vessels of humans assuming animal and mythical personas. The adoption of nonhuman personas through the use of masks and costumes is closely associated with complex shamanic behavior and beliefs throughout the Americas (Stone-Miller 2004).

As with aspects of color symbolism discussed earlier in this chapter, there appears to be a cross-cultural regularity of shamanic practices (Winkelman and White 1987) that might have a psychobiological basis and thus define a "shamanic paradigm" (Winkelman 2002: 72). Joralemon (1996: 52), noting their very ancient origins, has recently stated that: "Shamans were men and women called to a religious vocation centered on spiritual travel to different planes of the cosmos. Aided by animal familiars called nagual, into whose form a shaman could transform, these individuals visited other worlds to gain information about healing the sick, determining the cause of past events, and predicting the future." If one believes there is a biological basis or not, the ethnographic documentation of shamanic practices (especially across north Asia and the Americas) means that we should not be surprised to find artistic manifestations of it in Early Formative Mesoamerica (see Trigger 1998a: 20 and references therein). In fact, a number of authors interpret Middle Formative Olmec art as representing shamans transforming into jaguar spirit companions (see Reilly 1989, 1995; Furst 1995).[2] These two Initial Ceramic Period examples do not depict fierce, forest-dwelling animals like the jaguar but instead have an aquatic referent. The duck is an especially interesting creature as it floats on and dives beneath the water, walks on land and flies in the air. As such, it moves between the major elements so would have been a particularly apt symbol for the shaman's journey through different planes of existence.[3]

Initial Ceramic Period figurines and effigy vessels depict humans and animals in a literal manner as they would have appeared. Accordingly, ducks, clams, foxes and a range of mythical creatures appear to

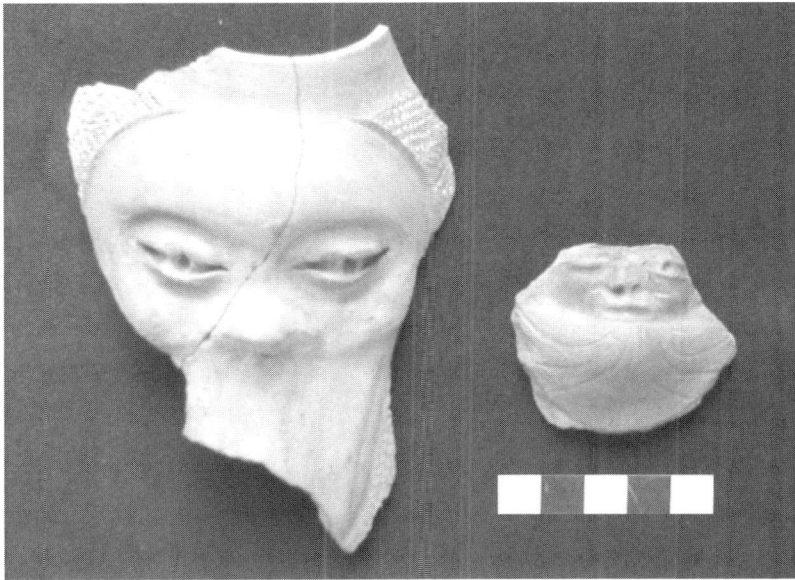

Figure 6.15
Locona-phase Papaya
Orange effigy pots. Left,
human with duck mask
on a tecomate recov-
ered from Cuauhtémoc.
Right, human with shell
mask on an effigy vessel
recovered from the site
of Aquiles Serdán in the
Mazatán zone (courtesy
of John E. Clark).

have been the focus of shamanic transformation and/or ritual enact-
ment. Rather than humans being depicted as transforming into such
animals, they were depicted wearing masks. The inhabitants of the
Soconusco employed various ceramic media to surround themselves
with objects that realistically depicted the world that they knew. Such
a seemingly naturalistic tradition of expression is more flexible than
the use of abstract symbolism because less of a distinction needs to be
made between the natural and the cultural worlds. Arbitrary signs
were soon to be adopted in the Soconusco, however, and their use distinguished Horizon I imagery from anything previously employed
in Mesoamerica.

Horizon I

We have seen that Horizon I ceramic vessels' shapes and colors differed from those employed during the Initial Ceramic Period and
that figurine representations of the human form also changed dramatically. It is therefore perhaps not surprising that the realistic Initial Ceramic Period effigy vessels were also replaced by stylized and
abstract decoration during Horizon I. Arbitrary signs were employed
during Horizon I to depict complex, culturally understood information – often with only a few simple lines. A part (and presumably a significant one) of complex Horizon I imagery was used to

represent the whole in what is sometimes referred to (by those with a penchant for Latin) as *pars pro toto*. Similar iconography, employing a comparable set of conventions, was found across Mesoamerica during Horizon I and at Cuauhtémoc is first documented during the Cuadros phase. Again, remember that I use the word Olmec as a descriptive stylistic term and that Olmec iconography is documented during both Horizon I and II and continues through Horizon III at sites such as Izapa. In the following discussion, I describe changing aesthetic standards in the Soconusco illustrated with examples from the small community of Cuauhtémoc.

The most elaborate Horizon I abstract iconography in the Soconusco has been documented on vases and serving dishes at Cantón Corralito (Cheetham 2006, 2007: Figures 5–49, 2010; Pérez 2002; Pool 2007: Figure 6.7), which appears to have been the regional center of the Mazatán zone during the Cuadros phase (Clark and Pye 2000). In the Mazatán zone, serving dishes with Olmec iconography were found during the Cuadros phase on Pampas Carved and Pampas Incised (local equivalents of Calzadas Carved and Limon Incised types from San Lorenzo) as well as Siltepec White and Tilapa Red-and-White ceramic types. During the following Jocotal phase, Olmec iconography was incised on vases and serving dishes of the Culebra Black, Culebra Gray (Figure 6.16A), Tacaná White and Xquic Red types and distributed more evenly across the Soconusco than had been the case during the previous phase (e.g., Coe and Flannery 1967: Figures 17, 22 and 23; Ekholm 1969: Figures 43, 46, 53 and 57; Pye et al. 1999: Figures 14 and 15). As discussed in Chapter 3, Olmec iconography can be represented at varying levels of abstraction. For example, at its most abstract, a single diagonal line with two downward facing arches can represent the jaw and teeth of the Olmec dragon (Joralemon 1976) as is shown by Figure 6.16D. The incised and painted representation of such mythical beings replaced the preexisting Initial Ceramic Period literal depictions of humans and animals on fancy serving vessels during the Cuadros and Jocotal phases.

The use of such abstract iconography on serving dishes likely served a political function. However, it is even more significant that the same abstract symbols also adorn Cuadros- and Jocotal-phase tecomates (see Figure 5.16; and see Ekholm 1969: Figure 33a). That similar symbols, especially in their most abstract form, are incised on unslipped tecomates (Figure 6.16, B and C) expands the

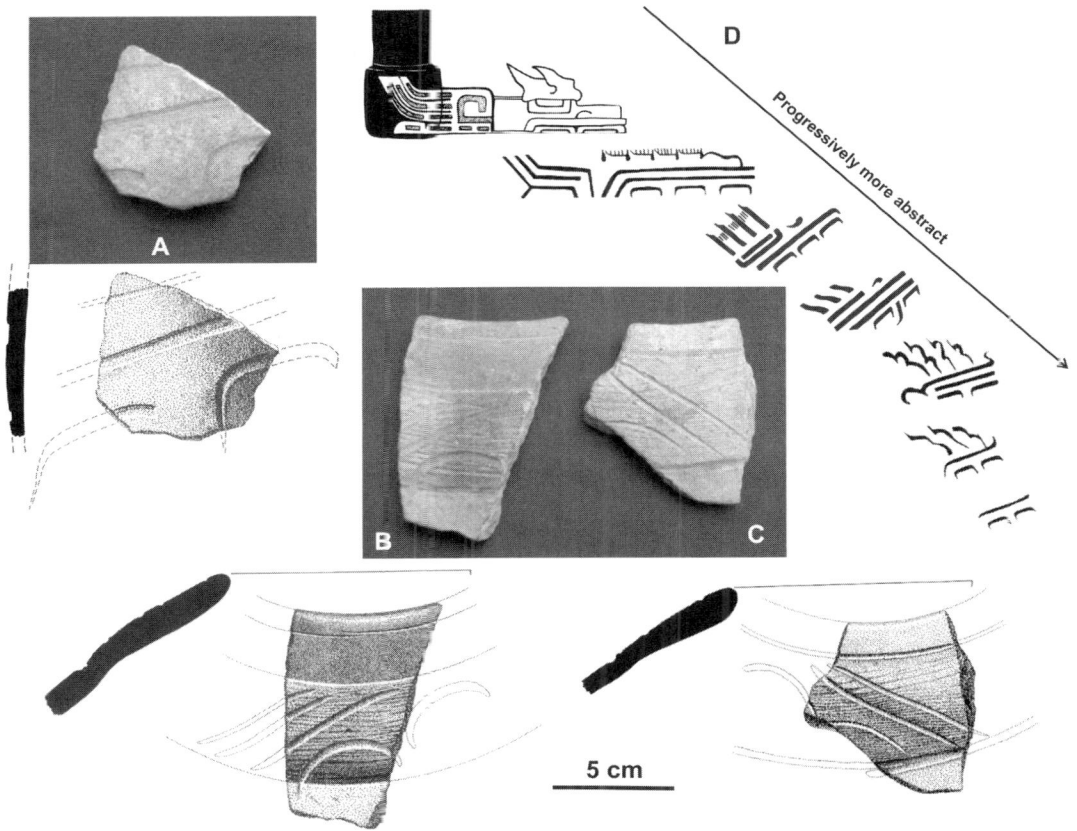

Figure 6.16
Horizon I iconography from Cuauhtémoc. Jocotal-phase Culebra Gray vase (A), Cuadros-phase Mendez Red and Buff tecomate (B), and Cuadros-phase Guamuchal Plain tecomate (C) rims. Olmec dragon motif represented at increasing levels of abstraction (D) – top image after Benson and de la Fuente (1996: 198) 2nd, 5th and 6th after Covarrubias (1957 taken from Lesure 2000: Figure 10); all other drawings by Ayax Moreno.

context of their use to include the domestic realm (see Pool 2007: 15). Furthermore, as the distribution of these vessels incised with Olmec imagery was not exclusively in elite contexts, all members of society were involved in their use, breakage, and discard. Olmec iconography appears to have been associated with Horizon I public and private realms among people of all social ranks. The ubiquitous nature of Horizon I iconography in the Soconusco is explained by Lesure (2000: 210) as follows: "...everyone might have known that propitiation of these forces was crucial to community well-being, while only elites knew how to perform rites of propitiation. This scenario would be especially likely if the symbolism bore an element of foreignness..." and further "...an emphasis on allegiance to large scale social groupings... would also have been advantageous to the elite of an increasingly divided society by providing cohesion at a higher level." This is precisely the sort of knowledge kula I discuss in Chapter 2. However, even if a restricted segment of the population fully understood their meaning, the aesthetic and cultural significance of this abstract set of symbols was adopted by all members of society.

Olmec symbols could have been used even if detailed knowledge of their meaning remained beyond the grasp of all who owned the vessels they adorned. Imperfect twentieth-century analogies are provided by the swastika and the hammer and sickle. Every member of society would not possess the same knowledge of the history of these symbols or of the political and social doctrines of German Nazism and Soviet Marxism–Leninism. Nor would all who used these symbols have known that the swastika owed its twentieth-century use to the fact that Hitler was an archaeology buff, and this symbol appeared on prehistoric pottery that covered the area of Indo-Europe, which he intended to conquer (Arnold 1990). Similarly, many would not have a detailed knowledge of how the hammer of the factory worker crossed with the sickle of the rural peasant was the crux of Lenin's doctrine of revolution in agrarian society and how this differed from Marx's theories that posited that class revolution would emerge solely from the industrialized urban proletariat. The use of either symbol on flags, carved into government buildings or depicted on coffee mugs had different connotations. Furthermore, these symbols used today in Italy, the United States, Cuba or Mexico depart even further from the original historical and geographic context of their use but nevertheless refer back to certain core concepts. The symbols depicted in Figure 6.16 and the swastika are similar in that a few simple lines carry a wealth of historical, geographical and political information. Simplicity and ease of identification are key characteristics of such symbols.

There is considerable literature that speculates on the emic meaning of Olmec imagery – to which I will not contribute here. Instead, I emphasize an understanding of formal aspects of these symbols and the context of their use (see Lesure 2002). This is not to deny that elaborate semantic meaning was associated with both Initial Ceramic Period and Horizon I imagery. In fact, the evident change in subject matter and increased abstraction during Horizon I provide important diachronic information to understand symbolic and political changes that were occurring. Lesure (2000: 206) sees the Initial Ceramic Period and Horizon I representational systems as "similar in the sense that both appear to reflect the symbolic manipulation of ideas about the natural and supernatural worlds and the development of those ideas in the negotiation of social relationships, especially those relationships activated in the presentation and consumption of food" (Lesure 2000: 206). He elaborates on the shift in meaning as follows:

> ...early period representations were naturalistic. Effigies were modeled to resemble the three dimensional form of their subjects. In the later period ... the motifs are two-dimensional abstractions composed of straight, curved, and hooked lines.... The shift from naturalism to stylization may signal an increase in the potential for ambiguity in the messages conveyed ... there was a new potential for restricting access to meaning. More ambiguous imagery could have provided greater scope for the development of esoteric interpretations that could be guarded as secret by a special segment of the community (Lesure 2000: 203).

Therefore, Horizon I imagery (and the ideology it represented) may have been easier to control by the elite at Cuauhtémoc and beyond. No longer did literal interpretations of the world (that everyone knew) provide the basis for the symbols that surrounded people during public rituals and domestic work. Instead, stylized images with arbitrary relationships to more complex concepts dominated. The increased ease with which the meaning of stylized Horizon I images could have their semantic content controlled may have been the key to their adoption in the Soconusco. In fact, James Scott (1998) notes that there is a tendency among complex societies toward standardization, legibility and simplification to increase elite control over society. Wengrow (1998, 2001) provides an archaeological example of this when he discusses the simplification of Late Ubaid through Uruk period pottery from Mesopotamia in the contexts of increasing elite control of society. In his words, the "... simplification of everyday practices may therefore be understood as a central feature of the state formation process, signifying progressive abdication of the responsibility for aesthetic labour, and the political power it confers, to a restricted sector of society" (Wengrow 2001: 182).

The control of Olmec symbols (cf their meaning, not their use) and the supernatural forces they explained could have made people with the knowledge to interpret them indispensable to society at large. Because political leaders attempted to increase the degree of social differentiation that was permitted within society, the control of arcane knowledge could have served as a powerful tool to differentiate them from the rest of society. Here I am thinking of the elite language and political knowledge that Cuna elite acquired from their voyages abroad, as discussed in Chapter 2.

The two-dimensional nature of Horizon I art also meant that it allowed a more narrative form of expression that would have facilitated making reference to time, location and other abstract concepts. A pot was not just a fish or a woman, as was the case during the Initial Ceramic Period. Instead, mythical creatures were depicted that could be portrayed interacting at a culturally understood time and in a specific place. The carving and painting on the interior surface of serving dishes with narrative scenes meant that in the process of consuming food mythical scenes appeared. This is also a change from the Initial Ceramic Period when the interiors of serving dishes were slipped but all decoration was depicted on vessel rims and exteriors.

Geometric designs on roller seals provide another example of the stylized nature of Horizon I representation at Cuauhtémoc (Figure 6.17). These seals would have been used to create repetitive patterns with pigment on cloth, bark, and/or the human body. Roller seals with abstract, geometric designs are also documented at Cantón Corralito from the Cuadros phase (Cheetham 2007: Figures 75–79). Although the images produced by these seals were not iconography per se, their geometric designs would have contributed to the nonrepresentational aesthetic dominant at the time. In addition to black and white being adopted as the dominant colors, the concomitant change from a naturalistic artistic tradition to one that was geometric and abstract meant that the Horizon I aesthetic in the Soconusco was a dramatic transformation from that of the Initial Ceramic Period. The cultural world was placed in more stark contrast to the natural world than had been the case before.

Figure 6.17
Horizon I cylinder seals from Cuauhtémoc with roll out drawings (right). Drawings by Ayax Moreno.

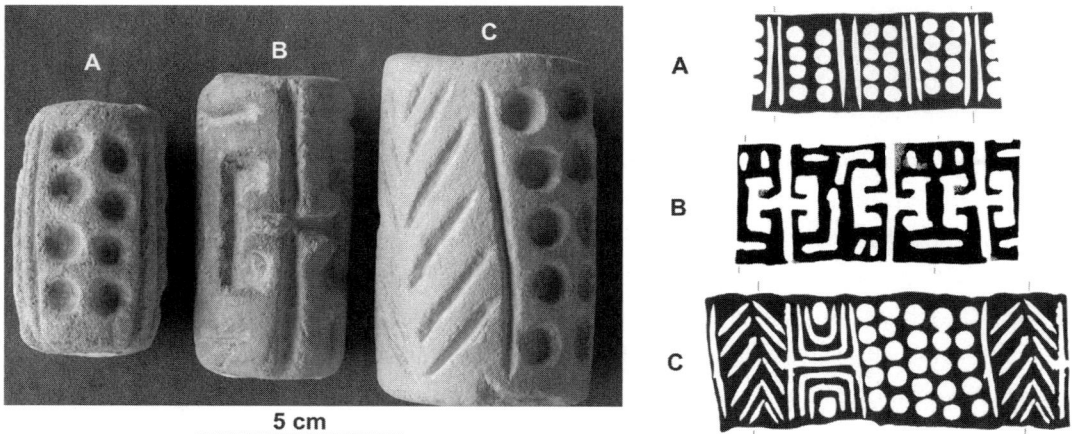

5 cm

Whereas Horizon I iconography was predominantly abstract, some ceramic effigy vessels were representational. By far the most common naturalistic depictions at Cuauhtémoc during Horizon I were fish faces on the bodies of unslipped tecomates (Figure 6.18). These effigies were placed below the design bands shown in Figure 6.16, C and D (see Figure 6.18A). These representations of fish were molded by pressing a finger out from the inside of the vessels to form the forehead when the clay was still soft (Figure 6.18, B and C). Holes for the eyes were pressed back into the wall of the tecomate and small appliqué disks were added. The upper lip of the mouth was formed by scraping up a piece of clay and the lower lip by adding appliqué. Coe and Flannery (1967: Plates 8i, j and k) represent similar decoration from Salinas la Blanca as does Ekholm (1969: Figure 27, n–q) from Izapa.

Surrounded by estuaries and rivers and with the ocean less than 10 km away, the inhabitants of Cuauhtémoc would have been surrounded by fish. Fish placed on the exterior of pots used to boil food and hold liquids would thus have been a straightforward association of fish and water. Remember, also, the predominance of fish

Figure 6.18
Cuadros and Jocotal fish effigy tecomate bodies from Cuauhtémoc. Sketches show an entire vessel with location of iconography and effigies (A) and examples of fish effigies on tecomates (B and C), as well as a Cherla-phase effigy bowl depicting a fish (D). Drawings by Ayax Moreno.

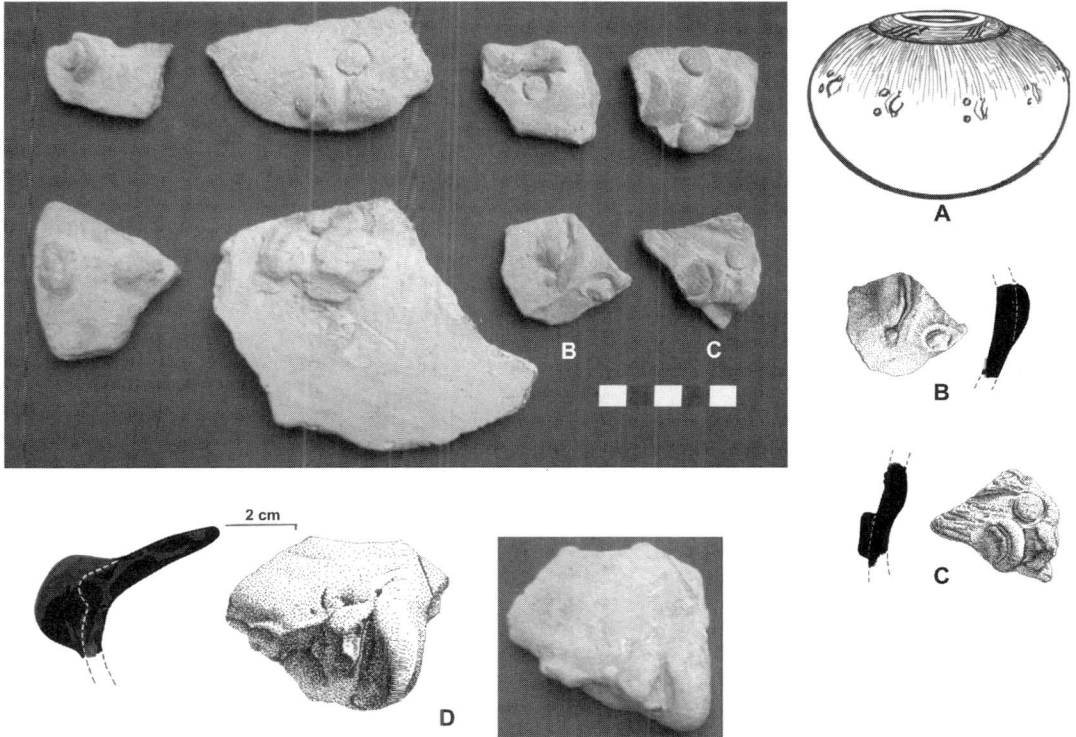

2 cm

and seafood documented in Chapter 4 from the Cuauhtémoc faunal assemblage. What is especially significant is that representational effigies were only molded on storage and cooking vessels during the Cuadros and Jocotal phases which created a contrast between the public realm of feasts and rituals where abstract symbols were employed and the domestic realm that employed both abstract symbols as well as more representational depictions of fish. The domestic realm thus remained more literal whereas abstract images were more often employed in the public realm.

I have been discussing Horizon I effigies and iconography but have so far failed to provide Cherla-phase examples. This omission is not an accident. Few effigy vessels have been recovered from the Cherla phase. Figure 6.18D is an example of a rare Cherla-phase effigy dish depicting a fish from Cuauhtémoc. Lesure (2000: Figure 8 bottom right) has published another example of a Cherla-phase fish effigy dish from Paso de la Amada. Furthermore, no abstract iconography is currently known from the Soconusco dating to the Cherla phase. It is possible that Olmec dragons were depicted on perishable materials such as wood, but there is no evidence of this. Although Olmec style heads were carved in wood at El Manatí (Ortiz and Rodríguez 2000), no wood dishes have been recovered. If abstract iconography really was not used until Cuadros/San Lorenzo A times, then the development of the new Olmec aesthetic was a gradual process during the course of Horizon I. The wholesale change of color at the beginning of the Cherla phase was accompanied by the progressive replacement of Xumay for Olmec figurines. However, it was not until the following Cuadros phase that the abstract iconography was adopted and Paqui female figurines ceased to be used. The recent work at Cantón Corralito will significantly augment our knowledge of the range of Cherla- and Cuadros-phase imagery (Cheetham 2006, 2007, 2009, 2010).

In sum, the inhabitants of Cuauhtémoc (as well as people across the Soconusco) employed imagery during Horizon I that made considerably less direct reference to the wildlife and natural world that surrounded them. Instead, culturally constructed symbols were employed to convey complex ideas. To have fully understood what these symbols likely meant, one needed the specific information possessed by shamans, chiefs and other community leaders. A deer or a fish depicted on a pot had the immediacy of something that was hunted, eaten and its remains left to be scavenged and decompose at the village. In contrast, the Olmec dragon existed only in the human imagination and was conveyed in stories, songs and rituals with its only physical manifestation being the (generally abstract) depictions in various media of material culture.

As discussed in Chapter 4, the fragmentary glimpse of changing architectural orientation also suggests that although a northwest–southeast orientation was the referent of house construction during the Initial Ceramic Period, by the end of Horizon I mound orientation was based on the cardinal directions. Abstract ceramic iconography and architecture orientated to the cardinal directions were also found across Mesoamerica at this time. Employing Horizon I imagery linked the residents of Cuauhtémoc to a larger world of meaning than had been the case during the Initial Ceramic Period.

Horizon II

During Horizon II there was a continuity of Olmec images from Horizon I that was evident in the iconography that adorned ceramic serving dishes. Figure 6.19 provides an example of a Conchas-phase carved and incised depiction of the Olmec dragon on the exterior of a large serving dish. Two upward facing arches represent the flame eyebrow above an eye formed by a horizontal carved area and surrounded by an incised line that had red pigment rubbed into it. Stylistically, the eyebrows (formed by upturned arches) were executed in much the same way as teeth were depicted during the previous Cuadros and Jocotal phases (see Figure 6.16). This elaborately decorated black dish was 38 cm in diameter and would have been used to serve food. Based on the wall angle of this sherd, and the scores of more complete dishes of this type, the vessel would have been no more than 10 to 15 cm deep. Serving food at feasts in vessels

Figure 6.19
Olmec dragon depicted on a Conchas-phase Melendrez Black dish from Cuauhtémoc. Drawing by Ayax Moreno.

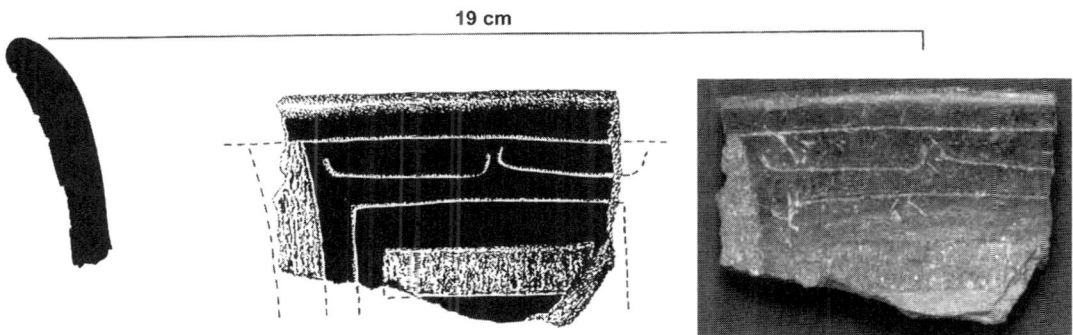

19 cm

with such iconography meant that Conchas-phase symbols such as the Olmec dragon continued a centuries-old practice that employed the same images in public discourse. Such iconographic continuities demonstrate clear aesthetic links between Horizon I and Horizon II.

Although there was an obvious continuity in imagery, this does not *necessarily* imply a semantic continuity or a correspondence in the social context of its use. As "the Olmec Dragon is a mythological beast with cayman, eagle, jaguar, human, and serpent attributes" (Joralemon 1976: 37) there would have been considerable scope to emphasize different aspects of its identity. In fact, Joralemon (1976: 58) associates the Olmec dragon with "earth, maize, agricultural fertility, clouds, rain, water, fire and kingship." My point here is simply that different aspects of these lists of animal and symbolic associations could have been emphasized at different times and in different places. Hypothetically then, clouds, rain and water could have been most important at first and then, after maize was employed as a staple crop, this aspect of the Olmec dragon could have been emphasized (or invented) along with agricultural fertility and kingship (see Rosenswig 2006a). A detailed example of diachronic divergence of the many aspects of the Olmec dragon into at least two distinct supernatural creatures popular later in Mesoamerica has recently been provided by Taube (1995).

Other examples of developments during Horizon II are provided by the elaboration of figurine types and changes in the color used to decorate pottery vessels, as previously discussed. The transference of facial characteristics from ceramic figurines during Horizon I to greenstone figurines and axes during the Middle Formative period suggests a similar shift in the meaning of the same image. A third example of change based on earlier patterns in the Soconusco was that black and white continue to be the dominant color of serving dishes during Horizon II but that the white-rimmed black ware dishes were no longer used (see Figure 6.2). Therefore, there was continuity in overall color scheme, but the technique of differential firing fell out of use and monochrome vessels were produced. These stylistic transformations during Horizon II all imply changes from their original Horizon I meaning.

A diachronic view of the Christian cross provides a comparative example of changing meaning of a single icon (that has changed little in appearance) over two millennia of use. Although the form of the image has remained the same, the meaning of this easily identifiable symbol would have been very different for a soldier of Richard the Lionheart, a sixteenth-century Franciscan friar in the Petén jungle, or a twenty-first-century suburban housewife in New Jersey – not to mention a twenty-first-century Maya shaman in Chiapas or Guatemala. Some would have associated it with love and peace, others with war and carnage, some with enlightenment and others with guilt. Also, that diversity is only among Christians. If the meaning of the cross is expanded to include the opinions of Jews, Muslims, Native Americans and so forth, in each of these historical epochs, then the range of symbolic association expands even more dramatically. Although the image remains the same, the associated meaning depends on the context, location and time of its use.

A number of new iconographic elements became common during Horizon II (see Clark and Pye 2000: 237–239); particularly noteworthy are those elements that made reference to maize (Diehl 2004: 87). Taube (1996; 2000: 299–300, 2004: 25–29) observes that maize imagery appears for the first time during the Middle Formative period, generally as a maize cob or axe emerging from a cleft in the head of an individual.[4] At Cuauhtémoc, the cleft and the double-line-break motifs became common during Horizon II (see Figure 6.20).[5] Viewed from the exterior of the vessel rim looking in, I interpret the double-line-break motif as the most abstracted version of the cleft motif.[6]

Figure 6.20
Horizon II double-line-break and cleft iconography from Cuauhtémoc. Exterior of a Melendrez Brown dish (A); double-line-break motif on Melendrez Red on Buff (B), Melendrez Black (C) and Melendrez White (D) dishes from Cuauhtémoc. Examples of cleft motif represented at increasing levels of abstraction (E); top two images are details from Middle Formative stone carvings after Benson and de la Fuente (1996: 258, 267). Drawing A by Ayax Moreno.

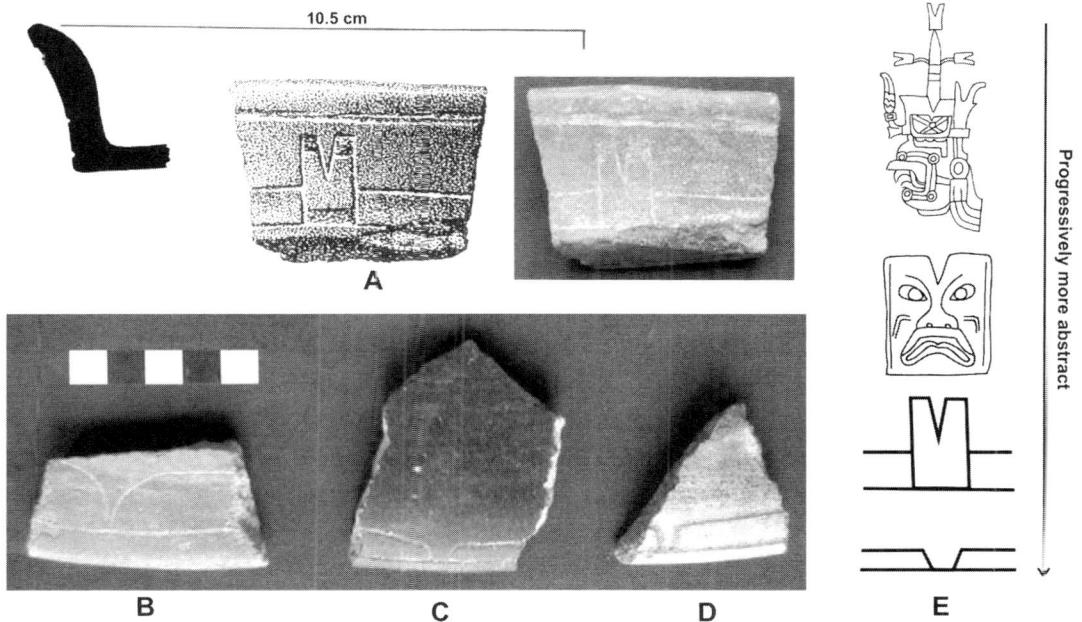

The new Horizon II maize imagery therefore also operated in the same manner, using a range of levels of abstraction that had been established during Horizon I. Three-dimensional creatures or, in this case, the importance of maize agriculture was rendered on a flat surface in two dimensions and depicted at increasing levels of abstraction (see Figure 6.20E). The narrative style on Horizon II serving dishes was thus maintained from Horizon I while the semantic content was expanded to include new subject matter. The use of maize as a staple crop for the first time was thus also reflected in the iconography.

Another indication of the change in meaning of Olmec iconography during Horizon II is that it was no longer employed to decorate cooking or storage vessels. This change in the contexts of its use suggests that during the Conchas phase such symbols became a characteristic of public discourse rather than being employed in all social realms. This restriction in the context of abstract iconography occurred as the range of images expanded. Therefore, an increasingly complex set of images filled the public and political world at Cuauhtémoc during the Conchas phase while the images were eliminated from the domestic realm.

A significant change to the economic base (i.e., significant increase in the reliance on maize) corresponded to an elaboration of the superstructure – as reflected in the expanded range of imagery. This change provides an example of the direction of the causative arrow from base to superstructure.[7] No one conceived of establishing maize as a staple crop and then set out to increase its cob size and convince people to eat more of it. Although this is the way that modern agribusiness and marketing departments work, it is not a credible interpretation of Formative Mesoamerica. Even after teocinte had been transformed into maize (e.g., Piperno and Flannery 2001), it was still a long time before maize was used as a staple crop that transformed society (Rindos 1984; Rosenswig 2006a). Macrobotanical data from Paso de la Amada provide preliminary evidence that maize cobs were progressively increasing in size during the Initial Ceramic Period (Feddema 1993). One plausible explanation for the selective force that led to the initial increase in cob size was to increase the sugar content of the stalk to ferment and make an alcoholic beer (Blake 2006; Smalley and Blake 2003). Increased cob size was also (but unintentionally) selected for (and found a new use as) a staple food in the Middle Formative period only after its caloric productivity had been increased.

Furthermore, such economic and ideological developments created the opportunity to sustain and maintain work parties to build some of Mesoamerica's earliest monumental architecture organized at centers across the La Blanca polity. Cuauhtémoc's economic base (and that of the entire La Blanca polity) was thus dramatically transformed from anything that had previously been known.

During Horizon II there was also a return to the naturalistic depiction of animals in much higher frequencies than before. Two things are remarkable about this change: 1) the wide range of naturalistically depicted animals and 2) the increased contexts of their use. Figure 6.21 represents some examples of Conchas-phase ceramic effigy vessels that depict animals that swam, ran and flew around the inhabitants of Cuauhtémoc. These naturalistic representations are depicted both on serving vessels and on those used for food storage. Again, the return of naturalistically depicted animals on serving dishes during Horizon II (as they had previously been depicted during the Initial Ceramic Period) would have produced a less stark aesthetic compared with Horizon I. Coupled with the increased range of iconography at this time, Horizon II serving wares resulted in a wealth of representational and abstract images depicted on the ceramic serving

Figure 6.21
Conchas-phase jar necks depicting a jaguar (A) and a bat (B), as well as serving dishes depicting a frog (C) and a fish (D). Drawings by Ayax Moreno.

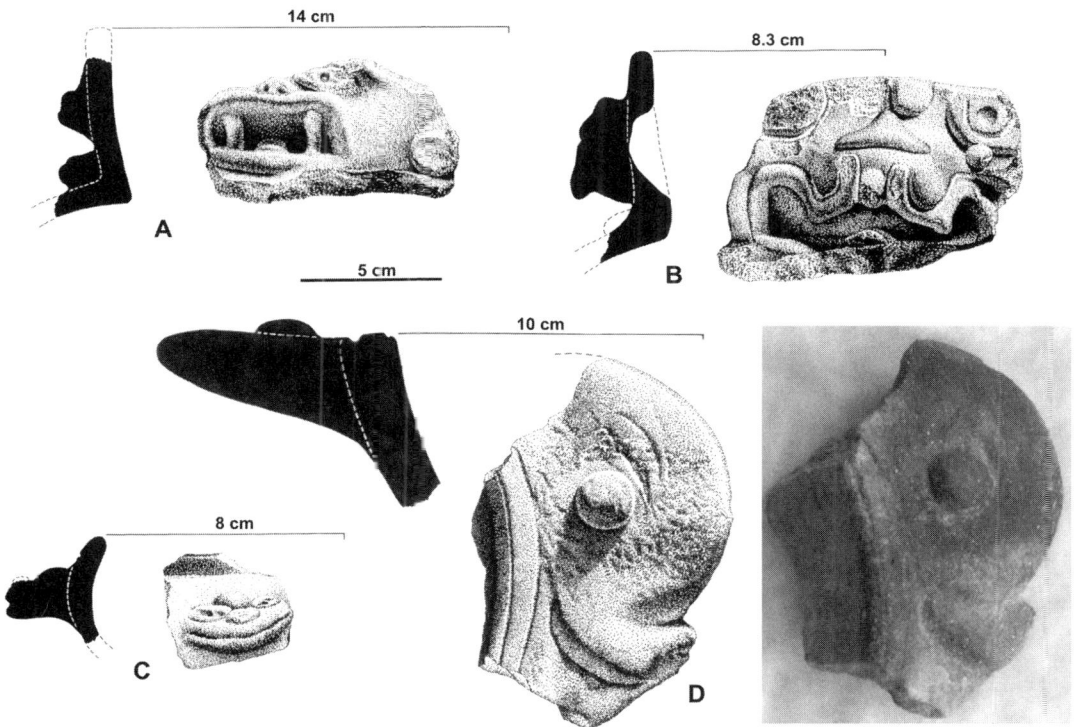

assemblage. The cooking and storage pottery assemble would have been less literal. Bats and jaguars (e.g., Figure 6.21, A and B) have no literal association with boiling food or storing liquids and so (unlike the fish on Horizon I tecomates) produce a more decorative Horizon II aesthetic (unless it was bat/jaguar stew being prepared).

In sum, the Horizon II aesthetic clearly derived from that of Horizon I. This was the case structurally (in terms of iconographic convention of depicting the same beings at varying degrees of abstraction) as well as formally (with specific continuities such as the importance of the Olmec dragon). However, there was an increase in the range of animals naturalistically depicted on both utilitarian and fancy vessels. Horizon II thus represents a loosening of the representative cannon at Cuauhtémoc that would have created an aesthetic evolution from the past. Cultural etymology is maintained but among a wider range of images.

SUMMARY OF CHANGING AESTHETICS AT CUAUHTÉMOC

The Initial Ceramic Period aesthetic was naturalistic, with people and animals represented as they appeared. Ceramic vessels were predominantly red and some had animals modeled around the outside of their rims. Figurines were relatively abundant and depicted young women who were standing as well as old individuals with large stomachs seated on stools. The seated figurines often wore a set of standardized masks – some depicting animals and others more fanciful creatures. These figurines have a parallel in a rare set of ceramic effigy vessels that depict humans wearing animal masks as both sets of objects portray human beings (likely shamans) in some sort of costume. Most ceramic effigy vessels depicted animals that would have been familiar to the inhabitants of Cuauhtémoc from the nearby environment. Overall, the Initial Ceramic Period aesthetic was realistic and literal. Even if shamans were thought to have transformed into a duck or a fox, they were depicted in clay as a human obviously wearing a mask rather than as a more abstract depiction of the transformed animal.

The Horizon I aesthetic replaced what came before. Ceramic vessels were predominantly black, white and/or unslipped, and during the Cherla and Cuadros phases, the largest size class of serving dishes was the white-rimmed black ware dishes so distinctive of this horizon. During the Cherla phase, figurines were relatively abundant.

Young standing women were still depicted, but the seated, and often masked, old men were replaced by Olmec figurines with slit eyes, fat cheeks and open mouths. During the following Cuadros and Jocotal phases, figurines were recovered in much lower frequencies, and no obviously female individuals were depicted. The age and gender of the individuals depicted by the figurines during these two phases appear to have been purposefully ambiguous. Horizon I also witnessed the first use of abstract iconography to stand for more complex concepts. Such iconography was incised on both fancy serving vessels and utilitarian cooking and storage containers, implying the internalization of the new stylistic elements and that the ideas they stood for permeated the domestic sphere.

The Horizon II representational system was an elaboration of iconographic elements based on the Horizon I aesthetic. The same manner of representing iconographic elements at varying degrees of abstraction continued, but more forms of such iconography were used. In particular, the double-line-break and cleft motifs, which made reference to maize, were frequently depicted. Black and white continued to be the dominant colors of pottery vessels, but the white-rimmed black wares were no longer made in the Soconusco. Figurines were produced in greater numbers at Cuauhtémoc and in more diverse forms than ever before. The most popular figurine types were not typically Olmec in style but nonetheless continued to represent the Horizon I practice of depicting the human form as ageless and sexless. In addition, the fact that a number of new, distinct figurine types were produced during this time indicates that the range of subject matter increased. Horizon II also saw the depiction of a wide range of animals from the surrounding environments molded on effigy vessels. The Horizon II representational system thus consisted of greater quantities, and more different types, of figurines; more forms of abstract iconography; and a return to common naturalistic depictions of animals on ceramic vessels.

During the course of Cuauhtémoc's occupation, the most dramatic changes in aesthetics occurred at the Initial Ceramic Period to Horizon I transition when a new pan-Mesoamerican representational system replaced a complex and well-developed indigenous one that had existed for many centuries. Beginning in the Cherla phase, red ceramics were replaced by black and white ones. Then, during the Cuadros and Jocotal phases, stylized, abstract and, at times, geometric forms of representation replaced the realistic aesthetic of the Initial Ceramic Period. During Horizon II, the range of abstract symbols expanded and realistic depiction of animals again became popular. However, the black-and-white color scheme and the practice of using abstract referents made connections to Horizon I explicit. The Initial Ceramic Period ideological superstructure at Cuauhtémoc thus seems to have been qualitatively transformed into a new Horizon I aesthetic whereas changes during the following Horizon II were derivative and of a more quantitative nature.

NOTES

1. I do not necessarily agree with the evolutionary scheme or the immutability of the eleven basic colors proposed by the Berlin and Kay paradigm but do credit their cross-cultural finding of the core triad of black, white, and red as a basic linguistic differentiation, especially in light of the corroborating ethnographic and archaeological evidence. See Chapman (2002: 45–53) for a comprehensive review of the problems with the Berlin and Kay paradigm and MacLaury (1997) for an extensive evaluation of it in relation to Mesoamerican languages. Regardless of problems with the Berlin and Kay paradigm, making a case for the existence of a limited number of cross-culturally relevant colors is not difficult. In fact, Wierzbicka (1990) argues that, due to some common universals of human experience, there may be cross-culturally consistent semantic meanings associated with the primary colors as well as black, white, green, and brown.

2. Recently there has been some debate among Mesoamerican art historians regarding the uncritical use of the concept of shamanism (Klein et al. 2002). Klein and her colleagues specifically criticize Kent Reilly and his discussion of Olmec shamanism. I am not sure how they would judge the Xumay figurines and effigy tecomates that depict animals and supernatural creatures as evidence of shamanic transformation during the Initial Ceramic Period in the Soconusco. I am also not sure how they might incorporate arguments for cross-cultural regularities in shamanic practices given that they claim "that much of the writing on the relation of Mesoamerican art to shamanism is predicated on a romantic vision of Mesoamericans that can be prejudicial when compared with the ways in which scholars characterize similar beliefs and practices in European history" (Klein and Stanfield-Mazzi 2004: 405).

3. Thanks are extended to Tomás Pérez for pointing out to me that ducks inhabit all of these environments while we were both analyzing ceramics at the NWAF in August of 2003.

4. Based on shared context of depiction, especially emerging from a cleft, maize cobs and greenstone axes appear to have been representationally interchangeable (Taube 2000). This interchangeability does not in itself provide us with specific semantic meaning. However, using the same logic of homologous replacement of Initial Ceramic Period to Cherla-phase seated figurines, axes and maize cob can be seen as homologous substitution that provides a contextual link between the two objects. It is then only a small interpretive leap to observe that axes would have been

important in clearing the forest and tilling the soil to plant maize. This logical association supports the contextual observation but still does not allow us to access the specifics of maize ideology during the Middle Formative period. That access can only be achieved using a direct historical analogy, and arguing for such links is beyond my purposes here.

5. Flannery and Marcus (2000: 24–25) claim that the double-line-break motif was developed first in Oaxaca on Atoyac White sherds dating to the San Jose phase. They argue that this makes the use of it 300 years earlier in Oaxaca than at San Lorenzo during the Nacaste phase. However, according to their own data (i.e., Flannery and Marcus 2000: Figure 18), the vast majority of Atoyac White were recovered from the late San Jose subphase (900–850 BCE), and they do specify whether the double-line-break is found in earlier deposits. Furthermore, they (Marcus 1989; Flannery and Marcus 2000: 29) note that the Olmec dragon was more common on black wares and that the cleft motif was more common on white wares. This change in color and iconography is actually a diachronic pattern from Horizon I to Horizon II that I discussed at length in Chapter 3 (in particular, see Chapter 3, note 6). Due to the conflation of 300 years into a single San Jose phase, they interpret this temporal change as evidence of the synchronic existence of two clans at San Jose Mogote that each used an iconographic symbol to signal group membership.

6. The double-line-break, and other incisions that decorate the interior of vessels lips, is often published upside down, thus obscuring the connection between this form of iconography and the larger and more representational corpus of iconography used at the time (e.g., Plog 1976: Figures 9.2 and 9.3). Plog's analysis employed frequencies of ninety-two incised design elements on Atoyac Yellow–white dishes to measure the intensity of intercommunity interaction in the Valley of Oaxaca. The orientation of such iconography was therefore irrelevant to his purposes. However, the presentation of this iconography upside down obscures its association with the larger corpus of icons that were popular at the time. Two excellent examples of clefts incorporated into the double-line-break on Atoyac Yellow–white vessels are presented by Flannery and Marcus (1994: Figures 12.17 and 12.18). Love (2002a: Figure 86) published a typology of Conchas-phase incised designs found on the interior rim of serving dishes, most of which are variants of the double-line-break. It is telling that one of these designs is a cleft (Love 2002a: Figure 86, #50 and see Figures 54b, 65e, 68c, 68e1, and 69b). I would argue that these are simply different levels of abstraction of the decoration along the interior rim of these dishes. Not all scholars concur with this interpretation that the double-line-break and cleft motif are referents to maize. Grove (1993: 98) sees the double-line-break as a representation of the gum line of the Olmec dragon. Arnold (2005) sees the cleft motif as the bifurcated tail of an Olmec "shark-monster." Rather than argue, I observe that iconography could well mean different things to different people both in the past and in the present. However, a strong contextual case can be made linking the double-line-break to the cleft and both to increased maize dependence due to the similar timing of both iconography and economic changes.

7. The double-line-break does decorate some dishes from the Jocotal phase (as noted in Chapter 3, note 5). The cleft motif was also carved in stone

monuments at San Lorenzo during Horizon I. I am therefore not arguing that the first usage of the cleft and the double-line-break was during Horizon II, simply that this was when they became much more frequently used. In the Soconusco, the Conchas phase saw a dramatic increase in the use of this imagery along with isotopic (Blake et al. 1992b) and other evidence (see Chapter 5) of a significant increase in maize dependence. Possibly due to the small sample of Cuadros and Jocotal burials, there is yet no conclusive isotopic evidence that maize was consumed as a staple prior to the Conchas phase. In fact, Blake et al. (1992b) do not have any isotope results from Jocotal-phase burials. Earlier use of the double-line-break can be seen as the seeds (or kernels!) of the Conchas-phase subsistence change having been planted at an earlier time. The Jocotal-phase use of the double-line-break iconography actually leads me to expect the increase in maize dependence during this phase but so far all other lines of evidence do not bear this out.

7

Inter-regional Exchange Patterns

> I also hope that I will not be held to have been overambitious
> for having felt the need and the desire for taking a wide view.
> Surely history need not simply be condemned to the study of
> well-walled gardens?
>
> Braudel 1980 [1966]: 4

The exchange of goods and ideas between regions is an important, and distinctly human, form of interaction. Exchange is defined here in the widest sense with no necessary assumption of the mechanisms through which objects were moved (Renfrew 1977: 72; Wright 1989: 268). Inter-regional exchange has long been linked to the emergence of sociopolitical ranking through resource exchange (Renfrew and Shennan 1982), craft specialization (Brumfiel and Earle 1987) and the control of esoteric knowledge (Helms 1979). Shelach (1999: 17–24) has made a case for the false dichotomy between processes internal and external to a given society and argues that both geographical scales must be integrated to understand the entirety of sociopolitical change. This argument is consistent with the core-periphery perspective discussed in Chapter 2 that addresses regional Mesoamerican processes to understand local developments at Cuauhtémoc. Although the degree to which inter-regional exchange accounts for local change can be challenging to demonstrate, the alternative – as Braudel notes – is to study small, well-walled gardens and miss the big picture.

Patterns of inter-regional exchange during Mesoamerica's Formative period have received considerable attention over the years. Such studies have focused largely on relations between highland and lowland regions (e.g., Clark 1987; Flannery 1968; Hirth 1984; Parsons and

Price 1971; Pires-Ferreira 1975; Rathje 1972), the assumption being that the more unevenly desired resources are distributed, the more interdependent areas will become to spread these objects around. This is the case when highland products (e.g., obsidian, jade, basalt) are not available in the lowlands and lowland products (e.g., cacao, cotton, tropical bird feathers) are not available in the highlands. Such highland–lowland exchange models are equally intelligible from a cultural ecology (e.g., Rappaport 1968) or a prestige goods (e.g., Freidman and Rowlands 1978) perspective. But what of two lowland areas like the Gulf Coast and the Soconusco that both possess similar resources? Purely functional exchange (in the sense of two regions each getting a product not locally available for one that is locally abundant) cannot explain why goods would have moved between such areas (see Sherratt and Sherratt 1991: 355).

Regardless of one's theoretical perspective, or the weight ascribed to external factors in explaining local changes, a factual basis must be established that documents the objects that moved from one location to another. Despite the various problems associated with prehistoric trade studies (Schortman and Urban 1992b: 236–237), the movement of goods provides an important baseline in documenting the nature of inter-regional exchange. In this chapter, I have two objectives – to document the movement of objects between the Soconusco, the Gulf Coast and Highland Guatemala as well as to estimate the travel time required for this movement to have occurred. I begin by using historical accounts to estimate exchange routes and travel times. Then, I present obsidian and ceramic sourcing data that document the actual movement of these goods. Next, I review other resources that were exchanged. Finally, I discuss a series of Cuadros- and Jocotal-phase estuary sites for what they might reveal of trade between the Soconusco and the Gulf Coast.

SOCONUSCO–GULF COAST EXCHANGE ROUTES
AND TRAVEL TIME

The Soconusco has always attracted attention from farther afield. In Chapter 1, I mentioned that the Soconusco was an important Spanish colonial territory and that previously the Aztec and the Quiché Maya had conquered the region. Why did this relatively small area attract so much attention in the past? Thanks to historical documents, we know that during Postclassic and early Colonial times it was

primarily cacao that brought successive waves of invaders to the area
(Gasco 1987, 2003a, 2006; Gasco and Voorhies 1989). The desirability
of the Soconusco lies in two aspects of the physical environment:
local environmental richness and a strategic location along a natural
transportation corridor.

High rainfall and productive alluvial soils provide high agricultural yields. Today, on much of the Soconusco coastal plain, three
maize crops can be harvested each year. In addition, estuary, lagoon,
swamp, forest, grassland and piedmont environments are all located
in close proximity to each other providing abundant and diverse
fauna and flora. As a result, the area is a virtual Garden of Eden
where any adaptive strategy can be successful with little effort.

The second explanation lies in the fact that the narrow coastal
plain (between the Pacific Ocean and Sierra Madre) funnels communication and transportation through the Soconusco. At the local level,
the narrow Soconusco region has resulted in a number of linear settlement systems over the millennia (see Rosenswig 2008). From a conti-
nental perspective (i.e., to get from Central Mexico and points north
to Central America and points south), the Pacific costal plain forces
lowland north–south travel through the Soconusco. In fact, to drive
from Mexico to Central America today there are only two routes:
along the Pacific coast, the colonial period *camino real* or through the
Central Depression of Chiapas (see Figure 7.1). Furthermore, to get
to the coastal route from the northern half of Mexico, the only break
in the Sierra Madre is at the Isthmus of Tehuantepec at the modern border of Chiapas and Oaxaca. The Gulf Coast and Isthmus of
Tehuantepec together with the Pacific coasts of Chiapas, Guatemala
and El Salvador form a geographically connected region with similar
environments, and the area has been considered to be a single-culture
area (Parsons and Price 1971: 170). The Soconusco has always been
(and still is) blessed by a tremendously rich local environment and a
central location along a natural transportation route.

Due to the rivers that cut the coastal plain, most land travel during
the early colonial times was along the edge of the Soconusco piedmont and primarily during the dry season. Early Colonial accounts
of this route are provided by both Fray Alonso Ponce from his 1574
journey to Guatemala City (see Coe 1961) and by Pedro de Alvarado
on his way to conquer Utatlán in 1524 (Navarrete 1978: 76). Both men
followed the coastal route to get from modern-day Mexico to the
Guatemalan highlands. In addition, a series of eighteenth-century

accounts describe basically the same travel conditions (Orellana 1995: 13). If we assume that travel conditions were similar in pre-Columbian times (i.e., before railways and paved roads were built), these historical sources provide a basis to estimate earlier exchange routes, travel conditions and voyage times.

Coastal route by foot

Based on the sources mentioned in the previous paragraph, it would have taken approximately twelve days to travel from Cuauhtémoc, up the coast, across the isthmus and on to San Lorenzo. Navarrete (1978: 77) estimates that, if he had traveled without stopping, it would have taken Fray Alonso Ponce five days to get from Tiltepec (near the modern town of Tonalá) to Ayutla, just over the modern Guatemalan border from Cuauhtémoc (see Figure 7.1). To make this trip they had to cross a total of forty rivers, creeks and arroyos. Beyond this, let us estimate – based on relative distance and similarity of environment – that it would have taken another seven days to cross through the break in the Sierra Madre (following the modern highway) and reach the Gulf Coast. This puts the distances being traveled in perspective at an estimated twelve days to walk from the modern Guatemala–Mexico border to the site of San Lorenzo, or a twenty-four-day return journey without factoring any time for rest, trade and so forth at the other end or along the way.

Based on the same historical sources, it would have taken ten days to travel from Cuauhtémoc to the El Chayal obsidian source. As I discuss later in this chapter, this source of high-quality obsidian, and the nearby Motagua Valley from which most blue jade was mined (Gendron et al. 2002), is key to understanding trade routes in the area. From the Soconusco it took Alvarado five days of straight travel to arrive in Quetzaltenango (Navarrete 1978: 76), so, based on similarity of distance and terrain, let us extrapolate that it would take another five days from Quetzaltenango to the Motagua River and the obsidian source of El Chayal – thus a total of ten days. Such an estimate would place the Soconusco at approximately the midpoint between San Lorenzo and El Chayal – a total one-way trip of twenty-two days. The Cuauhtémoc–El Chayal leg of the journey would have required approximately three weeks of travel time to make the return trip not including rest, resource procurement, trade and so forth.

Based on these rough estimates of travel time by foot along the coast, the total time required to get from Cuauhtémoc to El Chayal, back to Cuauhtémoc, over to San Lorenzo and then back to Cuauhtémoc would be a little more than six weeks. Of course, exchange ceremonies, feasts and so forth at each end might well have contributed more time to the length of the journey. Additional time might be added to these estimates to account for activities to have occurred along the way with nonsedentary peoples between the islands of complexity. However, if different individuals were responsible for each leg of the journey, then resources could have been delivered from one end of the exchange system to the other in less time. Let me emphasize that my purpose here is not to argue that a single group of individuals made the entire journey or even that they undertook an entire leg of the journey. Furthermore, the inhabitants of Cuauhtémoc never played more than a very modest role in inter-regional exchange. My goal is simply to approximate real travel times, and thus the relative effort required, for a Gulf Coast–Soconusco exchange system to have functioned.

Figure 7.1
Topography of
Mesoamerica.

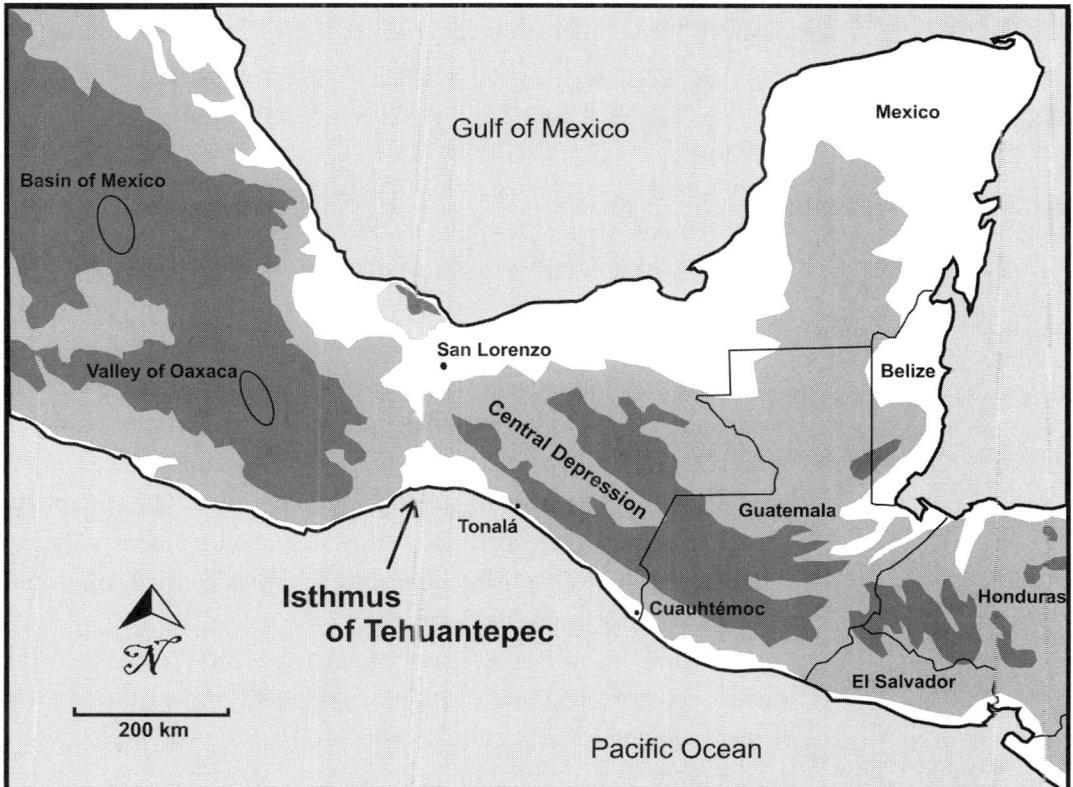

Coastal route by canoe

Another method of travel along the Pacific coast was by canoe through a system of estuary canals. These canals form when the coastal rivers are blocked by sandbars formed by discharge of the silt load they carry (Navarrete 1978: 80–81). Water is backed up behind the barrier beaches and creates a system of canals parallel to the coast. I estimate that this route would have taken approximately twenty days to get from Cuauhtémoc to San Lorenzo. A 1545 account, quoted by Navarrete (1978: 80), from Fray Tomás de la Torre states that "The natives of these towns communicate with one and other by means of drains and canals that they open in the marshes to make such a network that one could get lost in it if he should attempt to navigate them without a knowledgeable native." Archaeological data indicate that the estuary travel route was also important during the Post-classic period (Gasco 2003b). Another anonymous, late-eighteenth-century account quoted by Navarrete (1978: 80) states: "The products of this Province can be carried by the estuaries on the one hand to the Alcaldía Mayor of Escuintla, that is near Goatemala [i.e., mod-ern city of Antigua] and on the other hand to Teguantepeque [i.e., Oaxaca]." This covers three quarters of the El Chayal–Cuauhtémoc–San Lorenzo route that I am exploring here and is only missing the trip through the isthmus and down the Coatzacoalcos River to San Lorenzo.

In 1965, Navarrete began to collect accounts of this estuary canal route that was used up to the 1908 inauguration of the coastal rail-way line. Old merchants told him that, before the railway was built, convoys of up to forty canoes would make journeys up and down the coast transporting primarily cacao (but also crocodile hides, dried shrimp, fish and iguanas) out of the region and principally ceramics from Guatemala and Oaxaca into the Soconusco. During holiday or harvest seasons, these convoys would travel with much ceremony through the estuary canals singing hymns and the boat captains would announce their arrival by sounding shell trumpets. Shrimp continued to be transported along the Chiapas coast through this route into the 1960s (Pailles 1980: 11).

Navarrete (1978: 81) tells us that the trip from Cabeza de Torro (on the coast near Tonalá) to the Suchiate River (i.e., the modern border between Mexico and Guatemala) used to take ten to twelve days including the time required to receive and turn over cargo or, let us assume, nine days of pure travel time. Again, as with the travel times by foot, let us double the time to account for the trip to San Lorenzo and add another two days for the portage through the southern half of the isthmus. The total one-way travel time would be therefore approximately twenty days, or a little less than twice that of the voyage by foot. Although boat travel takes longer, greater quantities of goods can be transported per person and, according to estimates calculated by Drennan (1984: Table 2), boats would transport more than five times more goods per unit of effort. Furthermore, delicate items such as ceramic vessels would have had less chance of being damaged if packed in boats instead of being carried by porters. Traveling along the coast through the estuary would have required knowledge of tidal schedules as well as the routes through the mangrove swamp channels. This is precisely the type of knowledge that could be passed on between generation within the same family. During the nineteenth century, travel along these estuary canal systems extended as far south as El Salvador.

Highland routes

Travel between the Soconusco and Gulf Coast is also possible overland through the Chiapas highlands. There are four main passes that lead from the Pacific coast to the Central Depression of Chiapas and, from there, it is relatively easy to continue on to Tabasco. A late-sixteenth-century map of the coastal route, illustrated by Navarrete (1978: Figure 16), shows two roads leading north into the Central Depression. The first road was from the colonial coastal town of Xoconusco (near modern Mapastepec) to Xicimucelo (present day Chicomuselo) in the highlands. The second route was between Huitzla on the coast and Motozintla in the highlands – the same route that one of the two highways follows today. The other modern highway from the Central Depression to the coast is further north and crosses from Cintalapa to Arriaga; this road was the most common overland route during Colonial times (Navarrete 1978: 82). A fourth route leads from Tzutzuculi (near Tonalá) to Villa Corzo. The modern highways follow two of the four colonial routes through major mountain passes.

Travel through the Central Depression has always been important. This route was the main colonial route to get from Guatemala City to Mexico City if one wanted to avoid the Soconusco. The route leads through the Grijalva Valley and passes by Chiapa de Corzo, which is a mere 8 km from the current capital of Tuxtla Guitierez. The town was both the center of foot travel and an important port for river travel through the valley according to numerous late-sixteenth- and early-seventeenth-century sources (Navarrete 1978: 85). Furthermore, these historical sources attest to the extensive trade from the Grijalva Valley down to Tabasco (Navarrete 1978: 86–87; Lee 1978).

Foot travel through the mountains proceeds at approximately 30 km per day (Navarrete 1978: 83 quoting Waibel 1946). In the 1960s, an eighty-eight-year-old man who had been a tumpline porter traveling these passes reported to Navarrete (1978: 84) that it took eight days to travel from Trininaria to Huitztla. Furthermore, Torres's diaries relate the trip of a group of friars including Bartolomé de las Casas traveling from Campeche to Chiapas in 1545 (Navarrete 1978: 90). They left by canoe from Villahermosa and traveled up the Grijalva River. At Tacotalpa they hired local porters and continued on foot, making it to San Cristóbal in a total of twenty-two days. If they had headed down to Chiapa de Corzo via Ixtapa they would have saved a few days – therefore, let us say nineteen days. It would have taken another 8 days to get from Trinitaria to Huitztla according to Navarrete's informant, and 4 more days from Trinitaria to San Cristóbal at 30 km a day – or the same to travel by canoe down the Grijalva to Chiapa de Corzo. In all, it would have taken thirty-one days to go from the Soconusco to Tabasco through the mountains. Compare this to the estimated twelve-day journey from San Lorenzo to Cuauhtémoc by foot or the twenty-day voyage by canoe. In terms of travel time, the coastal route by foot was almost three times shorter than the inland route through the mountains. Furthermore, traveling by boat through the estuary would have taken two-thirds the time of the trip through the mountains – and could have transported greater quantities of goods more safely.

Inter-regional travel routes and the time it took to get from one island of complexity to the other are important backdrops for this book. Such is the case not only for the exchanged objects I discuss in this chapter but also for the exchanged ideas inferred by the shared artifact styles presented in the previous chapter. The discussion in this chapter so far should give the reader an idea of the time entailed to have traveled between the Soconusco and Gulf Coast as well as from the Soconusco to the Guatemalan highlands. With these estimates in mind, let us now turn to the evidence of the objects that moved to and from Cuauhtémoc.

OBSIDIAN EXCHANGE

Obsidian was transported from both the Guatemalan and Mexican highlands to San Lorenzo (Cobean et al. 1971, 1991). San Lorenzo lies approximately equidistant between these concentrations of obsidian sources (see Figure 7.2). El Chayal was by far the most common source of Guatemalan obsidian at San Lorenzo during the Initial Ceramic Period Ojochi phase through the Horizon III Palangana phase (Cobean et al. 1971: Table 1). This means that obsidian was traveling from Guatemala to San Lorenzo prior to Horizon I (when the site measured a modest 20 ha) and continued after the collapse evidenced by the Nacaste phase. Quantitatively, compared to both the preceding and subsequent periods, the importation of obsidian at San Lorenzo reached its peak during the San Lorenzo B phase with a

Figure 7.2
Map of Mesoamerica with obsidian sources indicated.

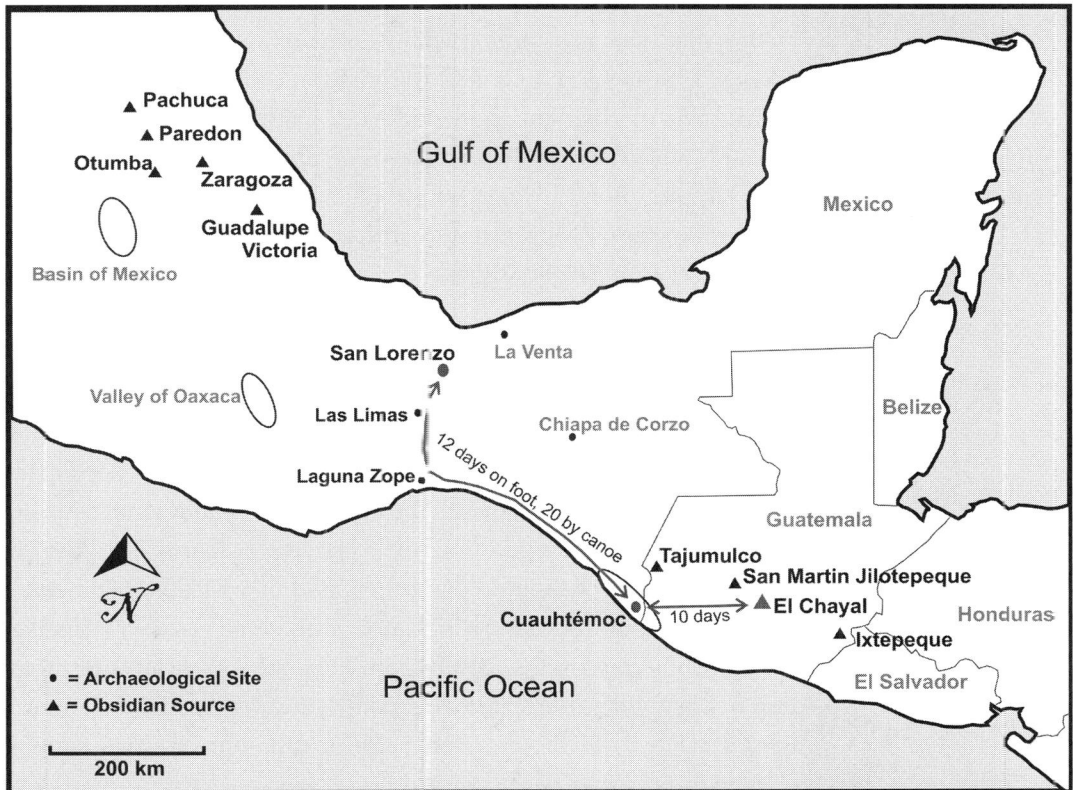

doubling in both the overall quantity as well as the number of sources from which this material was imported (Cobean et al. 1971: Figure 1, Table 3). In a recent analysis of obsidian from San Lorenzo, Jason De León (2008: 446) found that Nacaste-phase contexts, while not as numerous as those from Horizon I, had the highest documented obsidian density at the site as well as the earliest evidence of primary production of prismatic blades.

The significance of the Gulf Coast demand for El Chayal obsidian also can be documented indirectly by its scarcity in other parts of Mesoamerica. For example, Nelson (1985) suggests that the almost exclusive use of San Martín Jilotepeque obsidian by the inhabitants of the Maya lowlands during the Middle Formative period was the result of a monopoly over the El Chayal source by the inhabitants of coastal Chiapas who were transporting it to the Gulf Coast (also see Clark and Lee 1984). The subsequent decline in San Martín Jilotepeque obsidian and increase in material from the El Chayal source in the Maya lowlands during the Late Formative period is explained by these authors as the decline of economic power of Gulf Coast centers.

During the Early and Middle Formative Lagunita and Golfo phases, El Chayal and Guadalupe Victoria obsidian were the dominant types of obsidian recovered from Laguna Zope on the south coast of the Isthmus of Tehuantepec (Zeitlin 1978, 1979). This means that, although the El Chayal obsidian was rare across certain areas of Mesoamerica, a significant quantity of obsidian from this source made its way to the south side of the Isthmus of Tehuantepec (see Figure 7.2). This is exactly what would be expected if obsidian was being transported from the Guatemalan highland sources to the Gulf Coast along the Pacific coastal route.

As discussed in Chapter 5, Clark et al. (1989) explain the high quantity of obsidian at Initial Ceramic Period sites in the Soconusco (such as Paso de la Amada) as the result of aggrandizers acquiring this shiny material to give to their followers at feasts. The drop in overall levels of obsidian during the Cuadros phase – documented in the Mazatán zone and now at Cuauhtémoc as well (see Figure 5.15) – supports this contention. However, such an interpretation of obsidian patterns remains within the well-walled Soconusco gardens. How did the Horizon I use of different obsidian sources change from earlier periods?

Table 7.1. Counts and weights of obsidian from four sources recovered from Cuauhtémoc

	\multicolumn{10}{c}{Obsidian Source}									
	TAJ		SMJ		CHY		IXT		Total	
	#	grams	#	grams	#	grams	#	grams	#	grams
Barra/Locona	657	1,099.6	4	12.6	87	80.4	4	3.2	752	1,195.8
Locona	1,370	2,371.6	107	128.8	649	588.5			2,126	3,088.9
Ocós	534	1,003.8	8	12.8	160	115.9			702	1,132.5
Cherla	217	233.3	1	2.6	281	175.2			499	411.1
Cuadros	108	114.9	2	2.5	58	45.3			168	162.7
Jocotal	172	170.2	2	1.2	65	36.8			239	208.2
Conchas	1,240	1,353	35	30.9	745	479	1	0.7	2,021	1,863.6
Conchas Elite	125	139.8	4	4.4	69	76	2	3.2	200	223.4
Total:	4423	6486.2	163	195.8	2114	1597.1	7	7.1	6707	8286.2

Note: TAJ: Tajumulco; CHY: El Chayal; IXT: Ixtepeque; SMJ: San Martin Jilotepeque.

Cuauhtémoc obsidian sourcing results

All obsidian recovered from Cuauhtémoc came from major Guatemalan sources: Tajumulco, El Chayal, Ixtepeque and San Martin
Jiloltepeque. Obsidian from the latter two sources was recovered
in such low frequencies that I will exclude them from further discussion (see Table 7.1). More than 99% of all obsidian recovered
from unmixed midden context at Cuauhtémoc came from Tajumulco
(approximately 60 km to the northeast) and El Chayal (approximately
200 km directly east). Tajumulco obsidian is an opaque gray color,
pitted and full of impurities. Material from this source is difficult to
work and was never used to produce prismatic blades (Clark et al.
1989: 272; Jackson and Love 1991). In contrast, El Chayal obsidian is
of high-quality and prismatic blades are easily produced from it.

A total of 6,707 pieces of obsidian recovered at Cuauhtémoc from
temporally secure contexts (see Table 7.1) were visually sourced
by Travis Doering (2002), and seventy-seven samples were chemically checked by instrumental neutron activation analysis (INAA) at
the Missouri University Research Reactor (MURR) (Rosenswig et al.
2007). Based on these analyses, there was an overall increase in the
relative proportion of El Chayal obsidian and decrease in Tajumulco
obsidian over time (Figure 7.3). Measured as relative percentages
of pieces of obsidian, Tajumulco fell from accounting for approximately 90% of all obsidian discarded at Cuauhtémoc during the

Barra/Locona phase to 60% (measured by count) during the Conchas phase and by 90% to 70% (by weight). El Chayal obsidian rose from approximately 10% to 40% of all obsidian used during the same period (measured by count) and by 10% to 30% (by weight). In the Mazatán zone, obsidian from Tajumulco constituted more than 80% of that used during the Locona phase, and then the proportion fell consistently after that (Nelson and Clark 1998: 285).

Cherla-phase obsidian patterns stand out as El Chayal obsidian represents almost 60% of that recovered from Cuauhtémoc and Tajumulco obsidian fell to a little more than 40% of relative counts. An overall average of obsidian used in all sites in the Mazatán zone indicates that almost 75% of all obsidian used at this time came from El Chayal (Nelson and Clark 1998: 285). Therefore, at the beginning of Horizon I, the flow of obsidian from the Guatemalan highlands to San Lorenzo may have had an effect on the obsidian used by the inhabitants of the Soconusco. The dramatic increase in the quantity of obsidian from El Chayal used during the Cherla phase occurred at the same time as the ceramic color scheme and figurine styles were changing. Soconusco residents would have been aware that greater distances were being traveled (i.e., 200 km to El Chayal vs. 60 km to Tajumulco) to acquire the higher quality obsidian and that this resource was traveling through the Soconusco to the Gulf Coast.

The Cuadros phase represents a time when the relative quantity of obsidian recovered at Cuauhtémoc fell markedly (Figure 5.15). During the Cherla phase, overall obsidian counts remained high, but there was a dramatic change in the source from which this material originated. This change in source of obsidian puts a twist on the Clark et al. (1989) proposal that, during the Locona, Ocós and Cherla phases, aggrandizers were giving away obsidian at feasts and that, by the Cuadros phase, such practices had ceased. Judging from the number of pieces of obsidian at the site (Figure 5.15), it would appear that at Cuauhtémoc if gift giving occurred it had intensified during the Ocós phase and persisted into the Cherla phase. However, the dominant source of obsidian changed from the poor quality, but nearby, Tajumulco material during the Ocós phase to the high quality El Chayal obsidian (located more than three times as far away) during the Cherla phase. An increased Gulf Coast demand for El Chayal obsidian could have increased the quantity moving through the Soconusco and the prestige associated with giving it away at feasts during the Cherla phase. Therefore, an Initial Ceramic Period system of obsidian gift giving could have continued but been altered to incorporate the increased demand that placed a higher value on obsidian from El Chayal.

There was a subsequent drop in the proportion of El Chayal obsidian recovered from Cuadros- and Jocotal-phase contexts at Cuauhtémoc (Figure 7.3). The explanation might be the increased importance of exporting high quality obsidian from this source. Basic cutting needs could have been fulfilled with obsidian from the closer

Figure 7.3
Relative percentage of Cuauhtémoc obsidian by source for each phase.

El Chayal

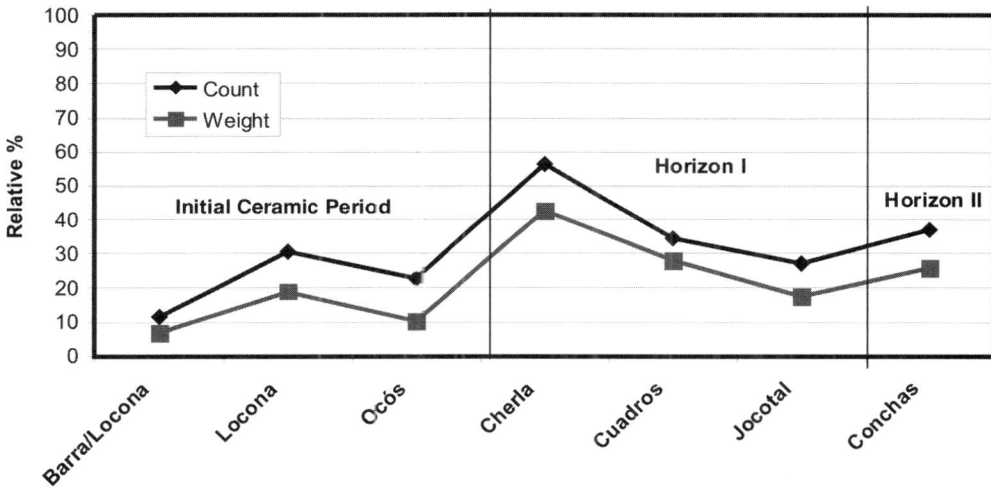

Tajumulco

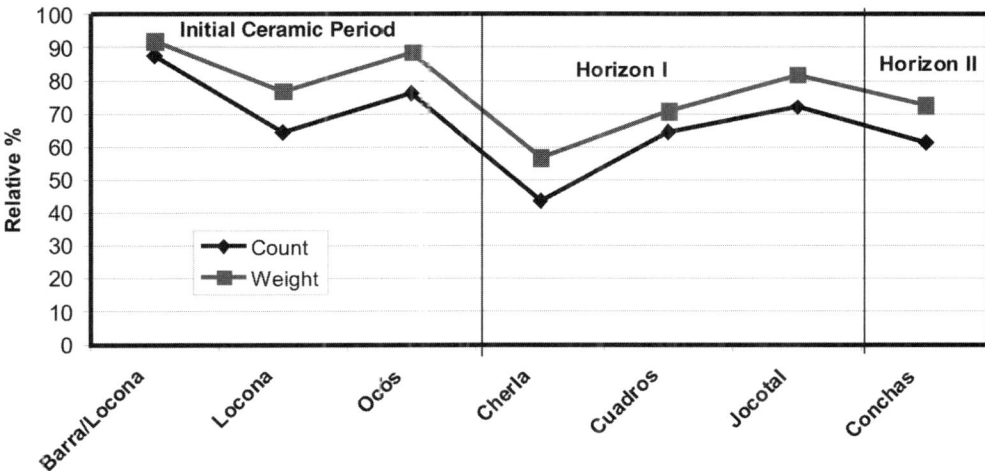

Tajumulco source as had been the case during the Initial Ceramic Period. This would have left relatively more El Chayal obsidian to be exported. While obsidian at San Lorenzo may not have been used for political purposes (De León 2008), in the Soconusco the increased demand may still have increased the value of obsidian from El Chayal.

Another pattern indicated by Figure 7.3 is that, on average, obsidian fragments deposited at Cuauhtémoc from Tajumulco were larger than those from El Chayal. This pattern would help to explain why the overall counts and weights do not correspond from Cherla-phase contexts (Figure 5.15). A significant shift in the dominant source of obsidian used at this time meant that a similar number of pieces of El Chayal obsidian was deposited at Cuauhtémoc during the Cherla phase compared to obsidian from Tajumulco during the Ocós phase (see Figure 7.3). However, although counts were similar, obsidian pieces were consistently smaller during the Cherla phase. Furthermore, the consistently smaller average size of El Chayal obsidian (during all phases) suggests that it was used more intensively than was the obsidian from Tajumulco.

Obsidian blades have been recovered in low frequencies at Cuauhtémoc. A total of thirty-two blades have been recovered, of which five were from systematic surface collection and another fifteen were from temporally mixed excavation contexts. The remaining twelve obsidian blades were recovered exclusively from Conchas-phase contexts. One of these blades has been chemically sourced to Ixtepeque and the rest are from El Chayal (Doering 2002).

To date, no obsidian blades have been recovered from secure Horizon I contexts at Cuauhtémoc. In contrast, Tomás Pérez has recovered obsidian blades from Cuadros levels in his test pits at Cantón Corralito. David Cheetham's dissertation will hopefully shed further light on this issue. Such a discrepancy in the distribution of blades is undoubtedly due to the regional prominence of the Cantón Corralito elite. However, it might also be due to their centrality in exchange relationships with the Gulf Coast. As Clark et al. (1989) note, the production of prismatic blades is only worthwhile when obsidian exchange occurs at an intensive level. Therefore, the presence of obsidian blades at Cantón Corralito and their absence at Cuauhtémoc suggest that the elite at the former site played a more central role in obsidian exchange than did inhabitants of Cuauhtémoc. Along with the lack of carved pottery at Cuauhtémoc and Salinas la Blanca

during the Cuadros phase, a lack of prismatic blades in the southeastern part of the Soconusco also contrasts with the Mazatán zone
during this phase.

CERAMIC EXCHANGE

Pottery is another ubiquitous material found in archaeological contexts that can be chemically sourced (Bishop 1980; Neff et al. 1988).
As we have seen, in historical times ceramics were one of the primary imports into the Soconusco from both Oaxaca and Guatemala
through the estuary canal system (Navarrete 1978). Ceramic vessels are therefore likely a good medium through which to document
Cuauhtémoc exchange.

Previous INAA studies from the Soconusco have documented
Gulf Coast ceramic imports during Horizon I. For example, at the
estuary site of Los Cerritos in the Acapetahua zone, Kennett et al.
(2004) have documented two sherds of an unnamed Cherla-phase
gray paste ware that were made of Gulf Coast clay. Lesure (2009:
Chapter 15) reports two Extranjero Black and White sherds and an
incised Tacaná White sherd that were of foreign manufacture from El
Varal in the Mazatán zone estuary. In addition, twenty-three Cherla-
and Cuadros-phase Gulf Coast imports have been documented in the
Mazatán zone at Cantón Corralito (Blomster et al. 2005; Cheetham
et al. 2009; Clark and Pye 2000: 234). However, as with the results
reported later in the text from Cuauhtémoc, the vast majority of
vessels recovered in the Soconusco from Horizon I deposits were
made locally (Blomster et al. 2005; Lesure 2009: Chapter 14).

Cuauhtémoc ceramic sourcing results

Serving dishes from all phases were the main target for this analysis.
Initial Ceramic Period effigy dishes, Horizon I white-rimmed black
wares and Horizon II monochrome serving dishes were judgmen-
tally selected for sourcing analysis. In addition, Horizon I utilitarian
tecomates, two Olmec-style figurines and an Initial Ceramic Period
Xumay figurine were also sourced as were a number of Conchas-
phase, fine white paste ceramics that were good candidates to be
made of Gulf Coast kaolin (based on visual inspection). Ceramic
products from the Soconusco and Gulf Coast are easily discriminated

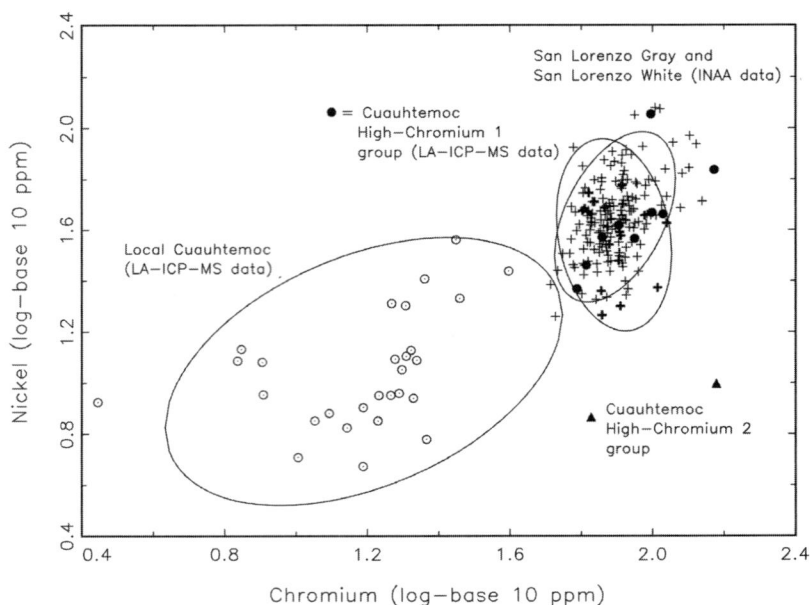

Figure 7.4
Chromium to nickel
bivariate plot of log-
concentrations of La
Blanca and Cuauhtémoc
Laser Ablation-
Inductively Coupled
Plasma-Mass Spectrome-
try data with INAA data
from the San Lorenzo
region. Ellipses represent
90% confidence inter-
vals. (Graph courtesy of
Hector Neff.)

on many projections of the data, including nickel and chromium (Fig-ure 7.4). Thirty-nine ceramic samples from Cuauhtémoc were initially characterized using Laser Ablation-Inductively Coupled Plasma-Mass Spectrometry, which divided the sample into three groups (Tejeda and Neff 2004). This is a relatively new technique that is point specific and can measure most elements at a parts-per-billion level (see Neff 2003). The majority of sherds we tested have relatively low chromium and are presumed local to the Soconusco region.

The two other groups, High-Chromium Group 1 (nine solid cir-cles) and High-Chromium Group 2, are probably from north of the Mazatán region. Two of the Cuauhtémoc samples that fall into the High-Chromium Group 1 are Cherla-phase Extranjero Black and White sherds (Figure 7.5, A and B) and another seven are Conchas-phase sherds made of fine white paste (Figure 7.5C). These nine sherds were then also analyzed at MURR by INAA, which permitted a direct comparison to the larger databases from Mazatán and the Gulf Coast. Although these are only a handful of sherds among more than ninety thousand recovered from Cuauhtémoc, a few prelimi-nary conclusions can be drawn.

Fine quality, white-rimmed black ware serving dishes were imported to Cuauhtémoc at the beginning of Horizon I during the Cherla phase (Figure 7.5, A and B). This means that at the same time as El Chayal obsidian was imported from the Guatemalan highlands in considerably higher frequencies, these serving dishes were imported from the Gulf Coast. Therefore, not only did white-rimmed black wares form the largest size class of serving dishes during the Cherla and Cuadros phases (Figure 6.3), but examples of this novel aesthetic style and firing technique were also imported from the Gulf Coast (Figure 7.5, A and B), broken and deposited at Cuauhtémoc during the Cherla phase (Rosenswig et al. 2007). These two sherds along with the concurrent increase of El Chayal obsidian provide us with a glimpse of the exchange patterns at the beginning of Horizon I. Despite the fragmentary nature of these data, they indicates a two-way flow of goods.

Twenty-nine samples were made from local sources of clay and include ceramic vessels and figurines from most of Cuauhtémoc's occupation. These ceramics are one Xumay figurine, an Initial Ceramic Period effigy fish pot (Figure 6.13D) and two effigy tecomates (one of which is the Papaya Orange individual with a duck mask pictured in Figure 6.15); six white-rimmed black ware, flat-bottomed serving dishes, two each from the Cherla, Cuadros and Jocotal phases; two Cuadros-phase tecomates with Olmec iconography (Figure 6.16, B and C); two Jocotal-phase Culebra Gray vases with Olmec iconography (one of which is pictured in Figure 6.16A); one dish from a Cherla-phase context and another from a Cuadros/Jocotal context with white paste (apparently local copies of Gulf Coast kaolin); one Cuadros- and one Jocotal-phase Olmec style figurine (Figure 6.8, D and A); three Conchas-phase fine wares

Figure 7.5
Two Cherla-phase, Extranjero Black and White sherds (A and B) recovered from Cuauhtémoc and Conchas-phase, fine paste white wares (C) made of clays with high chromium content sourced to the Gulf Coast.

A

B

C

5 cm

(two Ramirez Black and one Ramirez White); and six Conchas-phase Melendrez Black, White, Gray and Brown sherds, four of which have Olmec iconography or the double-line-break motif (Figures 6.19 and 6.20, A, C and D).

These locally made pottery vessels and figurines indicate that Cuauhtémoc was largely independent in terms of its ceramic production. Clay source data from within the Soconusco further suggest that Early and Middle Formative ceramics deposited at Cuauhtémoc were not made in the Mazatán zone (Neff and Glascock 2002). This local ceramic production indicates that, during the Initial Ceramic Period, effigy pots and figurines were made employing the same styles but from the clays available in their respective areas of the Soconusco 40 km apart. Therefore, shared ideas and regular contact can be inferred due to the independent production of a virtually identical representational system reflected in Initial Ceramic Period effigy pots and figurines.

The same situation of stylistically identical objects being produced from local clays persisted into Horizon I. Paso de la Amada was abandoned, and Cantón Corralito/Ojo de Agua replaced it as the largest center in the Soconusco. The ceramics and figurines used at Cuauhtémoc continued to stylistically resemble those from the new center up the coast and to use the same iconography. As during the Initial Ceramic Period, this intra-Soconusco representational unity was maintained with the local production of ceramics and figurines. The Cuauhtémoc elite were thus not dependent on others to supply them with these objects that tied into pan-Mesoamerican material culture styles and concepts. However, as mentioned earlier in the text, inhabitants of the southeast end of the Soconusco did not use carved pottery during the Cuadros phase as they did at Cantón Corralito, San Lorenzo and elsewhere.

OTHER EXCHANGED OBJECTS

The ubiquity of obsidian and ceramics in archaeological contexts, coupled with the ease of sourcing these materials, has resulted in archaeologists relying rather heavily on the information provided by these two types of data. However, as Nelson and Clark (1998: 278) note: "Given the constraints of physical geography, most exchange routes in any given region would probably have followed natural corridors. These routes would have been used for all commodities exchanged within the region. It follows, therefore, that obsidian exchange routes can serve as indicators of the exchange routes of other goods." As far as this is true, the movement of obsidian can be used as a proxy indicator of exchange routes more generally. Furthermore, obsidian and ceramic sourcing data from Cuauhtémoc together demonstrate the two-way flow of goods with the Gulf Coast. Other goods likely accompanied the ceramics brought to the Soconusco and the obsidian brought to the Gulf Coast. What might these other goods have been?

Objects such as Pacific marine shells, sea turtle and cotton constitute evidence of long-distance exchange when found in highland Mexico (e.g., Niederberger 2000: 157). These goods all would have been local products in the Soconusco and thus are promising candidates for exports. Furthermore, the Aztec tribute list for the Xoconusco province was primarily focused on cacao but also included colorful bird feathers, jaguar pelts and jade (Gasco and Voorhies 1989). Nineteenth-century trade items exported from the Soconusco were also primarily cacao but included crocodile hides, iguanas and dried shrimp (Navarrete 1978: 80). Thus, items originating from Soconusco primarily would have been cacao along with a variety of tropical animal hides and feathers. In addition, items that passed through the area would have included Guatemalan obsidian and a variety of greenstones.

It is possible to hypothesize, as Clark and Pye (2000: 234) do, that cacao was a Horizon I Soconusco export to the Gulf Coast, despite a lack of any physical evidence. However, the Gulf Coast was one of the primarily Postclassic and colonial production locales of these coveted beans (see Stark 1978). Therefore, if cacao was exported to the Gulf Coast from the Soconusco then economic factors would not have been the primary motivation. Jaguar pelts, crocodile hides and colorful feathers may have been exported as well. Again, like cacao, each of these products was equally available in the similar coastal plain and swamp systems of Veracruz. Although it is certainly possible that the items discussed in this paragraph were exchanged, there exists no evidence as yet.

There are, however, three other classes of lithic artifacts that were brought to Cuauhtémoc: 1) basalt used to make grinding tools; 2) greenstone used to make ornaments and axes; and 3) iron ore used to make mirrors. Clark (1988: 130) documents the two sources of basalt closest to the Soconusco as being in the area of Tajumulco. In

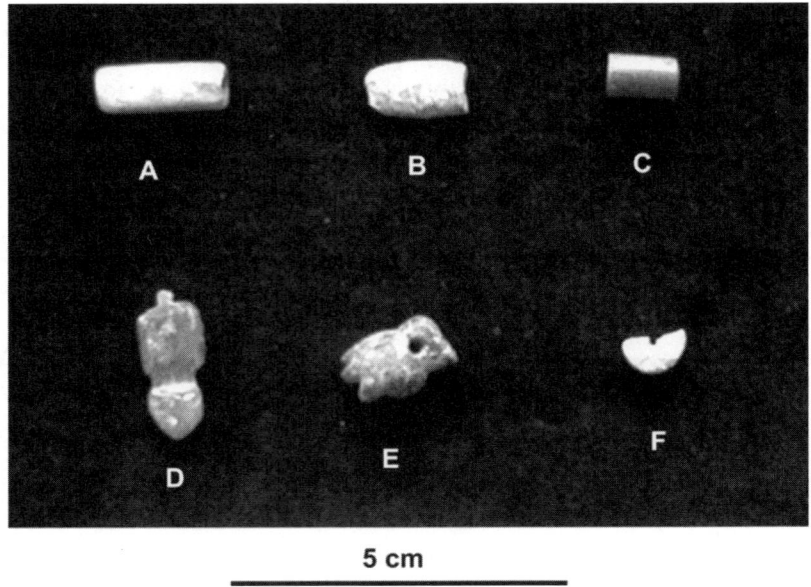

Figure 7.6
Greenstone adornments
from Cuauhtémoc. Tubu-
lar beads from Conchas
(A and B) and Locona
(C) midden contexts.
Abstract (D) and bird
(E) pendants found with
Burial #6 and broken disk
bead (F) recovered with
Burial # 7 – both dating to
the Locona phase.

Chapter 5, I suggested that ground stone from the Tajumulco area was likely brought in with obsidian. Therefore, the overall increase in abundance of obsidian during the Conchas phase is not surprising given the increased demand for manos and metates to process the maize that was becoming important at the time. Here I will just add that the exchange of basalt from the nearby Sierra Madre conforms to the highland–lowland exchange of practical goods that are not available in the immediate area of Cuauhtémoc.

The second class of imported lithic objects was jade and other green stones. Initial Ceramic Period objects of personal adornment made of greenstone were small pendants and beads that were in-cluded with burials and found in middens (Figure 7.6, C–F). By the Conchas phase, greenstone continued to be used to make beads (Fig-ure 7.6, A and B). Remember that greenstone also was used to carve a figurine with distinctive Olmec features during the Conchas phase (see Figure 6.12) as part of an overall pattern in Mesoamerica where greenstone was increasingly used.

Small greenstone axes were also recovered from Conchas-phase contexts at Cuauhtémoc (Figure 7.7). Two of these examples are from Conchas-phase construction fill, and so could have dated to Hori-zon I, but a third (Figure 7.7B) was recovered from a Conchas-phase midden. All of these objects show signs of wear and two were broken before being discarded. Therefore, unlike some of the axes known from the art market or excavated from caches and burials, these were tools from domestic contexts. Axes would have been increasingly important during the Conchas phase for felling trees to plant crops such as maize. However, due to their small size, these three examples do not appear to have been used to cut down trees. In addition, when tree-cutting tools break they are generally discarded in agricultural fields and would not be expected to be recovered in a village context. The axes pictured in Figure 7.7 are thus more likely to have been used for finer woodworking activities carried out in village contexts.

The basalt and greenstone objects recovered at Cuauhtémoc indicate the local movement of goods. This exchange occurred between the Sierra Madre and the Pacific coast of Chiapas and Guatemala. Ground stone was used in all periods but, as discussed in Chapter 5, went through a dramatic increase in importation during the Conchas phase. Greenstone objects also were found in deposits from all time periods, but the use of axes may have increased in popularity during the Conchas phase due to the role that these tools would have played in the increasingly important activity of agricultural production.

The final example of another class of imported lithic artifacts documented at Cuauhtémoc is a single iron ore mirror fragment (Figure 7.8). Although iron ore is not available on the Gulf Coast, much was imported to San Lorenzo from Oaxaca and the Central Depression of Chiapas (Agrinier 1984: 75–80; Di Castro 1997; Pires-Ferreira 1975). There have always existed close cultural ties between northern Chiapas and neighboring Tabasco and Veracruz (Lee 1978). That some of this material made its way to Cuauhtémoc is a testament

Figure 7.7
Greenstone axes from construction fill of Mound 1 (A), from Conchas midden (B) and from construction fill of Mound 2 (C).

5 cm

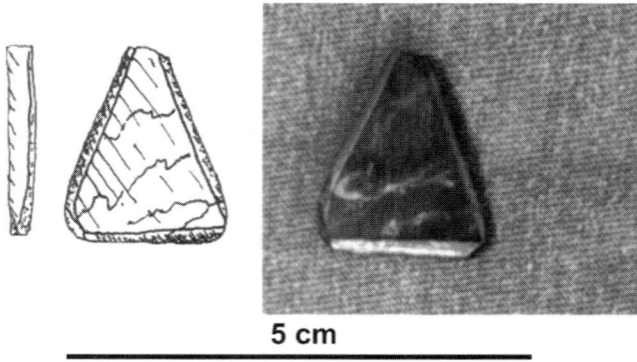

Figure 7.8
Triangular, polished
iron ore mirror from
Cuauhtémoc.

to the extent that prestige items were circulating at the time. Mirrors have a long history as symbols of status and were employed alongside Olmec imagery (Carlson 1981). Although this is only a single piece of one mirror, it does demonstrate the use of such objects at Cuauhtémoc. Cuauhtémoc was never more than a minor center in any period, but the elite nonetheless managed to acquire the status paraphernalia of the day. Such status items linked the leaders of Cuauhtémoc into larger intraelite exchange systems that must have helped provide evidence of their special status through knowledge of a larger world. Unfortunately, this object was recovered from the plough-zone and cannot be attributed to any specific epoch of Cuauhtémoc's occupation.

In sum, the objects presented in this chapter provide a glimpse of how Cuauhtémoc articulated into the larger Mesoamerican exchange networks – and how these networks changed through time. Although only a few objects made of ceramic and lithic materials survived, other objects were undoubtedly exchanged. The shared system of color use and abstract representations discussed in the previous chapter indicate the degree to which ideas were circulating along with the more tangible objects recovered. Obsidian, special ceramic vessels and iron mirrors found their way to Cuauhtémoc. As the Gulf Coast and the Soconusco have similar environments, any of the other locally available products – such as cacao, jaguar and crocodile pelts and colorful feathers – would not have fulfilled a functional purpose by providing either area with goods not locally available. However, to approach exchange according to purely functional criteria perhaps misses the point. In Chapter 8, I further explore the political function that exchange can play within society.

HORIZON I ESTUARY SITES

Another line of evidence that may illuminate Horizon I exchange patterns in the Soconusco is a series of sites located in the estuary/lagoon systems close to major rivers (see Figure 7.9). These sites include Pampa el Pajón, El Varal, Estero el Ponce Mound 2, Salinas la Blanca and El Mesak and were all built in the estuaries and swamps of the Soconusco or on tributaries leading to them. Some of these sites were first occupied during the Cuadros phase; all reached their peak (and final) occupation during the Jocotal phase. Clark and Pye (2000: 237) describe these sites as specialized resource extraction locales and speculate that salt or other products were being procured in much higher quantities than would have been required for local use. They note dense midden buildup at these sites that contained a full domestic artifact assemblage but one with more tecomates than inland sites

Figure 7.9
Cuadros- and Jocotal-
phase sites in the
Soconusco estuary and
coastal plain.

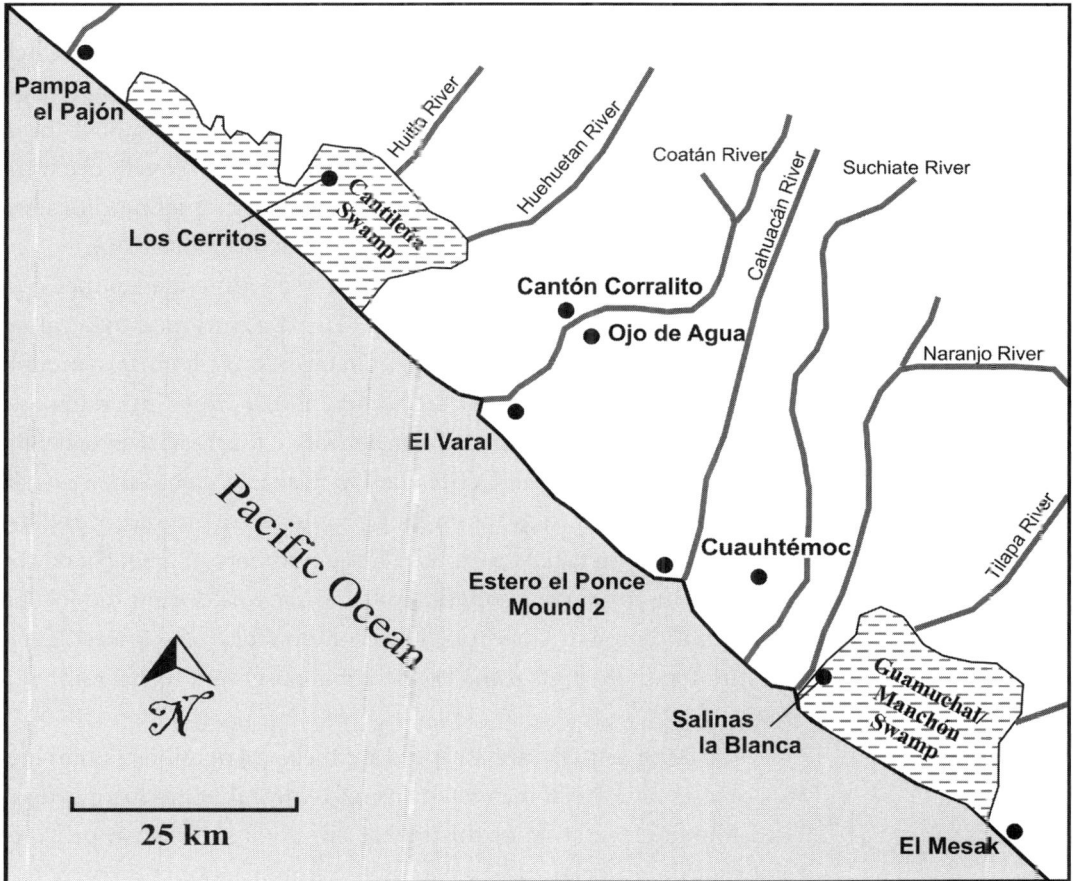

from this period (also see Lesure 2009). These sites in the Soconusco estuary appear to have served a domestic function (as this is what artifacts and features indicate), and the resource extraction hypothesis is a quite reasonable explanation. However, these sites also would have been advantageous locations if traders were passing through the estuary canal system discussed at the beginning of this chapter (as Pye and Demarest 1991: 96 have proposed also). Furthermore, regardless of the range of functions of these sites during Horizon I, none of these activities continued into Horizon II and all of these sites were abandoned.

The Pampa el Pajón site is located in the estuary northwest of the Cantileña swamp (see Figure 7.9). This site is formed by eleven mounds and contains one 4-m-high and 60-m-long mound dating to Horizon I where most excavations were conducted. The sherds from the earliest levels are from the Cuadros and Jocotal phases (Pailles 1980: 37–41, 70–71, 73) including a few Tacaná White sherds with Olmec iconography. Furthermore, the Pajón Group, Variety 2 ceramics (Pailles 1980: 42–44, 47) may date to the Cherla phase (which had not yet been defined at the time the materials were analyzed). Located just beyond the northwest edge of the area I have been focusing on for this book, this site is known for the discovery of a well-preserved adolescent burial with tabular-erect cranial modification that resembles that of many Olmec figurines (Romano 1980).

El Varal is located in the estuary on a lagoon edge southeast of the Coatán River (Lesure 1993, 2009). The site is formed by a raised platform 200 m long and 3.5 m high. On top of this platform, a mound rises another 3 m on the west side, and another rises 1 m on the east side. The west mound and platform beneath it that reach 6 m in height were excavated after being cut in half in the early 1990s when a canal was dug through it. Two 100-m-long profiles were produced, and the 15- to 25-m-wide canal cut spread large numbers of artifacts on the surface. The primary occupation of El Varal was during the Jocotal phase, but there is a Cuadros-phase component in the lowest levels (Lesure 2009: Chapters 8 and 10; personal observation of ceramics in 2003).

A striking pattern documented by these excavations is that status objects have been recovered from El Varal that are incongruous with the interpretation of this site as simply a salt or fish procurement locale. In particular, a complete ceramic stool and many fine examples of Olmec iconography on Culebra Black and Tacaná White sherds were recovered from this site. Furthermore, during the final period of occupation there was a significant increase in the quantity of figurines, obsidian and the relative proportion of serving dishes. Three ceramic masks were also recovered from this final occupation of the site (Lesure 2009: Chapter 10).

The site of Salinas la Blanca is formed by two mounds, and it was the larger one (measuring 100 m long and 4.5 m high) that was excavated by Coe and Flannery (1967). This site was the one at which both the Cuadros and Jocotal ceramic phases were originally defined, and it is approximately 15 km from Cuauhtémoc. A full range of ceramic types from these phases was recovered (Coe and Flannery 1967: 26–45, plates 6–16) as well as a few fine wares that may have been imported (Coe and Flannery 1967: Figures 39, a and b and 40, b and c).

El Mesak is a large site with more than fifty mounds located on the edge of the Guamuchal/Manchón swamp, just beyond the southern extent of the Soconusco (Pye 1995; Pye and Demarest 1991). The site was first occupied during the Locona and Ocós phases and then reoccupied during the Cuadros phase. A 26-m bulldozed cut in Mound 2 (which measures 100 m in diameter and 4.5 m high) was profiled and intensively excavated over two years. This mound contained Cuadros levels underlying Jocotal deposits, and three radiocarbon dates confirmed the age of the site. Tacaná White ceramics with Olmec iconography have been found from Jocotal-phase deposits, and Pye and Demarest (1991: 96) note that these fine ware ceramics and two greenstone axes are inconsistent with El Mesak's modest resource potential.

Estero el Ponce is the inland channel northwest of the Cahuacán River, that is visible at the center of the left side of Figure 4.1. During my initial reconnaissance in the area, a number of mounds were documented at this location (Rosenswig 2001). Most of these mounds were occupied during the Classic period, but Mound 2 was primarily built during the Jocotal phase. The site consists of a 7-m-high mound, approximately 100 m in diameter, and a second 2-m-high and 60-m-long mound to the northwest (Figure 7.10). No excavations have been undertaken at the site, but extensive armadillo burrows have littered the surface of these mounds with many sherds, most from the Jocotal phase with a few Cuadros-phase tecomates. In addition, nine low mounds were later built up against the base of the large mound. These nine small, Late Classic-period mounds contain abundant Plumbate ceramics as well as evidence of salt-boiling vessels. This site was thus occupied during Horizon I and a mound built up that would have kept people dry (but appears to be higher than would have been necessary had this been its only objective). As with the other Horizon I estuary sites, Estero el Ponce Mound 2 has no Conchas-phase occupation, despite being in the southeast end of the Soconusco where the La Blanca polity emerged. The abandonment of all these estuary sites at the end of the Jocotal phase is part of a change in Conchas-phase settlement strategy.

It is quite possible that all of these estuary sites were used to collect salt and/or fish as Clark and Pye (2000: 237) propose. However, five factors suggest to me that these were not simply isolated resource extraction sites hidden away deep in the mangrove swamps. First, all of these sites were located on or near what (from at least the sixteenth through the nineteenth centuries) served as a major transportation artery that ran from Tehuantepec to Guatemala and El Salvador. Second, most of these mounds were built higher than they needed to be if staying dry while extracting resources was the only objective of their construction. Third, at least at the sites that have been excavated (El Varal, Salinas la Blanca and El Mesak), more prestige goods were recovered than would be expected from a simple resource extraction locale. Fourth, all of these estuary sites were occupied during the Cuadros and Jocotal phases, a time when Soconusco exchange ties appear to have been more significant than either before or after. The primary occupation of all of these sites was during the Jocotal phase which may indicate an intensified use of the estuary canal system near the end of the San Lorenzo phenomenon. The detailed work at El Varal suggests that the final phase of occupation of this site at the very end of the Jocotal phase was when the greatest number of prestige goods were deposited. Fifth, all of these sites were abandoned after Horizon I when the San Lorenzo and the Ojo de Agua polities collapsed and the Soconusco population was reorganized around the La Blanca polity.

Based on the five factors listed above, an alternative to the resource extraction hypothesis is that these sites were part of the increased focus by the inhabitants of the Soconusco on contact with San Lorenzo and/or other distant polities. According to this alternative hypothesis, inter-regional travel during Horizon I was carried out, at least in part, through the estuary canal system discussed at the beginning of this chapter. Due to the lack of work at most of these

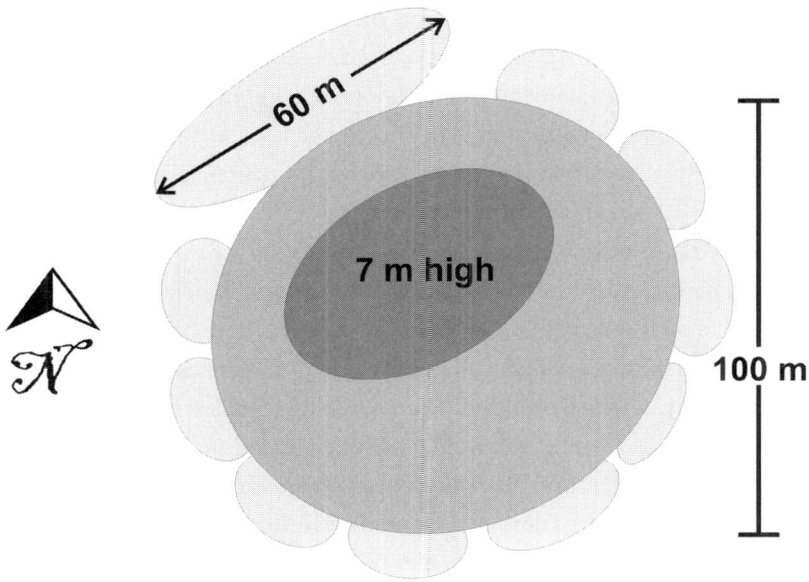

60 m

7 m high

100 m

Figure 7.10
Sketch of Estero el Ponce
Mound 2 located in the
estuary north of the
Cahuacán River.

estuary sites in the Soconusco, the validity of such a hypothesis will remain conjectural until further work is carried out and published. At present, the hypothesis that these sites were part of long-distance exchange networks through the estuary is as viable as the idea that they were solely resource extraction sites. This exchange hypothesis does not discount the importance of resource procurement at the Horizon I sites in the estuary. Instead, it is offered as a potentially complementary interpretation of these sites that may help to shed light on Soconusco exchange patterns during Horizon I.

SUMMARY OF THE CUAUHTÉMOC EXTERNAL ECONOMY

During the Initial Ceramic Period, most of the obsidian deposited at Cuauhtémoc came from the nearby Tajumulco source. Obsidian was recovered at relatively high levels during this period and, in addition to the utilitarian functions it served, may have played a political role by being given away at feasts. All of the Initial Ceramic Period ceramic effigy vessels and a Xumay figurine tested with laser ablation were made of clays from the immediate area. Therefore, despite clear links in the representational system with the Mazatán zone, it appears that the Cuauhtémoc elite produced their fanciest ceramics themselves. Small quantities of greenstone and basalt were imported from the nearby highlands by Initial Ceramic Period inhabitants of Cuauhtémoc.

The residents of Cuauhtémoc received some obsidian from El Chayal during all epochs, but a marked Cherla-phase increase is interpreted as evidence of the augmented presence of obsidian from this Guatemalan source due to the increased Gulf Coast demand. During the Cuadros and Jocotal phases, a decrease in the relative proportion of El Chayal obsidian may have been due to an increased level of exportation of this material to the Gulf Coast. Ceramic sourcing data indicate that two fine white-rimmed black ware serving dishes recovered from Cherla-phase contexts at Cuauhtémoc were made from Gulf Coast clays. Local copies of these vessels were made of local clays in the Cuauhtémoc area during the Cherla, Cuadros and Jocotal phases – as were vases, tecomates and figurines with Olmec imagery. Furthermore, a system of Cuadros- and Jocotal-phase sites were built in the estuary on a canal system posited by Navarrete (1978) to have been a significant transportation route to the Gulf Coast. These estuary sites were then all abandoned before the beginning of Horizon II.

During Horizon II, El Chayal obsidian continued to be imported at roughly the same proportion as during the Cuadros and Jocotal phases. However, for the first time prismatic blades are documented at Cuauhtémoc. The presence of prismatic blades may be due to the Cuauhtémoc elite's higher position in the local political order as well as a more central role played in inter-regional exchange. Although all sourced Horizon II fancy dishes recovered from Cuauhtémoc with Olmec iconography were made of local clays, a number of small, fine-paste white dishes were made of clay from the San Lorenzo area (Figure 7.5C). This finding indicates that long-standing exchange relations were not solely dependent on a powerful San Lorenzo elite for their existence, even if this polity had provided some of the impetus for intensified exchange during Horizon I. The residents of Cuauhtémoc received basalt from the highlands of Guatemala during Horizon II in greater quantities than before.

Most of the objects documented to have been exchanged in this chapter are not particularly surprising. Useful and beautiful materials not available in one region were exchanged for locally abundant materials to the mutual advantage of all involved. Not being surprising is, however, different from not being informative. The transport of ceramics, obsidian, greenstone and iron ore is demonstrated by artifacts recovered at Cuauhtémoc. Furthermore, the San Lorenzo polity's demand for El Chayal obsidian may have had an effect on the source used by the residents of Cuauhtémoc.

Ceramic vessels were clearly not imported to Cuauhtémoc (or anywhere in the Soconusco) from San Lorenzo due to lack of locally available clay. Therefore, the exchange of these vessels must have been motivated by either what they held or some aspect of their aesthetic/political value. Similar motivation also would have been the case if cacao, cotton or other lowland products were traded between the Soconusco and Gulf Coast. With all such resources equally available in both regions, the motivation for their movement was not functional.

SECTION III

DERIVING MEANING FROM THE ARCHAEOLOGICAL RECORD

8

Data and Expectations

> [Ideas] are given in experience and derived from the exter-
> nal world. [They] must therefore somehow correspond to that
> world . . .
>
> Childe 1956: 55

Some sort of empirical basis is required to evaluate competing theories proposed to explain the past. If not, archaeological fieldwork
does not expand our knowledge, and preference for one explanatory model over another is simply a matter of taste. Regardless of
the source of theories, or the manner of data presentation, better
explanations must be favored when they more fully, logically and
simply explain the material patterns documented by archaeologists.
This perspective gives equal weight to inductively and deductively
derived ideas, although I can think of no reason not to frame questions in a broadly deductive manner when possible (Nagel 1961:
15–28). Although deductive presentation is to some degree a matter
of style, it tends to generate a more logical explanatory scheme with
emphasis on the explicit treatment of expected material patterns. My
attempt to elaborate expected patterns for the three models presented
at the end of Chapter 3 might be a bit cumbersome but it forces a formal evaluation of who says what and exactly what data favor which
models. Even more importantly, it forces a formal evaluation and
choice of the model that best corresponds to the current state of the
data.

In this chapter, I propose that a pragmatic positivism most convincingly allows competing hypotheses to be evaluated. Then I turn
to the Cuauhtémoc data and evaluate them in terms of the expected
patterns laid out in Chapter 3. Next, I summarize why the elite

emulation model best accounts for the Cuauhtémoc and Soconusco data, especially when viewed diachronically over the centuries studied in this book. Finally, I examine the interpretive problems that result from using ceramic phases that last a century or more to reconstruct what was continuous change in the past. In particular, I explore the obstacles created by using such century-long segments of time for understanding the rise of La Blanca at the beginning of Horizon II and the fall of San Lorenzo and abandonment of the Mazatán zone of the Soconusco at the end of Horizon I.

EPISTEMOLOGY AND DATA

There are three basic epistemological positions – idealism, realism and positivism – that address how knowledge is created and what constitutes proof (see Trigger 1998a). An idealist epistemology places the locus of evaluation within the mind of the archaeologist. Collingwood (1946) long ago argued that those who study the past had to think themselves into the time they wanted to understand. This position was enthusiastically revived by a few prolific authors in the 1980s (e.g., Hodder 1982b, 1986; Shanks and Tilley 1987). In fact, Hodder continues to insist that "Archaeologists have always worked by thinking themselves into past cultural contexts – one cannot get very far otherwise" (Hodder and Hutson 2003: 237). This methodology of "sympathetic imagination" (Trigger 1995: 455) employs the hermeneutic mantra of "coherence and correspondence" (Hodder and Hutson 2003: 148–149, 240) – centered on the mind of the analyst – as the criteria of evaluating interpretations. This type of *post hoc plausibility testing* does not generate new knowledge about the past (see Arnold 2003: 58–60).

Trigger (1991, 1995, 1998a, 1998b, 2003a) and others (e.g., Gibbon 1989; McGuire 1992; Wylie 2002) have proposed a realist epistemology be employed by archaeologists. Proponents of this position argue that a real world exists regardless of our ability to study or measure it. Realism is said to be less constraining to the production of knowledge than the positivism advocated by successive generations of processual archaeologists (Trigger 1998a: 6–7, 2003b: 28–29). Alison Wylie goes further in her critique of logical positivism for not really testing hypotheses as its advocates claim. She states:

If it is the case that interesting hypotheses invariably overreach the available evidence, perhaps even all imaginable evidence, and that the evidence itself is often ambiguous then it follows that empirical adequacy alone cannot account for the choices scientists make among competing hypotheses. With ingenuity, alternative hypotheses can always be formulated that account for the evidence just as well as the hypothesis we favor...all science, not just failed science, is much more open-ended and much more profoundly shaped by contextual factors...than had been acknowledged by traditional positivist and empiricist philosophers of science (Wylie 2002: 11).

She argues that it is important to account for the social, political and institutional context of archaeology as well as to pay special attention to the "knowledge" that remains stable through changes in style of reasoning and changing theoretical orientation (Wylie 2002: 12). Although these are certainly valid observations, there is nothing that *necessarily* ties Wylie's caveats to a specific epistemological position.

Positivism was originally formulated by Hume to keep the use of God out of scientific explanation. To do so, positivism requires the evaluation of empirical evidence (i.e., measurable by one of the human senses) to evaluate competing hypotheses (Bell 1994; Salmon 1982; Watson 1990, 1991). Unfortunately, the application of Hempelian logical positivism by processual archaeologists (e.g. Fritz and Plog 1970) was based on "the conviction that cultural systems and processes can be treated as law-governing phenomena" (Wylie 2002: 4). Although such early processualists should be lauded for the optimism and enthusiasm they generated, the past forty years of investigation have failed to produce any such laws. Cultural systems do not appear to be governed by simple overarching principles just as they cannot be explained by straightforward, monocausal models (e.g., population pressure, control of irrigation systems), and few scholars are still pursuing them. Instead, it has become increasingly obvious that although similarities exist between people in different regions faced by similar problems, historical processes in each area can significantly shape the course of cultural developments. Therefore, positivists have adapted "...to the complexity and messiness of human behavior by advocating a statistical-relevance model of explanation in place of a deductive-nomological one" (Trigger 1998a: 6 and see Kelly and Hanen 1988: 173–175, 195–200).

The basic quandary of epistemology, especially relevant to the archaeologist faced with piles of stones and bones, is to establish what constitutes proof. To reject the Hempelian "covering law" model is not the same as rejecting positivism. A pragmatic positivism then is simply one that uses human sensory perception as the criteria to favor one explanatory position over another. Although I am sympathetic to a realist epistemology, this position allows too much latitude on the practical level when evaluating interpretations against the often spotty available data. Although an objective reality certainly does exist regardless of the human ability to perceive it (as realists argue), observable phenomena are the only reliable criteria to limit social, political and/or idiosyncratic pressures on archaeological interpretation. From the realist position, there is no reason to reject the monocausal models discussed in the previous paragraph – perhaps archaeologists have not yet found the evidence or the one true cause. The pragmatic positivist, however, would have to observe that after so many years of searching we are no closer to finding any single causes to explain the development of society. Said positivist should therefore reject monocausal models as not accounting for enough of the complex nature of human society. The scientific method is a positivist undertaking that need only be as restrictive or inclusive as we define it to be.

Rather than limit researchers' creative breadth, positivism (at its most productive) can simply hold ideas to a stricter level of proof than the other two epistemologies. It is primarily on this point that I diverge from those advocating a realist perspective. Followed to its logical conclusion, realism provides no criteria for rejecting God (or space aliens) from archaeological interpretation. Furthermore, the pragmatic positivist can acknowledge that "...models that could not initially be tested by direct evidence frequently turned out to be verifiable in the long run" (Trigger 1998a: 6). The creativity of scholars (not to mention their desire for career advancement) will continue to generate alternative hypotheses. Such hypotheses are often unsubstantiated and motivate new data to be gathered for them to be proven or refuted. Instead of a logical positivism divorced from the actual production of knowledge, a pragmatic positivism need not be limited by an insistence on empirical evidence at the stage of generating hypotheses, only when it comes time to evaluate them. In keeping with a classical Marxist approach, a pragmatic positivism should further strive to account for archaeology's place within society to achieve a greater objectivity (Kelly and Hanen 1988: 162).

EVALUATING THE SOCONUSCO DATA

From this position of pragmatic positivism I evaluate the Soconusco data. In the preceding four chapters I have presented twenty-six lines of quantitative and twenty-two lines of qualitative evidence (Table 8.1). My purpose in listing the data in a single table is to concisely summarize the lines of evidence I have employed and the inferences I have drawn. Presented in such a stripped-down manner, my inferences can be more easily evaluated and, if necessary, refuted. One might ask – why set myself up in such a way? To ask such a question assumes that my goal in undertaking this study was to produce the definitive word on the subject. My goal is more modest. I simply wish to provide new data to better approximate the nature of Gulf Coast–Soconusco relations and by extension contribute to a better understanding of the "Olmec Problem." If presenting my arguments in an accessible manner allows a number of them to be more easily refuted, it will simply increase the credibility of those claims that fail to be refuted.

In light of the data presented in Chapters 4 through 7, let us return to the expectations presented in Chapter 3. Was San Lorenzo the seat of an empire that conquered the Soconusco? Was it more politically complex than any other Mesoamerican polity at the time and, if so, were its customs worth emulating? Was San Lorenzo simply one among many equal partners in an Early Formative Mesoamerican interaction sphere? In the remainder of this chapter, I evaluate these hypotheses for the Initial Ceramic Period, Horizon I and Horizon II in light of Cuauhtémoc and Soconusco data. For each epoch I also identify gaps in our knowledge that inhibit interpretation and suggest some directions for future research.

INITIAL CERAMIC PERIOD

Settlement/political organization

The Soconusco appears to have been the single most politically developed region in Mesoamerica during this early sedentary period, and Paso de la Amada the largest site. Rather than consisting only of the competing polities around Mazatán (Clark and Blake 1994), related peoples using virtually identical material culture were also present 40 km down the coast. The Cuauhtémoc survey expands our knowledge of just how developed the Soconusco was as it provides a glimpse of another political system operating down the coast from the Mazatán zone. This type of political complexity is exactly what the Elite Emulation Model (EEM) predicts for the societies that will develop the most intensive relations with the Gulf Coast. However, the degree of Soconusco complexity is not necessarily incompatible with either of the other models.

Table 8.1. Data presented in this book and inferences drawn

Type of data	Presented in	Quantitative data	Pattern observed	Inference made	Epoch of major change
CHAPTER 4					
Survey					
Cuauhtémoc 28-sq-km survey	Fig 4.4	x	Small Locona peak, significant increase in Jocotal and highest level during Conchas	Corresponds to Mazatán during Initial Ceramic Period and Horizon I, and tracks emergence of La Blanca in Horizon II	
Comparison to other regions	Table 4.1	x	Mazatán reorganized as San Lorenzo rises in Horizon I and they collapse together	Mazatán and San Lorenzo's fortunes are intertwined during Horizon I rise and Horizon II collapse	
Architecture					
Architectural orientation	Figs 3.1, 3.3, 4.8 and 4.10		Initial Ceramic Period residences oriented northwest–southeast, Horizon I and Horizon II on cardinal directions	Initial Ceramic Period naturalistic, Horizon I and Horizon II based on nonlocal principle	Horizon I
Mound building	Figs 4.7 and 4.10		Earliest system of central pyramid mounds in Mesoamerica during Horizon II	New level of political integration established in the Soconusco	Horizon II
CHAPTER 5					
Diet					
Overall faunal classes	Fig 5.1	x	Similar patterns in all periods	Mixed economy in all periods	
Proportion of mammals	Fig 5.3	x	Horizon II increase of deer and dog exploitation	Horizon II intensification of fewer animal species	
Maize density	Fig 5.4	x	Increased density of maize remains in Horizon II contexts	Greater reliance on maize	Horizon II
Elite context Conchas fauna	Rosenswig 2007	x	Considerably more dog	Horizon II use of dog at feasts	
Isotope data	Blake et al. 1992a	x	C4 signature increases in Horizon II	Maize becomes a staple crop	
Net weights	Fig 5.6	x	Presence of net weight in all periods	Intensive exploitation of aquatic environments in all periods	

Food Processing

Proportion undecorated tecomates	Fig 5.7	x	Fewer in use over time	Fewer tecomates but …	
Size of undecorated tecomates	Fig 5.8	x	Horizon I and Horizon II increase over Initial Ceramic Period size	… they are bigger indicating more intensive food preparation	} Horizon I
Density of fire-cracked rock	Fig 5.9	x	Horizon I decrease	Archaic pit roasting food preparation technique decreases	
Density of ground stone	Fig 5.10	x	Horizon II increase in overall quantity of grinding occurring	More grinding in Horizon II	
Mano/metate: Pestle/mortar	Fig 5.11	x	Horizon II increase in relative proportion of manos and metates	More grinding in Horizon II	} Horizon II
Grater bowls and round pestles	Figs 5.12–5.14		Horizon II expansion of grating technologies	Short supply of basalt due to increased grinding in Horizon II	
Density of obsidian	Fig 5.15	x	Decrease in Horizon I and Horizon II	End of obsidian gift giving after Cherla phase	} Horizon I

Feasting

Serving to cooking vessels	Fig 5.16	x	Consistent through time with slight increase in Horizon I and Horizon II	Increasing emphasis on serving food	
Size of decorated tecomates	Figs 5.17 and 5.18	x	Horizon I increase	Larger groups being served food and drink beginning in Horizon I	
Proportion of decorated dishes	Fig 5.19	x	Horizon I increase	Serving food becomes relatively more important/frequent	
Size of decorated dishes	Table 5.4	x	Horizon I increase from Initial Ceramic Period levels	Larger groups being served food beginning in Horizon I	} Horizon I
Distribution of Initial Ceramic Period and Horizon I dishes	Fig 5.20	x	Three size classes in Initial Ceramic Period and Horizon I	Serving vessels used for distinct functions	
Distribution of Horizon II dishes	Fig 5.21	x	Clear elite size distribution	Formalized elite serving vessel assemblage documented for this phase	

(continued)

Table 8.1 (*continued*)

Type of data	Presented in	Quantitative data	Pattern observed	Inference made	Epoch of major change
CHAPTER 6					
Ceramic Vessels					
Overall ceramic color	Fig 6.2	x	Initial Ceramic Period dominated by red wares; Horizon I and Horizon II by black and white wares	Aesthetic disjuncture begins in Horizon I and persisted through Horizon II	
Gulf Coast white-rimmed black wares			Used at San Lorenzo during Horizon I and persists on the Gulf Coast through Classic period	Indigenous Gulf Coast style employed in the Soconusco only for the duration of Horizon I	
Horizon I serving dish color by size	Fig 6.3	x	Cherla white-rimmed black ware comprise the largest size class of serving dishes	Meaning of the novel color aesthetic suggested by use to serve food to large groups of people	
Figurines					
Density through time	Fig 6.4	x	Horizon I decrease and Horizon II increase	Horizon I restriction of human representation	Horizon I
Initial Ceramic Period naturalism	Figs 6.5–6.7		Seated, fat elders and standing young females	Naturalistic, emphasizing aspects of age and sex	
Horizon I thematic narrowing	Fig 6.8		Naked sexless individuals	Disjuncture from Initial Ceramic Period	
Cherla transition	Fig 6.9		Combines elements of Initial Ceramic Period and Horizon I traditions	Developed local representational system, gradually replaced by foreign system but variability in rate of such change between Mazatán and Cuauhtémoc	
Horizon II diversification	Figs 6.10–6.12		More sizes, types and materials used to make figurines during Horizon II	Broadened use of human representations evolve out of Horizon I cannon	
Effigies + Iconography					
Initial Ceramic Period representation and technique	Fig 6.13		Naturalism and manufacture technique same as figurines	Together they form a cohesive, indigenous Soconusco representational tradition	
Initial Ceramic Period tecomate effigy supports	Fig 6.14		Tecomate supports in the form of female legs or animal heads	Naturalistic representations suggesting the sex of pots	
Initial Ceramic Period humans effigy vessels	Fig 6.15		Duck and shell masks worn over lower face	Thematically consistent with Xumay figurines and are part of the indigenous Soconusco tradition	

Horizon I abstract iconography	Fig 6.16		Olmec dragon represented as diagonal lines and two downward facing arches	Break from the Initial Ceramic Period naturalism by coding complex information using simple symbols
Horizon I cylinder seals	Fig 6.17		Geometric designs	Break from the Initial Ceramic Period naturalism
Horizon fish effigy vessels	Fig 6.18		Fish represented on utilitarian tecomates that held water	Naturalism not part of public discourse
Horizon II depiction of Olmec dragon	Fig 6.19		Same subject matter and method of abstraction as during Horizon I	Continuity from Horizon I
Horizon II double-line-break and cleft motifs	Fig 6.20		Same method of increasing levels of abstraction	Elaboration of meaning using symbolic conventions established in Horizon I
Horizon II animal effigies	Fig 6.21		A variety of animals depicted	Broadening of subjects represented

(Figs 6.16–6.21 bracketed as **Horizon I**)

CHAPTER 7

Ethnohistory of travel times and routes			San Lorenzo to Cuauhtémoc: 12 days by foot along the coast and 20 by boat; 31 days through the highlands	Natural corridors dictate travel routes
Obsidian sources	Table 7.1	x	Most from Tajumulco and El Chayal sources	Former: poor quality, 60 km away; later: good quality, 200 km away
Proportion of obsidian sources	Fig 7.3	x	Increase in El Chayal with spike during Cherla phase	Guatemala obsidian coming through Soconusco as San Lorenzo emerges as a center
Obsidian blades		x	Only in Horizon II contexts at Cuauhtémoc yet present in Horizon I contexts at both Cantón Corralito and San Lorenzo	Restricted geographic distribution suggests Cuauhtémoc elite may have been excluded from such exchange
Ceramic sourcing	Figs 7.4 and 7.5	x	Two Cherla-phase sherds and seven Conchas-phase sherds from Gulf Coast	Ceramics arrived at Cuauhtémoc during Horizon I and Horizon II
Greenstone	Figs 7.6 and 7.7		Present in all epochs but more from Horizon II, including axes	Local highland–lowland exchange networks had always existed
Iron ore	Fig 7.8		Single piece of mirror	Another class of material brought in from further north
Horizon I estuary sites	Figs 7.9 and 7.10		Located along travel route and abandoned with fall of San Lorenzo	Intensification of interaction, especially during Jocotal phase

(Fig 7.3 bracketed as **Horizon I**; Figs 7.6 and 7.7 bracketed as **Horizon II**; Figs 7.9 and 7.10 bracketed as **Horizon I**)

Subsistence and technology

There is no direct evidence that addresses the intensity of resource exploitation in the Soconusco during the Initial Ceramic Period. However, the quantity of fauna from the estuary and net weights do indicate that aquatic resources were intensively harvested at this early date. The rich local environment, the lack of maize dependence, as well as changes in fire-cracked rock and tecomate patterns (possibly reflecting food being steamed) indicate that subsistence patterns may have been only very gradually changing from Archaic times. Indirect evidence of Initial Ceramic Period intensification was the progressive increase in the size of corn cobs recovered from Paso de la Amada (Feddema 1993).

Food and drink were served in fancy vessels in the Soconusco from the beginning of the Initial Ceramic Period. In fact, feasting may have been why ceramics were first adopted in the region (Clark and Blake 1994; Clark and Gosser 1995). As with settlement data, subsistence and feasting patterns are consistent with what the EEM predicts regarding the islands of complexity that will be the societies most interested in establishing ties to the Gulf Coast. However, there is nothing about Initial Ceramic Period subsistence data that is inconsistent with either the Peer Polity Model (PPM) or the Aztec Analogy Model (AAM).

Symbolism

The distinctive and indigenous nature of the Soconusco Initial Ceramic Period representational system has been convincingly presented by others (e.g., Clark and Pye 2000; Lesure 2000). The Cuauhtémoc ceramic and figurine data confirm that this was an integrated Soconusco-wide phenomenon that extended from one end of the land between the swamps to the other. This artistic tradition used naturalistic conventions to accurately depict a wide range of humans and animals. Primordial themes certainly could have been modeled in clay as posited by some proponents of the PPM. In fact, an effigy tecomate depicting a human wearing a duck mask (see Figure 6.15) does seem to have thematic similarity in later Olmec art (see Rosenswig 2003). This object may further be part of a pan-American tradition of shamanism that dates back to the original peopling of the New World. Therefore, this is an example of a primordial theme executed in the indigenous Soconusco style that was later re-interpreted using Olmec aesthetics. However, the documentation of a well-developed representational system (employed across the Soconusco) during the Initial Ceramic Period and its subsequent replacement by a new aesthetic in Horizon I provides one of the strongest arguments against the PPM.

Exchange

Greenstone, basalt and obsidian were finding their way to Cuauhtémoc from the Guatemalan highlands throughout the Initial Ceramic Period. In fact, obsidian was also brought into the Soconusco during Archaic times (Nelson and Voorhies 1980). Thus, the exchange of goods from nearby, yet geographically and environmentally distinct, regions was established prior to the Initial Ceramic Period. El Chayal obsidian was also making its way to San Lorenzo in significant quantities during the Initial Ceramic Period.

There is no evidence from the Soconusco of goods traded in from (or out to) more distant regions at this time. However, the ceramic similarities that define a Locona interaction sphere across the southern part of Mesoamerica indicate that at least ideas were traveling between the Soconusco and Gulf Coast (through the Isthmus of Tehuantepec) during this time. The technical knowledge of how to make ceramics at all was also spreading across Mesoamerica at this time (see Clark and Cheetham 2002: Figure 2). The Initial Ceramic Period patterns of exchange do not favor one model over the others.

Directions for future work

At a Mesoamerican-wide scale, a worthwhile endeavor would be to more precisely define the extents of the Locona interaction sphere. Are the sites that share Initial Ceramic Period ceramic styles the same ones that were occupied during Horizon I? Furthermore, how does this interaction sphere (that encompasses both the Soconusco and Gulf Coast) integrate with the neighboring Red-on-Buff interaction sphere? Both Clark (1991: Figure 8) and Flannery and Marcus (2000: Figure 3) indicate a zone where the two spheres overlap, but do not elaborate on what this implies for the societies on the borderland. Defining the Early Formative history of these borderland sites would provide a better understanding of if and/or how the

Horizon I phenomenon (however it is explained) transformed the Initial Ceramic Period world.

Another worthwhile endeavor would be to systematically source Initial Ceramic Period ceramics from both the Soconusco and Gulf Coast. This is rarely done as the assumption is that they are all locally produced – as all of the Cuauhtémoc examples in fact were (see Chapter 7). However, documenting (or failing to do so) the transport of Initial Ceramic Period ceramics between the Soconusco and Gulf Coast would indicate the type of inter-regional exchange that resulted in the Locona interaction sphere.

In the Cuauhtémoc zone, extending the survey and excavating at other Initial Ceramic Period sites will be necessary to determine if the Cuauhtémoc site was a solitary center 40 km down the coast from the Mazatán zone or whether it was part of a more integrated local system that replicated the competing Mazatán polities on a smaller scale. Significant in its own right in illuminating the process of emergent rank society, documenting a larger area around Cuauhtémoc also would contribute to a more complete understanding of how the Soconusco political landscape was then transformed during Horizon I.

HORIZON I

Settlement/political organization

Settlement patterns in the Soconusco changed significantly during Horizon I. In the Mazatán zone, Paso de la Amada was three times larger than any other site during the Locona and Ocós phases (covering 140 ha and 74 ha, respectively) (Clark, personal communication 2004). During the Cherla phase, Paso de la Amada measured 41 ha, and Cantón Corralito was at least half of that size but could well have been larger (current data do not document the extents). Paso de la Amada was then abandoned by the time of the Cuadros phase, and Cantón Corralito and Ojo de Agua were the largest sites in the Soconusco for the remainder of Horizon I. It is therefore difficult to argue that the settlement system in the Soconusco was not dramatically transformed during Horizon I. In contrast to the situation in Morelos, Oaxaca and elsewhere, the Soconusco appears to have undergone a significant political reorganization and population loss during the Cherla and Cuadros phases. Furthermore, this reorganization occurred in tandem with events occurring on the Gulf Coast.

This finding is inconsistent with the predictions of the PPM as defined in Chapter 3.

The AAM also seems inconsistent with settlement data. Clark (1997, 2007) uses the settlement reorganization during the Cuadros phase as one of his main arguments to support Gulf Coast imperialism in the Soconusco. However, according to Stark's (1990) criteria, the establishment of a colonial outpost at a new location is only to be expected in a situation of direct imperial administration (i.e., empires like those established by the Romans or the Inca). Even the Spanish did not change the location of Mexico City or Cuzco, nor did the British when they ruled India. On this point, Clark may be overinterpreting the significance of Cantón Corralito's location.

Furthermore, it appears that Cantón Corralito was established as a relatively large center during the Cherla phase (Peréz 2002; the final results of David Cheetham's 2004 field season will help determine this). Although the full dimensions during the Cherla phase are still unknown, Cantón Corralito was at least half (i.e., 20 ha) the size of Paso de la Amada at this time and thus comparable to other centers such as Aquiles Serdán (which was also occupied throughout Horizon I). Therefore, Cantón Corralito's even larger size during the subsequent Cuadros phase cannot simply be due to the founding of an outpost ruled by Gulf Coast invaders. Instead, the regional prominence of Cantón Corralito during the Cuadros phase is more easily explained as the success of one set of local leaders over the traditional Initial Ceramic Period seat of power at Paso de la Amada. Cantón Corralito was located on the Coatán River (compared to the other Mazatán centers during the Initial Ceramic Period that were landlocked on the coastal plain), possibly because of the importance of long-distance ties. Local competition between elites at large sites, rather than imperial decree, more parsimoniously accounts for the passing of Paso de la Amada from local prominence and the ascendance of Cantón Corralito. Local competition accounting for the establishment of Cantón Corralito as the largest Soconusco center is exactly what is predicted by the EEM.

Clark (1997: 228) argues that a complex chiefdom was established during the Cuadros phase with Cantón Corralito as a paramount center. The problem with this interpretation is that, during the Locona, Ocós and Jocotal phases, there is evidence of a settlement system with three levels, but during the Cherla and Cuadros phases only two levels are indicated by site sizes in the Mazatán zone. With all of the alluvium deposited in the Mazatán zone it is possible that other sites will be found in the future, and excavation may determine that known sites were larger. However, based on my current understanding of the data, there is as yet no settlement evidence to support arguments for a complex chiefdom during the Cuadros phase. Three levels of settlement are, however, suggested during the subsequent Jocotal phase, so perhaps one emerged with Ojo de Agua as its paramount center. An independent complex chiefdom in the Mazatán zone of the Soconusco and a more complex chiefdom (or even an incipient state) at San Lorenzo are consistent with the EEM.

The Cuauhtémoc zone demographic patterns parallel those from the Mazatán zone. This means that the Horizon I demographic disturbance in the Soconusco beginning in the Cherla phase occurred on a regionwide scale. Population levels reached their highest Early Formative level during the Jocotal phase, and the Cuauhtémoc site (at 7.5 ha) was larger than ever before. However, due to Cuauhtémoc's peripheral (geographical and political) position it was apparently spared the fate of Paso de la Amada and Ojo de Agua and survived into Horizon II.

No transshipment or storage facilities have been encountered at Cantón Corralito but, due to the relatively small amount of work done there and the lack of stone building materials, even if such facilities had ever existed we might not expect to find any.

Subsistence and technology

There is isotopic and faunal as well as multiple lines of artifactual evidence (see Table 8.1) that the local diet remained relatively unchanged from the Initial Ceramic Period through Horizon I (see Rosenswig 2006a). Furthermore, increased scale of feasting (based on data from village midden contexts) may be interpreted as indicating an improvement of the standard of living during Horizon I. An improved standard of living could be consistent with all of the models. It certainly is what the EEM predict.

As for the AAM, all we can conclude is that if tribute was being extracted from the residents of the Soconusco (or just the Mazatán zone) and shipped to the Gulf Coast, it was not having an adverse affect on the local standard of living. It is curious that the data presented in Chapter 5 indicate a dramatic reorganization of the economy during the Conchas phase with increased reliance on intensifiable fauna and flora. The timing of this intensification could be construed as evidence against the AAM as economic intensification occurred after the collapse of San Lorenzo. Later in this chapter I present a more detailed discussion of this subsistence pattern as a cause or as an effect of political processes.

Symbolism

The replacement of the indigenous Initial Ceramic Period representational system with the new Olmec aesthetic in the Mazatán zone is well established (e.g., Clark and Pye 2000; Lesure 2004). The Cuauhtémoc data are consistent with evidence from the Mazatán zone and show that the complete replacement of the traditional Initial Ceramic Period representational system occurred on a Soconusco-wide scale. The Initial Ceramic Period system was representational and made direct reference to the surrounding environment whereas during Horizon I stylized and geometric symbols were used to stand for more abstract concepts. This transition is demonstrated by changes to the color of the pottery assemblage as well as the style of effigy vessels and figurines, and by the novel Horizon I practice of using roller seals and incising or painting abstract iconography on ceramic vessels. In addition, architectural orientation suggests that, during the Initial Ceramic Period, northwest–southeast orientation was important for house construction and there was a common local referent in both the Mazatán and Cuauhtémoc zones. Then, at some point during Horizon I, mounds were built in relation to the cardinal directions.

The Cuauhtémoc data hint at some differences in the rate at which Horizon I symbolism was adopted across the Soconusco. First, during the Cherla phase, the replacement of seated Xumay figurines by Olmec figurines may have occurred more gradually than was the case at the larger polities up the coast, such as Paso de la Amada. Second, the use of elaborately carved ceramic serving dishes with Olmec iconography is documented at Cantón Corralito and nearby sites in the Mazatán zone during the Cuadros phase and is virtually identical to that at San Lorenzo during the San Lorenzo phase (Cheetham 2007). In contrast, there are only two examples of Cuadros-phase carved dishes from Cuauhtémoc and none from Salinas la Blanca, where the Cuadros phase was originally defined (Coe and Flannery 1967). However, abstract depictions of the Olmec dragon were carved into utilitarian cooking and storage vessels at Cuauhtémoc, Salinas la Blanca and Izapa during the Cuadros phase. Olmec iconography was then commonly incised and painted on serving vessels at these sites during the Jocotal phase. These intraregional differences in the incised pottery used during the Cuadros phase suggest that the inhabitants of the Mazatán zone were involved with inter-regional relationships in a different manner than their neighbors down the coast during the century or so that this phase lasted.

Across the Soconusco, the Cherla-phase introduction of Olmec figurines and the disappearance of standing, female figurines by the following Cuadros phase indicate a gradual integration of foreign imagery into a preexisting representational system. Such integration is also suggested by the use of Olmec iconography on utilitarian tecomates. As figurines and utilitarian vessels would have been used in domestic contexts, this integration is inconsistent with any of Stark's (1990) imperialism models in which imperial rituals are carried out in public contexts and indigenous rituals are expected to persist in private contexts. Instead, all residents of the Soconusco appear to have internalized the new Horizon I aesthetic by using white-rimmed black ware vessels during the Cherla phase and incising Olmec iconography on tecomates during the Cuadros phase as well as using Olmec-style figurines in all Horizon I phases. These patterns are not consistent with the AAM or expected patterns from the literature on imperial conquest.

Because of a number of coarse-grained local chronologies, there is to date no conclusive evidence that vessels with carved or incised Olmec iconography were used on the Gulf Coast earlier than in other areas of Mesoamerica. However, if we limit the comparison to just the Gulf Coast and the Soconusco, such iconography appears simultaneously in contemporaneous Cuadros and San Lorenzo A assemblages. Based on the published literature, carved and incised pottery was absent during both the preceding Cherla and Chicharas phases.[1] This would appear to be consistent with the PPM expectations. However, when viewed from a more general aesthetic perspective, the persistence of white-rimmed black wares into the Late Classic period at sites in Tabasco and Veracruz, I argue that this was a core Gulf Coast aesthetic. In contrast, white-rimmed black wares were adopted in the Soconusco (and elsewhere) during Horizon I and then fell out of use after the collapse of San Lorenzo. The short-lived use of white-rimmed black ware vessels serves as the clearest Horizon I style marker. The adoption of a Gulf Coast aesthetic by residents of the Soconusco during Horizon I is inconsistent with the PPM.

In summary, the use of the Olmec figurine style and iconography on utilitarian vessels in the Soconusco is not consistent with the AAM. A Gulf Coast origin of black and white ceramics argues against the PPM. However, each of these lines of evidence is consistent with the EEM. As mentioned in the previous section, when evaluating Initial Ceramic Period patterns, the complete replacement during Horizon I of the indigenous Soconusco representational system is one of the strongest arguments against the PPM. Cherla- and Cuadros-phase ceramic data from Cuauhtémoc suggest how the novel Olmec color aesthetic was employed politically in the Soconusco by decorating the largest serving dishes used at public rituals.

Exchange

There is no evidence for the unidirectional flow of tribute from the Soconusco to the Gulf Coast. The Cuauhtémoc data indicate that obsidian was traded north to the Gulf Coast and that ceramic vessels and iron ore mirrors traveled back down south. Obsidian data could be rationalized by proponents of any of the hypotheses. However, if obsidian was the material sought by a San Lorenzo empire then we would expect it to have increased in popularity at the beginning of Horizon I and not during the San Lorenzo B and Nacaste phases (i.e., Jocotal and Conchas phases in the Soconusco) as Cobean et al. (1971) and De León (2008) document. However, the Jocotal phase is also when a series of estuary sites expanded in size, and this suggests that trade through the Soconusco estuary intensified at this time.

At Cuauhtémoc (as in the Mazatán zone) there was an overall decrease in the quantity of obsidian disposed of at the site beginning in the Cuadros phase. There was also a decrease in the proportion of El Chayal obsidian recovered from Cuauhtémoc during the Cuadros and Jocotal phases when its demand was greatest at San Lorenzo. This pattern could be used to reject the AAM. However, following the argument formulated by Zeitlin (1990) for *Spondylus* shell, an increased foreign demand could have resulted in reduced levels of local use as it all was being exported. This second scenario finds some support because, during the Cuadros phase, prismatic blades made from El Chayal obsidian were recovered at Cantón Corralito, as they were at San Lorenzo but not at more peripheral sites such as Cuauhtémoc. It appears that Cantón Corralito had a unique role in the exchange of obsidian compared to other sites in the Soconusco.

Directions for future work

The single most important thing that needs to be done in the Soconusco is to determine the extent and layout of both Cantón Corralito and Ojo de Agua – the Horizon I regional centers of the Mazatán zone. Are these two sites or one? Was there a formal architectural plan and were there large elite residences? Work by David Cheetham (2006) at Cantón Corralito as well as that of John Hodson and John Clark at Ojo de Agua (Pinkowski 2006) should begin to shed light on some of these issues. I treat these as two components of the same site, as they were located across the Coatán River from each other and Cantón Corralito's occupation ended due to an extreme flooding event that caused the site to be buried under 1 m of sediment. The precise sequence of occupation remains to be determined with future excavations. Due to the alluvium in this part of the Soconusco, an extensive test-pitting program likely will be required to determine the extents of occupation on both sides of the river. Furthermore, it remains to be determined if there was an extensive Cherla- and/or Cuadros-phase occupation of Ojo de Agua. Based on the presence of diagnostic figurine types, some portion of Cantón Corralito continued to be occupied during the Jocotal phase (see Cheetham 2007: Figures 70–72).

In the Cuauhtémoc zone, extending the systematic survey and excavating at other sites will be necessary to determine how this zone was integrated with the changes occurring in the Mazatán zone during Horizon I. The initial 28-sq-km survey suggests that little settlement reorganization occurred, and, if this is confirmed in a larger area, it would help further contextualize the changes occurring in the Mazatán zone.

I have called the scenario whereby San Lorenzo is postulated to have turned the Soconusco into a subjugated tributary the Aztec Analogy Model. Because those scholars who have advocated such a position employ (in varying degrees of explicitness) the late Postclassic Aztec colonization of the area as an analogy for their Early

Formative predecessors. However, an examination of the archaeological data for the Soconusco being an Aztec colony during the century prior to the Spanish conquest is itself revealing. The Codex Mendoza lists the quantity of Soconusco tribute payments and names eight towns that were responsible for this tribute as well as the two Aztec administrators who supervised its collection and transport. Some of these eight towns have been located on rivers and in areas that still bear their Aztec names. This corroboration of large Late Postclassic sites and the names used by the Aztec helps to validate the historical dependability of the codices. However, if no documentary evidence existed, it is unclear that we would be able to infer that the Soconusco was a province of the Aztec empire based solely on archaeological evidence. Therefore, although there seems to be little convincing evidence to accept the Soconusco as a tributary province of San Lorenzo during Horizon I, the Aztec data warn us that this possibility cannot be ruled out. Data from the 28-sq-km Cuauhtémoc survey and reconnaissance in the surrounding area together suggest that there was an increase in settlement nucleation during this time (Rosenswig 2001, 2002, 2008). Future survey in the region, and excavation at Late Postclassic sites, may provide an analogy for expected patterns of what local integration into a known foreign empire looked like archaeologically in the Soconusco.

HORIZON II

Settlement/political organization

The collapse of political centers in the Mazatán zone occurred periodically during the Early Formative period. Paso de la Amada rose to power during the Locona and Ocós phases and then Cantón Corralito/Ojo de Agua took its place during the Cuadros and Jocotal phases. However, these sites were located within a few hours walk of each other. What transpired with the Jocotal-to-Conchas transition was different. The Mazatán region was completely abandoned, and La Blanca emerged at the opposite end of the land between the two large Soconusco swamps.

Soconusco settlement data are incompatible with the PPM. Political fluctuations, and resulting demographic changes, in the Cuauhtémoc zone and across the entire Soconusco seem too closely associated with the political fortunes of San Lorenzo to have occurred by chance alone. First, the disruption of the Initial Ceramic Period system is evident during the Cherla phase with overall population drops in both the Cuauhtémoc and Mazatán zones. During the Joco-tal phase there was both a population explosion across the Soconusco (but see Rosenswig 2009) and significant growth of a series of sites along the estuary system. These two facts suggest a society geared to long-distance trade operating in the Soconusco at the same time that the San Lorenzo polity was at, or just past, its peak.

The subsequent and simultaneous collapse of San Lorenzo and the Mazatán zone corresponds to the establishment of La Blanca at the other end of the Soconusco. Such disruption as well as boom and bust in the Mazatán zone are consistent with both the EEM and the AAM, but it is difficult to differentiate between the two based on survey data alone. It is worth noting, however, that the collapse of the Mazatán zone resulted in more nucleated and hierarchical polity at La Blanca (Love 2002a; Rosenswig 2007). The collapse of the San Lorenzo polity coincided with the emergence of the most powerful polity that had existed to that point in the Soconusco.

Subsistence and technology

During Horizon II, maize was used as a staple crop for the first time. Cuauhtémoc data show a marked increase in the density of maize remains in Conchas-phase contexts. The consumption of mammals doubled in relative frequency at this time, and dog and deer were much more intensively exploited. The increased reliance on maize resulted in a diversification of the ceramic vessel forms employed (including grater bowls) and increased overall use of ground stone as well as the proportion of manos and metates used. The transition to a full-fledged agriculture adaptation corresponding to the fall of San Lorenzo does not clearly conform to or deny any of the models examined.

In contrast to the adoption of agriculture, feasting behavior demonstrates remarkably little structural change from Horizon I. This lack of change at first appears inconsistent with the AAM as the collapse of the imperial masters might be expected to result in a dramatic reformulation of public ritual. The elaboration of the number of vessel forms could indicate changes in ritual practices. However, changes to the ceramic assemblage in the Soconusco (such as the addition of grater bowls) associated with the increased reliance on maize could have been responsible for such changes and therefore make it difficult to differentiate between the EEM and the AAM. As with settlement patterns, the timing of technological changes accompanied the collapse of both the San Lorenzo and Mazatán polities. The correspondence of collapse in two such distant lands is too much of a coincidence if the impact of San Lorenzo was really no more than a "sack of sawdust" as Marcus (1989: 194) posits.

Symbolism

The Horizon II aesthetic established throughout the La Blanca polity was derivative of that employed during Horizon I. The pottery assemblage was still predominantly decorated with white and/or black – but red and orange became increasingly popular. Iconography of the Olmec dragon continued to be used to decorate ceramic vessels, but new images were added, or significantly increased in frequency. During Horizon II, the representational convention of depicting images at varying levels of abstraction was maintained. Therefore, the structure of presentation endured from Horizon I, but the content was elaborated upon. This symbolic elaboration of Horizon I standards is also exemplified in household ritual by the increased number of distinct Horizon II figurine types produced in a wider range of sizes and on a wider range of materials. The most common figurine type was still sexless and chubby during the Conchas phase, with a continued emphasis on open mouths and detailed depictions of ears suggesting the making and hearing of sound. However, a new "cast of characters" was depicted by Conchas phase figurines.

Symbolic patterns are inconsistent with the PPM. Olmec iconography does not disappear in the Soconusco after Horizon I. The Soconusco appears to have been tightly integrated into the San Lorenzo system and aesthetic standards internalized during Horizon I. During the following Horizon II period, the Conchas- and Nacaste-phase ceramics and figurines were also very similar and indicate that inhabitants of the Soconusco remained in close contact with residents of the Gulf Coast.

Exchange

The EEM predicts that San Lorenzo's decline and collapse would have left a cadre of leaders in the Soconusco geared to inter-regional trade. Removal of the San Lorenzo elite might have resulted in cultivating a new range of trade associates and distant social ties. In contrast, the AAM should predict that the collapse of the colonial centers would result in a major disruption of the local political system. The PPM predicts that no significant change would be expected at this time.

Gulf Coast ceramics, such as the fancy vessels made of kaolin clay, continued to be desired by the residents of the Soconusco. Vessels made of this kaolin and other Gulf Coast clays were recovered from Cuauhtémoc, Los Cerritos, El Varal and Cantón Corralito during the Cherla and Cuadros phases. During the Conchas phase, small, fine-paste white vessels were produced on the Gulf Coast and imported to Cuauhtémoc. This continued Soconusco-Gulf Cost trade during Horizon II indicates a continuity in trade networks from the past. Even when San Lorenzo was no longer a large polity, nearby potters still produced ceramics desired by the residents of the Soconusco. In addition, El Chayal obsidian continued to be found in Nacaste-phase deposits, albeit at lower frequencies than during Horizon I (Cobean et al. 1991). These two facts lend support to the EEM as fancy ceramics and high-quality obsidian continued to be exchanged after the San Lorenzo and Mazatán polities collapsed. Although there is currently no ceramic sourcing evidence of a wider range of Soconusco trading partners, stylistic evidence ties the Soconusco to the Basin of Mexico during the Jocotal phase (see Chapter 3, note 3).

Directions for future work

At present, the Conchas phase is known only from La Victoria, where Coe (1961) originally defined it, from La Blanca (Love 2002a) and now from Cuauhtémoc.[2] In addition, there are Conchas-phase remains in the Izapa collections held at the New World Archaeological Foundation (NWAF). These remains were originally defined as being from the Duende phase (Ekholm 1969) – what Clark and Cheetham (2005) call the following Middle Formative phase. An extremely important objective of future investigations is to determine the temporal extents of the Conchas phase with stratified contexts. Excavations from Cuauhtémoc have documented Conchas-phase deposits stratigraphically above Jocotal and have a number of accelerator mass spectrometry (AMS) dates from these two phases (Rosenswig 2005:

Appendix 3). Excavations are required from a site with Conchas-phase deposits below Duende, Escalón and Frontera occupation levels.

Another extremely important goal is to more fully define the geographic extents of sites with Conchas-phase occupation. The southeastern extent of these sites appears to be the Guamuchal swamp next to La Blanca as no Conchas-phase remains are known from further down the Guatemalan coast. Izapa is the northern extent of known Conchas-phase sites, and Cuauhtémoc is the westernmost site where excavations have been conducted. However, a number of other Conchas-phase sites are known further northwest such as the Niño site (Figure 2.1). The number, extents and distribution of Conchas-phase sites will document the overall population levels and the internal organization of this polity.

Another important research gap in our knowledge is if there were any Conchas-phase estuary sites that fulfill more than just resource extraction activities. Their lack would bolster the argument that I present in Chapter 7 that the Cuadros- and Jocotal-phase estuary sites were somehow ties into Soconusco–Gulf Coast trade relationships. The extent of Conchas-phase estuary use is also significant in documenting how the adoption of maize affected the overall adaptive system in the region. Documenting the distribution of Conchas-phase sites is significant for understanding how the emergence of agriculture in the Soconusco affected land-use patterns.

ELITE EMULATION IN DIACHRONIC PERSPECTIVE

I have argued that the AAM and PPM do not correspond to the material patterns as well as the EEM does. The timing of settlement pattern changes and the replacement of indigenous Soconusco iconography by the Olmec aesthetic during the course of Horizon I are incompatible with the PPM. In addition, settlement pattern changes and the ubiquity of Olmec imagery on utilitarian vessels do not support the AAM. Furthermore, there is a lack of evidence for tribute extraction. In contrast, although a number of lines of evidence are ambiguous, none are inconsistent with the EEM; thus, based on the current evidence, this model is favored. In this section, I review the key points that support the emulation by Soconusco elites of their Gulf Coast contemporaries. I present seven anchors that hold the

EEM in place while the other two models are rocked by the tides of evidence. My approach to interpreting the data is diachronic, so, rather than attempting to describe a static Horizon I situation, the EEM is supported by the way material patterns changed from the Initial Ceramic Period to Horizon I and how they changed again to Horizon II.

First, the disruption of the Initial Ceramic Period settlement system in the Soconusco corresponded to the rise of San Lorenzo during the Chicharras phase. Cantón Corralito was established as a center during the Cherla phase. Although the specifics are not completely understood at present, Paso de la Amada's position appears to have been challenged by Cantón Corralito. By the Cuadros phase, the former site was abandoned whereas the Cantón Corralito polity grew larger. At the southern end of the Soconusco, Cuauhtémoc was on the periphery of these political developments and continued to be occupied through Horizon I.

Second, the abandonment of the Mazatán zone after the Jocotal phase corresponds to the fall of the San Lorenzo polity. Not only did the Ojo de Agua polity collapse, but the entire population of the Mazatán zone appears to have relocated to the other end of the fertile land between the two Soconusco swamps. With the disappearance of the San Lorenzo polity, the Horizon I political system in the Mazatán zone appears to have lost its ideological (and likely its economic) base and so was replaced by a new political phenomenon. This new polity was nucleated around the site of La Blanca, and the surrounding Mazatán and Jesús river zones were abandoned.

Third, the Soconusco adoption of a Gulf Coast black and white color aesthetic during the Cherla phase suggests the direction of influence. This assertion is based on five observations: 1) black and white colors were used to decorate some ceramic vessels on the Gulf Coast during the Initial Ceramic Period Bajío phase and the Soconusco Ocós phase; 2) this color scheme was dominant in the Soconusco during each of the subsequent Horizon I phases when, in particular, the distinctive white-rimmed black wares were first adopted during the Cherla phase and continued to be used through the Cuadros and Jocotal phases; 3) white-rimmed black wares were no longer used in the Soconusco by the Conchas phase but persisted on the Gulf Coast through the Middle Formative and on into the Late Classic period (Pool and Britt 2000; von Nagy 2003). Although black and white ceramics were popular across Mesoamerica during Horizon II, the distinctive white-rimmed black wares appear to have been a stylistic convention employed outside of the Gulf Coast only during Horizon I when the San Lorenzo polity was at the height of its power; 4) The political function of this novel color symbolism in the Soconusco is suggested by its use as the largest size class of Cherla- and Cuadros-phase serving dishes; and 5) Sourcing data demonstrate that Gulf Coast serving vessels with this novel color scheme were imported to many sites across the Soconusco (including Cuauhtémoc) during the Cherla phase.

Fourth, local Initial Ceramic Period Soconusco symbolic conventions were discarded during Horizon I. In general terms, a naturalistic and representational aesthetic was replaced by an abstract and more geometric system. Data that support this claim are from four sources: 1) the change in the orientation of the long-axis of residences at Paso de la Amada and Cuauhtémoc from northwest–southeast to an alignment on the cardinal directions; 2) the replacement of a well-established naturalistic indigenous figurine tradition by an abstract pan-regional Olmec one; 3) the replacement of a system of three-dimensional ceramic vessels modeled to depict animals and humans dressed as animals by a two-dimensional system where abstract symbols were carved into the surface of domestic and fancy ceramic wares (Horizon I symbols were depicted at variable levels of abstraction to represent a limited set of themes); and 4) the novel use of geometric roller seals during Horizon I where no such implements were previously employed.

Fifth was the use of a wider range of abstract iconographic themes at the same time as a renewal of naturalistic depictions of animals from the local environment during Horizon II. Data that support this are from four sources: 1) figurines made in a wider range of sizes, styles and materials during the Conchas phase; 2) serving and storage vessels adorned with a wide range of animals that were depicted three-dimensionally; 3) the double-line-break and cleft motif popularity (providing one example of the range of iconographic themes expanding); and 4) Horizon I abstract images, such as the Olmec dragons, that continued to be depicted and the persistence of black and white as the most common colors used to decorate pottery vessels (both suggest clear links between Horizon I and Horizon II aesthetics).

Sixth, there was a significant reorganization of the Soconusco economy during Horizon II. This reorganization was a shift from a broad-based horticultural adaptation to the emergence of maize-based agriculture along with a more intensive use of domestic animals such as dogs and those that are attracted to human crops such as deer (Rosenswig 2007). Data that support this are from seven sources: 1) carbon isotopic evidence from human remains that indicate the Conchas phase marks the beginning of maize as a staple crop (Blake et al. 1992a); 2) densities of maize remains from Cuauhtémoc that show a significant increase in Conchas-phase deposits. The increased importance of maize is also evident by changes in grinding technology; 3) A dramatic increase in the overall use of ground stone; 4) a higher proportion of manos and metates relative to mortars and pestles; 5) the use of grater bowls as a new grinding tool perhaps to compensate for increased demand for basalt; 6) iconographic representations of maize and maize growing from clefts in the ground and from the heads of individuals for the first time (Taube 2000); and 7) faunal evidence that dog and deer were exploited in higher relative proportions than ever before. Therefore, along with multiple lines of evidence for increased reliance on maize, faunal remains demonstrate that, during the Conchas phase, the entire diet shifted to exploiting more easily controlled and intensifiable species.

Seventh, the development of a new form of labor organization occurred during the Conchas phase. Increased labor control was likely due to the advent of agriculture and the resulting ability to increase population nucleation. The ability to concentrate people and provision them would have allowed for more time to be spent on nonsubsistence, elite-directed activities. Increased labor organization is documented by three lines of evidence: 1) the construction of a system of monumental architecture at political centers, which looms the largest on the local horizon and is the most obvious end product of intensive labor projects (Rosenswig 2010); and other craft objects, including 2) the much more widespread production of obsidian prismatic blades; and 3) the increased use of greenstone, particularly axes. Axes would have been increasingly important due to the increase in maize agriculture that would have required clearing more forests.

The EEM more fully and simply accounts for the available data than does either the PPM or the AAM. As I indicated at the end of Chapter 3, all authors acknowledge (implicitly in the case of Flannery, Marcus and Grove; explicitly in the case of Clark, Diehl, Coe and Demarest) that the EEM provides a sound interpretation of

the data. Therefore, I will not belabor the point. I end this chapter
with a brief discussion of the difficulty in establishing causality using
archaeological data, with the Horizon I to Horizon II transition as an
example.

285

CAUSATION,
TEMPORAL
RESOLUTION AND
THE HORIZON I TO
HORIZON II
TRANSITION

CAUSATION, TEMPORAL RESOLUTION AND THE
HORIZON I TO HORIZON II TRANSITION

Correlation, as the statisticians tell us, is not the same as causation.
There was a temporal co-occurrence at the Horizon I to Horizon II
transition of 1) the collapse of the San Lorenzo polity; 2) the abandonment of the Mazatán zone; 3) the rise of La Blanca; as well as 4)
the emergence of agriculture; and 5) the building of the first system
of monumental conical mounds in the center of first-, second-, and
third-tier centers. However, observing the co-occurrence of these five
processes is not the same as establishing causative relations between
them. At the local level, the collapse of the Mazatán zone could have
been the cause or a result of the rise of La Blanca. Furthermore, a
significantly increased reliance on food production could be cast as
the cause or a result of the replacement of one political system by
the other. Similarly, the building of monumental architecture could
be the cause or a result of the La Blanca polity establishment in the
southeast end of the Soconusco.

One factor that obscures causation is that archaeologists (even
those that use the most refined chronologies) separate prehistoric
data into discrete, century-long phases. If we had year-by-year or
month-by-month information then we could know the exact order
of events and therefore be more confident on which events caused
which others to occur. Due to the separation of time into phases and
the resulting homogenization of segments of time within each phase
we cannot achieve such resolution. This archaeological reality necessarily makes change appear to be punctuated at phase borders and
followed by equilibrium for the duration of the phase (O'Shea and
Barker 1996). It is difficult to establish causal relationships between
the fall of the San Lorenzo polity and the rise of the one at La Blanca.
Did the rise of La Blanca result in the fall of Ojo de Agua and this
in turn contribute to the fall of the San Lorenzo polity? Or, was it
the reverse (that the collapse of San Lorenzo created a power vacuum that facilitated the emergence of the La Blanca polity in the
Soconusco)?

The second (which I believe to be the most plausible) scenario might go something like this. The San Lorenzo polity began to fall apart at the end of Horizon I. The eventual collapse might have been foreshadowed for years by an increase in the cost of San Lorenzo's elite staying in power due to increased internal factionalism (see Pool 2007: 195), deteriorating environmental conditions and so forth. More obsidian and other goods were imported during the latter part of Horizon I (i.e., the Jocotal and San Lorenzo B phases) in an attempt to maintain the old world order. During the next few years, stories of this dissolution (perhaps explained as the disfavor of the gods) began reaching the Soconusco as exchange parties arrived less frequently and those who made the trip from the Soconusco through the Isthmus of Tehuantepec returned with the disturbing news. The Soconusco elite might have tried to suppress such reports, but could not do so for long. Other groups may have traveled further north at this time and contacted people in the Basin of Mexico, and elsewhere in the Mexican highlands. Although inhabitants of the Soconusco perhaps were previously aware of such other lands, more direct contact was now established. New sites were established along the estuary canal system, and mounds up to 7 m in height were constructed. Local resources were extracted, but the goal of these sites may have been to launch and/or receive trading parties engaged in trans-Isthmian voyages. This use of the Horizon I estuary sites would explain the presence of a ceramic stool and ceramic masks during the fourth and final occupation of El Varal (Lesure 2009) and all the fancy objects at El Mesak (Pye and Demarest 1991).

From within the politically uncertain environment during the final years of the Jocotal phase, an elite faction and their followers established a new polity at La Blanca. Perhaps these individuals were from Ojo de Agua or elsewhere in the Mazatán zone or perhaps they were from the southeast end of the Soconusco. Either way, within the rich local environment of the land between the two large Soconusco swamp systems, they established the center of the new polity as far away as possible from Mazatán and set themselves up at the previously unoccupied location that was to become La Blanca. Maize had been grown for centuries, perhaps to make beer, and it was undoubtedly widely known that it could be eaten. Dogs and deer were also long-established food sources. If the more intensive reliance on dog, deer and maize was an innovation dreamed up at La Blanca or whether it was borrowed from elsewhere does not alter the fact that this subsistence change occurred at the same time in the Soconusco as the establishment of the La Blanca polity. The newly forming La Blanca polity thus relied more heavily on intensifiable sources of food than anyone in the Soconusco had before.

In creating a more controllable and intensifiable resource base, a greater division of labor was possible and more people could be provisioned and thus devote increasing amounts of time to building the 25-m-high central mound at La Blanca. Others could devote more time to craft and political specializations during the Conchas phase. A new, tributary mode of production (*sensu* Wolf 1982) is evident at La Blanca based on the extraction of labor, and it fundamentally transformed society from that which had existed in the Early Formative Mazatán centers of Paso de la Amada or Cantón Corralito/Ojo de Agua. The expenditure of labor in mound construction was a goal in itself. After more and more people were concentrated in the La Blanca area, the elite required projects to keep them busy. What better than working on a communal project that purportedly benefited all members of society? Otherwise, what would stop them from melting back into the forests and swamps? Let's build a mountain! A mountain created by human toil and organized by the most powerful segment of society. This mountain will bring us closer to the gods that have forsaken those in the Mazatán zone. The building of this mountain would unite people through the act of its construction and reinforce the controlling role of the elite (as Joyce 2004a argues). In doing so, it would counter the strife and insecurity resulting from the dramatic changes occurring with the collapse of Cantón Corralito/Ojo de Agua up the coast and the collapse of San Lorenzo across the Isthmus (in a similar way as Kolb 1994 argues for Hawaii). Furthermore, after being completed, these new architectural features would have provided a universally recognizable symbol of the authority of the individuals who ruled La Blanca (as Trigger [1990, 2004] argues the case cross-culturally).

Maize was the new foundation on which Conchas-phase society was built in the Soconusco. Successful crops became the basis of both political authority and life itself. In establishing this new polity, existing legends and myths were elaborated to explain the La Blanca elite's political fortune as well as the newly important role played by maize. A new aspect of the Olmec dragon was emphasized in Conchas-phase iconography. By portraying this long-established mythical being from the front (rather than in profile), new aspects of

287

CAUSATION,
TEMPORAL
RESOLUTION AND
THE HORIZON I TO
HORIZON II
TRANSITION

its powers could be depicted alongside preexisting ones. The cleft motif depicted the emergence of corn from the ground and also portrayed it as growing from the head of rulers (Taube 2000). This iconography, and an increased reliance on maize, may not have been new. In fact, there are examples of the double-line-break on Jocotal-phase dishes. Based on current evidence, however, maize agriculture did not transform Soconusco society until Conchas times (Rosenswig 2006a). As a result, these precocious maize referents reflect the kernels of economic transformation planted in the very fabric of Horizon I society.

Symbolically, maize (the essence of life) emerged from the ruler's head. For many members of the La Blanca polity, it actually was the case that their existence depended on the elite to sustain them. Those people devoting significant quantities of time to architectural projects and craft objects were no longer fulfilling all of their own sub-sistence needs. Instead, they were dependent on the elite to receive (extract) it from others and pass it along to them. The producers of maize and other food were also increasingly cut off from the spiri-tual world as increasingly specialized individuals undertook more elaborate and arcane rituals to access. Again, it was the elite who positioned themselves as the mediators between these two worlds either as the religious specialists themselves or in control of the peo-ple who fulfilled religious functions. Society was more integrated than before, and a limited sector of the population had inserted themselves as the fulcrum of integration (as argued in Rosenswig 2007). Religion functioned as a legitimizing ideology of elite rule by providing an explanatory framework for how the non-elite major-ity of society articulated with the larger political landscape. As well as providing authority to the elite, however, the new ideology also embedded them in a system of obligation – if the maize crop failed, so too did the evidence of their divine support.

Preexisting elites in the southeast end of the Soconusco, such as those at Cuauhtémoc, quickly saw the opportunities provided by their integration into the La Blanca polity, not to mention the dangers in failing to align themselves. Alternatively, the rulers of La Blanca could have employed some form of threat or supported a rival faction within smaller polities such as Cuauhtémoc. Although the method of incorporation is unclear, the fact that Horizon I political and economic organization were replaced by those of Horizon II is not. Imitating the practices of their new allies, a relatively large amount of labor was employed to expand the high ground on which Cuauhtémoc's residents lived and to build two new mounds at the site (Rosenswig 2010). Paralleling La Blanca, at Cuauhtémoc a larger 5-m-high mound was built to the south and a smaller one to the north.

289

CAUSATION,
TEMPORAL
RESOLUTION AND
THE HORIZON I TO
HORIZON II
TRANSITION

As things fell apart in the Mazatán zone, increasing waves of people flowed south. The elite of the swelling La Blanca polity grew increasingly powerful and more stratified than had any previous system of political organization in the Soconusco. The obvious power of the La Blanca elite and equally obvious dissolution of the old Mazatán system, not to mention its distant allies on the Gulf Coast, created a feedback loop. Within a relatively brief time, and one too short to be archaeologically visible, the Mazatán zone was abandoned and La Blanca formed the heart of a powerful new polity. As more people arrived, the La Blanca site eventually covered upwards of 200 ha. This was the largest center the Soconusco had ever witnessed, and at its center was a 25-m-high mound – the largest ever constructed in Mesoamerica to that point.

In the scenario I have just outlined, San Lorenzo and Ojo de Agua crumbled together concurrent with La Blanca's rise to regional prominence within a relatively short period of time. For the idealist the loss of faith in the old ideology would explain the Mazatán collapse whereas for the vulgar materialist the emergence of agriculture would account for the rise of La Blanca. However, in real life things are rarely so simple. Without a crisis of faith perhaps the San Lorenzo elite would have survived longer. Without a new basis for economic intensification, the La Blanca polity might not have risen so meteorically, or not at all.

The basic archaeological method of data divided into century-long phases creates a problem for differentiating the independent variables from the dependent ones. All we can know for sure is how events turned out. In the case at hand, the Mazatán and Jesús river zones were abandoned, La Blanca rose as a political force, its people were fed by maize, and they built the largest mound yet built in the Soconusco. This narrative presents one possible interpretation of the end of Horizon I and the transition to Horizon II in the Soconusco. In the next chapter, I return to the Initial Ceramic Period–Horizon I transition and explore the cultural processes behind Mesoamerica emerging as an interacting world.

NOTES

1. David Cheetham's work at Cantón Corralito may document this iconography in Cherla-phase sherds, and Ann Cypher's work at San Lorenzo may on Chicharras sherds. Or, one or the other of these assemblages may predate the other in the use of abstract iconography by the residents of either site. Regardless of how this evidence pans out, there is yet no reason for one area to claim this innovation.

2. In addition to excavations at the Cuauhtémoc site, the Soconusco Formative Project carried out test excavations at two other sites with Conchas-phase components: Las Palmas (Rosenswig 2002) and San Martín. Both sites are located close to Cuauhtémoc (1 km and 2.5 km distance, respectively) and represent a lower tier in the Conchas-phase settlement system (Rosenswig 2008). At San Martín, the undisturbed evolution of Jocotal-into Conchas-phase ceramic styles is clearly documented. Neither of these sites, however, helps us to understand the extents of Conchas-phase sites.

9

Conclusion

> ...the most powerful, economically dominant class, which, through the medium of the state, becomes also the politically dominant class...thus acquires new means of holding down and exploiting the oppressed class.
>
> Engels [1891] 1972: 216–217

This book is built from the data presented in Chapters 4 through 7. Around this substantive core, Chapters 3 and 8 create an interpretive lens through which three competing models are presented and then evaluated. Chapter 2 lays out an anthropological perspective that employs ethnographic and archaeological data to flesh out the types of behavior that articulate local political organization (in this case the Soconusco) and interaction with societies further afield (such as those on the Gulf Coast). A historical materialist perspective situates the Early and Middle Formative Mesoamerican case study presented here within a broader understanding of emergent complexity.

In this final chapter, I summarize the substantive contributions of the Cuauhtémoc data, tie up some loose ends raised in the course of my discussion and highlight the important transformations in the Soconusco that occurred during Horizons I and II. First, I summarize the demographic, economic, ideological and exchange data from Cuauhtémoc. Next, I discuss how the definition of a knowledge kula operating in an archipelago of complexity helps with an understanding of Horizon I Mesoamerica. I then address the structure of the mother versus sister culture debate and argue that San Lorenzo was an important (if distant) ancestor of later Mesoamerican civilizations. Then, I review how the disagreement over whether to classify San Lorenzo as a chiefdom or a state has resulted in more confusion than clarity. I propose instead that it is more productive to understand early complex societies based on the presence or absence of exploitation. Therefore, the changing mode of production more effectively organizes the documentation of cultural evolution than does a list of traits. I end this chapter by summarizing the significance of the Mesoamerica's first stylistic horizons (i.e., Horizon I and Horizon II) from a historical materialist perspective.

SUBSTANTIVE CONTRIBUTION

The Cuauhtémoc data provide a unique opportunity to document developments at a single Mesoamerican community during the period from 1600 to 800 BCE. Not only was the site occupied before, during and after the Horizon I apogee of the San Lorenzo polity, but, during this entire period, Cuauhtémoc occupied a similar political position as a modest local center. Therefore, the effects of the rise and fall of the political centers such as Paso de la Amada, Cantón Corralito/Ojo de Agua and La Blanca can be examined in terms of the effect they had on the inhabitants of this one community over time. The Cuauhtémoc data thus provide contextualizing regional evidence with which to evaluate competing views on the nature of Soconusco–Gulf Coast relations.

Settlement and architecture

In Chapter 4, the Early and Middle Formative results of a full coverage, systematic survey from around the Cuauhtémoc site indicate that Early Formative demographic patterns in the Cuauhtémoc zone correspond to those in the Mazatán zone (see Rosenswig 2008 for results from all time periods). Survey results from both zones document a small peak during the Locona phase and a dramatic increase in the hectares of occupation during the Jocotal phase. Furthermore, the Cuauhtémoc survey is the first to quantitatively document the dramatic population increase in the southeastern part of the Soconusco during the Conchas phase when the La Blanca polity emerged as the political center in the region. This survey contrasts with the Mazatán zone survey that documents no occupation in that region during the Conchas phase.

Architectural data from the Cuauhtémoc site are more fragmentary but provide some informative hints. Two Locona-phase

structures were documented by post molds and associated pit features, burials and a hearth. These are currently the only detailed Early
Formative residential structures from the Soconusco documented
outside of the Mazatán zone. The northwest–southeast orientation
of the two structures aligns their long axes in the same direction as
Mound 6, a chiefly residence at Paso de la Amada. Domestic architecture from both ends of the lands between the large Soconusco
swamps thus align similarly during the Initial Ceramic Period.

Cuauhtémoc also contained a Jocotal-phase mound measuring
approximately 100 m in length and 25 m in width that was similar
to mounds documented at other sites in Soconusco from this period.
Significantly, the long axis of this mound was oriented east–west,
which was a change from the Initial Ceramic Period orientation.
During the following Conchas phase, the east side of the site was built
up above the season flood level, and two more mounds were built. A
5-m-high mound was constructed on the newly enlarged area of the
site and, directly north, a 3-m-high mound was constructed. These
two mounds continued an architectural program based on cardinal
direction alignments, and the Jocotal mound was expanded during
the Conchas phase. This architectural alignment replicates that at La
Blanca, where the largest 25-m-high Mound 1 was also located at the
south of the site and the second highest mound was located directly
north. To date, Cuauhtémoc is the only site in the Soconusco where
both Jocotal- and Conchas-phase occupation has been documented
from domestic contexts (at Izapa, ceramics from these two phases
were documented in construction fill). It thus provides a unique case
from which to study the local effects of the Horizon I to Horizon II
transition that occurred with the collapse of the San Lorenzo polity
on the Gulf Coast.

Domestic economy

In Chapter 5, I presented data on the changing nature of the
Cuauhtémoc domestic economy. Faunal and isotopic data provide
a reconstruction of a diversified diet during the Early Formative
period that then changed considerably during the early Middle Formative Conchas phase beginning at 900 BCE. At this time, considerably more dog, deer and maize were consumed than had previously
been the case. The Conchas phase thus represents the earliest full-
fledged adoption of an agricultural adaptation in the region, and the

inhabitants of Cuauhtémoc depended on controllable and intensifiable plant and animal resources for the first time (see Rosenswig 2006a).

Food processing and preparation practices were documented at Cuauhtémoc employing patterns of ceramic vessel, fire-cracked rock and obsidian data. Each of these classes of data indicates gradual changes through the six phases that constitute the Early Formative period in the Soconusco (see Table 3.1). During the Conchas phase, there were then dramatic increases in the quantity of ground stone used overall as well as the proportion of manos and metates employed compared to mortars and pestles. Along with the adoption of a new ceramic form (i.e., grater bowls), these data indicate an increased focus on grinding tools, presumably to process increasing quantities of maize.

Ceramic vessels were also employed to document changing food-serving practices at Cuauhtémoc. In contrast to the timing of changes in food processing, there was a marked transformation in food presentation during Horizon I. More, and larger serving vessels were used at this time than during the preceding Initial Ceramic Period. These changes to food presentation practices suggest that social and political transformations occurred during Horizon I but that it was only during Horizon II that the Cuauhtémoc economy was significantly altered.

Ideology

In Chapter 6, I presented data that indicate major ideological changes occurred at Cuauhtémoc during the course of its occupation. The Initial Ceramic Period naturalistic, indigenous Soconusco artistic and ideological tradition, previously documented in the Mazatán zone by Clark (1994) and Lesure (2000), is also present in the Cuauhtémoc zone in the same range of images and themes. Thus, from northwest to southeast, the Soconusco appears to have formed an intensively interacting cultural system beginning with the first sedentary villagers (Rosenswig n.d.). The ceramic vessels employed during the Initial Ceramic Period were mostly small and red with a wide range of animals depicted on them. Figurines were numerous and clearly depict 1) old, seated individuals often wearing costumes; and 2) young, standing, naked women.

During Horizon I, aesthetic standards changed significantly from previous naturalistic imagery and employed much more abstract and geometric standards. These changes are consistent with the results in Chapter 5 that show Horizon I to have been a time when political transformations occurred (as reflected in changing food presentation patterns). Ceramics were predominantly colored black and white during Horizon I – a dramatic visual contrast from the Initial Ceramic Period's red wares. The fact that the largest Cherla- and Cuadros-phase serving vessels were white-rimmed black wares indicates that the new color aesthetic played a political role at food presentation events. Figurines were much less common during Horizon I than before and depicted individuals of ambiguous age and sex. Ceramic effigy vessels were rarer than before, but when they were made it was generally to depict fish faces around the midsection of tecomates. Much of the artistic energy during Horizon I was put into depicting mythological creatures such as the so-called Olmec dragon. At this time, the Olmec dragon and other mythical creatures were depicted at varying degrees of abstraction so that a few simple lines could be understood to represent more complex concepts.

During Horizon II there was an expansion of Horizon I aesthetic standards. Black and white remained the most common colors used to decorate pottery, but monochrome black, white and gray wares replaced the white-rimmed black wares that had been so common during Horizon I. Figurines were more numerous than ever before, and their subject matter expanded to include a host of new characters depicted in a wider range of sizes and on a greater range of materials. A broader range of abstract imagery was depicted during Horizon II, but the Horizon I practice of representing mythological creatures at varying degrees of abstraction continued. Effigy vessels also became more common during Horizon II, and the range of animals that were depicted returned to Initial Ceramic Period levels. The Horizon II aesthetic was, however, clearly derivative of Horizon I conventions and themes but demonstrates an elaboration of subject matter.

Exchange

In Chapter 7, ethnohistorical data on travel routes and voyage times were reviewed. I estimated that it would have taken approximately twelve days to travel along the Pacific Coast and through the

Isthmus of Tehuantepec from San Lorenzo to Cuauhtémoc by foot. This same voyage would have taken approximately twenty days by canoe, whereby fewer people could have transported more goods. In addition, the route from Cuauhtémoc through the mountains to the obsidian source at El Chayal would have taken another ten days of travel. These estimated travel times put the effort required for inter-regional exchange into a comparative framework.

Obsidian and ceramic sourcing data were also presented in Chapter 7. Almost all of the obsidian recovered from Cuauhtémoc was from the nearby (and poor quality) source of Tajumulco and the high quality source of El Chayal located 200 km to the northeast. Over time there was a relative increase in the quantity of El Chayal obsidian deposited at Cuauhtémoc. Most notably, there was a dramatic increase in the relative quantity of El Chayal obsidian during the Cherla phase, which is interpreted as being the result of increased Gulf Coast demand.

Most sourced ceramic sherds were produced from clays local to the Cuauhtémoc and La Blanca area. These samples include Initial Ceramic Period effigy vessels and figurines that are stylistically indistinguishable from those in the Mazatán zone. This local production in the southeast end of the Soconusco means that the Paso de la Amada and surrounding sites were not the center of production of these fine wares and that sites around the Cahuacán, Suchiate and Naranjo Rivers were fully integrated into the cultural system of the land between the two large swamps. Other ceramic samples include Horizon I white-rimmed black wares as well as figurines with Olmec features and sherds with Olmec iconography from the Conchas phase that were also all produced from local clays. These results demonstrate that the international Olmec style was reproduced locally even at small sites such as Cuauhtémoc. Nine of thirty-nine sherds tested are interpreted as having been produced on the Gulf Coast. Two very fine white-rimmed black ware, Cherla-phase sherds were made of Gulf Coast clays. These findings, along with other ceramic sourcing data from the Mazatán and Acapetahua zones of the Soconusco, indicate that prestigious fine wares decorated with the new color scheme were imported at the beginning of Horizon I. Furthermore, seven fine-paste white wares from Conchas-phase deposits were also made in the area of San Lorenzo. This finding indicates that even after the collapse of the San Lorenzo polity, potters in the area continued to produce vessels desired by the inhabitants of the Soconusco.

Summary

Evidence presented in this book indicates that, during Horizon I, elite emulation contributed to a reorganization of Soconusco society. This reorganization was expressed by the adoption of new aesthetic conventions and intensified feasting practices. Such changes suggest that the transformations to society during Horizon I were predominantly political in nature. It was only during the following Conchas phase that the economic base of Cuauhtémoc society was reformulated due to a significantly increased reliance on food production. Earlier in this chapter, I briefly summarized how the data presented in this book expand our understanding of Early and Middle Formative developments in the Soconusco. In the following sections of this chapter, I place these local developments into a broader context and explore how the Olmec style may have tied together people inhabiting distant lands.

AN EARLY FORMATIVE MESOAMERICAN ARCHIPELAGO OF COMPLEXITY

Many local developments at Cuauhtémoc (and in the Soconusco more generally) occurred as the result of elite participation in a system of inter-regional relationships. The comparative ethnographic and archaeological examples presented in Chapter 2 suggest how the dynamism of an elite emulation system is often driven by the existence of a more developed distant center. Political competition is fueled as local elites seek out foreign objects and exotic ideas. Flannery (1968: 106) originally proposed that "the areas most likely to form exchange systems with, and truly emulate the behavior and symbolism of, the Olmec were not the least developed regions of the highlands, but the most developed." Such Initial Ceramic Period communities in Mesoamerica can be conceptualized as a preexisting archipelago of cultural complexity. This initial cultural archipelago was strengthened and "internationalized" during Horizon I due to the emergence of the political phenomenon on the Gulf Coast that employed a novel aesthetic.[1]

Following Flannery, Richard Wilk (2004: 86) has noted that "...when you find stylistic similarity, or even the same goods in two places, there may not be simple domination or incorporation, but an internal dynamic that drives external contact." Wilk makes

297

AN EARLY
FORMATIVE
MESOAMERICAN
ARCHIPELAGO
OF COMPLEXITY

the unlikely comparison between the Olmec horizon style and the standardization of female beauty produced by the proliferation of pageants during the late twentieth century. In Belize, where Wilk works, beauty pageants take local forms, but the dimensions of beauty (if not its content) are determined by Euroamerican standards. The standardization of the criteria through which beauty is judged (to include women from around the world) does not mean that everyone has to look the same. Instead, a mutually intelligible idiom (what Wilk calls a system of common difference) is created through which only certain aspects of beauty can be compared. Beauty is thus defined by the pageants as being purely physical, and such characteristics as wisdom or kindness are excluded from consideration. As a result, the ideological changes accompanying such a restricted standard of female beauty have contributed to making Belizeans more dependent on U.S. consumer beauty products (Wilk 2004: 93). As with twentieth-century beauty pageants:

> The "Olmec" art style was clearly a common arena of competition over large parts of Mesoamerica, with many diverse players. As with any system of common difference, though, some groups had more power to define what Olmec art was and they had institutional channels for judging it, deciding what met the standards and what did not. It is likely that the actual groups that controlled the arena and the rules – the showroom – changed several times over the approximately 650 years the style lasted. It would not be surprising if there were two contending Olmec styles at some times (e.g., Miss Universe – Miss World, National League – American League, USA – USSR), or at times when the whole system broke down into chaos before reforming under new management.   Wilk 2004: 94

Participation in a system of common difference may well have occurred between centers of complexity in Horizon I Mesoamerica. A pan-regional aesthetic idiom would have been useful in facilitating interaction between groups of culturally unrelated people. As Schortman and Urban (1992b: 240) note: "Sharing an identity, founded on commonly held assumptions, values, and beliefs, creates personalistic ties which encourage trust and communication among people who would otherwise be isolated by the absence of such bonds..." Furthermore, Wilk's description, just quoted, of a change in management might well describe the Horizon I to Horizon II transformation instituted with the rise of the La Blanca polity (as described at the end of Chapter 8).

The idea of an archipelago of complexity helps to describe the large areas (such as the entire Maya lowlands) that were devoid of Olmec iconography, or other signs of external contact, until the very end of Horizon I or during Horizon II. A lack of Olmec iconography is thus interpreted as a lack of interest in (and equally important – a lack of interest *from*) people in these regions. Not only were the inhabitants of such areas politically and economically uninteresting to elites in other areas, but they could also be dangerous, thus adding to the prestige of persons who traveled through their lands to bring back exotic goods and ideas. During the Initial Ceramic Period and Horizon I, the Soconusco can be envisioned as an island in a cultural archipelago that included other such islands as the Gulf Coast, Valley of Oaxaca, Basin of Mexico, Chalcatzingo and the Copán Valley. The Soconusco was separated from the Gulf Coast by the Sierra Madres, the coastal desert of Oaxaca and the less fertile northwestern half of the Chiapas coast. Environmental richness of the land between the two large Soconusco swamp systems appears to have resulted in Initial Ceramic Period population growth and incipient rank with little economic differentiation (Lesure and Blake 2002). Thus leaders in such areas would have been enthusiastic in embracing novel sources of foreign prestige

In certain areas of the Pacific coast of North America there are analogous examples of economically egalitarian society with unexpectedly developed political superstructures (Lightfoot 1993). On both the Pacific Northwest and Californian coasts, relatively high population levels developed along with signs of incipient social rank (see Arnold 1995). Interestingly, boat travel also emerged in both these regions and appears "...to have facilitated sociopolitically important activities, such as information exchange, elite manipulations of goods and services...and controlling the intensity and direction of social contacts" (Arnold 1995: 736). These rich, non–agriculturally adapted peoples are thus similar to the Initial Ceramic Period inhabitants of the Soconusco in terms of having access to extremely abundant resources in the local environment that allowed sedentarism, population nucleation and incipient rank to develop without relying on domesticates. However, what the Soconusco had during Horizon I that groups in British Columbia and California lacked was a cultural archipelago that included a more politically developed neighbor. One can only speculate what would have

299

AN EARLY
FORMATIVE
MESOAMERICAN
ARCHIPELAGO
OF COMPLEXITY

happened to either the Chumash or the Haida had the San Lorenzo polity arisen a two- or three-week journey away. Left to their own devices, local elites in California and British Columbia were limited by the productivity of the local physical environment. This is not to say that there were no differences in complexity between societies from these two regions. In contrast, the Trobriand and Cycladic elites I describe in Chapter 2 possessed external ties but lacked the local environmental potential in their island setting (given their level of technology) to sustain larger concentrations of people. From this comparative perspective, local environmental richness in a few discrete regions and the existence of distant peoples to interact with on the Pacific side of Mexico and Peru may, in fact, explain why hierarchical peoples first emerged and formed the basis for later civilizations. Setting aside such hemisphere-wide conclusions, let us review some of the interpretations of Early Formative Mesoamerican society.

WAS SAN LORENZO MESOAMERICA'S MOTHER?

Did the Early Formative elite at San Lorenzo birth a new social structure and a set of innovative material culture conventions that spawned the subsequent civilizations of Mesoamerica? It cannot be put more simply than that. Framing the debate in terms of mother and sister cultures (e.g., Blomster et al. 2005; Clark 1997; Diehl and Coe 1995; Flannery and Marcus 2000; Flannery et al. 2005) does not at first appear to lend itself to an anthropological treatment of Mesoamerican prehistory. However, the debate highlights the nature of emergent hierarchy in Mesoamerica – as I discuss in the following sections of this chapter.

In this section, I address the debate over which female relative best describes San Lorenzo's relationship to subsequent Mesoamerican people. The question cannot be answered, however, until we define exactly what constitutes the area to which we refer today as Mesoamerica. Kirchoff's (1952) canonical definition of Mesoamerica was based on the presence of certain traits: 1) a calendar; 2) hieroglyphic writing; 3) books; 4) astronomy; 5) the ballgame; 6) specialized markets and trade; 7) the use of cacao as money; 8) wars for sacrifice; 9) auto-sacrifice; and 10) a complex pantheon of gods. Most of these traits are not easy to document archaeologically, particularly for the Early Formative period. Instead, I evaluate Joyce's (2004b:

Figure 1.2) reformulation of archaeologically identifiable practices that can be used to define Mesoamerica. These are:

1. *subsistence production* – a) agriculture based on corn, beans and squash; b) agricultural intensification including raised fields; c) plants, such as cacao, amaranth and maguey raised for specialized use; and d) corn processed by soaking with lime and grinding on metate
2. *long-distance exchange* of valuables such as obsidian, cacao and jade
3. *cosmology and ritual* – a) shared calendars, both 365 and 260 days; b) use of writing and positional mathematics; c) ritual warfare using special costumes and performing human sacrifice; and d) specialized ritual architecture such as ball courts, temples and observatories
4. *social stratification* expressed in a) costumes (such as role- and gender-specific dress and headdresses); and b) ornaments (such as lip and ear plugs as well as pyrite and obsidian mirrors)

1. Subsistence production

It is difficult to characterize the San Lorenzo polity's subsistence strategy and even harder to generalize about all of Mesoamerica during Horizon I. In the Soconusco, it was during the Conchas phase that the first use of maize as a staple crop is documented. Therefore, Joyce's subsistence characteristics 1a, 1b and 1d postdate Horizon I. There is, however, recent evidence of cacao use dating to the Initial Ceramic Period (Powis et al. 2007). Cacao use in the Soconusco therefore precedes Horizon I, and intensified maize use postdates it. Based on the current state of our knowledge, no qualitative changes can be attributed to subsistence practices during Horizon I.

2. Long-distance exchange

Horizon I exchange was not distinctive in terms of the types of objects that were moved from one region to another. Obsidian moved hundreds of kilometers into the Soconusco during the Archaic period (Nelson and Voorhies 1980) and the Initial Ceramic Period (see Chapter 6), and jade was included in Initial Ceramic Period burials at

Cuauhtémoc, Paso de la Amada and elsewhere. The intensification of jade use, especially for making axes, occurred during the Middle Formative period. The movement of each of these resources between different regions did not originate during Horizon I. However, the movement of obsidian did increase during Horizon I as did that of iron ore and mica – this movement was, however, a change in degree and not in kind.

In contrast, a novel, pan-regional aesthetic emerged for the first time during Horizon I. This is evident in the widespread use of the black and white color aesthetics, first evident at San Lorenzo at the end of the Initial Ceramic Period and then adopted across Mesoamerica (as outlined in Chapters 5 and 6). Another Horizon I novelty was the invention and use of a standardized set of abstract iconography. Due to the problem with which archaeologists are faced in determining precise contemporaneity using century-long phases, vessels with this iconography appear to spring up across Mesoamerica simultaneously. However, based on chemical sourcing data, ceramic vessels with the Olmec aesthetic were exported in only one direction at this time – from the Gulf Coast to Oaxaca (Blomster 2004: 132–145), the Soconusco (see Chapter 7; Kennett et al. 2004; Lesure 2009) and elsewhere (Blomster et al. 2005). Therefore, it appears to have been the movement of valuable ideas and not valuable commodities that defined Horizon I exchange.

3. Cosmology and ritual

There is no evidence that the cosmological and ritual complexes that united Mesoamerica at the time of Spanish contact were established during Horizon I. The earliest evidence of a long count date is from a Late Formative stela at Chiapa de Corzo (Lowe 1962). The earliest published evidence of a glyph does come from the Gulf Coast but dates to the late Middle Formative period (Pohl et al. 2002), and Stephen Houston (Popson 2003) questions whether this speech scroll depicted on a roller seal is sufficient to infer a written language or whether it was simply an elaborated form of the abstract symbolism that had originated during Horizon I. The same can surely also be said of the Cascajal block (Rodríguez et al. 2006). So, although the use of writing (#3b) likely postdates San Lorenzo, the use of abstract symbols (to represent such concepts as the Olmec dragon) did originate during Horizon I.

There is no convincing evidence of ritual warfare or of human sacrifice (#3c) during Horizon I. Although a lack of evidence does not necessarily mean that ritual war and human sacrifice did not occur, it is incautious to assume that it did without evidence. Ritual architecture such as the ball court is documented in the Soconusco during the Initial Ceramic Period (Hill et al. 1998). Furthermore, as discussed in Chapter 4, it was in the Middle Formative period that conical mounds were first built. Therefore, the Mesoamerican calendar, writing and large mounds all postdate Horizon I whereas the earliest documented ball court in Mesoamerica predates this epoch.

4. Social stratification

Little evidence exists, prior to the Middle and Late Formative period carving of stelae, of costumes and headdresses depicting elite status (#4a). The one conspicuous exception is from Horizon I sculpture at San Lorenzo (Cyphers 2004). The precise meaning of the headgear worn by the individuals depicted by Olmec colossal heads is debatable. However, headdresses depicted on thrones at San Lorenzo (e.g., Monument 14; Cyphers 2004: 71–73) and at Loma del Zapote (e.g., Monuments 8 and 9; Cyphers 2004: 249–253) are surely associated with social rank. The Initial Ceramic Period Xumay figurines from the Soconusco provide early evidence of specialized costumes and masks associated with elders (who were presumably leaders). Earspools (#4b) are found in midden contexts and depicted on figurines beginning in the Initial Ceramic Period. Also, during the Initial Ceramic Period, mirrors have been documented in burial contexts (e.g., Clark 1991). Elaborate burials with formal crypts containing elaborate jewelry and ceramic vessels are known only from the Middle Formative period at sites like La Venta (Drucker et al. 1959) and Chiapa de Corzo (Agrinier 1962). Therefore, indicators of social differentiation are present before, during and after Horizon I. I argue elsewhere that social stratification is first conclusively documented with the rise of the La Blanca polity (Rosenswig 2007, 2010).

Summary

Based on either Kirchoff's or Joyce's list, there is insufficient evidence to claim that San Lorenzo was Mesoamerica's mother. A number of Joyce's traits were present before Horizon I (#1c, 2, 3d, 4) and many more, especially related to agricultural practices and monumental architecture, date to the Middle Formative period (#1a, 1b, 1d, 3b, 3d). Although a number of other traits could have begun during Horizon I (such as writing, ritual warfare, status-related costumes) there is at present no evidence to claim that they did.

San Lorenzo did not birth Mesoamerica (that was a labor that took many centuries), but it was certainly its most crucial ancestor. Therefore, the Early Formative San Lorenzo elite should not be cast in the role of Mesoamerica's mother or sister, but instead as a grandmother.[2] Forging the first stratified society, the elite of San Lorenzo were responsible for a political transformation that established the exploitive relations that defined all subsequent Mesoamerican societies. Diehl (2004: 28) notes that by Horizon I there existed "...a new rich and flamboyant civilization of such a sort that never existed before in Mesoamerica" and further that "San Lorenzo was the primary hearth of this new civilization." I agree with Diehl but caution that this early civilization lacked most of the cultural traits possessed by the peoples first encountered by the Spanish during the sixteenth century.

WAS SAN LORENZO A CHIEFDOM OR A STATE?

A traditional anthropological approach to understanding the changes that were occurring during Horizon I is to situate San Lorenzo in the history of Mesoamerican political evolution. As we have seen, all scholars acknowledge that San Lorenzo was more politically complex than any other polity in Mesoamerica during Horizon I. The San Lorenzo polity had four settlement tiers (Symonds et al. 2002: Figure 4.5). The San Lorenzo site itself measured 500 ha and contained dozens of stone monuments including the colossal heads and thrones. There were two second-tier sites with stone monuments, as well as third- and fourth-tier sites. In contrast, all other political centers across Mesoamerica ranged in size from 10 ha to 70 ha; all had modest architecture, no stone monuments, and a single lower tier of smaller sites.[3] By traditional standards, San Lorenzo was at least a complex chiefdom and all other Horizon I centers were simple chiefdoms (Steponaitis 1978; Wright 1984). Flannery (1999: 16–21) argues that four levels of settlement size indicate the existence of an archaic state (consistent with Johnson's [1973] original formulation) but that this many tiers were lacking in the San Lorenzo polity.

On one hand, Diehl and Coe (1995) and especially Clark (1997, 2007) argue that San Lorenzo was the seat of an empire. As state infrastructure is required to administer an empire, these authors propose (with varying degrees of explicitness) that San Lorenzo was a state and that other complex polities at the time were chiefdoms. Although these authors employ the Soconusco as their best case of Gulf Coast imperialism during Horizon I (Clark 1997: 228–229, 2007; Diehl and Coe 1995: 23–24), as I argued in Chapter 8 evidence supporting this position is far from convincing (and see Chapter 3, note 8).

On the other hand, Flannery and Marcus (2000) argue forcefully that San Lorenzo was not a state. This typological distinction is important to their argument because if San Lorenzo was not a state then it was a chiefdom and a number of other chiefdoms also existed in Mesoamerica by Horizon I. Citing Goldman's (1970) Polynesian typology, they describe San Lorenzo as a paramount chiefdom and all other societies as open and traditional chiefdoms (Flannery and Marcus 2000: 2). If San Lorenzo was a chiefdom, then (their argument goes) differences with other polities at the time were quantitative rather than qualitative.

One line of reasoning that Flannery and Marcus (2000: 3–6) present against interpreting San Lorenzo as a state is that examples of similar levels of monumental labor investments and production of prestige goods are present from examples around the world among societies they call chiefdoms. First, they point out that San Lorenzo covered a smaller area than Cahokia did. Second, they note that San Lorenzo did not have any architecture to rival Cahokia's Monks Mound.[4] Third, they observe that the inhabitants of Easter Island carved 100 times more stone monuments of important ancestors and that many of the Polynesian examples are much larger than those from Mesoamerica (Flannery and Marcus 2000: Figure 1). Fourth, they note that the Maori of New Zealand were renowned carvers of jade.[5]

A problem with this logic is that none of Flannery and Marcus's examples comes from Horizon I Mesoamerica. There simply was no Mesoamerican polity comparable to San Lorenzo in terms of size or complexity during Horizon I. We can acknowledge that Cahokia was larger and had a bigger mound, that more and larger heads were carved on Easter Island, and that the Maori were master jade carvers, but how does this help their case that other societies in

Mesoamerica were equally as complex as San Lorenzo during Horizon I? It does not. These examples of cultural accomplishment from the American Southeast and Polynesia have no bearing on differences between Early Formative Mesoamerican societies. To make the case that the elite at San Lorenzo did not establish the first stratified society in Mesoamerica, they need a single example of an equally complex polity having existed anywhere else in Mesoamerica during, or before, Horizon I.

Wrestling with the chiefdom/state distinction, Clark (1997: 215) proposes that San Lorenzo falls somewhere between a complex chiefdom and an archaic state. Pool (2007: 24) notes that one of the important limitations of evolutionary typologies is that "...there will always be some societies, such as the Olmec, that lie at the margins of the types." Encountering the same terminological problem more than three decades ago, Renfrew (1972: 369) referred to Mycenaean society as "something more than chiefdoms, something less than states." Contemplating the evolutionary line between chiefdom and state with regard to Polynesian societies such as Tahiti, Tonga and Hawaii, Webster (1999: 312) observes that "Such confusion of terminology itself is revealing, since it signals the existence of complex sociopolitical forms for which our comparative or evolutionary terminology is inadequate." Marcus and Flannery (1996: 171) face this same typological problem when describing the emergence of the Monte Albán polity that "cannot easily be fitted into one of these two evolutionary stages." All of these scholars are grappling with the same problem – early stratified societies do not conform easily to abstract, ethnographically derived typologies.

A MORE MEANINGFUL WAY TO INTERPRET CULTURAL CHANGE

An underlying obstacle in sorting out the "Olmec Problem" is created by the continued use of the concepts of chiefdoms and states (see discussions by Grove 1997: 74 and Pool 2007: 18–25). It is worth noting that the reality of the chiefdom as an evolutionary stage was quickly questioned by its creator (Service 1967). After initial attempts to group societies with emergent complexity together under the chiefdom umbrella (e.g., Renfrew 1973) and distinguish between chiefdoms and less complex societies (e.g., Creamer and Haas 1985), many archaeologists laid the chiefdom concept to rest (e.g., Feinman and Neitzel 1984; McGuire 1983). For more than a decade now it has been widely argued that chiefdoms do not actually describe an identifiable form of political organization that has cross-cultural significance (e.g., Gilman 1995; McIntosh 1999; Yoffee 1993; but see Drennan and Peterson 2006; Earle 1997).

Early (or archaic) states are no simpler to identify than chiefdoms. Some archaeologists continue to employ trait lists to define such states (e.g., Flannery 1999; Marcus and Feinman 1999: 6–7). However, if statehood is defined using criteria such as the number of settlement tiers, then city-states (one of the two basic forms of preindustrial political organization according to Trigger [2003a]) do not gain access to this pinnacle of the evolutionary ladder. In fact, Stein (1998: 26–27) has effectively refuted the appropriateness of using the number of settlement tiers to define states in Mesopotamia (contra Flannery 1999). More generally, Kristiansen (1991: 17) identifies the problem with the evolutionary trait list approach as being that "... a few variables have been studied without due consideration of their implications for the organization of production in the society under study."

Even if we were to accept the use of a list of traits to define modern and historically known states, archaeological data provide ambiguous indicators of those from prehistory. In particular, defining states as using legitimized force is difficult to document without written records. Furthermore, there is often no clear qualitative division between the uses of force in what are called complex chiefdoms from that in what are called archaic states (see Webster 1999). In addition, the idea of bureaucratic rather than kin-based government is not particularly easy to document without the help of written documents. Wright (1984: 69) once proposed that in both Mesoamerica and Mesopotamia class relations were established *before* state formation. If this were the case, then one has to wonder: What was so significant about the development of states in these two areas?

For the historical materialist, exploitation is the qualitative, watershed characteristic that irrevocably changed social, political and economic relations between human beings (Chapman 2003: 88–99; Kristiansen 1998: 54–61). In societies where such exploitive relations exist, a nonproducing class succeeded in appropriating land, labor or material products from other members of society. It is the resulting unequal structural relationships that define class-based society – rather than the individual forms that such exploitation takes. The most significant qualitative distinction is between exploitive societies and those that were not. Therefore, divisions between what are called tribes and simple chiefdoms on the one hand from complex chiefdoms and states on the other can provide a clearer distinction in social structure based on the presence or absence of exploitation by a small segment of society over the masses. Or, as Smith (2003: 25) has noted, "The suffocating focus on the evolution of the state has left the study of early complex polities without the theoretical apparatus for attending to the central problem of political analysis: what did early complex polities actually do?" Exploitation exists in some early complex polities but not in others.

Chapman (2003: 195) describes the Argaric Bronze Age of southeast Spain as consisting of small-scale, unstable states (but see Gilman 2001). He argues that to call such societies, with demonstrable exploitation, chiefdoms "confuses a structural model of the state with the various material forms it might take" and that by doing so "we are trying to 'fit' our archaeological research on past societies into existing evolutionary typologies, rather than find out how far past social forms were similar or different from those known in the ethnographic record" (Chapman 2003: 196). Chapman uses both San Lorenzo and Cahokia as examples of other societies that are not always considered states but where exploitive relations are clearly evident. In fact, he specifically presents the Clark (1997) versus Flannery and Marcus (2000) difference of interpretation as an example of typological disagreement hindering the understanding of underlying cultural processes (Chapman 2003: 91, 93, 195). I end this chapter with an interpretation of Mesoamerica during Horizon I informed by a historical materialist perspective.

HISTORICAL MATERIALISM AND MESOAMERICA'S FIRST HORIZONS

As I discussed in Chapter 6, one of the most striking characteristics of the art from Horizon I in the Soconusco was the reduction in the range of images used. This was undoubtedly the point. A narrow cannon of abstract representation was a strategy to increase control over political and religious ideology (*sensu* Scott 1998). The same images were repeated again, and again, and again, and again. Today a president's picture and a country's flag are displayed most often by authoritarian regimes whose authority is in constant need of being reaffirmed. Horizon I iconography in Mesoamerica shares much with twentieth-century totalitarian imagery. A limited set of symbols represents the state along with portraits of the current ruler and a limited number of his venerated predecessors. The repetitious political strategy reflects insecurity on the part of the elite and their perception of their tenuous grasp of power when they are attempting to control unequal social and economic relations.

Flannery and Marcus (2000: 12–13) claim that the 176 Olmec motifs Joralemon (1971) long ago identified are simply stylistic variants of a handful of mythological creatures. They point out that the majority of the stylistic variability comes from the Mexican highlands. San Lorenzo was the most politically complex society at the time and had a narrower range of images. The elaboration of Olmec symbols in the Mexican highlands (when compared to the range used on the Gulf Coast) shows that this imagery was employed for different purposes in the two regions.

This disparate range of symbols used at San Lorenzo compared to the highlands might parallel hammer-and-sickle imagery used in the former USSR in a much more restricted manner than, for example, among Latin American revolutionary groups where such iconography has often been embedded within local mediums of folk art. In the former case, state ideology is controlled in a purposeful manner whereas in the latter the same icons are sometimes appropriated in creative ways for local use. In Early Formative Mesoamerica, I would predict that there was an inverse relationship between the diversity of iconographic images and the degree to which they were employed in the formation of political power. This proposal inverts Flannery and Marcus's (2000: 15) claim that "To argue a specific area was the center of origin . . . you should be able to show . . . that it displayed greater variety in that area." At the political center, the symbols of power would be kept pure and simple. Out on the periphery, local creativity and syncretism would likely generate more diversity.

Any assumption that origins equal greater diversity seems unwarranted unless the types of behavior that would necessitate simplification through borrowing can be elaborated. Like the childhood game of broken telephone, logic dictates that the more a message moves the more it will tend to change. In the Mexican highlands, different Olmec images may well have been borrowed by village factions to emphasize descent lines, as Marcus (1989: 169) proposes, whereas on the Gulf Coast powerful rulers could have employed a narrower range of symbols for political ends. As Scott (1998) so eloquently argues, strong political authority simplifies many aspects of a society so as to more effectively control people. It is therefore to be expected that, as a more stratified society, "San Lorenzo displays fewer pan-Mesoamerican motifs than either Tlapacoya or San José Mogote" (Flannery and Marcus 2000: 27). Such an "impoverished" set of motifs can be interpreted as evidence of a more effectively controlled political discourse.

A detailed treatment of exploitation at San Lorenzo is beyond the scope of this book. However, in the Soconusco there is no convincing evidence of economic exploitation during Horizon I. There was, however, a clear iconographic and ideological break from the past that was expressed by local imagery being replaced with the new pan-regional Olmec aesthetic. Based on size classes and ceramic sourcing data (presented in Chapters 6 and 7), this new aesthetic appears to have played a political role. However, the political aspirations of Early Formative Soconusco elites outstripped their economic means during Horizon I.

The economic base in the Soconusco appears to have come to the "support" of the superstructure only during Horizon II (Rosenswig 2006a, 2007). With the emergence of agriculture, the Soconusco economy could underwrite the social inequality that the elite had been haltingly attempting to establish for centuries. During the Initial Ceramic Period, a political strategy relying on local symbols of authority was employed by aggrandizers, as Clark and Blake (1994) convincingly explain. During Horizon I, the strategy shifted to one that emphasized ties to distant elites expressed in abstract terms. During both the Initial Ceramic Period and Horizon I, elites faced the problem of not being able to exert sufficient control over the economy of the societies they were attempting to rule (e.g., Lesure and Blake 2002). Lightfoot (1993: 183–185) notes a similar limitation for the elite on the Northwest Coast, when compared with agricultural groups. In each of these cases, the superstructure hits a limit to the degree that labor can be mobilized and surplus appropriated until agriculture provided a more intensifiable base.

This limitation is opposite that described by McIntosh (1999) for West Africa, in which she claims that ritual authority was used to overcome limitations in economic organization. Cobb (2003) suggests a similar use of ritual authority among Mississippian society.

These cases contradict the traditional materialist view that the base determines the superstructure. Brumfiel (1983: 264) concisely summarizes this critique: "Marxists have erred in focusing on the political implications of economics rather than the economic implications of politics." Her observation is that economic divisions within society are the inadvertent result of emerging rulers creating social and political divisions between themselves and other members of society. As I argue at the beginning of Chapter 6, rather than decide a priori whether it is the political superstructure or the economic base that determines change, the point simply can be left open for empirical documentation.

The significance of the Conchas phase in the Soconusco was that developments in the economic base at this time provided a mechanism by which the elite could cement their superstructural political power. This transformation occurred because technological developments in agricultural productivity (and the population concentration that this new form of production could provision) allowed for the base to "catch up" to the superstructure. When this occurred, the local prestige provided to the Horizon I Mazatán center through links to San Lorenzo was replaced by the economic power that established the La Blanca polity. The erosion of esoteric power at the end of Horizon I may therefore explain the collapse of San Lorenzo. During Horizon II, the range of iconography that was employed increased compared to Horizon I as elite claims to power were less tenuous. The La Blanca elite had economic power to reinforce the elevated social statuses established by their Horizon I predecessors.

Horizon I then corresponds to one of the historical moments, referred to by Marx in the epigraph to Chapter 6, when the superstructure is more developed than would be expected given the economic base. This superstructural explosion likely contributed to Mesoamerica's first pan-regional style horizon. Horizon II, then, represents a realignment during which the base "caught up" to the superstructure. The iconography and overall aesthetic of this second style horizon was derivative of what came before.[6] Certain elements (such as the cleft motif) became increasingly popular, however, and were used to explain changes to people's everyday lives. The economic base that supported the Soconusco was transformed, and this transformation provided economic power with which certain local elite factions could undermine the prestige of other elite factions that relied on associations with the distant lands to bolster their authority. For their part, loosening the network of allies that could supply such raw materials as obsidian, the San Lorenzo polity collapsed and further fueled the power of newly established centers such as La Blanca.

The scenario presented in the last two paragraphs is not terribly different from the one proposed by Rathje (1972) more than three decades ago (summarized in Chapter 3). The main limitation with his model, steeped as it was in the cultural ecology of the time, was that Rathje tried to establish an economic rationale for the initial exchange of goods between the highlands and the lowlands. The insight of Rathje's model was that he peered around the materialist blinkers of the day and identified esoteric knowledge as a viable Gulf Coast export. However, his explanation for the collapse of this system was rather weakly attributed to a difficulty of the Gulf Coast elite to maintain a monopoly over such knowledge. Although plausible, there was no trigger for his explanation of collapse.

In contrast, I propose that a segment of the local Soconusco elite trumped the Gulf Coast esoteric knowledge with an increased ability to control the economy. Undermining the authority of the elite at the Cantón Corralito/Ojo de Agua center actually may have begun during the Jocotal phase. As a result of failing authority, there may have been an intensification of trips to and from the Gulf Coast by the Soconusco elite (see discussion in the final section of Chapter 8) and a search for other distant allies. The overflow of the Coatán River appears to have destroyed much of the Cantón Corralito site at the end of the Cuadros phase and resulted in the center of this polity relocating on the other side of the Coatán River at Ojo de Agua. Such an auspicious sign appears to have signaled that the end of this regime was at hand – and the Mazatán zone was then abandoned at the end of the Jocotal phase.

By the Conchas phase, the Horizon I Mazatán political system collapsed. A rival segment of the regional elite established a new polity around La Blanca at the other end of the land between the two large Soconusco swamps. Due to its integrative virtues (and the disappearance of local competition), the La Blanca polity was so successful that it drew in all of the surrounding population. The Mazatán zone, center of political activity for centuries, was completely abandoned. A new political capital sprang up on the Naranjo River around a 25-m-high mountain that was built on the flat coastal plain through the directed labor of thousands. This was not the only center, however – a handful of second- and third-tier centers, of which Cuauhtémoc was one, were established each with its own mountain built of human toil.

The story of political development in the Soconusco does not end here. La Blanca was an experiment that lasted for a century or two before it too collapsed at the end of the Conchas phase. The Cuauhtémoc site and surrounding area were also abandoned at this time – after more than 800 years of occupation. This small local center had weathered the rise and fall of Paso de la Amada and Cantón Corralito/Ojo de Agua in the Mazatán zone up the coast and then had been swept up in the fervor of the nearby La Blanca phenomenon. Flying so close to the political flame, Cuauhtémoc was then burned along with the rest of the La Blanca political and demographic experiment. The next chapter in the political evolution of the area was to be the rise of Izapa, 20 km north on the piedmont below the Sierra Madres. Perhaps based on the lessons learned from La Blanca's collapse, the Izapa elite persisted at this new center for the next millennium – but that is another tale.

For the historical materialist, it is less useful to decide whether to designate San Lorenzo as a mother, a sister, a chiefdom or a state and more productive to understand how structural inequality developed in Mesoamerica. As Cobb (2003: 79) notes, by doing so we are "thereby moving from how complex to why complex." Some scholars suggest that the economic base determines the political superstructure. This is clear in Engels's epigraph to this chapter as he proposes that economic power translates directly into political power. The Soconusco example explored in this book suggests that this is too simple as political power outstripped economic control during the centuries of Horizon I. However, during Horizon II economic exploitation qualitatively transformed Soconusco society and came to support the superstructure. Engels's epigraph also emphasizes that the emergence of exploitation fundamentally altered the structure of human relations. With this I agree. It is not difficult to argue that Mesoamerican civilization emerged in earnest during the Late Formative period when sites like Izapa, Kaminaljuyu, Monte Albán and El Mirador dominated the political landscape. The exploitive relations that define each of these polities trace their structural phylogeny back to the transformation that originally occurred within polities such as San Lorenzo on the Gulf Coast and then La Blanca on the Soconusco coast.

1. My ultimate objective in this book is to understand Soconusco society during Horizon I and the effects of contact with the inhabitants of the Gulf Coast. I have not explored why the San Lorenzo polity emerged when and how it did – this issue unfortunately remains an explanatory black box. Exploring the precocious developments at San Lorenzo (as Ann Cyphers is currently doing) is one of the most important problems that confront Mesoamerican archaeology and the comparative development of complex society worldwide.

2. Flannery and Marcus (2000: 11) satirically attribute the Initial Ceramic Period to the role of Mesoamerica's grandmother. If San Lorenzo is to be grandmother, Initial Ceramic Period society would have to be a great-grandmother – and really stretch the analogy of female ancestry.

3. In Chapter 4, I compared settlement density between the San Lorenzo polity and the Soconusco. Settlement hierarchies are much more difficult to infer due to the incomplete nature of settlement data from across the Soconusco. Meaningful comparisons can be made, however, with the Basin of Mexico and the Valley of Oaxaca where regional surveys have been completed. At no polity other than San Lorenzo can a four-tier settlement system even be entertained during Horizon I.

4. Flannery and Marcus (2000: 4–5) compare Monks Mound (which is 30 m high and covers an area 300 m by 212 m) to Mound C-1 at La Venta, which is the same height but considerably smaller in the area it covered. However, La Venta is irrelevant to the subject of Horizon I society in Mesoamerica. During Horizon I, San Lorenzo had no large central mound but a clearly hierarchical political organization as discussed in Chapter 3.

5. Again, compared to latter periods, significant quantities of jade and other greenstones were not carved during Horizon I, and little of this material has been recovered from San Lorenzo. Conflating the political phenomena that occurred at San Lorenzo and La Venta under the heading "Olmec" obscures the process of incipient hierarchy in Mesoamerica. For this reason I have restricted my use of the term Olmec to describe an art style and my discussion of the primary establishment of hierarchy to the San Lorenzo polity.

6. Separating an Initial Ceramic Period, Horizon I and Horizon II is useful for dating and cross-dating purposes. However, the continuity (or lack thereof) between the dominant aesthetic from each epoch also informs us of the cultural values and what regard a society had for the past.

Appendix 1 Temporally secure excavation contexts at Cuauhtémoc with detailed ceramic data

Subop	Lot	Level	Volume	MNV
		BARRA/LOCONA MIDDEN		
7b	66	12	0.192	14
7b	79	13	0.188	8
7b	82	14	0.074	1
7b	83	14	0.151	3
7b	86	15	0.212	1
7b	91	16	0.216	2
7b	96	13	0.397	2
		Total:	1.429	31
		LOCONA FEATURES		
7a	99	13	0.164	12
8e	41/162/163	5/6	0.384	34
8d	221/234/288	5/6	0.193	17
		LOCONA MIDDEN		
1	20	13	0.352	12
1d	76	8	0.328	51
1d	79	9	0.324	23
2b	115	10	0.232	4
2b	119	11	0.248	1
2b	126	13	0.940	1
2l	189	13	0.164	5
2l	190	14	0.140	2
2l	194	15	0.188	7
2l	196	16	0.220	6
3b	43	22	0.200	4

(continued)

(*continued*)

Subop	Lot	Level	Volume	MNV
3c	57	–	0.063	3
7b	41	7	0.488	46
7b	50	8	0.528	29
7b	53	9	0.328	27
7b	64	11	0.328	10
7d	63	8	0.488	43
7d	75	9	0.014	5
7d	76	9	0.014	3
7d	84	10	0.148	24
7d	106	11	0.268	10
7d	107	12	0.128	14
7d	110	13	0.204	7
7d	111	14	0.268	2
		Total:	7.345	402

OCÓS FEATURE

Subop	Lot	Level	Volume	MNV
2L	230/231		0.096	8

OCÓS MIDDEN

Subop	Lot	Level	Volume	MNV
1c	77	9	0.124	1
1c	80	11	0.126	2
1c	85	13	0.216	1
1d	72	7	0.328	32
2b	45	7	0.358	7
2b	47	7	0.284	8
2b	50	8	0.144	5
2b	52	9	0.065	2
2l	186	12	0.412	4
2n	220	10	0.070	1
3b	40	21	0.144	10
7b	36	6	0.496	16
7d	62	8	0.048	2
		Total:	2.911	99

CHERLA FEATURE

Subop	Lot	Level	Volume	MNV
3c	50/51/52		0.430	45

CHERLA MIDDEN

Subop	Lot	Level	Volume	MNV
1c	74	7	0.440	1
1d	71	6	0.326	34
2b	40	5	0.350	6
2b	38	6	0.328	9
2n	217	8	0.520	4
3b	30	18	0.200	14
3b	31	19	0.200	13
3c	54	–	0.115	8
3c	55	–	0.182	4

(continued)

Subop	Lot	Level	Volume	MNV
			3.091	**138**
2g	110	18	**0.106**	**1**
2m	187	11	**0.308**	**1**
3a	21	12	**0.920**	**12**
3a	25	13	**0.620**	**11**
3a	26	14	**0.102**	**13**
3a	32	15		**7**
7b	28	4	**0.400**	**34**
7c	20	3	**0.408**	**33**
7c	26	4	**0.392**	**50**
		Total:	**3.256**	**162**

JOCOTAL FEATURE

Subop	Lot	Level	Volume	MNV
2L	172	11	**0.152**	**17**

JOCOTAL MIDDEN

Subop	Lot	Level	Volume	MNV
1d	69	5	**0.324**	**24**
2e	56	5	**0.122**	
2n	219	9	**0.170**	**2**
3b	27	17	**0.136**	**18**
3b	28	18	**0.200**	**4**
4	6	5	**0.388**	**2**
4	8	7	**0.204**	No rims
4	9	8	**0.204**	No rims
4	10	9	**0.200**	No rims
7d	24	4	**0.344**	**43**
		Total:	**2.444**	**110**

CONCHAS DOMESTIC FEATURES

Subop	Lot	Level	Volume	MNV
8a/3f	280/286/289	5/6	**0.469**	**37**
8i	104	4	**0.001**	**13**
1	7	4	**0.390**	**15**
1	8	5	**0.360**	**40**
1	9	6	**0.428**	**46**
1c	62	3	**0.314**	**16**
1c	63	3	**0.400**	**4**
1c	64	3	**0.101**	**5**
1d	66	3	**0.700**	**10**
1d	67	4	**0.460**	**22**
2b	25	4	**0.326**	**28**
2b	31	4	**0.470**	**9**
2b	34	5	**0.191**	**19**
2m	161	4	**0.216**	**7**
2m	162	5	**0.228**	**11**
2m	163	5	**0.228**	**33**

(continued)

Subop	Lot	Level	Volume	MNV
2m	164	7	**0.208**	**17**
2m	165	8	**0.316**	**27**
2n	204	4	**0.760**	**3**
2n	209	5	**0.114**	**8**
2n	212	6	**0.156**	**7**
2n	222	9	**0.144**	**5**
3b	19	13	**0.300**	**1**
3b	24	16	**0.186**	**21**
10	13	6	**0.008**	**1**
10	14	6	**0.160**	**5**
10	16	7	**0.076**	**9**
10	20	8	**0.140**	**8**
10	20	9	**0.109**	**15**
10	25	10	**0.084**	**12**
10	28	11	**0.052**	**24**
10	31	12	**0.088**	**27**
10	34	13	**0.116**	**43**
10	37	14	**0.096**	**18**
10	39	15	**0.076**	**21**
10	41	16	**0.080**	**9**
10	44	17	**0.168**	**7**
10b	10	2	**0.124**	**4**
10b	12	3	**0.208**	**2**
10b	15	4	**0.212**	**1**
10b	19	6	**0.212**	**1**
10b	21	7	**0.184**	**6**
10b	23	8	**0.108**	**9**
10b	24	9	**0.100**	**9**
10b	26	10	**0.072**	**16**
10b	29	11	**0.116**	**47**
10b	38	13	**0.100**	**39**
10b	40	14	**0.100**	**39**
10b	45	15	**0.128**	**16**
10b	46	16	**0.040**	**16**
10b	48	17	**0.064**	**14**
10b	49	18	**0.104**	**12**
		Total:	**10.591**	**834**

CONCHAS ELITE FEATURES

Subop	Lot	Level	Volume	MNV
7	34/48	6	**0.456**	**57**
7a	42	10	**0.083**	**7**

CONCHAS ELITE MIDDEN

Subop	Lot	Level	Volume	MNV
2l	145	4	**0.232**	**12**
2l	146	5	**0.168**	**21**
2l	148	6	**0.200**	**10**
2l	153	7	**0.224**	**11**
2l	154	8	**0.188**	**7**

(continued)

Subop	Lot	Level	Volume	MNV
2l	155	9	**0.196**	**9**
2l	156	1C	**0.260**	**5**
2l	173	11	**0.228**	**5**
2l	174	11	**0.288**	**3**
2l	175/176	11	**0.220**	**5**
2l	178	11	**0.108**	**1**
7d	19	3	**0.352**	**12**
		Total:	**3.203**	**165**

Appendix 2 Temporally secure excavation contexts at Cuauhtémoc without detailed ceramic data

Subop	Lot	Level	Volume	MNV
		BARRA/LOCONA MIDDEN		
8c	126	6	0.352	
8c	188	7	0.042	
8c	190	7	0.346	
2	7	6	0.294	
2	8	7	0.303	
2	9	8	0.307	
2	11	9	0.163	
2m	169	9	0.300	2
7a	92	15	0.184	
7a	95	16	0.184	
7a	98	17		
7b	94	17	0.204	No rims
7b	103	19	0.061	No rims
7c	59	8	0.376	17
7c	61	9	0.336	27
7c	67	10	0.392	17
7c	78	11	0.212	12
7c	80	12	0.052	No rims
7c	81	12	0.183	5
7c	88	13	0.101	No rims
7c	101	14	0.089	1
8b	113	4	0.440	
8b	116	5	0.520	
8b	130	6	0.006	
8b	144	6	0.007	
8g	117	5	0.244	
8g	156	7	0.168	
		Total:	5.866	81

Subop	Lot	Level	Volume	MNV
		LOCONA MIDDEN		
1	23	14	0.428	
1	24	14	0.384	
1	29	15	0.440	
1	91	—		
1b	47	8	0.192	37
1b	49	9	0.220	23
1b	50	10	0.228	7
1b	51	11	0.200	2
1b	54	12	0.180	No rims
1b	57	12	0.180	No rims
2a	16	3	0.396	
2a	17	4	0.376	
2c	27	2	0.270	3
2c	28	3	0.980	4
2c	29	3		1
2c	30	5	0.148	
2c	32	6	0.400	2
2l	197	17		
2m	184	10	0.168	2
2m	181	11	0.960	1
3a	36	16	0.561	2
3a	39	18	0.460	No rims
3a	32	20		
3a	35	20		
3b	45	24	0.260	No rims
3c	56	—	0.561	
7c	52	7	0.304	13
7d	113	14	0.600	
7c	115	14	0.009	
7d	116	15	0.120	
7d	118	15	0.164	
8	7	5	0.168	
8	9	6	0.236	
8	10	7	0.208	
8c	118	5	0.212	
8d	221	5	0.147	
8d	239	5	0.005	
8d	270	5	0.240	
8d	251	6	0.201	
8d	288	6	0.046	
8e	161	6	0.052	
8e	165	6	0.133	
8e	249	7	0.325	
8e	253	7	0.014	
8e	254	7	0.021	
8e	264	8	0.022	
8h	143	6	0.141	
8h	260	6	0.216	

(continued)

(*continued*)

Subop	Lot	Level	Volume	MNV
8h	158	7	**0.000**	
8h	160	7		
8i	234	7	**0.195**	
8i	258	7	**0.165**	
9	7	5	**0.240**	7
9	10	6	**0.005**	No rims
9	11	6	**0.002**	No rims
9	12	6	**0.006**	No rims
9	15	6	**0.200**	No rims
9	17	6	**0.160**	No rims
9	18	7	**0.208**	5
9	19	8	**0.196**	No rims
9	21	10	**0.304**	1
9	22	11	**0.196**	No rims
9	26	13	**0.415**	4
9	23	17		No rims
10a	57	17	**0.124**	3
10a	59	18	**0.140**	1
10a	69	19		No rims
10a	70	20	**0.172**	1
10a	78	20		No rims
		Total:	**14.305**	119

	CONCHAS VILLAGE MIDDEN			
1a	25	5	**0.222**	3
1a	26	5	**0.216**	1
1a	27	6	**0.186**	7
1a	30	7	**0.178**	9
1a	31	8	**0.212**	21
1a	35	9	**0.186**	16
1b	35	4		13
2f	74	12	**0.294**	10
2f	79	13	**0.324**	17
2f	80	14	**0.300**	10
2f	85	15	**0.650**	30
2f	86	15	**0.500**	19
2f	91	16	**0.250**	92
2g	76	1	**0.240**	4
2g	77	2	**0.188**	No rims
2g	78	3	**0.188**	7
2g	82	5	**0.220**	No rims
2g	83	6	**0.224**	4
2g	84	7	**0.168**	4
2g	87	8	**0.200**	2
2g	88	9	**0.216**	2
2g	89	10	**0.244**	4
2g	90	11	**0.416**	2
2g	93	13	**0.208**	3
2g	94	14	**0.196**	4

Subop	Lot	Level	Volume	MNV
2g	95	15	0.220	12
2g	100	16		15
2g	109	17	0.140	4
2h	102	4	0.252	
2h	104	5	0.176	
2k	140	8	0.192	13
2k	147	9	0.296	17
2k	149	10	0.216	35
2k	150	11	0.284	50
2m	177	10	0.156	17
2m	182	11		1
2p	206	1	0.660	4
2p	207	2	0.118	3
2p	208	3	0.122	8
2p	210	4	0.540	5
2p	211	5	0.216	9
2p	214	6	0.480	7
3b	22	14	0.060	No rims
3b	23	15	0.180	No rims
4	5	4	0.144	3
6	2	1	0.196	5
6	3	2	0.216	10
6	7	3	0.168	8
6	8	4	0.236	10
6	9	5	0.200	10
6	10	6	0.192	15
6	11	7	0.204	7
6	12	8	0.200	2
6	13	9	0.200	3
10	43	17	0.004	No rims
10	51	18	0.124	No rims
10	64	19	0.080	No rims
10a	5	2	0.140	3
10a	7	3	0.184	1
10a	9	4	0.172	No rims
10a	17	5	0.064	8
10a	27	6	0.068	18
10a	30	7	0.076	6
10a	30	8		4
10a	35	9	0.068	2
10a	36	10	0.140	5
10a	40	11	0.248	5
10a	47	12	0.112	5
10a	50	13	0.096	2
10a	52	14	0.100	3
10b	18	5	0.060	No rims
10c	88	2	0.248	
10c	90	3	0.136	
10c	92	4	0.112	
10c	94	5	0.150	

(continued)

(continued)

Subop	Lot	Level	Volume	MNV
10d	86	2	**0.564**	
10d	89	3	**0.140**	
10d	91	4	**0.172**	
10d	93	5	**0.396**	
		Total:	**16.144**	**619**
CONCHAS ELITE MIDDEN				
7	8	2	**0.257**	**17**
7	9	2	**0.005**	**10**
7	11	3	**0.255**	**15**
7	30	4		No rims
7	33	5	**0.022**	**6**
7	46	5	**0.605**	**59**
7a	32	10	**0.370**	
7a	38	10	**0.012**	
7a	39	10	**0.020**	
7a	42	10	**0.083**	
7c	16	2	**0.376**	**33**
9	4	2	**0.100**	**14**
9	5	3	**0.288**	**11**
		Total:	**2.392**	**165**

References Cited

Abu-Lughod, Janet L. 1989 *Before European Hegemony: The World System A.D. 1250–1350*. Oxford University Press, New York.

Adams, Jenny L. 1999 Refocusing the Role of Food-Grinding Tools as Correlates for Subsistence Strategies in the U.S. Southwest. American Antiquity 64: 475–498.

Adams, Richard N. 1975 *Energy and Structure: A Theory of Social Power*. University of Texas Press, Austin.

Adams, Ron L. 2004 An Ethnoarchaeological Study of Feasting in Sulawesi, Indonesia. Journal of Anthropological Archaeology 23: 56–78.

Agrinier, Pierre 1962 The Archaeological Burials at Chiapa de Corzo and their Furniture. Papers of the New World Archaeological Foundation No. 16. Brigham Young University, Provo, UT.

———— 1984 The Early Olmec Horizon at Mirador, Chiapas, Mexico. Papers of the New World Archaeological Foundation 48. Provo, UT.

Andrews V., E. Wyllys 1986 Olmec Jades from Chacsinkin, Yucatan, and Maya Ceramics from La Venta Tabasco. In *Research and Reflections in Archaeology and History*, edited by E. W. Andrews V., American Institute Publication 57. Tulane University, New Orleans.

Appadurai, Arjun 1981 Gastropolitics in Hindu South Asia. American Ethnologist 8: 494–511.

———— 1986 *The Social Life of Things: Commodities in Cultural Perspective*. Cambridge University Press, Cambridge.

Arnold, Benita 1990 The Past as Propaganda: Totalitarian Archaeology in Nazi Germany. Antiquity 64: 464–478.

Arnold, Jeanne E. 1995 Transportation Innovation and Social Complexity among Maritime Hunter-Gatherer Societies. American Anthropologist 97: 733–747.

Arnold III, Philip J. 1999 Tecomates, Residential Mobility, and Early Formative Occupation in Coastal Lowland Mesoamerica. In *Pottery and People: A Dynamic Interaction*, pp. 157–170. Edited by J. M. Skibo and G. M. Feinman. University of Utah Press, Salt Lake City.

———— 2000 Sociopolitical Complexity and the Gulf Coast Olmecs: A View from the Tuxtla Mountains, Veracruz, Mexico. In *Olmec Art and Archaeology in Mesoamerica*, pp. 117–136. Edited by J. E. Clark and M. E. Pye. National Gallery of Art, Washington, DC.

———— 2003 Back to Basics: The Middle-Range Program as Pragmatic Archaeology. In *Essential Tensions in Archaeological Method and Theory*. University of Utah Press, Salt Lake City.

———— 2005 Gulf Olmec Variation and Implications for Interaction. In *New Perspectives on Formative Mesoamerican Cultures*, pp. 73–84. Edited by Terry G. Powis. British Archaeological Reports International Series 1377. Oxford.

Arroyo, Barbara 2002 Appendix I: Classification of La Blanca Figurines. In *Early Complex Society in Pacific Guatemala: Settlements and Chronology of the Rio Naranjo, Guatemala*, pp. 205–235. Edited by Michael W. Love. Papers of the New World Archaeological Foundation 66. Brigham Young University, Provo, UT.

Ashmore, Wendy 1984 Quirigua Archaeology and History Revisited. Journal of Field Archaeology 11: 365–386.

———— 1989 Construction and Cosmology: Politics and Ideology in Lowland Maya Settlement Patterns. In *Word and Image in Maya Culture: Explorations in Language, Writing and Representations*, pp. 272–286. Edited by W. F. Hanks and D. S. Rice. University of Utah Press, Salt Lake City.

———— 1991 Ode to a Dragline: Demographic Reconstructions at Classic Quirigua. In *Precolumbian Population History in the Maya Lowlands*, pp. 63–82. Edited by T. P. Culbert and D. S. Rice. University of New Mexico Press, Albuquerque.

Awe, Jaime 1992 Dawn in the Land between the Rivers: Formative Occupation at Cahal Pech, Belize and Its Implications for Preceramic Developments in the Central Maya Lowlands. Unpublished Ph.D. dissertation, University of London, England.

Beck, Charlotte and George T. Jones 1994 On-Site Artifact Analysis as an Alternative to Collection. American Antiquity 59: 304–315.

Bell, James A. 1994 *Reconstructing Prehistory; Scientific Method in Archaeology*. Temple University Press, Philadelphia.

Benson, Elizabeth P. and Beatriz de la Fuente 1996 Catalogue. In *Olmec Art of Ancient Mesoamerica*, pp. 153–273. Edited by E. P. Benson and B. de la Fuente. National Gallery of Art, Washington, DC.

Berlin, Brent and Paul Kay 1969 *Basic Color Terms: Their Universality and Evolution*. University of California Press, Berkeley.

Bishop, Ronald L. 1980 Aspects of Ceramic Compositional Modeling. In *Models and Methods in Regional Exchange*, pp. 47–66. Edited by R. Fry. Society for American Archaeology Papers, No.1, Washington, DC.

Blackman, M. James, Sophie Mery and Rita P. Wright 1989 Production and Exchange of Ceramics on the Oman Peninsula from the Perspective of Hili. Journal of Field Archaeology 16: 61–77.

Blake, Michael 1991 An Emerging Early Formative Chiefdom at Paso de la Amada, Chiapas, Mexico. In *The Formation of Complex Society in Southeastern Mesoamerica*, pp. 27–45. Edited by W. R. Fowler, Jr. CRC Press, Boca Raton.

———— 2006 Dating the Initial Spread of *Zea mays*. In *Histories of Maize: Multidiciplinary Approaches to the Prehistory, Linguistics, Biogeography, Domestication and Evolution of Maize*, edited by J. Staller, R. Tykot and B. Benz, pp. 55–72. Academic Press, New York.

Blake, Michael, John E. Clark, Brian S. Chisholm and Karen Mudar 1992a Non-agricultural Staples and Agricultural Supplements: Early Formative Subsistence in the Soconusco Region, Mexico. In *Transitions to Agriculture in Prehistory*, pp. 133–151. Edited by A. B. Gebauer and T. D. Price. Prehistory Press, Madison, WI.

Blake, Michael, B. S. Chisholm, John E. Clark, Barbara Voorhies and Michael W. Love 1992b Prehistoric Subsistence in the Soconusco Region. Current Anthropology 33: 83–94.

Blake, Michael and John E. Clark 1999 The Emergence of Hereditary Inequality: The Case of Pacific Coastal Chiapas. In *Pacific Latin America in Prehistory*, pp. 55–73. Edited by M. Blake. Washington State University Press, Seattle.

Blake, Michael, John E. Clark, Barbara Voorhies, George Michaels, Michael W. Love, Mary E. Pye, Arthur A. Demarest and Barbara Arroyo 1995 Radiocarbon Chronology for the Late Archaic and Formative Periods on the Pacific Coast of Southeastern Mesoamerica. Ancient Mesoamerica 6: 161–183.

Blake, Michael, Richard G. Lesure, Warren D. Hill, Luis Barba and John E. Clark 2006 The Residence of Power at Paso de la Amada, Mexico. In *Palaces and Power in the Americas: From Peru to the Northwest Coast*, pp. 191–210. Edited by J. J. Cristie and P. J. Sarro. University of Texas Press, Austin.

Blanton, Richard and Gary Feinman 1984 The Mesoamerican World Systems. American Anthropologist 86: 673–682.

Blanton, Richard E., Gary M. Feinman, Stephen A. Kowalewski and Laura Finsten 1996 A Dual-Processual Theory for the Evolution of Mesoamerican Civilization. Current Anthropology 37: 1–14.

Blanton, Richard E., Stephen A. Kowalewski, Gary Feinman and Jane Appel 1982 Monte Alban's Hinterland, Part 1: The Prehispanic Settlement Patterns of the Central and Southern Parts of the Valley of Oaxaca, Mexico. University of Michigan Museum of Anthropology Memoirs No. 15, Ann Arbor.

Blitz, John 1993 Big Pots for Big Shots: Feasting and Storage in a Mississippian Community. American Antiquity 58: 80–96.

Blomster, Jeffrey P. 1998 Context, Cult and Early Formative Period Public Ritual at Mixteca Alta: Analysis of a Hollow-Baby Figurine from Etlatongo, Oaxaca. Ancient Mesoamerica 9: 309–326.

——— 2004 *Etlatongo: Social Complexity, Interaction, and Village Life in the Mixteca Alta of Oaxaca, Mexico*. Wadsworth, Belmont, CA.

Blomster, Jeffrey P., Hector Neff and Michael D. Glascock 2005 Olmec Pottery Production and Export in Ancient Mexico Determined Through Elemental Analysis. Science 307: 1068–1072.

Bornstein, Joshua A. 2001 Tripping Over Colossal Heads: Settlement Patterns and Population Development in the Upland Olmec Heartland. Unpublished PhD dissertation. Department of Anthropology, Pennsylvania State University.

Braudel, Fernand 1972 *The Mediterranean and the Mediterranean World in the Age of Philip II*. Collins, London.

——— 1980 [1966] From the preface to La Méditerranée et le monde méditerranéen a l'époque de Philipe II, 2e édition. In On History, translated by S. Mathews. University of Chicago Press, Chicago.

——— 1992 *The Perspective of the World, Civilization and Capitalism, 15th – 18th Century.* Vol. III. University of California Press, Berkeley.

Braun, David P. 1983 Pots as Tools. In *Archaeological Hammers and Theories*, pp. 107–134. Edited by J. Moore and A. Keene. Academic Press, New York.

——— 1995 Coevolution of Sedentism, Pottery Technology and Horticulture in the Central Midwest, 200 bc-ad 600. In *Evolutionary Archaeology: Theory and Application*, pp. 270–283. Edited by M. J. O'Brien. University of Utah Press, Salt Lake City.

Broodbank, Cyprian 2000 *An Island Archaeology of the Early Cyclades*. Cambridge University Press, Cambridge.

Brumfiel, Elizabeth M. 1983 Aztec State Making: Ecology, Structure, and the Origins of the State. American Anthropologist 85: 261–284.

Brumfiel, Elizabeth M. and Timothy K. Earle (editors) 1987 *Specialization, Exchange and Complex Societies.* Cambridge University Press, Cambridge.

Brunton, Ron 1975 Why Do the Trobriands Have Chiefs? Man 10: 544–558.

Burger, Richard L. 1992 *Chavín and the Origins of Andean Civilization.* Thames and Hudson, London.

——— 1993 The Chavín Horizon: Stylistic Chimera or Socioeconomic Metamorphosis? In *Latin American Horizons*, pp. 41–82. Edited by D. S. Rice. Dumbarton Oaks, Washington, DC.

Burger, Richard L. and Ramiro Matos Mendieta 2002 Atalla: A Center on the Periphery of the Chavín Horizon. Latin American Antiquity 13: 153–177.

Caldwell, Joseph R. 1964 Interaction Spheres in Prehistory. Illinois State Museum Scientific Papers 12 (6): 133–143.

Carlson, John B. 1981 Olmec Concave Iron-Ore Mirrors: The Aesthetics of a Lithic Technology and the Lord of the Mirror. In *The Olmec and Their Neighbors, Essays in Memory of Mathew W. Sterling*, pp. 117–132. Edited by E. P. Benson. Dumbarton Oaks, Washington, DC.

Carmack, Robert M. 1981 *The Quiché Maya of Utatlan: The Evolution of a Highland Guatemala Kingdom.* University of Oklahoma Press, Norman.

Carr, Christopher 1995 Building a Unified Middle-Range Theory of Artifact Design: Historical Perspective and Tactics. In *Style, Society and Person: Archaeological and Ethnological Perspectives*, pp. 151–170. Edited by C. Carr and J. E. Neitzel. Plenum, New York.

Carr, Christopher and Jane E. Neitzel (editors) 1995 *Style, Society and Person: Archaeological and Ethnological Perspectives.* Plenum, New York.

Ceja Tenorio, Jorge F. 1985 Paso de la Amada: An Early Preclassic site in the Soconusco, Chiapas. Papers of the New World Archaeological Foundation No. 49. Brigham Young University, Provo, UT.

Champion, Timothy 1989 Introduction. In *Center and Periphery: Comparative Studies in Archaeology*, pp. 1–21. Edited by T. Champion. Routledge, New York.

Chapman, John 2002 Colourful Prehistories: The Problem with the Berlin Kay Colour Paradigm. In *Colouring the Past: The Significance of Colour in Archaeological Research*, pp. 45–72. Edited by A. Jones and G. MacGregor. Berg, Oxford and New York.

Chapman, Robert 2003 *Archaeologies of Complexity.* Routledge, London.

Chase-Dunn, Christopher 1992 The Comparative Study of World-Systems. *Review* 15: 313–333.

Chase-Dunn, Christopher and Thomas D. Hall 1991 *Core/Periphery Relations in Precapitalist Worlds*. Westview Press, Boulder, CO.

——— 1993 Comparing World Systems: Concepts and Working Hypotheses. Social Forces 71: 851–886.

——— 1995 Cross-World-System Comparisons: Similarities and Differences. In *Civilizations and World Systems: Studying World-Historical Change*, pp. 109–135. Edited by S. K. Sanderson. Altamira Press, Walnut Creek, CA.

Cheetham, David 1998 Interregional Interaction, Symbol Emulation, and the Emergence of Socio-political Inequality in the Central Maya Lowlands. Unpublished MA thesis, Department of Anthropology and Sociology, University of British Columbia, Vancouver.

——— 2006 America's First Colony? A Possible Olmec Outpost in Southern Mexico. Archaeology 59 (1): 42–46.

——— 2007 Cantón Corralito: Objects from a Possible Gulf Olmec Colony. Accessed from FAMSI webpage http://www.famsi.org/reports/05021/index.html on September 3, 2009.

——— 2009 Early Olmec Figurines from Two Regions: Style as Cultural Imperative. In *Mesoamerican Figurines: Small-Scale Indices of Large-Scale Social Phenomena*, pp. 149–179. Edited by C. T. Halperin, K. A. Faust, R. Taube and A. Giheut. University Press of Florida, Gainesville.

——— 2010 Cultural Imperatives in Clay: Early Olmec Carved Pottery from San Lorenzo and Cantón Corralito. *Ancient Mesoamerica*, in press.

Cheetham, David, Susana E. Gonzáles, Richard J. Behl, Michael D. Coe, Richard A. Diehl and Hector Neff 2009 Petrographic Analyses of Early Formative Olmec Carved Pottery. *Mexicon* 31: 69–72.

Childe, V. Gordon 1946 Archaeology and Anthropology. Southwestern Journal of Anthropology 2: 243–251.

——— 1949 *Social Worlds of Knowledge*. Oxford University Press, London.

——— 1950 The Urban Revolution. Town Planning Review 21: 2–17.

——— 1956 *Society and Knowledge*. Harper and Brothers, New York.

Clark, Grahame 1986 *Symbols of Excellence*. Cambridge University Press, Cambridge.

Clark, John E. 1987 Politics, Prismatic Blades and Mesoamerican Civilization. In *The Organization of Core Technology*, pp. 259–284. Edited by J. K. Johnson and C. A. Morrow. Westview Press, Boulder, CO.

——— 1988 The Lithic Artifacts of La Libertad, Chiapas, Mexico: An Economic Perspective. Papers of the New World Archaeological Foundation, No. 23. Brigham Young University, Provo, UT.

——— 1990 Olmecas, Olmequismo, y Olmequizacion en Mesoamerica. Arqueologia 3: 49–56.

——— 1991 The Beginnings of Mesoamerica: Apologia for the Soconusco Early Formative. In *The Formation of Complex Society in Southeastern Mesoamerica*, pp. 13–26. Edited by W. R. Fowler, Jr. CRC Press, Boca Raton.

——— 1994 The Development of Early Formative Rank Societies in the Soconusco, Chiapas, Mexico. Unpublished Ph.D. dissertation, Department of Anthropology, University of Michigan, Ann Arbor.

——— 1996 Craft Specialization and Olmec Civilization. In *Craft Specialization and Social Evolution: In Memory of V. Gordon Childe*, pp. 187–200.

Edited by B. Wailes. University Museum Monograph 93. The University Museum of Archaeology and Anthropology University of Pennsylvania, Philadelphia.

———— 1997 The Arts of Government in Early Mesoamerica. Annual Review of Anthropology 26: 211–234.

———— 2004 Mesoamerica Goes Public: Early Ceremonial Centers, Leaders and Communities. In *Mesoamerican Archaeology: Theory and Practice*, pp. 43–72. Edited by J. A. Hendon and R. A. Joyce. Blackwell, Oxford.

———— 2007 Mesoamerica's First State. In *The Political Economy of Ancient Mesoamerica: Transformations during the Formative and Classic Periods*, pp. 11–48. Edited by V. L. Scarborough and J. E. Clark. University of New Mexico Press, Albuquerque.

Clark, John E. and Michael Blake 1989 El Origen de la Civilización en Mesoamerica: Los Olmecas y Mokaya del Soconusco de Chiapas, México. In *El Preclassico o Formativo: Avances y Perspectivas*, pp. 385–403. Edited by M. Carmona Macias. Museo Nacional de Antropología, México, DF.

———— 1994 The Power of Prestige: Competitive Generosity and the Emergence of Rank Societies in Lowland Mesoamerica. In *Factional Competition and Political Development in the New World*, pp. 17–30. Edited by E. M. Brumfiel and J. W. Fox. Cambridge University Press, Cambridge.

Clark, John E. and David Cheetham 2002 Mesoamerica's Tribal Foundations. In *The Archaeology of Tribal Societies*, pp. 278–339. Edited by W. Parkinson. International Monographs in Prehistory, Ann Arbor.

———— 2005 Cerámica del Formativo de Chiapas. In *La Producción Alfarera en el México Antiguo I*, pp. 285–433. Edited by Beatriz Leonor Merrino de Carrión and Ángel García Cook. Instituto Nacional de Antropología e Historia, Mexico, DF.

Clark, John E., Jon L. Gibson and James A. Zeidler 2006 First Towns in the Americas: Searching for Agriculture and Other Enabling Conditions. In *Pathways to Complexity: The Archaeology of Subsistence and Authority in Middle Range Societies*. Edited by I. Kuijt and W. C. Prentiss, in press.

Clark, John E. and Dennis Gosser 1995 Reinventing Mesoamerica's First Pottery. In *The Emergence of Pottery: Technology and Innovation in Ancient Societies*, pp. 209–221. Edited by W. K. Barnett and J. W. Hoopes. Smithsonian Institution Press, Washington, DC.

Clark, John E. and John G. Hodgson 2004 A Millennium of Wonders in Coastal Mesoamerica (1700–700 BC). Paper presented at the Annual Meetings of the American Anthropological Association, Atlanta. December 15–19.

Clark, John E. and Thomas A. Lee, Jr. 1984 Formative Obsidian Exchange and the Emergence of Public Economies in Chiapas, Mexico. In *Trade and Exchange in Early Mesoamerica*, pp. 235–274. Edited by K. Hirth. University of New Mexico Press, Albuquerque.

Clark, John E., Thomas A. Lee and Tamara Salcedo 1989 The Distribution of Obsidian. In *Ancient Trade and Tribute: Economics of the Soconusco Region of Mesoamerica*, pp. 268–284. Edited by B. Voorhies. University of Utah Press, Salt Lake City.

Clark, John E. and Mary E. Pye 2000 The Pacific Coast and the Olmec Question. In *Olmec Art and Archaeology in Mesoamerica*, pp. 217–251. Edited by J. E. Clark and M. E. Pye. National Gallery of Art, Washington, DC.

Cobb, Charles R. 2003 Mississippian Chiefdoms: How Complex? Annual Review of Anthropology 32: 63–84.

Cobean, Robert H., Michael D. Coe, Edward A. Perry, Karl D Turekian and Dinkar P. Kharker 1971 Obsidian Trade at San Lorenzo Tenochtitlán, Mexico. *Science* 174: 666–671.

Cobean, Robert, James Vogt, Michael Glascock and Terrance Stocker 1991 High-Precision Trace-Element Characterization of Major Mesoamerican Obsidian Sources and Further Analysis of Artifacts from San Lorenzo Tenochtitlán. Latin American Antiquity 2: 69–91.

Coe, Michael D. 1961 La Victoria: An Early Site on the Pacific Coast of Guatemala. Papers of the Peabody Museum of Archaeology and Ethnology, Vol. 53, Peabody Museum, Cambridge, MA.

———— 1965a The Olmec Style and its Distribution. In *Handbook of Middle American Indians*, pp. 739–775. Vol. 3. Edited by R. Wauchope and G. R. Willey. University of Texas Press, Austin.

———— 1965b *The Jaguar's Children: Pre-Classic Central Mexico*. Museum of Primitive Art, New York.

———— 1977 Olmec and Maya: A Study in Relationships. In *The Origins of Maya Civilization*, pp. 183–195. Edited by R. E. W. Adams. University of New Mexico Press, Albuquerque.

———— 1989 The Olmec Heartland: Evolution of Ideology. In *Regional Perspectives on the Olmec*, pp. 68–82. Edited by R. J. Sharer and D. C. Grove. Cambridge University Press, Cambridge.

Coe, Michael D. and Richard A. Diehl 1980a *In the Land of the Olmec*. Vol. 2. University of Texas Press, Austin.

———— 1980b *In the Land of the Olmec: The Archaeology of San Lorenzo Tenochtitlán*. Vol. 1. University of Texas Press, Austin.

———— 1991 Reply to Hammond's *"Cultura Hermana*: Reappraisal of the Olmec." Review of Archaeology 12: 30–35.

Coe, Michael D. and Kent V. Flannery 1967 *Early Cultures and Human Ecology in South Coastal Guatemala*. Smithsonian Contributions to Anthropology. Vol. 3. Smithsonian Institution Press, Washington, DC.

Collingwood, Robin G. 1946 *The Idea of History*. Oxford University Press, Oxford.

Conkey, Margaret and Christine Hastorf (editors) 1990 *The Uses of Style in Archaeology*. Cambridge University Press, Cambridge.

Cooke, Richard G., Máximo Jiménez, Conrado Tapia and Barbara Voorhies 2004 A Closer Look at the Late Archaic Fish Fauna. In *Coastal Collectors in the Holocene: The Chantuto People of Southwest Mexico*, pp. 207–299. University Press of Florida, Gainesville.

Costin, Catherine L. and Timothy Earle 1989 Status Distinction and Legitimation of Power as Reflected in Changing Patterns of Consumption in Late Prehispanic Peru. American Antiquity 54: 691–714.

Cowgill, George L. 1986 Archaeological Applications of Mathematical and Formal Methods. In *American Archaeology Past and Future*, pp. 369–393. Edited by D. J. Meltzer, D. D. Fowler and J. A. Sabloff. Smithsonian Institution Press, Washington, DC.

———— 1990 Toward Refining Concepts of Full-Coverage Survey. In *The Archaeology of Regions: A Case for Full Coverage Survey*, pp. 249–259. Edited by S. K. Fish and S. A. Kowalewski. Smithsonian Institution Press, Washington, DC.

Creamer, W. and J. Haas 1985 Tribe versus Chiefdom in Lower Central America. American Antiquity 50: 738–754.

Cruz Lara Silva, Adriana and Eugenia Guevara Muños 2002 La Restauración de Cerámica Olmeca de San Lorenzo Tenochtitlán. UNAM, Mexico, DF.

Cunningham, Jerimy J. 2003 Rethinking Style in Archaeology. In *Essential Tensions in Archaeological Method and Theory*, pp. 23–40. Edited by T. L VanPool and C. S. Vanpool. University of Utah Press, Salt Lake City.

Curet, L. Antonio 1998 New Formulae for Estimating Prehistoric Populations for Lowland South American and the Caribbean. Antiquity 72: 359–375.

Cyphers Guillen, Ann 1988 Thematic and Contextual Analyses of Chalcatzingo Figurines. Mexicon 10: 98–102.

———— 1993 Women, Rituals, and Social Dynamics at Ancient Chalcatzingo. Latin American Antiquity 4: 209–224.

———— 1997a Olmec Architecture at San Lorenzo. In *Olmec to Aztec: Settlement Patterns in the Ancient Gulf Coast Lowlands*, pp. 98–114. Edited by B. L. Stark and P. J. Arnold. University of Arizona Press, Tucson.

———— 1997b La Arquitectura Olmeca en San Lorenzo Tenochtitlán. In *Población, Subsistencia y Medio Ambiente en San Lorenzo Tenochtitlán*, pp. 91–117. Edited by A. Cyphers. UNAM, Mexico, DF.

———— 1997c Crecimiento y Desarrollo de San Lorenzo Tenochtitlán. In *Población, Subsistencia y Medio Ambiente en San Lorenzo Tenochtitlán*, pp. 255–274. Edited by A. Cyphers. UNAM, Mexico, DF.

———— 2004 *Escultura Olmec de San Lorenzo Tenochtitlán*. UNAM, Mexico, DF.

Davis, Dave D. 1975 Patterns of Early Formative Subsistence in Southern Mesoamerica, 1500–1100 BC. Man 10: 41–59.

Deal, Michael 1998 *Pottery Ethnoarchaeology in the Central Maya Highlands*. University of Utah Press, Salt Lake City.

DeBoer, Warren R. 1975 The Archaeological Evidence for Manioc Cultivation: A Contemporary Tale. American Antiquity 40: 419–433.

———— 2003 Ceramic Assemblage Variability in the Formative of Ecuador and Peru. In *Archaeology of Formative Ecuador*, pp. 289–336. Edited by J. S. Raymond and R. L. Burger. Dumbarton Oaks Research Library and Collection, Washington, DC.

De León, Jason P. 2008 The Lithic Industries of San Lorenzo-Tenochtitlán: An Economic and Technological Study of Olmec Obsidian. Unpublished Ph. D. dissertation, Department of Anthropology. Pennsylvania State University, State Park PA.

Demarest, Arthur A. 1989 The Olmec and the Rise of Civilization in Eastern Mesoamerica. In *Regional Perspectives on the Olmec*, pp. 303–311. Edited by R. J. Sharer and D. C. Grove. Cambridge University Press, Cambridge.

———— 2004 *Ancient Maya: The Rise and Fall of a Rainforest Civilization*. Cambridge University Press, Cambridge.

DeMarrais, Elizabeth, Luis J. Castillo and Timothy Earle 1996 Ideology, Materialization, and Power Strategies. Current Anthropology 37: 15–32.

Dewar, Robert 1991 Incorporating Variation in Occupation Span into Settlement Pattern Analysis. American Antiquity 56: 604–620.

Di Castro Stringher, Anna 1997 Los Bloques de Ilmenito de San Lorenzo. In *Población, Subsistencia y Medio Ambiente en San Lorenzo Tenochtitlán*, pp. 153–160. Edited by A. Cyphers. UNAM, Mexico, DF.

Diehl, Richard A. 1981 Olmec Architecture: A Comparison of San Lorenzo and La Venta. In *The Olmec and Their Neighbors: Essays in Memory of Mathew W. Sterling*, pp. 69–82. Edited by E. P. Benson. Dumbarton Oaks, Washington, DC.

———— 2004 *The Olmecs: America's First Civilization*. Thames and Hudson, London and New York.

Diehl, Richard A. and Michael D. Coe 1995 Olmec Archaeology. In *The Olmec World: Ritual and Rulership*, pp. 11–26. Edited by J. Guthrie. The Art Museum, Princeton University, Princeton.

Dietler, Michael 1990 Driven by Drink: The Role of Drinking in the Political Economy and the Case of Early Iron Age France. Journal of Anthropological Archaeology 9: 352–406.

———— 1996 Feasts and Commensal Politics in the Political Economy: Food, Power and Status in Prehistoric Europe. In *Food and the Status Quest: An Interdisciplinary Perspective*, pp. 87–125. Edited by P. Wiessner and W. Schiefenhövel. Berghahn Books, Providence, RI.

———— 2001 Theorizing the Feast: Rituals of Consumption, Commensal Politics, and Power in African Contexts. In *Feasts: Archaeological and Ethnographic Perspectives on Food, Politics and Power*, pp. 65–114. Edited by M. Deitler and B. Hayden. Smithsonian Institution Press, Washington, DC.

Dietler, Michael and Brian Hayden (editors) 2001 *Feasts: Archaeological and Ethnographic Perspectives on Food, Politics and Power*. Smithsonian Institution Press, Washington and London.

Doering, Travis 2002 Preliminary Obsidian Results from Cuauhtémoc. In *Soconusco Formative Project: Preliminary Technical Report 2002*, pp. 50–60. Edited by R. M. Rosenswig. Submitted to the Instituto Nacional de Antropología e Historia, México, DF.

Downum, Christian E. and Gregory B. Brown 1998 The Reliability of Surface Artifact Assemblages as Predictors of Subsurface Remains. In *Surface Archaeology*, pp. 111–123. Edited by A. P. Sullivan. University of New Mexico Press, Albuquerque.

Drennan, Robert D. 1976a Religion and Social Evolution in Formative Mesoamerica. In *The Ancient Mesoamerican Village*, pp. 345–368. Edited by K. V. Flannery. Academic Press, Orlando.

———— 1976b *Fábrica San José and the Middle Formative Society in the Valley of Oaxaca, Mexico*. Memoir 8. Museum of Anthropology, University of Michigan, Ann Arbor.

———— 1983 Appendix: Radiocarbon Dates from the Oaxaca Region. In *The Cloud People: Divergent Evolution of the Zapotec and Mixtec Civilizations*, pp. 363–370. Edited by K. V. Flannery and J. Marcus. Academic Press, New York.

———— 1984 Long-Distance Transport Costs in Pre-Hispanic Mesoamerica. American Anthropologist 86: 105–112.

Drennan, Robert D. and Christian E. Peterson 2006 Patterned Variation in Prehistoric Chiefdoms. Proceedings of the National Academy of Sciences 103: 3960–3967.

Drucker, Philip 1947 *Some Implications of the Ceramic Complex of La Venta.* Smithsonian Misc. Collection Vol. 107, No. 8. Smithsonian Institution, Washington DC.

———— 1948 Preliminary Notes on an Archaeological Survey of the Chiapas Coast. Middle American Research Records. Vol. 1, 11: 151–169. Middle American Research Institute, Tulane University, New Orleans.

———— 1952 La Venta, Tabasco: A Study of Olmec Ceramics and Art. Smithsonian Institution, Bureau of American Ethnology, Bulletin 153. Washington, DC.

Drucker, Philip and Robert F. Heizer 1967 *To Make My Name Good: A Reexamination of the Southern Kwakiutl Potlatch.* University of California Press, Berkeley.

Drucker, Philip, Robert F. Heizer and Robert J. Squier 1959 Excavations at La Venta Tabasco, 1955. Bureau of American Ethnology Bulletin 170, Smithsonian Institution, Washington, DC.

———— 1992 The Notion of Site. In *Space, Time and Archaeological Landscapes*, pp. 21–41. Edited by J. Rossignol and L. Wandsnider. Plenum, New York.

Dunnell, Robert C. and William S. Dancey 1983 The Siteless Survey: A Regional Scale Data Collection Strategy. Advances in Archaeological Method and Theory 6: 267–287.

Earle, Timothy 1990 Style and Iconography as Legitimation in Complex Chiefdoms. In *The Use of Style in Archaeology*, pp. 73–81. Edited by M. Conkey and C. Hastorf. Cambridge University Press, Cambridge.

———— 1997 *How Chiefs Come to Power: The Political Economy in Prehistory.* Stanford University Press, Stanford.

Ekholm, Gordon 1944 *Excavations at Tampico and Panuco in the Huasteca, Mexico.* American Museum of Natural History, New York.

Ekholm, Kasja and Jonathan Friedman 1985 Towards a Global Anthropology. Critique of Anthropology 5: 97–119.

Ekholm, Susanna M. 1969 Mound 30A and the Early Preceramic Sequence of Izapa, Chiapas, Mexico. Papers of the New World Archaeological Foundation No. 25. Brigham Young University, Provo, UT.

———— 1989 Las Figurillas Preclasicas Ceramicas de Izapa, Chiapas: Tradición Mixe-Zoque. In *El Preclassico o Formativo: Avances y Perspectivas*, pp. 333–352. Edited by M. Carmona Macias. Museo Nacional de Antropología, México, DF.

Emery, Kitty L., Lori E. Wright and Henry Schwarcz 2000 Isotopic Analysis of Ancient Deer Bone: Biotic Stability in Collapse Period Maya Land-use. Journal of Archaeological Science 27: 537–550.

Engels, Frederick 1972 [1891] *The Origins of the Family, Private Property and the State.* Pathfinder Press, New York.

Evans, Susan T. 2004 *Ancient Mexico and Central America: Archaeology and Culture History.* Thames and Hudson, London.

Fash, William L. 2001 *Scribes, Warriors and Kings: The City of Copan and the Ancient Maya*, 2nd Edition. Thames and Hudson, New York.

Feddema, Vicki 1993 Early Formative Subsistence and Agriculture in Southeastern Mesoamerica. Unpublished Masters Thesis, Department of Anthropology and Sociology, University of British Columbia, Vancouver.

Feinman, Gary M. and Jill Neitzel 1984 Too Many Types: An Overview of Sedentary Prestate Societies in the Americas. Advances in Archaeological Method and Theory 7: 39–102.

Flannery, K. V., A. K. Balkansky, G. M. Feinman, D. C. Grove, J. Marcus, E. M. Redmond, R. G. Reynolds, R. J. Sharer, C. S. Spencer and J. Yaeger 2005 Implications of New Petrographic Analysis for the Olmec "Mother Culture" Model. Proceedings of the National Academy of Sciences 102: 11219–11223.

Flannery, Kent V. 1968 The Olmec and the Valley of Oaxaca: A Model for Interregional Interaction in Formative Times. In *Dumbarton Oaks Conference on the Olmec*, pp. 79–110. Edited by E. Benson. Dumbarton Oaks, Washington, DC.

———— 1969 An Analysis of Animal Bones from Chiapa de Corzo, Chiapas. In *The Artifacts of Chiapa de Corzo, Chiapas, Mexico*, pp. 209–218. Edited by T. A. Lee, Jr. Papers of the New World Archaeological Foundation, No. 26. Brigham Young University, Provo, UT.

———— 1999 The Ground Plans of Archaic States. In *Archaic States*, pp. 15–57. Edited by G. M. Feinman and J. Marcus. School of American Research, Sante Fe, NM.

Flannery, Kent V. and Joyce Marcus 1994 Early Formative Pottery of the Valley of Oaxaca, Mexico. Memoirs of the Museum of Anthropology 27. University of Michigan, Ann Arbor.

———— 2000 Formative Mesoamerican Chiefdoms and the Myth of the "Mother Culture." Journal of Anthropological Archaeology 19: 1–37.

———— 2003 The Origins of War: New 14C Dates from Ancient Mexico. Proceedings of the National Academy of Sciences 100: 11803–11805.

Frank, Andre G. 1990 A Theoretical Introduction to 5000 Years of World Systems History. Review 12: 155–248.

———— 1993 Bronze Age World System Cycles. Current Anthropology 34: 383–429.

———— 1995 The Modern World System Revisited: Rereading Braudel and Wallerstein. In *Civilization and World Systems: Studying World-Historical Change*, pp. 163–194. Edited by S. K. Sanderson. Alta Mira Press, Walnut Creek, CA.

Frank, Andre G. and Barry K. Gills (editors) 1993 *The World System: Five Hundred Years or Five Thousand?* Routledge, London.

Frankenstein, Susan and Michael Rowlands 1978 The Internal Structure and Regional Context of Early Iron Age Society in South Western Germany. Bulletin of the Institute of Archaeology 15: 73–112.

———— 1985 The Internal Structure and Regional Context of Early Iron Age Societies in Southeast Germany. Bulletin of the Institute of Archaeology of London 15: 73–112.

Friedman, Jonathan and Michael J. Rowlands 1978 Notes towards an Epigenetic Model of the Evolution of "Civilization." In *The Evolution of Social Systems*, pp. 201–276. Edited by J. Friedman and M. J. Rowlands. Duckworth, London.

Fritz, John M. and Fred T. Plog 1970 The Nature of Archaeological Explanation. American Antiquity 35: 405–412.

Furst, Peter T. 1995 Shamanism, Transformation, and Olmec Art. In *The Olmec World: Ritual and Rulership*, pp. 69–81. The Art Museum, Princeton University, Princeton.

Gasco, Janine L. 1987 Economic Organization in Colonial Soconusco, New Spain: Local and External Influences. Research in Economic Anthropology 8: 105–137.

——— 2003a The Polities of Xoconuchco. In *The Postclassic World*, pp. 50–54. Edited by M. E. Smith and F. F. Berdan. University of Utah Press, Salt Lake City.

——— 2003b Soconusco. In *The Postclassic World*, pp. 282–296. Edited by M. E. Smith and F. F. Berdan. University of Utah Press, Salt Lake City.

——— 2006 Soconusco Cacao Farmers Past and Present: Continuity and Change in an Ancient Way of Life. In *Chocolate in Mesoamerica: A Cultural History of Cacao*, pp. 322–337. Edited by C. L. McNeil. University of Texas Press, Austin.

Gasco, Janine L. and Barbara Voorhies 1989 The Ultimate Tribute: The Role of Soconusco as an Aztec Tributary. In *Ancient Trade and Tribute: Economies of the Soconusco Region of Mesoamerica*, pp. 48–94. Edited by B. Voorhies. University of Utah, Salt Lake City.

Gendron, François, David C. Smith and Aïcha Gendron-Badou 2002 Discovery of Jadteite-Jade in Guatemala Confirmed by Non-Destructive Raman Microscopy. *Journal of Archaeological Science* 29: 837–851.

Gerritsen, Fokke (editor) 2000 Food and Foodways. Archaeological Dialogues 7 (2).

Gibbon, Guy 1989 *Explanation in Archaeology*. Blackwell, Oxford.

Gillespie, Susan D. 1989 *The Aztec Kings*. University of Arizona Press, Tucson.

——— 1994 Llano del Jícaro: An Olmec Monument Workshop. Ancient Mesoamerica 5: 231–242.

Gilman, Antonio 1995 Prehistoric European Chiefdoms: Rethinking "Germanic" Societies. In *Foundations of Social Inequality*, pp. 235–251. Edited by T. D. Price and G. M. Feinman. Plenum, New York and London.

——— 2001 Assessing Political Development in Copper and Bronze Age Southeast Spain. In *From Leaders to Rulers*, pp. 59–81. Edited by J. Haas. Kluwer Academic Plenum Publishers, New York.

Godelier, Maurice 2004 What Mauss Did Not Say: Things You Give, Things You Sell, and Things That Must Be Kept. In *Values and Valuables: From the Sacred to the Symbolic*, pp. 3–20. Edited by C. Werner and D. Bell. Altamira Press, Walnut Creek, CA.

Goldman, Irwin 1970 *Ancient Polynesian Society*. University of Chicago Press, Chicago.

Gonzalez Lauck, Rebeca 1989 Recientes Investigaciones en La Venta, Tabasco. In *El Preclásico o Formativo: Avances y Perspectivas*, pp. 81–89. Edited by M. Carmona Macias. Museo Nacional de Antropología, México, DF.

——— 1996 La Venta: An Olmec Capital. In *Olmec Art of Ancient Mexico*, pp. 79–110. Edited by E. P. Benson. National Gallery of Art, Washington, DC.

Gosden, Chris and Jon Hather 1999 *The Prehistory of Food*. Routledge, London.

Gosden, Chris 1985 Gifts and Kin in Early Iron Age Europe. *Man*: 475–493.

——— 1989 Debt, Production, and Prehistory. Journal of Anthropological Archaeology 8: 355–387.

——— 2001 Making Sense: Archaeology and Aesthetics. World Archaeology 33: 163–167.

Graeber, David 1996 Beads and Money: Notes toward a Theory of Wealth and Power. American Ethnologist 23: 4–24.

——— 2002 *Toward an Anthropological Theory of Value: The False Coin of Our Own Dreams*. Palgrave, New York.

Grayson, Donald K. 1984 *Quantitative Zooarchaeology*. Academic Press, Orlando.

Green, Dee F. and Gareth W. Lowe 1967 Altamira and Padre Piedra, Early Preclassic Sites in Chiapas, Mexico. Papers of the New World Archaeological Foundation 20. Provo, UT.

Grove, David C. 1970 The Olmec Paintings of Oxtotitlan Cave, Guerrero, Mexico. Studies in Pre-Columbian Art and Archaeology, No. 6. Dumbarton Oaks, Washington, DC.

——— 1987 *Ancient Chalcatzingo*. University of Texas Press, Austin.

——— 1989 Olmec: What's in a Name? In *Regional Perspectives on the Olmec*, pp. 8–14. Edited by R. J. Sharer and D. C. Grove. Cambridge University Press, Cambridge.

——— 1993 "Olmec" Horizons in Formative Period Mesoamerica: Diffusion or Social Evolution? In *Latin American Horizons*, pp. 83–111. Edited by D. S. Rice. Dumbarton Oaks, Washington, DC.

——— 1996 Archaeological Contexts of Olmec Art Outside of the Gulf Coast. In *Olmec Art of Ancient Mexico*, pp. 105–117. Edited by E. P. Benson and B. de la Fuente. National Gallery of Art, Washington, DC.

——— 1997 Olmec Archaeology: Half a Century of Research and Its Accomplishments. Journal of World Prehistory 11: 51–101.

——— 1999 Public Monuments and Sacred Mountains: Observations on Three Formative Period Sacred Landscapes. In *Social Patterns in Preclassic Mesoamerica*, pp. 255–299. Edited by D. C. Grove and R. Joyce. Dumbarton Oaks, Washington, DC.

——— 2000 The Preclassic Societies of the Central Highlands of Mesoamerica. In *The Cambridge History of Native Peoples of the Americas*, pp. 122–151. Vol. II Mesoamerica. Edited by R. E. W. Adams and M. J. MacLeod. Cambridge University Press, Cambridge.

Guernsey, Julia 2006 Rulership and Power in Stone: The Performance of Rulership in Mesoamerican Izapan Style Art. University of Texas Press, Austin.

——— n.d. Rulers, Gods, and Potbellies: A Consideration of Sculptural Forms and Themes from Preclassic Pacific Coast and Piedmont of Mesoamerica. In *The Place of Stone Monuments in Mesoamerica's Preclassic Tradition: Context, Use and Meaning*. Edited by J. Guernsey, J. E. Clark and B. Arroyo. Dumbarton Oaks, Washington, DC, in press.

Guernsey Kappelman, Julia 2003 Reassessing the Late Preclassic Pacific Slope: The Role of Sculpture. Mexicon 25: 39–42.

——— 2004 Demystifying the Late Preclassic Izapan-style Stela Alter "Cult." RES 45: 99–122.

Gummerman IV, George 1997 Food and Complex Societies. Journal of Archaeological Method and Theory 4: 105–139.

Hall, Thomas D. 1986 Incorporation in the World-System: Toward a Critique. American Sociological Review 51: 390–402.

Hammond, Norman 1989a Cultura Hermana: Reappraising the Olmec. Quarterly Review of Archaeology 9 (4): 1–4.

———— 1989b The Function of Maya Middle Preclassic Pottery Figurines. Mexicon 11: 111–113.

Hayden, Brian 1990 Nimrods, Piscators, Pluckers and Planters: The Emergence of Food Production. Journal of Anthropological Archaeology 9: 31–69.

———— 1995 Pathways to Power: Principles for Creating Socioeconomic Inequalities. In *Foundations of Social Inequality*, pp. 15–86. Edited by T. D. Price and G. M. Feinman. Plenum Press, New York.

Hayden, Brian and Aubrey Cannon 1983 Where the Garbage Goes: Refuse Disposal in the Maya Highlands. Journal of Anthropological Archaeology 2: 117–163.

Hayden, Brian and Rick Schulting 1997 The Plateau Interaction Sphere and Late Prehistoric Cultural Complexity. American Antiquity 62: 51–85.

Heilbroner, Robert 1980 *The Worldly Philosophers: The Lives and Times of Great Economic Thinkers*. Simon and Schuster, New York.

Helms, Mary W. 1979 *Ancient Panama: Chiefs in Search of Power*. University of Texas Press, Austin.

———— 1988 *Ulysses' Sail: An Ethnographic Odyssey of Power, Knowledge and Geographical Distance*. Princeton University Press, Princeton.

———— 1992 Long-Distance Contacts, Elite Aspirations, and the Age of Discovery in Cosmological Context. In *Resources, Power and Interregional Interaction*, pp. 157–174. Edited by E. M. Schortman and P. A. Urban. Plenum Press, New York.

———— 1993a *Craft and the Kingly Ideal: Art, Trade and Power*. University of Texas Press, Austin.

———— 1993b Cosmological Chromatics: Color-Related Symbolism in the Ceramic Art of Ancient Panama. In *Reinterpreting Prehistory of Central America*, pp. 209–252. Edited by M. M. Graham. University Press of Colorado, Boulder.

Henderson, John S. 1979 Atopula, Guerro and the Olmec Horizon in Mesoamerica. Yale University Publications in Anthropology 77, New Haven.

Henrickson, Elizabeth and Mary M. A. McDonald 1983 Ceramic Form and Function: An Ethnographical Search and an Archaeological Application. American Anthropologist 85: 360–643.

Hill, Warren D., Michael Blake and John E. Clark 1998 Ball Court Design Date Back 3,400 Years. Nature 392: 878–879.

Hill, Warren D. and John E. Clark 2001 Sports, Gambling and Government: America's First Social Conquest? American Anthropologist 103: 331–345.

Hirth, Kenneth G. (editor) 1984 *Trade and Exchange in Early Mesoamerica*. University of New Mexico Press, Albuquerque.

Hodder, Ian 1982a Toward a Contextual Approach to Prehistoric Exchange. In *Contexts for Prehistoric Exchange*, pp. 199–212. Edited by J. E. Ericson and T. K. Earle. Academic Press, New York.

———— 1982b *Symbols in Action: Ethnoarchaelogical Studies of Material Culture.* Cambridge University Press, Cambridge.

———— 1986 *Reading the Past: Current Approaches to Interpretation in Archaeology.* Cambridge University Press, Cambridge.

———— 1990 *The Domestication of Europe.* Blackwell, Oxford.

Hodder, Ian and Scott Hutson 2003 *Reading the Past: Current Approaches to Interpretation in Archaeology*, 3rd Edition. Cambridge University Press, Cambridge.

Hodgson, John G. 2006 Informe Técnico por el Proyecto Ojo de Agua. National Institute of Anthropology and History (INAH), Mexico, DF.

Hovers, Erella, Shimon Ilani, Ofer Bar-Yosef and Bernard Vandermeersch 2003 An Early Case of Color Symbolism: Ochre Use by Modern Humans in Qafzeh Cave. Current Anthropology 44: 491–522.

Hudson, Jean, Barbara Voorhies and Philip L. Walker 1989 Changing Patterns of Faunal Exploitation. In *Ancient Trade and Tribute: Economies of the Soconusco Region of Mesoamerica*, pp. 133–154. Edited by B. Voorhies. University of Utah Press, Salt Lake City.

Hudson, Mark J. 2004 The Perverse Realities of Change: World System Incorporation and the Okhotsk Culture of Hokkaido. Journal of Anthropological Archaeology 23: 290–308.

Iceland, Harry B. 1997 The Preceramic Origins of the Maya: Results of the Colha Preceramic Project in Northern Belize. Unpublished Ph.D. dissertation, Department of Anthropology, University of Texas, Austin.

Irwin, Geoffrey 1983 Chieftainship, Kula and Trade in Massim Prehistory. In *The Kula: New Perspectives on Massim Exchange*, pp. 29–72. Edited by J. W. Leach and E. Leach. Cambridge University Press, Cambridge.

Ivic de Monterroso, Matilde 2004 Las Figurillas de La Blanca, San Marcos. In XVII Simposio de Investigaciones Arqueológicas en Guatemala, 2003, pp. 392–404. Edited by Juan P. Laporte, Barbar Arroyo, Hector Escobedo and H. Mejía. Museo Nacional de Arqueología y Etnología, Guatemala.

Jackson, Thomas L. and Michael W. Love 1991 Bladerunning: Obsidian Production and the Introduction of Prismatic Blades at La Blanca, Guatemala. Ancient Mesoamerica 2: 47–59.

Johnson, Gregory A. 1973 Local Exchange and Early State Development in Southwestern Iran. Museum of Anthropology, Papers 51. University of Michigan, Ann Arbor.

Jonaitis, Aldona (editor) 1991 *Chiefly Feasts: The Enduring Kwakiutl Potlatch.* University of Washington Press, Seattle.

Joralemon, Peter D. 1971 *A Study of Olmec Iconography.* Studies in Precolumbian Art and Archaeology 7. Dumbarton Oaks, Washington, DC.

———— 1976 The Olmec Dragon: A Study of Pre-Columbian Iconography. In *Origins of Religious Art and Iconography in Preclassic Mesoamerica*, pp. 27–71. Edited by H. B. Nicholson. Dumbarton Oaks, Washington, DC.

———— 1996 In Search of the Olmec Cosmos: Reconstructing the World View of Mexico's First Civilization. In *Olmec Art of Ancient Mexico*, pp. 51–59. Edited by E. P. Benson and B. de la Fuente. National Gallery of Art, Washington, DC.

Joyce, Rosemary A. 2004a Unintended Consequences? Monumentality as a Novel Experience in Formative Mesoamerica. Journal of Anthropological Method and Theory 11: 5–29.

———— 2004b Mesoamerica: A Working Model for Archaeology. In *Mesoamerican Archaeology: Theory and Practice*, pp. 1–42. Edited by J. A. Hendon and R. A. Joyce. Blackwell, Oxford.

Joyce, Rosemary A. and John S. Henderson 2001 Beginnings of Life in Eastern Mesoamerica. Latin American Antiquity 12: 5–24.

Junker, Laura L. 1999 Raiding, Trading and Feasting: The Political Economy of Philippine Chiefdoms. University of Hawaii Press, Honolulu.

———— 2001 The Evolution of Ritual Feasting Systems in Prehispanic Philippine Chiefdoms. In *Feasts: Archaeological and Ethnographic Perspectives on Food, Politics and Power*, pp. 267–310. Edited by M. Deitler and B. Hayden. Smithsonian Institution Press, Washington and London.

———— 2003 Economic Specialization and Inter-ethnic Trade between Foragers and Farmers in the Prehispanic Philippines. In *Forager-Traders in South and Southeast Asia: Long-Term Histories*, pp. 203–241. Edited by Kathleen D. Morrison and Laura L. Junker. Cambridge University Press, Cambridge.

Justeson, John S. and Peter Mathews 1983 The Seating of the Tun: Further Evidence concerning a Late Preclassic Lowland Maya Stela Cult. American Antiquity 48: 586–593.

Kaplan, Jonathan 2008 Hydraulics, Cacao, and Complex Developments at Preclassic Chocolá, Guatemala: Evidence and Implications. Latin American Antiquity 19: 399–413.

Kaplan, Jonathan and Juan Antonio Valdés 2004 Chocolá, an Apparent Regional Capital in the Southern Maya Preclassic: Preliminary Findings from the Proyecto Arqueológico Chocolá (PACH). Mexicon 26: 77–86.

Kay, Paul, Brent Berlin and W. Merrifield 1997 Color Naming across Languages. In *Color Categories in Thought and Language*, pp. 21–56. Edited by C. L. Hardin and L. Maffi. Cambridge University Press, Cambridge.

Kelly, Jane H. and Marsha P. Hanen 1988 *Archaeology and the Method of Science*. University of New Mexico Press, Albuquerque.

Kennett, Douglas J., Hector Neff, Barbara Voorhies, Andrew Roberts and Michael D. Glascock 2004 Evidence for Early Olmec Influences on the Soconusco Coast. Paper presented at the 69th Annual Meeting of the Society of American Archaeology, Montreal. March 31-April 4.

Kennett, Douglas J., Barbara Voorhies and Dean Martorana 2006 An Ecological Model for the Origins of Maize-Based Food Production on the Pacific Coast of Southern Mexico. In *Behavioral Ecology and the Transition to Agriculture*, pp. 103–136. Edited by Douglas J. Kennett and Bruce Winterhalder. University of California Press, Berkeley.

Killion, Thomas W. and Javier Urcid 2001 The Olmec Legacy: Cultural Continuity and Change in Mexico's Southern Gulf Coast Lowlands. Journal of Field Archaeology 28: 3–25.

Kintigh, Keith W. 1994 Contending with Contemporaneity in Settlement-pattern Studies. American Antiquity 59: 143–148.

Kirchoff, Paul 1952 Meso-America: Its Geographical Limits, Ethnic Composition and Cultural Characteristics. In *Heritage of Conquest*, pp. 17–30. Edited by S. Tax. The Free Press, New York.

Klein, Cecelia F., Eulogio Guzman, Elisa C. Mandell and Maya Stanfield-Mazzi 2002 The Role of Shamanism in Mesoamerican Art: A Reassessment. Current Anthropology 43: 383–419.

Klein, Cecelia F. and Maya Stanfield-Mazzi 2004 Reply to "On Sharpness and Scholarship in the Debate on Shamanism." Current Anthropology 45: 404–406.

Kohl. Phillip L. 1987 The Use and Abuse of World Systems Theory: The Case of the Pristine West Asian State. Advances in Archaeological Method and Theory 11: 1–35.

Kolb, Michael J. 1994 Monumentality and the Rise of Religious Authority in Precontact Hawai'i. Current Anthropology 34: 521–547.

——— 2006 The Origins of Monumental Architecture in Ancient Hawai'i. Current Anthropology 47: 657–665.

Komter, Aafke E. 2005 Social Solidarity and the Gift. Cambridge University Press, Cambridge.

Kowalewski, Stephen A. 1990 Merits of Full-Coverage Survey: Examples from the Valley of Oaxaca, Mexico. In The Archaeology of Regions: A Case for Full Coverage Survey, pp. 33–85. Edited by S. K. Fish and S. A. Kowalewski. Smithsonian Institution Press, Washington, DC.

Kowalewski, Stephen A., Gary M. Feinman, Laura Finsten, Richard E. Blanton and Linda M. Nicholas 1989 Monte Alban's Hinterland, Part II: Prehispanic Settlement Patterns in Tlacolula, Etla and Ocotlan, the Valley of Oaxaca, Mexico. Memoirs of the University of Michigan Museum of Anthropology, No. 23, Ann Arbor.

Kristiansen, Kristian 1987 Centre and Periphery in Bronze Age Scandinavia. In Centre and Periphery in the Ancient World, pp. 74–85. Edited by M. Rowlands, M. Larsen and K. Kristiansen. Cambridge University Press, Cambridge.

——— 1991 Chiefdoms, States and Systems of Social Evolution. In Chiefdoms: Power, Economy and Ideology, pp. 16–43. Edited by T. Earle. Cambridge University Press, Cambridge.

——— 1998 Europe before History. Cambridge University Press, Cambridge.

Kristiansen, Kristian and Thomas B. Larsson 2005 The Rise of Bronze Age Society: Travels, Transmissions and Transformations. Cambridge University Press, Cambridge.

Kubler, George 1990 The Art and Archaeology of Ancient America, 3rd Edition. Yale University Press, New Haven.

Lawrence, Denise L. and Setha M. Low 1990 The Built Environment and Spatial Form. Annual Review of Anthropology 19: 453–505.

Lee Jr., Thomas W. 1978 The Historical Routes of Tabasco and Northern Chiapas and Their Relationship to Early Cultural Developments in Central Chiapas. In Mesoamerican Communication Routes and Cultural Contacts, pp. 75–106. Edited by T. A. Lee, Jr. and C. Navarrete. Papers of the New World Archaeological Foundation 40. Provo, UT.

Lentz, Carola (editor) 1999 Changing Food Habits: Case Studies from Africa, South America, and Europe. Hardwood, Amsterdam.

Lesure, Richard G. 1993 Salvamento Arqueológico en El Varal. Un Perspectiva Sobre la Organización Sociopolítica Olmeca de la Costa de Chiapas. In Segundo y Tercer Foro de Arqueología de Chiapas, pp. 211–227. Gobierno del Estado de Chiapas, Tuxtla Gutierrez.

——— 1995 Paso de la Amada: Sociopolitical Dynamics in an Early Formative Community. Unpublished Ph.D. dissertation, Department of Anthropology, University of Michigan, Ann Arbor.

———— 1997a Figurines and Social Identities in Early Sedentary Societies of Coastal Chiapas, Mexico 1150–800 b.c. In *Women and Prehistory: North America and Mesoamerica*, pp. 225–248. Edited by C. Claasen and R. A. Joyce. University of Pennsylvania Press, Philadelphia.

———— 1997b Early Formative Platforms at Paso de la Amada, Chiapas, Mexico. Latin American Antiquity 8: 217–235.

———— 1998 Vessel Form and Function in an Early Formative Ceramic Assemblage from Coastal Mexico. Journal of Field Archaeology 25: 19–36.

———— 1999a Platform Architecture and Activity Patterns in an Early Mesoamerican Village in Chiapas, Mexico. Journal of Field Archaeology 26: 391–406.

———— 1999b Figurines as Representations and Products at Paso de la Amada, Mexico. Cambridge Archaeological Journal 9: 209–220.

———— 1999c On the Genesis of Value in Early Hierarchical Societies. In *Material Symbols: Culture and Economy in Prehistory*, edited by J. E. Robb. Center for Archaeological Investigations, Occasional Paper No. 26. Southern Illinois University, Carbondale.

———— 2000 Animal Imagery, Cultural Unities, and Ideologies of Inequality in Early Formative Mesoamerica. In *Olmec Art and Archaeology in Mesoamerica: Developments in Formative Period Social Complexity*, pp. 193–215. Edited by J. E. Clark and M. E. Pye. National Gallery of Art, Washington DC.

———— 2002 The Goddess Diffracted: Thinking about the Figurines of Early Villages. Current Anthropology 43: 587–610.

———— 2004 Shared Art Styles and Long-Distance Contact in Early Mesoamerica. In *Mesoamerican Archaeology: Theory and Practice*, pp. 73–96. Edited by J. A. Hendon and R. A. Joyce. Blackwell, Oxford.

———— 2009 Settlement and Subsistence in Early Formative Soconusco: El Varal and the Problem of Inter-Site Assemblage Variation. Cotsen Institute, Los Angeles., in press.

Lesure, Richard G. and Michael Blake 2002 Interpretive Challenges in the Study of Early Complexity: Economy, Ritual and Architecture at Paso de la Amada, Mexico. Journal of Anthropological Archaeology 21: 1–24.

Lesure, Richard G. and John E. Clark 2001 Working copy of Mazatán figurine description dated June 15, 2001. Ms in possession of author.

Lightfoot, Kent G. 1993 Long-term Developments in Complex Hunter-Gatherer Societies: Recent Perspectives from the Pacific Coast of North America. Journal of Archaeological Research 1: 167–201.

Linares, Olga F. 1976 Garden Hunting in the American Tropics. Human Ecology 4: 331–349.

Lohse, Jon, Jaime Awe, Cameron Griffith, Robert Rosenswig and Fred Valdez, Jr. 2006 Preceramic Occupations in Belize: Updating the Paleoindian and Archaic Record. Latin American Antiquity 17: 209–226.

Lorenzo, José Luis 1955 Los Concheros de la Costa de Chiapas. Anales del Instituto Nacional de Antropología e Historia 7: 41–50.

Love, Michael W. 1991 Style and Social Complexity in Formative Mesoamerica. In *The Formation of Complex Society in Southeastern Mesoamerica*, pp. 47–76. Edited by W. R. Fowler, Jr. CRC Press, Boca Raton.

———— 1999a Economic Patterns in the Development of Complex Society in Pacific Guatemala. In *Pacific Latin America in Prehistory: The Evolution of Archaic and Formative Cultures*, pp. 89–100. Edited by M. Blake. University of Washington Press, Pullman.

———— 1999b Ideology, Material Culture and Daily Practice in Pre-Classic Mesoamerica: A Pacific Coast Perspective. In *Social Patterns in Pre-Classic Mesoamerica*, pp. 127–154. Edited by D. G. Grove and R. A. Joyce. Dumbarton Oaks, Washington, DC.

———— 2002a Early Complex Society in Pacific Guatemala: Settlements and Chronology of the Rio Naranjo, Guatemala. Papers of the New World Archaeological Foundation 66. Brigham Young University, Provo, UT.

———— 2002b Ceramic Chronology of Preclassic Period Western Pacific Guatemala and Its Relationship to Other Regions. In *Incidents of Archaeology in Central America and Yucatán: Essays in Honor of Edwin M. Shook*, pp. 51–73. Edited by M. Love, M. Popenoe de Hatch and H. L. Escobedo. University Press of America, Lanham, MD.

Love, Michael and Julia Guernsey 2007 Monument 3 from La Blanca, Guatemala: A Middle Preclassic Earthen Sculpture and Its Ritual Associations. Antiquity 81: 920–932.

Low, Setha M. 2000 *On the Plaza: The Politics of Public Space and Culture*. University of Texas Press, Austin.

Lowe, Gareth W. 1962 Mound 5 and Minor Excavations, Chiapa de Corzo, Chiapas Mexico. Papers of the New World Archaeological Foundation 12. Brigham Young University, Provo, UT.

———— 1967 Discussion. In *Altamira and Padre Piedra, Early Preclassic Sites in Chiapas, Mexico*, pp. 53–79. By D. F. Green and G. W. Lowe. Papers of the New World Archaeological Foundation 20. Provo, UT.

———— 1971 The Civilizational Consequences of Varying Degrees of Agricultural and Ceramic Dependency within the Basic Ecosystems of Mesoamerica. In *Observations on the Emergence of Civilization in Mesoamerica*, pp. 212–248. Edited by R. F. Heizer and J. A. Graham. Contributions of the University of California Research Facility, No 11. University of California, Berkeley.

———— 1975 Early Preclassic Barra Phase of Altamira, Chiapas. Papers of the New World Archaeological Foundation 38. Provo, UT.

———— 1977 The Mixe-Zoque as Competing Neighbors of the Early Lowland Maya. In *The Origins of Maya Civilization*, pp. 197–248. Edited by R. E. W. Adams. University of New Mexico Press, Albuquerque.

———— 1978 Eastern Mesoamerica. In *Chronologies in New World Archaeology*, pp. 331–393. Edited by R. E. Taylor and C. W. Meighan. Academic Press, New York.

———— 1981 Olmec Horizons Defined in Mound 20, San Isidro, Chiapas. In *The Olmec and Their Neighbors: Essays in Honor of Mathew W. Sterling*, pp. 231–255. Edited by E. P. Benson. Dumbarton Oaks, Washington, DC.

———— 1989 The Heartland Olmec: Evolution of Material Culture. In *Regional Perspectives on the Olmec*, pp. 33–67. Edited by R. J. Sharer and D. C. Grove. Cambridge University Press, Cambridge.

———— 1998 Mesoamérica Olmeca: Diez Preguntas. Colección Científica Nacional Institute of Anthropology and History/(INAH/UNAM), México, DF.

Lowe, Gareth W., Thomas A. Lee, Jr., and E. M. Espinoza 1982 Izapa: An Introduction to the Ruins and Monuments. Papers of the New World Archaeological Foundation 31. Provo, UT.

Luttwak, Edward N. 2007 Dead End: Counterinsurgency Warfare as Military Malpractice. Harpers 314 (1881 Feb.): 32–42.

Lyman, R. Lee 1994 Quantitative Units and Terminology in Zooarchaeology. American Antiquity 59: 36–71.

MacLaury, Robert E. 1997 *Color and Cognition in Mesoamerica: Constructing Categories as Vantages*. University of Texas Press, Austin.

MacNeish, Richard S. 1954 An Early Archaeological Site near Panuco Vera Cruz. Transactions of the American Philosophical Society Vol. 44 Part 5, American Philosophical Society, Philadelphia.

Malinowski, Bronislav 1922 *Argonauts of the Western Pacific: An Account of Native Enterprise and Adventure in the Archipelagoes of Melanesian New Guinea*. Routledge and Kegan, London.

———— 1935 *Coral Gardens and Their Magic*. Allen & Unwin, London.

Marcus, Joyce 1983 The Conquest Slabs of Building J, Monte Alban. In *The Cloud People: Divergent Evolution of the Zapotec and Mixtec Civilizations*, pp. 106–108. Edited by K. V. Flannery and J. Marcus. Academic Press, New York.

———— 1989 Zapotec Chiefdoms and the Nature of Formative Religions. In *Regional Perspectives on the Olmec*, pp. 148–197. Edited by R. J. Sharer and D. C. Grove. Cambridge University Press, Cambridge.

———— 1996 The Importance of Context in Interpreting Figurines. Cambridge Archaeological Journal 6: 285–291.

———— 1998 Woman's Ritual in Formative Oaxaca: Figurine-making, Divination, Death and the Ancestors. University of Michigan Museum of Anthropology, Ann Arbor.

Marcus, Joyce and Gary M. Feinman 1999 Introduction. In *Archaic States*, pp. 3–13. Edited by G. M. Feinman and J. Marcus, School of American Research, Sante Fe, New Mexico.

Marcus, Joyce and Kent V. Flannery 1996 *Zapotec Civilization: How Urban Society Evolved in Mexico's Oaxaca Valley*. Thames and Hudson, London.

Marx, Karl 1973 [1857–8] *Grundrisse: Foundations to the Critique of Political Economy*. Vintage Books, New York.

———— 1977 [1867] *Capital*. Vol. 1. Random House, New York.

———— 1978 The Gundrisse. In *The Marx-Engels Reader*, 2nd Edition, pp. 221–293. Edited by R. C. Tucker. Norton & Company, New York.

Mauss, Marcel 1990 *The Gift: The Form and Reason for Exchange in Archaic States*. W. W. Norton, London.

McC. Adams, Robert 2001 Complexity in Archaic States. Journal of Anthropological Archaeology 20: 345–360.

McGuire, Randall H. 1983 Breaking Down Cultural Complexity: Inequality and Heterogeneity. Advances in Archaeological Method and Theory 6: 91–142.

———— 1987 The Papaguerian Periphery: Uneven Development in the Prehistoric US Southwest. In *Politics and Partitions: Human Boundaries and* the Growth of Complex Societies, pp. 123–139. Edited by K. M. Trinkaus. Anthropological Research Paper 37, Arizona State University.

——— 1992 A Marxist Archaeology. Academic Press, San Diego.

——— 1996 The Limits of the World-Systems Theory for the Study of Prehistory. In Pre-Columbian World Systems, pp. 51–64. Edited by P. N. Perigrine and G. M. Feinman. Prehistory Press, Madison, WI.

McIntosh, Susan K. 1999 Pathways to Complexity: An African Perspective. In Beyond Chiefdoms: Pathways to Complexity in Africa, pp. 1–30. Edited by S. K. McIntosh. Cambridge University Press, Cambridge.

Miles, Suzanne W. 1965 Sculpture of the Guatemalan-Chiapas Highlands and Pacific Slopes and Associated Hieroglyphs. In Archaeology of Southern Mesoamerica, pp. 237–275. Edited by G. R. Willey. Handbook of Middle American Indians. Vol. 2. University of Texas Press, Austin.

Miller, Daniel 1982 Structures and Strategies: An Aspect of the Relationship between Social Hierarchy and Cultural Change. In Symbolic and Structural Archaeology, pp. 89–98. Edited by I. Hodder. Cambridge University Press, Cambridge.

Mills, Barbara J. 1989 Integrating Functional Analyses of Vessel and Sherds through Models of Ceramic Assemblage Formation. World Archaeology 21: 133–147.

Mintz, Sidney W. 1985 Sweetness and Power: The Place of Sugar in Modern History. Viking Press, New York.

Mintz, Sidney W. and Christine M. Du Bois 2002 The Anthropology of Food and Eating. Annual Review of Anthropology 31: 99–119.

Mollon, J. D. 1997 "'Tho' she kneel'd in that place where they grew . . . ": The Uses of Primate Colour Vision. In Readings in Color, Vol. 2. The Science of Color, pp. 379–396. Edited by A. Byrne and D. R. Hilbert. MIT Press, Cambridge.

Morris, Donald H. 1990 Changes in Ground Stone following the Introduction of Maize into the American Southwest. Journal of Anthropological Research 46: 177–194.

Nagel, Ernest 1961 The Structure of Science: Problems in the Logic of Scientific Explanation. Harcourt, Brace and World, New York.

Navarrete, Carlos 1970 Evidencias de la Lengua Quiché en el Soconusco. Boletín Escritura Maya 11 (2): 32–33.

——— 1978 The Prehispanic System of Communication between Chiapas and Tabasco. In Mesoamerican Communication Routes and Cultural Contacts, pp. 75–106. Edited by T. A. Lee, Jr. and C. Navarrete. Papers of the New World Archaeological Foundation 40. Provo, UT.

Neff, H., J. P. Blomster, R. L. Bishop, M. J. Blackman, M. D. Coe, G. L. Cowgill, R. A. Diehl, S. Houston, A. A. Joyce, C. P. Lipo, B. L. Stark and M. Winter 2006a Methodological Issues in the Provenance Investigation of Early Formative Mesoamerican Ceramics. Latin American Antiquity 17: 54–76.

Neff, H., J. P. Blomster, R. L. Bishop, M. J. Blackman, M. D. Coe, G. L. Cowgill, A. Cyphers, R. A. Diehl, S. Houston, A. A. Joyce, C. P. Lipo and M. Winter 2006b Smokescreens in the Provenance Investigation of Early Formative Mesoamerican Ceramics. Latin American Antiquity 17: 104–118.

Neff, Hector 2002 Sources of Raw Material Used in Plumbate Pottery. In Incidents of Archaeology in Central America and Yucatan: Essays in Honor of

Edwin M. Shook, pp. 217–231. Edited by M. Love, M. Popenoe de Hatch and H. L. Escobedo. University Press of America, Lanham, MD.

——— 2003 Analysis of Mesoamerican Plumbate Pottery Surfaces by Laser Ablation-Inductively Coupled Plasma-Mass Spectrometry (LA-ICP-MS). Journal of Archaeological Science 30: 21–35.

Neff, Hector, Ronald L. Bishop and Dean E. Arnold 1988 Reconstructing Ceramic Production and Ceramic Compositional Data: An Example from Guatemala. Journal of Field Archaeology 15: 339–348.

Neff, Hector and Michael D. Glascock 2002 Instrument Neutron Activation Analysis of Ceramics from the Mazatán Region, Chiapas, Mexico. Ms available on the MURR Archaeometry Laboratory web site. http://archaeometry.missouri.edu/datasets/resource/Neff_Glascock_2002.html Accessed on September 3, 2009.

Neff, Hector, Deborah M. Pearsall, John G. Jones, Bárbara Arroyo, Shawn K. Collins and Dorothy E. Freidel 2006c Early Maya Adaptive Patterns: Mid-Late Holocene Paleoenvironmental Evidence from Pacific Guatemala. Latin American Antiquity 17: 287–315.

Nelson Jr., Fred W. 1985 Summary of the Results of Analysis of Obsidian Artifacts from the Maya Lowlands. *Scanning Electron Microscopy* II: 631–649.

Nelson Jr., Fred W. and John E. Clark 1998 Obsidian Production and Exchange in Eastern Mesoamerica. In *Rutas de Intercambio en Mesoamerica:* Vol. III. *Coloquio Pedro Bosch-Gimpera*, pp. 277–333. Edited by E. Childs Rattray. Universidad Nacional Autónoma de México, México DF.

Nelson, Fred W. and Barbara Voorhies 1980 Trace Element Analysis of Obsidian Artifacts from Three Shell Midden Sites in the Littoral Zone, Chiapas, Mexico. American Antiquity 45: 540–550.

Nichols, Deborah L. 1996 An Overview of Regional Settlement Pattern Survey in Mesoamerica: 1960–1995. In *Arqueología Mesoamericana: Homenajo a William T. Sanders*, pp. 59–95. Edited by A. G. Mastache, J. R. Parsons, R. S. Santley and M. C. Serra Puche,. Vol. 1. Instituto Nacional de Antropología e Historia, Mexico City.

Niederberger, Christine 1987 Paléopaysages et Archéologie Pre-urbaine du Bassin de Mexico. Centre d'Études Mexicaines et Centraméricaines. CEMCA, Colección Études Mésoaméricaines, Mexico, DF.

——— 2000 Ranked Societies, Iconographic Complexity, and Economic Wealth in the Basin of Mexico toward 1200 BC. In *Olmec Art and Archaeology in Mesoamerica*, pp. 169–188. Edited by J. E. Clark and M. E. Pye. National Gallery of Art, Washington, DC.

Odell, George H. 2001 Research Problems R Us. American Antiquity 66: 679–685.

Odess, Daniel 1998 The Archaeology of Interaction: Views from Artifact Style and Material Exchange in Dorset Society. American Antiquity 63: 417–435.

Orellana, Sandra L. 1995 Ethnohistory of the Pacific Coast. Labyrinthos, Lancaster, CA.

Ortiz Pérez, Mario Arturo and Ann Cyphers 1997 La Geomorfología y las Evidencias Arqueológicas en la Región de San Lorenzo Tenochtitlán, Veracruz. In *Población, Subsistencia y Medio Ambiente en San Lorenzo Tenochtitlán*, pp. 31–53. Edited by A. Cyphers. Uiversidad Nacional Autonomo de Mexico, Mexico, DF.

Ortiz. Ponciano and María del Carmen Rodríguez 2000 The Sacred Hill at El Manatí: A Preliminary Discussion of the Site's Ritual Paraphernalia. In Olmec Art and Archaeology in Mesoamerica: Developments in Formative Period Social Complexity, edited by J. E. Clark and M. E. Pye, pp. 75–93. National Gallery of Art, Washington, DC.

Orton, Clive 2000 Sampling in Archaeology. Cambridge University Press, Cambridge.

O'Shea, J. M. and Alex W. Barker 1996 Measuring Social Complexity and Variation: A Categorical Imperative? In Emergent Complexity: The Evolution of Intermediate Societies, pp. 13–24. Edited by J. E. Arnold. International Monographs in Prehistory, Ann Arbor

Pailles, Maricruz H. 1980 Pampa El Pajón, An Early Estuarine Site, Chiapas, Mexico. Papers of the New World Archaeological Foundation, No. 44. Brigham Young University, Provo, UT

Parsons, Lee A. 1981 Post-Olmec Stone Sculpture: The Olmec-Izapan Transition on the Southern Pacific Coast and Highlands. In The Olmec and Their Neighbors: Essays in Memory of Matheu W. Sterling, pp. 257–288. Edited by M. Coe, D. Grove and E. P. Benson. Dumbarton Oaks, Washington, DC.

Parsons, Lee A. and Barbara J. Price 1971 Mesoamerican Trade and Its Role in the Emergence of Civilization. In Observations on the Emergence of Civilization in Mesoamerica, pp. 169–195. Edited by R. F. Heizer and J. A. Graham. Contributions of the University of California Research Facility, No 11. University of California, Berkeley.

Patterson, Thomas C. 2003 Marx's Ghost: Conversations with Archaeologists. Berg, Oxford and New York.

Pauketat, Timothy R. 2004 Ancient Cahokia and the Mississippians. Cambridge University Press, Cambridge.

Pauketat, Timothy R. and Thomas E. Emerson 1991 The Ideology of Authority and the Power of the Pot. American Anthropologist 93: 919–941.

Pauketat, Timothy R., Lecretia S. Kelly, Gayle J. Fritz, Neal H. Lopinot, Scott Elias and Eve Hargrave 2002 The Residues of Feasting and Public Ritual at Early Cahokia. American Antiquity 67: 257–279.

Peebles, Christopher S. and Susan M. Kus 1977 Some Archaeological Correlates of Ranked Societies. American Antiquity 42: 421–448.

Pérez Suárez, Tomás 2002 Cantón Corralito: Un Sitio Olmeca en el Litoral Chiapaneco. In Arqueología Mexicana, Historia y Esencia. Siglo XX: En Reconocimiento al Dr. Román Piña Chán, pp. 71–92. Edited by J. Nava Rivero. Instituto Nacional de Antropología e Historia, Mexico, DF.

Pérez Suárez, Tomás and Richard G. Lesure 1998 Informe del Proyecto Arqueologico de las Aldeas a los Centros de Poder en la Costa de Chiapas 1997. Entregado al Instituto Nacional de Antropología e Historia, Mexico, DF.

Perigrine, Peter N. and Gary M. Feinman (editors) 1996 Pre-Columbian World Systems. Prehistory Press, Madison, WI.

Phillips, Philip and Gordon R. Willey 1953 Method and Theory in American Archaeology: An Operational Basic for Culture-Historical Integration. American Anthropologist 55: 615–631.

Pinkowski, Jennifer 2006 A City by the Sea: Early Urban Planning on Mexico's Pacific Coast. Archaeology 59 (1):46–49.

Piperno, Dolores R. and Kent V. Flannery 2001 The Earliest Archaeological Maize (Zea mays L.) from Highland Mexico: New Accelerator Mass

Spectrometry Dates and Their Implications. Proceedings of the National Academy of Sciences 98: 2101–2103.

Pires-Ferreira, Jane W. 1975 Formative Mesoamerican Exchange Networks with Special Reference to the Valley of Oaxaca. Memoirs of the Museum of Anthropology No. 7. University of Michigan, Ann Arbor.

Plog, Fred T. 1974 *The Study of Prehistoric Change*. Academic Press, New York.

Plog, Stephen 1976 Measurement of Prehistoric Interaction between Communities. In *The Early Mesoamerican Village*, pp. 255–272. Edited by K. V. Flannery. Academic Press, Orlando.

Pohl, Mary D., Kevin O. Pope and Christopher von Nagy 2002 Olmec Origins of Mesoamerican Writing. Science 298: 1984–1987.

Pool, Christopher A. 2005 Perspectives on Variation in Olmec Settlement and Polity Using Mississippian Models. In *Gulf Coast Archaeology: The Southeastern United States and Mexico*, pp. 223–244. Edited by N. M. White. University Press of Florida, Gainesville.

———— 2007 *Olmec Archaeology and Early Mesoamerica*. Cambridge University Press, Cambridge.

Pool, Christopher A. and Georgia Mudd Britt 2000 A Ceramic Perspective on the Formative to Classic Transition in Southern Veracruz, Mexico. Latin American Antiquity 11: 139–161.

Pool, Christopher A. and M. A. Ohnersorgen 2003 Archaeological Survey and Settlement at Tres Zapotes. In *Settlement Archaeology and Political Economy at Tres Zapotes, Veracruz, Mexico*, pp. 7–31. Monograph 50, Cotsen Institute of Archaeology, University of California, Los Angeles.

Popson, Colleen P. 2003 Earliest Maya Writing? Archaeology 56: 10.

Potter, James M. 2000 Pots, Parties, and Politics: Communal Feasting in the American Southwest. American Antiquity 65: 471–492.

Powell, H. A. 1960 Competitive Leadership in Trobriand Political Organization. Journal of the Royal Anthropological Institute 90: 118–145.

———— 1969 Territoriality, Hierarchy and Kinship in Kiriwina. Man 4: 580–604.

Powis, Terry G., W. Jeffrey Hurst, María del Carmen Rodriguez, C. Ponciano Ortíz, Michael Blake, David Cheetham, Michael D. Coe and John G. Hodgson 2007 Oldest Chocolate in the New World. Antiquity 81 (314). http://antiquity.ac.uk/Projgall/powis. Accessed on September 3, 2009.

Pye, Mary E. 1995 Settlement, Specialization, and Adaptation in the Rio Jesus Drainage, Retalhuleu, Guatemala. Unpublished Ph.D. Dissertation, Department of Anthropology, Vanderbilt University, Nashville.

Pye, Mary E. and Arthur A. Demarest 1991 The Evolution of Complex Societies in Southeastern Mesoamerica: New Evidence from El Mesak, Guatemala. In *The Formation of Complex Societies in Southeastern Mesoamerica*, pp. 77–100. Edited by W. R. Fowler, Jr. CRC Press, Boca Raton.

Pye, Mary E., Arthur A. Demarest and Barbara Arroyo 1999 Early Formative Societies in Guatemal and El Salvador. In Pacific Latin America in Prehistory: The Evolution of Archaic and Formative Cultures, pp. 75–88. Edited by M. Blake. Washington State University Press, Pullman, WA.

Rapoport, Amos 1982 *The Meaning of Built Environment: A Nonverbal Communication Approach*. Sage Publications, Beverly Hills.

———— 1988 Levels of Meaning in the Built Environment. In *Cross-cultural Perspectives in Nonverbal Communication*, pp. 317–336. Edited by Fernando Poyatos. CF Hogrefe, Toronto.

———— 1990 Systems of Activities and Systems of Settings. In *Domestic Architecture and the Use of Space: An Interdisciplinary Cross-Cultural Study*, pp. 9–20. Edited by Susan Kent. University of Cambridge Press, Cambridge.

Rappaport, Roy A. 1968 *Pig for the Ancestors: Ritual in the Ecology of a New Guinea People*. Yale University Press, New Haven and London.

Rathje, William L. 1971 The Origins and Development of Lowland Classic Maya Civilization. American Antiquity 36: 275–286.

———— 1972 Praise the Gods and Pass the Metates: A Hypothesis of the Development of Lowland Rainforest Civilization. In *Contemporary Archaeology: A Guide to Theory and Contributions*, pp. 365–392. Edited by M. Leone. Southern Illinois Press, Carbondale.

Redman, Charles L. 1987 Surface Collection, Sampling, and Research Design. American Antiquity 52: 249–265.

Reilly III, Kent 1989 The Shaman in Transformation Pose: A Study of the Theme of Rulership in Olmec Art. Record of the Art Museum, Princeton University 48 (2): 4–21.

———— 1990 Cosmos and Rulership: The Function of Olmec-Style Symbols in Formative Period Mesoamerica. Visible Language 24: 12–37.

———— 1995 Art, Ritual and Rulership in the Olmec World. In *The Olmec World: Ritual and Rulership*, pp. 27–46. The Art Museum, Princeton University, Princeton.

———— 1999 Mountains of Creation and Underworld Portals: The Ritual Function of Olmec Architecture at La Venta, Tabasco. In *Mesoamerican Architecture as a Cultural Symbol*, pp. 15–39. Edited by J. K. Kowalski. Oxford University Press, New York.

Renfrew, Colin 1972 *The Emergence of Civilization*. Methuen, London.

———— 1973 Monuments, Mobilization and Social Organization in Neolithic Wessex. In *The Explanation of Culture Change: Models in Prehistory*, pp. 539–558. Duckworth, London.

———— 1977 Alternative Models for Exchange and Spatial Distribution. In *Exchange Systems in Prehistory*, pp. 71–90. Edited by T. K. Earle and J. E. Ericson. Academic Press, New York.

———— 1986a Introduction: Peer Polity Interaction and Socio-Political Change. In *Peer Polity Interaction and Socio-Political Change*, pp. 1–18. Edited by C. Renfrew and J. F. Cherry. Cambridge University Press, Cambridge.

———— 1986b Varna and the Emergence of Wealth in Prehistoric Europe. In *The Social Life of Things: Commodities in Cultural Perspective*, pp. 141–168. Edited by A. Appadurai. Cambridge University Press, Cambridge.

———— 1993 Trade beyond the Material. In *Trade and Exchange in Prehistoric Europe*, pp. 5–16. Edited by C. Scarre and F. Healy. Oxbow, Oxford.

Renfrew, Colin and John F. Cherry (editors) 1986 *Peer Polity Interaction and Socio-Political Change*. Cambridge University Press, Cambridge.

Renfrew, Colin and Stephan Shennan (editors) 1982 *Ranking Resources and Exchange*. Cambridge University Press, Cambridge.

Rice, Don S. (editor) 1993 *Latin American Horizons*. Dumbarton Oaks, Washington, DC.

Rindos, David 1984 *The Origins of Agriculture: An Evolutionary Perspective*. Academic Press, New York.

Robb, John E. 1998 The Archaeology of Symbols. Annual Review of Anthropology 27: 327–346.

Rodríguez Martínez, Ma. del Carmen, Ponciano Ortíz Ceballos, Michael D. Coe, Richard A. Diehl, Stephen D. Houston, Karl A. Taube and Alfredo Delgado Calderón 2006 Oldest Writing in the New World. Science 313: 1610–1614.

Romano Pacheco, Arturo 1980 Appendix 3: The Skull from Pajón, Chiapas. In *Pampa El Pajón, An Early Estuarine site, Chiapas, Mexico*, pp. 95–114. Edited by Maricruz H. Pailles. Papers of the New World Archaeological Foundation, No. 44 Brigham Young University, Provo, UT.

Roseberry, William 1989 *Anthropologies and Histories: Essays in Culture, History and Political Economy*. Rutgers University Press, New Brunswick.

Rosenswig, Robert M. 2000 Some Political Processes of Ranked Societies. Journal of Anthropological Archaeology 19: 413–460.

———— 2001 Informe Técnicos Parcial del Proyecto Formativo Soconusco 2001. Por el Instituto Nacional de Antropología e Historia, México, DF.

———— 2002 Informe Técnicos Parcial del Proyecto Formativo Soconusco 2002. Por el Instituto Nacional de Antropología e Historia, México, DF.

———— 2003 Earliest Mesoamerican Human-duck Imagery from Cuauhtémoc, Chiapas, Mexico. Antiquity 77 (298): http://antiquity.ac.uk/ProjGall/rosenswig/. Accessed on September 3, 2009.

———— 2004 New Archaeological Excavation Data from the Late Archaic Occupation of Northern Belize. Research Reports in Belizean Archaeology 1: 267–277.

———— 2005 From the Land between Swamps: Cuauhtémoc in an Early Olmec World. Unpublished Ph.D. dissertation. Department of Anthropology, Yale University, New Haven.

———— 2006a Sedentism and Food Production in Early Complex Societies of the Soconusco, Mexico. World Archaeology 38: 329–354.

———— 2006b Northern Belize and the Soconusco: A Comparison of the Late Archaic to Formative Transition. Research Reports in Belizean Archaeology 3: 59–71.

———— 2007 Beyond Identifying Elites: Feasting as a Means to Understand Early Middle Formative Society on the Pacific Coast of Mexico. Journal of Anthropological Archaeology 26: 1–27.

———— 2008 Prehispanic Settlement in the Cuauhtémoc Region of the Soconusco, Chiapas, Mexico. Journal of Field Archaeology 33: 389–411.

———— 2009 Early Mesoamerican Garbage: Ceramic and Daub Discard Patterns from Cuauhtémoc, Soconusco, Mexico. Journal of Archaeological Method and Theory 16: 1–31.

———— 2010 The Origins of Monumental Architecture and Social Stratification at Cuauhtémoc, Mexico. In *The Origins of New World Monumentality*. Edited by R. L. Burger and R. M. Rosenswig. University Florida Press, Gainesville, in press.

———— n.d. An Early Mesoamerican Archipelago of Complexity: As Seen from Changing Population and Human Depictions at Cuauhtémoc. In *Sociopolitical Transformation in Early Mesoamerica: Archaic to Formative in the Soconusco Region*. Edited by Richard Lesure. University of California Press, Berkeley, under review.

Rosenswig, Robert M., Travis Doering, Hector Neff and Ana Tejada 2007 Early Formative Pottery and Obsidian Exchange from Cuauhtémoc, Chiapas, Mexico. Poster presented at the 72nd Annual Meetings of the Society for American Archaeology, Austin. April 25–29.

Rosenswig, Robert M. and Marilyn A. Masson 2001 Seven New Preceramic Sites Documented in Northern Belize. Mexicon 23 (6): 138–140.

———— 2002 Transformation of the Terminal Classic to Postclassic Architectural Landscape at Caye Coco, Belize. Ancient Mesoamerica 13: 213–235.

Rowlands, Michael, M. Larsen and Kristian Kristiansen 1987 Centre and Periphery in the Ancient World. University of Cambridge Press, Cambridge.

Rust, William F. 1992 New Ceremonial and Settlement Evidence at La Venta, and Its Relationship to Preclassic Maya Cultures. In New Theories on the Ancient Maya, pp. 23–29. Edited by E. Danien and R. Sharer. University Museum Monograph 77, The University of Pennsylvania, Philadelphia.

Rust, William F. and Robert J. Sharer 1988 Olmec Settlement Data from La Venta, Tabasco, Mexico. Science 242: 102–104.

Sabloff, Jeremy A. 1975 Excavations at Seibal: Ceramics. Memoirs of the Peabody Museum of Archaeology and Ethnology 13(2).

Sagona, A. 1994 The Quest for the Red Gold. In Bruising the Red Earth: Ochre Mining and Ritual in Tasmania, pp. 8–38. Edited by A. Sagoma. Melbourne University Press, Melbourne.

Sahlins, Marshall 1972 Stone Age Economics. Aldine de Gruyter, New York.

———— 1992 Historical Ethnography. Anahulu: The Anthropology of History in the Kingdom of Hawaii, Vol. 1. Edited by P. V. Kirch and M. Sahlins. University of Chicago Press, Chicago.

———— 1994 Cosmologies of Capitalism: The Trans-Pacific Sector of the World System. In Culture/Power/History: A Reader in Contemporary Social Theory, pp. 412–455. Edited by N. B. Dirks, G. Eley and S. B. Ortner. Princeton University Press, Princeton.

Saitta, Dean J. 1997 Power, Labor, and the Dynamics of Change in Chacoan Political Economy. American Antiquity 62: 7–26.

Salmon, Merrilee H. 1982 Philosophy and Archaeology. Academic Press, New York.

Salzman, Philip C. 1999 Is Inequality Universal? Current Anthropology 40: 31–61.

Sanders, William, Jeffery Parsons and Robert Santely 1979 The Basin of Mexico: Ecological Processes in the Evolution of a Civilization. Academic Press, New York.

Sanders, William T. and Barbara J. Price 1968 Mesoamerica: The Evolution of a Civilization. Random House, New York.

Santley, Robert S. and Rani T. Alexander 1992 The Political Economy of Core-Periphery Systems. In Resources, Power and Inter-regional Interaction, pp. 23–49. Edited by E. M. Schortman and P. A. Urban. Plenum, New York.

Santley, Robert S. and Philip J. Arnold III 1996 Prehispanic Settlement Patterns in the Tuxtla Mountains, Southern Veracruz, Mexico. Journal of Field Archaeology 23: 225–249.

Santley, Robert S., Philip J. Arnold and Thomas P. Barrett 1997 Formative Period Settlement Patterns in the Tuxtla Mountains. In Olmec to Aztec: Settlement Patterns in the Ancient Gulf Coast Lowlands, pp. 174–205. Edited by B. Stark and P. J. Arnold. University of Arizona Press, Tucson.

Saunders, Nicholas J. 2001 A Dark Light: Reflections on Obsidian in Mesoamerica. World Archaeology 33: 220–236.

Scarre, Chris 2002 Epilogue: Colour and Materiality in Prehistoric Society. In *Colouring the Past: The Significance of Colour in Archaeological Research*, pp. 227–242. Edited by A. Jones and G. MacGregor. Berg, Oxford and New York.

Schacht, Robert M. 1981 Estimating Past Population Trends. Annual Review of Anthropology 10: 119–140.

———— 1984 The Contemporaneity Problem. American Antiquity 49 (4): 678–695.

Scheffler, Hal W. 1965 *Choiseul Island Social Structure*. University of California Press, Berkeley.

Schiffer, Michael B. 1972 Archaeological Context and Systemic Context. American Antiquity 37: 156–165.

———— 1987 *Formation Processes of the Archaeological Record*. University of Utah Press, Salt Lake City.

Schneider, Jane 1977 Was There a Pre-capitalist World-system? Peasant Studies 6: 20–29.

Schortman, Edward M. and Patricia A. Urban 1987 Modeling Interregional Interaction in Prehistory. Advances in Archaeological Method and Theory 11: 37–95.

———— 1992a *Resources, Power and Inter-regional Interaction*. Plenum, New York.

———— 1992b Current Trends in Interaction Research. In *Resources, Power and Interregional Interaction*, pp. 235–255. Edited by E. M. Schortman and P. A. Urban. Plenum Press, New York.

———— 1994 Living on the Edge: Core/Periphery Relations in Ancient Southeastern Mesoamerica. Current Mesoamerica 35: 401–430.

Schulting, Rick J. and Michael P. Richards 2002 Dogs, Ducks, Deer and Diet: New Stable Isotope Evidence on Early Mesolithic Dogs from the Vale of Pickering, North-east England. Journal of Archaeological Science 29: 327–333.

Scott, James C. 1998 *Seeing Like a State: How Schemes to Improve the Human Condition Have Failed*. Yale University Press, New Haven.

Service, Elma R. 1967 Our Contemporary Ancestors: Extant Stages and Extinct Ages. In *War: The Anthropology of Armed Conflict and Aggression*, pp. 160–167. Edited by M. Fried, M. Harris and R. Murphy. American Museum of Natural History, Chicago.

Shanks, Michael and Christopher Tilley 1987 *Social Theory and Archaeology*. Polity Press, Cambridge.

Sharer, Robert J., Andrew K. Balkansky, James H. Burton, Gary M. Feinman, Kent V. Flannery, David C. Grove, Joyce Marcus, Robert G. Moyle, T. Douglas Price, Elsa M. Redmond, Robert G. Reynolds, Prudence M. Rice, Charles S. Spencer, James B. Stoltman and Jason Yaeger 2006 On the Logic of Archaeological Inference: Early Formative Pottery and the Evolution of Mesoamerican Societies. Latin American Antiquity 17: 90–103.

Shelach, Gideon 1999 *Leadership Strategies, Economic Activity, and Interregional Interaction: Social Complexity in Northeast China*. Kluwer Academic/Plenum Publishers, New York.

Shennan, Stephan 1997 *Quantifying Archaeology*, 2nd Edition. Edinburgh University Press, Edinburgh.

Sherratt, Andrew and Susan Sherratt 1991 From Luxuries to Commodities: The Nature of Mediterranean Bronze Age Trading Systems. In *Bronze Age Trade in the Mediterranean*, pp. 351–386. Edited by N. H. Gale. Paul Astroms Forlag, Jonsered.

Shook, Edwin M. 1948 Guatemalan Highlands. Institute of Washington Yearbook, 1946–1947. No. 46: 179–184.

———— 1965 Archaeological Survey of the Pacific Coast of Guatemala. In *Archaeology of Southern Mesoamerica, Part 1*, pp. 180–194. Edited by G. R. Willey. Handbook of Middle American Indians, Vol. 2. University of Texas Press, Austin.

Simmons, Alan H. 1998 Exposed Fragments and Buried Hippos: Assessing Surface Archaeology. In *Surface Archaeology*, pp. 159–167. Edited by A. P. Sullivan III. University of New Mexico Press, Albuquerque.

Skibo, James M., Michael B. Schiffer and Nancy Kowalski 1989 Ceramic Style Analysis in Archaeology and Ethnoarchaeology: Bridging the Analytical Gap. *Journal of Anthropological Archaeology* 8: 388–409.

Smalley, John and Michael Blake 2003 Sweet Beginnings: Stalk Sugar and the Domestication of Maize. Current Anthropology 44: 675–703.

Smith, Adam T. 2000 Rendering the Political Aesthetic: Political Legitimacy in Urartian Representations of the Built Environment. Journal of Anthropological Archaeology 19: 131–163.

———— 2003 *The Political Landscape: Constellations of Authority in Early Complex Polities*. University of California Press, Berkeley.

Smith, Michael E. 1987 The Expansion of the Aztec Empire: A Case Study in Correlation of Diachronic Archaeological and Ethnohistorical Data. American Antiquity 52: 37–54.

———— 1992 Braudel's Temporal Rhythms and Chronology Theory in Archaeology. In *Archaeology, Annales and Ethnohistory*, pp. 23–34. Edited by A. Bernard Knapp. Cambridge University Press, Cambridge.

Smith, Michael E. and Lisa Montiel 2001 The Archaeological Study of Empires and Imperialism in Pre-Hispanic Central Mexico. Journal of Anthropological Archaeology 20: 245–284.

Spencer, Charles S. 1982 *Cuicatlán Cañada and Monte Albán: A Study of Primary State Formation*. Academic Press, New York.

Spencer, Charles S. and Elsa M. Redmond 1997 Archaeology of the Cañada de Cuicatlán, Oaxaca. Anthropological Papers, Vol. 80. American Museum of Natural History, New York.

———— 2003 Militarism, Resistance, and Early State Development in Oaxaca, Mexico. Social Evolution and History 2: 25–70.

———— 2004 Primary State Formation in Mesoamerica. Annual Review of Anthropology 33: 173–199.

Spielman, Katherine A. 2002 Feasting, Craft Specialization, and the Ritual Mode of Production in Small-scale Societies. American Anthropologist 104: 195–207.

Stark, Barbara L. 1978 An Ethnohistoric Model for Native Economy and Settlement Patterns of Southern Veracruz, Mexico. In *Prehistoric Coastal Adaptations: The Economy and Ecology of Maritime Middle America*, pp. 211–238. Edited by B. L. Stark and B. Voorhies. Academic Press, New York.

——— 1990 The Gulf Coast and the Central Highlands of Mexico: Alternative Models for Interaction. Research in Economic Anthropology 12: 243–285.

——— 1997 Gulf Lowland Ceramic Styles and Political Geography in Ancient Veracruz. In Olmec to Aztec: Settlement Patterns in the Ancient Gulf Lowlands, pp. 278–309. Edited by B. L. Stark and P. J. Arnold III. University of Arizona Press, Tucson.

——— 2000 Framing the Gulf Olmecs. In *Olmec Art and Archaeology in Mesoamerica*, pp. 31–53. Edited by J. E. Clark and M. E. Pye. National Gallery of Art, Washington, DC.

Steadman, David W., Marcus P. Tellkamp and Thomas A. Wake 2003 Prehistoric Exploitation of Birds on the Pacific Coast of Chiapas, Mexico. The Condor 105: 572–579.

Stein, Gil J. 1998 Heterogeneity, Power and Political Economy: Some Current Research Issues in the Archaeology of Old World Complex Societies. Journal of Archaeological Research 6: 1–44.

——— 1999 *Rethinking World-Systems: Diasporas, Colonies, and Interaction in Uruk Mesopotamia*. University of Arizona Press, Tucson.

——— 2002 Passive Periphery to Active Agents: Emerging Perspectives in the Archaeology of Interregional Interaction. American Anthropologist 104: 903–916.

Steponaitis, Vincas P. 1978 Locational Theory and Complex Chiefdoms: A Mississippian Example. In *Mississippian Settlement Patterns*, pp. 417–453. Edited by B. D. Smith. Academic Press, New York.

Stirling, Matthew W. 1955 Stone Monuments of the Rio Chiquito, Veracruz, Mexico. Bureau of American Ethnology, Bulletin 157. Smithsonian Institution, Washington, DC.

Stoltman, J. B., J. Marcus, K. V. Flannery, J. H. Burton and R. G. Moyle 2005 Petrographic Evidence Shows that Pottery Exchange between the Olmec and Their Neighbors Was Two Way. Proceedings of the National Academy of Sciences 102: 11213–11218.

Stone-Miller, Rebecca 2004 Human-Animal Imagery, Shamanic Visions, and Ancient American Aesthetics. RES: Anthropology and Aesthetics 45: 47–68.

Strathern, Andrew 1971 *The Rope of Moka: Big-men and the Ceremonial Exchange in Mont Hagen, New Guinea*. Cambridge University Press, Cambridge.

Stuart, David 2000 "The Arrival of Strangers": Teotihuacan and Tollan in Classic Maya History. In Mesoamerica's Classic Heritage: From Teotihuacan to the Aztecs, edited by D. Carrascow, L. Jones and S. Sessions, pp. 465–514. University Press of Colorado, Boulder.

Symonds, Stacey C. 2000 The Ancient Landscape at San Lorenzo Tenochtitlan, Veracruz, Mexico: Settlement and Nature. In *Olmec Art and Archaeology in Mesoamerica*, pp. 55–74. Edited by J. E. Clark and M. E. Pye. National Gallery of Art, Washington, DC.

Symonds, Stacey C., Ann Cyphers and Roberto Lunagomez 2002 *Asentamiento Prehispánico en San Lorenzo Tenochtitlán*. Universidad Nacional Autónoma de México, México, DF.

Taube, Karl 1995 The Rainmakers: The Olmec and Their Contribution to Mesoamerican Belief and Ritual. In *The Olmec World: Ritual and Rulership*, pp. 83–104. Edited by J. Guthrie. The Art Museum, Princeton University, Princeton.

——— 1996 The Olmec Maize God: The Faces of Corn in Formative Mesoamerica. RES: Anthropology and Aesthetics 29–30: 39–81.

——— 2000 Lightning Celts and Corn Fetishes: The Formative Olmec and the Development of Maize Symbolism in Mesoamerica and the American Southwest. In *Olmec Art and Archaeology in Mesoamerica*, pp. 297–337. Edited by J. E. Clark and M. E Pye. National Gallery of Art, Washington, DC.

——— 2004 Olmec Art at Dumbarton Oaks. Dumbarton Oaks, Washington, DC.

Tejeda, Ana and Hector Neff 2004 Laser Ablation-Inductively Coupled Plasma-Mass Spectrometry (LA-ICP-MS) Analysis of Fine Paste Ceramics of La Blanca, Guatemala. Paper presented at the 69th Annual Meeting of the SAA, Montreal. March 31-April 4.

Tolstoy, Paul 1989a Coapexco and Tlatilco: Sites with Olmec Materials in the Basin of Mexico. In *Regional Perspectives on the Olmec*, pp. 85–121. Edited by R. J. Sharer and D. C. Grove. Cambridge University Press, Cambridge.

——— 1989b Western Mesoamerica and the Olmec. In *Regional Perspectives on the Olmec*, pp. 275–302. Edited by R. J. Sharer and D. C. Grove. Cambridge University Press, Cambridge.

Tolstoy, Paul and Susane K. Fish 1975 Surface and Subsurface Evidence for Community Size at Coapexco, Mexico. Journal of Field Archaeology 2: 97–104.

Tolstoy, Paul, Suzanne K. Fish, Martin W. Boksenbaum, Kathryn Blair Vaugh and C. Earle Smith, Jr. 1977 Early Sedentary Communities of the Basin of Mexico: A Summary of Recent Investigations. Journal of Field Archaeology 4: 92–106.

Trigger, Bruce G. 1989 *A History of Archaeological Thought*. Cambridge University Press, Cambridge.

——— 1990 Monumental Architecture: A Thermodynamic Explanation of Symbolic Behaviour. World Archaeology 22: 119–132.

——— 1991 Distinguished Lecture in Archaeology: Constraint and Freedom – A New Synthesis for Archaeological Explanation. American Anthropologist 93: 551–569.

——— 1993 Early Civilizations: Ancient Egypt in Context. American University in Cairo Press, Cairo.

——— 1995 Expanding Middle Range Theory. Antiquity 69: 449–458.

——— 1998a Archeology and Epistemology: Dialogue across the Darwinian Chasm. American Journal of Archaeology 102: 1–34.

——— 1998b *Sociocultural Evolution: Calculation and Contingency*. Blackwell, Oxford.

——— 2003a *Understanding Early Civilizations: A Comparative Study*. Cambridge University Press, Cambridge.

——— 2003b Introduction: Understanding the Material Remains of the Past. In *Artifacts and Ideas: Essays in Archaeology*, pp. 1–30. Edited by B. G. Trigger. Transaction Publishers, New Brunswick and London.

——— 2004 Settlement Patterns in the Postmodern World: A Study of Monumental Architecture in Early Civilizations. In *The Archaeologist: Detective and Thinker*, pp. 237–248. Edited by L. Vishnyatsky, A. Kovalev and O. Scheglova. St. Petersburg University Press, St. Petersburg.

Turbitt, Mary Beth D. 2000 Mound Building and Prestige Goods Exchange: Changing Strategies in the Cahokia Chiefdom. American Antiquity 65: 669–690.

Turkon, Paula 2004 Food and Status in the Prehispanic Malpaso Valley, Zacatecas, Mexico. Journal of Anthropological Archaeology 23: 225–251.

Turner, Victor 1967 *The Forest of Symbols: Aspects of Ndembu Ritual*. Cornell University Press, Ithaca.

Uberoi, J. P. Singh 1962 *Politics of the Kula Ring: An Analysis of the Findings of Bronislaw Malinowsi*. Manchester University Press, Manchester.

Upham, Steadman 1992 Interaction and Isolation: The Empty Spaces in Pan-regional Political and Economic Systems. In *Resources, Power and Interregional Interaction*, pp. 139–152. Edited by E. M. Schortman and P. A. Urban. Plenum Press, New York.

———— 2000 Scale, Innovation, and Change in the Desert West: A Macroregional Approach. In *The Archaeology of Regional Interaction: Religion, Warfare, and Exchange across the American Southwest and Beyond*, pp. 235–256. Edited by M. Hegmon. University Press of Colorado, Boulder.

Urban, Patricia, Edward Schortman and Marne Ausec 2002 Power without Bounds? Middle Preclassic Political Developments in the Naco Valley, Honduras. Latin American Antiquity 13: 131–152.

VanDerwarker, Amber M. 2005 Field Cultivation and Tree Management in Tropical Agriculture: A View from Gulf Coastal Mexico. World Archaeology 37: 275–289.

———— 2006 *Farming, Hunting and Fishing in the Olmec World*. University of Texas Press, Austin.

Veblen, Thorstein 1994 [1899] *The Theory of the Leisure Class*. Macmillan, New York.

von Nagy, Christopher L. 1997 The Geoarchaeology of Settlement in the Grijalva Delta. In *Olmec to Aztec: Settlement Patterns in the Ancient Gulf Lowlands*, pp. 253–277. Edited by B. L. Stark and P. J. Arnold III. University of Arizona Press, Tucson.

———— 2003 Of Meandering Rivers and Shifting Towns: Landscape Evolution and Community within the Grijalva Delta. Ph.D. Dissertation, Department of Anthropology, Tulane University, New Orleans.

von Nagy, Christopher L., Mary D. Pohl and Kevin O. Pope 2002 Ceramic Chronology of the La Venta Olmec Polity: The View from San Andrés, Tabasco. Paper presented at the 67th Annual Meeting of the Society for American Archaeology, Denver, March 20–24.

Voorhies, Barbara 1989a Settlement Patterns in the Western Soconusco: Methods of Site Recovery and Dating Results. In *New Frontiers in the Archaeology of the Pacific Coast of Southern Mesoamerica*, pp. 103–124. Edited by F. Bove and L. Heller. Anthropological Research Papers No. 39. Arizona State University, Tempe.

———— 2004 *Coastal Collectors in the Holocene: The Chantuto People of Southwest Mexico*. University Press of Florida, Gainesville.

Voorhies, Barbara and Douglas Kennett 1995 Buried Sites on the Soconusco Coastal Plain, Chiapas, Mexico. Journal of Field Archaeology 22: 65–79.

Voorhies, Barbara, Douglas J. Kennett, John G. Jones and Thomas A. Wake
2002 A Middle Archaic Archaeological Site on the West Coast of Mexico. Latin American Antiquity 13: 179–200.

Wake, Thomas A. 2004 Vertebrate Archaeofauna from the Early Formative Period Site of Paso de la Amada, Chiapas, Mexico. In *Maya Zooarchaeology: New Directions in Method and Theory*, pp. 209–222. Edited by K. Emery. Cotsen Institute of Archaeology Monograph 51, Los Angeles.

Wake, Thomas A. and Lady R. Harrington 2002 Appendix II: Vertebrate Faunal Remains from La Blanca, Guatemala. In *Early Complex Society in Pacific Guatemala: Settlements and Chronology of the Rio Naranjo, Guatemala*, pp. 237–252. By Michael W. Love. Papers of the New World Archaeological Foundation 66. Brigham Young University, Provo, UT.

Wallerstein, Immanuel 1974 *The Modern World-System: Capitalist Agriculture and the Origins of Capitalist World-Economy in the Sixteenth Century*. Academic Press, New York.

——— 1991 The Invention of TimeSpace Realities: Towards an Understanding of our Historical System. In *Unthinking Social Sciences*. Edited by I. Wallerstein. Polity Press, Cambridge.

——— 1995 Hold the Tiller Firm: On Method and the Unit of Analysis. In *Civilization and World Systems: Studying World-Historical Change*, pp. 239–247. Edited by S. K. Sanderson. Alta Mira Press, Walnut Creek, CA.

Watson, Richard 1990 Ozymandias, King of Kings: Postprocessual Radical Archaeology as Critique. American Antiquity 41: 210–215.

——— 1991 What the New Archaeology Has Accomplished. Current Anthropology 32: 275–291.

Webster, David 1999 Warfare and Status Rivalry: Lowland Maya and Polynesian Comparisons. In *Archaic States*, pp 311–351. Edited by G. M. Feinman and J. Marcus. School of American Research, Sante Fe, NM.

Weiner, Annette B. 1976 *Woman of Value and Men of Renown*. University of Texas Press, Austin.

Welch, Paul D. 1991 *Moundville's Economy*. University of Alabama Press, Tuscaloosa.

Welch, Paul D. and C. Margaret Scarry 1995 Status-Related Variation in Foodways in the Moundville Chiefdom. American Antiquity 60: 397–419.

Wells, Peter S. 1992 Tradition, Identity, and Change beyond the Roman Frontier. In *Resources, Power and Interregional Interaction*, pp. 175–188. Edited by E. M. Schortman and P. A. Urban. Plenum Press, New York.

——— 1999 Production within and beyond Imperial Boundaries: Goods, Exchange and Power in Roman Europe. In *World-Systems Theory in Practice: Leadership, Production and Exchange*, pp. 85–101. Edited by P. N. Kardulias. Rowman & Littlefield, Lanham, MD.

Wendt, Carl J. 2005a Excavations at El Remolino: Household Archaeology in the San Lorenzo Olmec Region. Journal of Field Archaeology 30: 163–180.

——— 2005b Using Refuse Disposal Patterns to Infer Olmec Site Structure in the San Lorenzo Region, Veracruz, Mexico. Latin American Antiquity 16: 449–466.

Wengrow, David 1998 The Changing Face of Clay: Continuity and Change in the Transition from Village to Urban Life in the Near East. Antiquity 72: 783–795.

——— 2001 The Evolution of Simplicity: Aesthetic Labour and Social Change in the Neolithic Near East. World Archaeology 33: 168–188.

White, Christine D., Mary E. D. Pohl, Henry Schwarcz and Fred J. Longstaffe 2001 Isotopic Evidence for Maya Patterns of Deer and Dog Use at Preclassic Colha. Journal of Archaeological Science 28: 89–107.

——— 2004 Feasts, Fields and Forests: Deer and Dog Diets at Lagartero, Tikal and Copan. In *Maya Zooarchaeology: New Directions in Method and Theory*, pp. 141–158. Edited by K. Emery. Cotsen Institute of Archaeology Monograph 51, Los Angeles.

Whitehouse, Harvey (editor) 2001 *The Debated Mind: Evolutionary Psychology versus Ethnography*. Berg, Oxford.

Wierzbicka, Anna 1990 The Meaning of Color Terms: Semantics, Culture and Cognitive. Cognitive Linguistics 1: 99–150.

Wiessner, Polly 1990 Is There a Unity to Style? In *The Uses of Style in Archaeology*, pp. 105–112. Edited by M. Conkey and C. Hastorf. Cambridge University Press, Cambridge.

——— 2002 The Vines of Complexity: Egalitarian Structures and the Institutionalization of Inequality among the Enga. Current Anthropology 43: 233–269.

Wilk, Richard 2004 Miss Universe, the Olmec and the Valley of Oaxaca. Journal of Social Archaeology 4: 81–98.

Willey, Gordon R. 1945 Horizon Styles and Pottery Traditions in Peruvian Archaeology. American Antiquity 11: 49–56.

——— 1948 Functional Analysis of "Horizon Styles" in Peruvian Archaeology. In *A Reappraisal of Peruvian Archaeology*. Memoirs of the Society for American Archaeology 4: 8–15.

——— 1962 The Early Great Styles and the Rise of the Pre-Columbian Civilization. American Anthropologist 64: 1–14.

——— 1991 Horizonal Integration and Regional Diversity: An Alternating Process in the Rise of Civilizations. American Antiquity 56: 197–215.

Willey, Gordon R. and Philip Phillips. 1958 Method and Theory in American Archaeology. University of Chicago Press, Chicago.

Willey, Gordon R. and Jeremy A. Sabloff 1993 *A History of American Archaeology*, 3rd Edition. Freeman, New York.

Williams Howel and Robert F. Heizer 1965 Sources of Rocks Used in Olmec Monuments. Contributions to the University of California Archaeological Research Facility 1: 1–39.

Wing, Elizabeth S. 1978 Use of Dogs for Food: An Adaptation to the Coastal Environment. In *Prehistoric Coastal Adaptations: The Economy and Ecology of Maritime Middle America*, pp. 29–41. Edited by B. L. Stark and B. Voorhies. Academic Press, New York.

Winkelman, Michael 2002 Shamanism and Cognitive Evolution. Cambridge Archaeological Journal 12: 71–101.

Winkelman, Michael and D. White 1987 A Cross-Cultural Study of Magico-Religious Practitioners and Trance States: Data Base. In *Human Relations Area Files Research Series in Quantitative Cross-cultural Data*, Vol. 3. Edited by D. Levinson and R. Wagner. HRAF Press, New Haven.

Wobst, Martin 1977 Stylistic Behavior and Information Exchange. In *Papers for the Director*, pp. 317–342. Edited by C. E. Moore. Anthropological Papers, Museum of Anthropology, No. 61. University of Michigan, Ann Arbor.

———— 1999 Style in Archaeology or Archaeologists in Style. In *Material Meanings: Critical Approaches to the Interpretation of Material Culture*, pp. 118–132. Edited by E. S. Chilton. University of Utah Press, Salt Lake City.

Wolf, Eric 1982 *Europe and the People without History*. University of California Press, Berkeley.

Wright, Henry T. 1984 Prestate Political Formations. In *On the Evolution of Complex Societies: Essays in Honor of Harry Hoijer*, pp. 41–77. Edited by T. Earle. Undena Publications, Malibu, CA.

Wright, Rita P. 1989 New Tracks on Ancient Frontiers: Ceramic Technology on the Indo-Iranian Borderlands. In *Archaeological Thought in America*, pp. 268–279. Edited by C. C. Lamberg-Karlovsky. Cambridge University Press, Cambridge.

Wylie, Alison 2002 *Thinking from Things: Essays in the Philosophy of Archaeology*. University of California Press, Berkeley.

Yoffee, Norman 1993 Too Many Chiefs? (or, Safe Texts for the 90s). In *Archaeological Theory: Who Sets the Agenda?* pp. 60–78. Edited by N. Yoffee and A. Sherratt. Cambridge University Press, Cambridge.

Zeitlin, Robert N. 1978 Long-distance Exchange and the Growth of a Regional Center: An Example from the Southern Isthmus of Tehuantepec, Mexico. In *Prehistoric Coastal Adaptations*, pp. 183–210. Edited by B. L. Stark and B. Voorhies. Academic Press, New York.

———— 1979 Prehistoric Long-distance Exchange on the Southern Isthmus of Tehuantepec, Mexico. Unpublished Ph.D. Dissertation, Department of Anthropology, Yale University, New Haven.

———— 1990 The Isthmus and the Valley of Oaxaca: Questions about Zapotec Imperialism in Formative Period Mesoamerican. American Antiquity 55: 250–261.

Zeitlin, Robert N. and Judith F. Zeitlin 2000 The Paleoindian and Archaic Cultures of Mesoamerica. In *The Cambridge History of Native Peoples of the Americas*. Vol. II. *Mesoamerica*. Edited by R. E. W. Adams and M. J. MacLeod. Cambridge University Press, Cambridge.

Zipf, G. K. 1949 *Human Behavior and the Principle of Least Effort*. Addison-Wesley, Cambridge, MA.

Index